The Obligation of Perfect and Perpetual Continence

The Obligation of Perfect and Perpetual Continence

And Married Deacons in the Latin Church

Anthony McLaughlin

✸*ENROUTE*
Make the time

⊛ENROUTE

Make the time

ENROUTE Books & Media, LLC

5705 Rhodes Avenue, St. Louis, MO 63109

Contact us at contactus@enroutebooksandmedia.com

© 2018 by ENROUTE Books & Media, LLC

LCCN: 2018940391

Cover design by T.J. Burdick

Paperback ISBN: 978-1-952464-13-3

E-book ISBN: 978-0-9998814-5-3

Printed in the United States of America

1 3 5 7 9 10 8 6 4 2

PREFACE

Through the reception of diaconate a man becomes a cleric. Canon 277 §1 states: "Clerics are obliged to observe perfect and perpetual continence for the sake of the kingdom of Heaven and therefore are bound to celibacy...." Accordingly, it would seem that clerics have two distinct obligations: sexual continence (no sexual relations) and celibacy (no marriage) with continence presented as the fundamental norm. With the restoration of the permanent diaconate by Paul VI in 1967 and the admission of married men to this order, a fundamental question arises: "Are married deacons, though dispensed from the obligation of celibacy, unless their wife dies, obliged to observe perfect and perpetual continence?" The book has five chapters. Chapter one presents a general historical overview of clerical continence, chastity and celibacy in the Latin Church. Chapter two examines the 1917 code's dispositions on clerical continence, chastity and celibacy. Chapter three follows both the discussions of the Fathers at the Second Vatican Council and post-conciliar norms concerning the restoration of the permanent diaconate in the Latin Church. It also presents the conciliar teaching on sexuality and marriage, with particular focus given to the compatibility of marriage and orders. Chapter four examines canon 277 §1 of the 1983 code, with special attention given to the revision process. Chapter five considers whether married deacons in the Latin Church are obliged to observe perfect and perpetual continence. The book demonstrates that how one understands the law of continence is dependent upon how one understands the law of celibacy. If celibacy is understood narrowly as the legal condition of being unmarried then only celibate clerics are bound to observe the law of continence (the "Celibacy School"). However, if celibacy is understood broadly in terms of the *lex continentiae,* no sexual relations *post ordinationem,* then married deacons are bound to observe the law of continence ("the Continence School"). In clarifying the fundamental issues and analyzing the implicit suppositions of the two "schools" this book will help to illustrate why the obligation of continence for married deacons is even a question.

On two different occasions in 2011, the Pontifical Council for Legislative Texts (PCLT), responded to questions concerning whether married deacons are bound to observe the continence prescribed in canon 277 § 1. The questions were posed by Archbishop Timothy Dolan, President of the United States Conference of Catholic Bishops, on behalf of various conference committees seeking clarification on the matter. The first response, dated March 4, 2011, signed by the President, Archbishop Coccopalmerio, was published in *Roman Replies and CLSA Advisory Opinions 2011.*[1] It stated: "Permanent deacons who are married prior to ordination do not have the obligation of celibacy (and therefore continence) during marriage. They do have the obligation of celibacy in case of widowhood."

In a second response dated 17 December 2011, signed by the President and

---

[1]   PCLT 12959/2011. *Roman Replies and CLSA Advisory Opinions 2011* (Canon Law Society of America, 2011) 18-20.

counter-signed by the Secretary, the PCLT offered an extended clarification of the continence obligations of married deacons. The PCLT again concluded that married deacons are not bound to observe the continence prescribed in canon 277§ 1. This letter was sent to all members of the United States Conference of Catholic Bishops with a cover letter dated 31 January 2012. It was published in *Roman Replies and CLSA Advisory Opinions 2012*.[2] The cover letter from Bishop Robert J. Carlson, Chairman, Committee on Clergy, Consecrated Life and Vocations, and Archbishop Timothy P. Broglio, Chairman, Committee on Canonical Affairs and Church Governance stated, "…that married deacons are not bound to observe perfect and perpetual continence, as long as their marriage lasts."

The PCLT clarifications are a most significant contribution to a disputed canonical question. This author finds two things of interest in the clarifications: (1) there was no articulation as to why the long canonical tradition of clerical continence had been set aside and (2) "continence" and "celibacy" at times seem to be understood as synonymous.[3] Without question, the PCLT clarifications have "authority" and cannot be discounted, and those arguing on either side

---

2   PCLT 13095/2011. *Roman Replies and CLSA Advisory Opinions 2012* (Canon Law Society of America, 2012) 12-14.

3   For example: PCLT 12959/2011: "Permanent deacons who are married prior to ordination do not have the obligation of celibacy (and therefore of continence) during the marriage." Celibacy and continence are presented as the same obligation. PCLT 13095/2011: "In canon 277.1 the requirement of perfect and perpetual continence is inseparably linked to the obligation of celibacy to which all clerics, in principle, are bound." Celibacy, not continence is presented as the fundamental obligation. Later in this article we will examine the long canonical history of clerical continence; how continence and celibacy were understood as distinct obligations; and how continence, not celibacy, was the fundamental norm that bound all major clerics, married or unmarried.

of the question must consider and address the clarifications.[4] Yet, though they have "authority" they are not "authoritative." They do not have the force of law because they were not given *per modum legis*.[5] The competencies of the PCLT are outlined in John Paul II's, apostolic constitution *Pastor bonus*.[6] Article 155 states that regarding the universal laws of the Church, the Council (PCLT) is competent to publish authentic interpretations which are confirmed by pontifical authority, after having heard the views of various dicasteries concerned with the subject matter.[7] However the PCLT's clarifications were not confirmed "gener-

---

4   The PCLT's second response builds on the shorter clarification offered in its first response. It has three main points: "1. In can. 277, § 1 CIC, the requirement of perfect and perpetual continence is inseparably linked to the obligation of celibacy to which all clerics, in principle, are bound. Also, can. 1037 CIC requires that unmarried candidates for the permanent diaconate must assume the obligation of celibacy prior to ordination. Furthermore, can. 1087 CIC establishes an impediment to marriage for those in sacred orders. For this reason, permanent deacons who are widowers cannot marry, unless being dispensed, and therefore are bound to observe perfect and perpetual continence. The particular discipline of these two last canons, 1037 and 1087 CIC, applicable to certain situations of permanent deacons, explains on the one hand why can. 288 CIC did not exempt in a general way "all" permanent deacons from the obligation of continence established by the can. 277 § 1 CIC; and on the other hand how it is evident from all these norms that the canon wanted to exempt married permanent deacons from such obligation of continence so long as their marriage lasts.
2. Indeed, can. 1031 § 2 CIC admits married men to the clerical state in the particular case of permanent deacons, but states nothing about a hypothetical obligation to observe perfect and perpetual continence, as the Legislator would indicate if such an obligation were to be established. Ultimately, the fact that in order for a married
man to be admitted to the order of the diaconate, the consent of his wife is required (c. 1031, § 2) implies that an explicit consent would have been required for reasons of justice if the condition of permanent deacon had entailed the obligation of perfect and perpetual continence (c. 1055).
3. Naturally, this canonical discipline does not state anything apart from what the Church's Magisterium has already affirmed in this regard. In fact, the Dogmatic Constitution *Lumen gentium*, n. 29 (§ 2), and other successive normative documents of the Holy See, appear to take for granted that married permanent deacons live their marriage in the ordinary way (see Congregatio De Institutione Catholica Ratio fundamentalis institutionis diaconorum permanentium, Institutio diaconorum of February 22, 1998 (nn. 36-38, 62-63, 68); Congregatio Pro Clericis, Directorium pro ministerio et vita diaconorum permanentium, Diaconatus originem of February 22, 1998 (nn. 7, 27, 33, 45, 50, 59-62, and particularly n. 61)." See PCLT 13095/2011. *Roman Replies and CLSA Advisory Opinions 2012* (Canon Law Society of America, 2012) 12-14.
5   83 *CIC*, c. 16§ 2. Authentic interpretations are promulgated in the *Acta Apostolicae Sedis* (*AAS*) in accord with canon 8§ 1. To date there has been no such promulgation of these PCLT clarifications.
6   John Paul II, apostolic constitution *Pastor bonus* 154-158, June 28, 1988: *AAS* 80 (1988) 901-902. Hereafter *PB*.
7   *PB* 155, *AAS* 80 (1988) 901.

ically" or "specifically" by pontifical authority.[8] Also none of the formalities prescribed for the promulgation of an authentic interpretation of the law were observed.[9] Therefore in the absence of an authentic interpretation this author believes that the question of whether married deacons are bound to the continence obliged by canon 277 §1 remains unresolved.[10]

---

8   "Under the regime of the present two codes, the promulgated interpretation notes that the pope was informed of the interpretation in an audience granted to the President of the PCLT, at which time the pope decided that it should be promulgated. *In Audienta die NN...de supradictis decisionibus (de supradicta decisione) certior factus, eas (eam) publicari iussit.*" John M. Huels, "Classifying Authentic Interpretations of Canon Law," *The Jurist* 72 (2012) 612. These formalities were not observed in the 2011 PCLT clarifications concerning diaconal continence.

9   "An interpretation given by PCLT *per modum legis* is the exercise of ordinary legislative power accorded it by the supreme legislator in *Pastor bonus,* art. 155.....An interpretation *per modum legis,* however, must be promulgated; promulgation is a constitutive element of the act without which such interpretation does not exist." See John M. Huels, "Classifying Authentic Interpretations of Canon Law," 612, 613. See also canons 8 and 16.

10   For more on authentic interpretations and the competencies of PCLT see Lawrence G. Wrenn, *Authentic Interpretations on the 1983 Code,* (Washington, DC: CLSA, 1993); Francisco Javier Urrutia, "De Pontificio Consilio de legume textibus interpretandis," *Periodica* 78 (1989) 503-521 and Huels, "Classifying Authentic Interpretations of Canon Law," 605-640.

CONTENTS

ABBREVIATIONS

1980 *Schema*   Pontificia Commissio Codici Iuris Canonici Recognoscendo, *Schema Codicis Iuris Canonici iuxta animadversiones S. R. E. Cardinalium, Episcoporum Conferentiarum, Dicasteriorum Curiae Romanae, Universitatum Facultatumque ecclesiasticarum necnon Superiorum Institutorum vitae consecrata recognitum.* (Vatican City: Typis Polyglottis Vaticanis, 1980)

1981 *Relatio*   Pontificia Commissio Codici Iuris Canonici Recognoscendo, *Relatio Complectens Synthesim Animadversionum ab Em. mis. atque Exc. mis. Patribus Commissionis ad Novissimum Schema Codicis Iuris Canonici Exhibitarum, cum Responsionibus a Secretaria et Consultoribus datis* (Vatican City: Typis Polyglottis Vaticanis, 1981)

1982 *Schema*   Pontificia Commissio Codici Iuris Canonici Recognoscendo, *Codex Iuris Canonici: Schema Novissimum iuxta placita Patrum Commissionis Emendatum atque Summo Pontifici Praesentatum* (Vatican City: Typis Polyglottis Vaticanis, 1982)

AC   Pius XI. Encyclical *Ad catholici sacerdotii*, December 20, 1935: AAS 28 (1936) 390-395

ADA   *Vatican Council II, Acta et Documenta Concilio Oecumenico Vaticano II Apparando, Series 1 Antepraeparatoria* (Vatican City: Typis Polyglottis Vaticanis, 1960)

AHC   Annuarium historiae conciliorum: internationale Zeitschrift für Konziliengeschichtsforschung

AP   Paul VI. Motu proprio *Ad pascendum,* August 15, 1972: *AAS* 64 (1972) 534-540

ASS   *Acta Sanctae Sedis* (Rome: Ex Typographia Polyglotta S. C. de Propaganda Fide, 1865-1908).

Anthony McLaughlin

AAS	*Acta Apostolicae Sedis, Commentarium Officiale* (Rome: 1908-1928. Vatican City: 1929-)
Bruns	Herman Theodore Bruns, *Canones Apostolorum et Conciliorum Saeculorum: Saeculorum IV. V. VI. VII* (Berlin: G. Reimeri, 1839)
CDoc	Catholic Documents
CDTA	*Concilium Tridentinum Diariorum, Actorum, Epistularum, Tractum Nova Collectio.* The Commission of Theologians of the Council of Trent, ed. Societas Goerresiana (Freiburg: Herder, 1901)
17 *CIC*	*Codex Iuris Canonici Pii X Pontificis Maximi iussu digestus Benedicti Papae XV auctoritate promulgatus* (Rome: Typis Polyglottis Vaticanis,1917)
83 *CIC*	*Codex Iuris Canonici auctoritate Ioannis Pauli PP. II promulgatus* (Vatican City: Libreria Editrice Vaticana, 1983)
CCL	*Corpus Christianorum, Series Latina* (Turnhout: Typographi Brepols Editores Pontificii, 1954-)
CM	Benedict XV. Allocution *Cum multa hoc*, December 16, 1920: *AAS* 12 (1920) 585-588.
COD	*Conciliorum Oecumenicorum Decreta*, ed. Iosepho Alberigo et al. (Bologna: Institutio per le Scienze Religiose, 1973)
CON	*Concilium, International Journal of Theology*
Coustant	*Epistolae Romanum Pontificum et Quae ad Eos Scriptae sunt: Clemente I usque Ad Inocentium III,* ed. Pierre Coustant (Braunsberg: Eduard Peter, 1868)
DDC	*Dictionnaire de droit canonique,* ed. Raoul Naz (Paris: Librairie Letouzey et Ané, 1935-1965)
Discorsi	*Discorsi e radiomessagi de Sua Santita Pio XII* (Milan: Societa Editrice 'Vita e pensiero,' 1943)
DMC	*Dictionarium Morale et Canonicum,* ed. Pietro Palazzini (Rome: Officium Libri Catholici, 1962-1968)

DSAM	*Dictionnaire de spiritualité ascétique et mystique: doctrine et histoire,* ed. Marcel Viller et al. (Paris: G. Beauchesne et fils, 1937-.)
DThC	Dictionnaire de théologie Catholique
DV	Vatican II. Dogmatic constitution *Dei verbum,* November 18, 1965: *AAS* 58 (1966) 817-830
FC	John Paul II. Apostolic exhortation *Familiaris consortio,* November 22, 1981: *AAS* 74 (1982) 81-191
FKDG	Forum für Katholische Theolgie
Fontes	*Codicis Iuris Canonici Fontes,* ed. Pietro Gasparri (Rome: Typis Polylottis Vaticanis, 1923-1939)
Friedberg	*Corpus Iuris Canonici,* ed. Emil Friedberg (Graz: Akademische Druck- u. Verlagsanstalt, 1959)
Gia	Pius XII. Allocution to Roman Rota, *Gia per la terza volta,* October 31, 1941: *AAS* 33 (1941) 421-426
GS	Vatican II. Pastoral constitution *Gaudium et spes,* December 7,1965: *AAS* 58 (1966) 1025-1115
Incrementa	*Incrementa in Progressu 1983 Codicis Iuris Canonici,* ed. Edward Peters (Montréal: Wilson & Lafleur, 2005)
Joannou	Périclès-Pierre Joannou, *Discipline* générale antique. (Grottaferrata: Pontificia Commissione per la Redazione del Codice di Diritto Canonico Orientale, 1962)
JTS	*Journal of Theological Studies*
Lewis & Short	Charlton T. Lewis & Charles Short eds., *A Latin Dictionary* (Oxford, England: Clarendon Press, 1962)
LG	Vatican II. Dogmatic constitution *Lumen gentium,* November 21, 1964: *AAS* 57 (1965) 5-67
LMD	*La Maison Dieu*
LThK	*Lexikon für Theologie und Kirche*

Mansi	*Sacrorum Conciliorum: Nova et Amplissma Collectio,* ed. Ioannes Dominicus Mansi (Paris: Herbert Welter, 1902)
MC	Pius XII. Encyclical *Mystici Corporis,* July 24, 1943: *AAS* 35 (1943) 193-248
MN	Pius XII. Apostolic exhortation *Menti nostrae,* September 23, 1950: *AAS* 42 (1950) 657-702
MQ	Paul VI. Motu proprio *Ministeria quaedam,* August 15, 1972: *AAS* 64 (1972) 529-534
NI	John Paul II. Letter *Novo incipiente,* April 8, 1979: *AAS* 71 (1979) 393-417
NRT	*Nouvelle revue théologique*
OT	Vatican II. Decree *Optatam totius,* October 28, 1965: *AAS* 58 (1966) 713-727
PC	Vatican II. Decree *Perfectae caritatis,* October 28, 1965: *AAS* 58 (1966) 702-712
Percival	*Seven Ecumenical Councils of the Undivided Church,* ed. Henry Percival (New York, NY: Charles Scribner's Sons, 1900)
PG	*Patrologia Cursus Completus. Series Graeca,* ed. J. P. Migne. 162 vols. (Belgium: Brepols Press, 1857-1866)
PH	Congregation for the Doctrine of the Faith, *Persona humana: Declaration on Certain Questions Concerning Sexual Ethics,* December 29, 1975: *AAS* 68 (1976) 77-96.
PL	*Patrologia Cursus Completus. Series Latina,* ed. J. P. Migne. 221 vols. (Belgium: Brepols Press, 1857-1866)
PO	Vatican II. Decree *Presbyterorum Ordinis,* December 7, 1965: *AAS* 58 (1966) 991-1024.
PPF	*Iuris Pontificii De Propaganda Fide* (Rome: Ex Typographia Polyglotta S. C. de Propaganda Fide, 1888-1909)
RAC	*Reallexikon für Antike und Christentum.*

RE	Sacred Congregation for the Propagation of the Faith. Decree *Romanae Ecclesiae*, May 1, 1897: *ASS* 30 (1897-1898) 635-636.
RH	John Paul II. Encyclical *Redemptor hominis,* March 4, 1979: *AAS* 71 (1979) 257-324
Roskovány	*Caelibatus et Breviarum: Duo Gravissima Clericorum Officina, e Monumentis Omnium Seculorum Demonstrata,* ed. Augustino De Roskovány. 11 vols. (Pestini: Typis Beimel et Basilii Kozma, 1861)
RRDec	*Sacrae Romanae Rotae Decisiones Seu Sententiae* (Vatican City: Libreria Editrice Vaticana, 1909-.)
SCo	Leo XIII. Encyclical *Satis cognitum,* June 29, 1896: *ASS* 28 (1895-96) 708-73
Schema de Populi Dei	Pontificia Commissio Codici Iuris Canonici Recognoscendo, *Schema Canonum Libri II De Populo Dei* (Vatican City: Typis Polyglottis Vaticanis, 1977)
Schroeder	*Disciplinary Decrees of the General Councils,* ed. H. J. Schroeder (St. Louis, MO: B. Herder Book Co., 1937)
SDO	Paul VI. Motu proprio *Sacram diaconatus ordinem,* June 18, 1967: *AAS* 59 (1967) 697-704
SV	Pius XII. Encyclical *Sacra virginitas*, March 25, 1954: *AAS* 46 (1954) 161-191
Tanner	*Decrees of the Ecumenical Councils,* ed. Norman P. Tanner. 2 vols. (Washington: Sheed & Ward and Georgetown University Press, 1990)
TPS	*The Pope Speaks*
UT	Synod of Bishops, decree on the ministerial priesthood *Ultimis temporibus,* November 30, 1971: *AAS* 63 (1971) 898-922
ZKTh	*Zeitschrift für Katholische Theologie*

This book is dedicated to the Most Blessed Trinity, my patron saints, Anthony of Padua and Martin De Porres, and my mother and father, Isobelle and Kevin, who taught me that if something is worth doing, it is worth doing well.

In memory of Dr. Joseph Keenan and with deep thanks to his lovely wife, Sally.

INTRODUCTION

Through the reception of diaconate a man becomes a cleric.[1] Canon 277 §1 states: "Clerics are obliged to observe perfect and perpetual continence for the sake of the kingdom of Heaven and therefore are bound to celibacy...."[2] Accordingly, it would seem that clerics have two distinct obligations: sexual continence (no sexual relations) and celibacy (no marriage) with continence presented as the fundamental norm. With the restoration of the permanent diaconate by Paul VI, in 1967 through *Sacrum diaconatus ordinem*,[3] and the admission of married men to this order, a fundamental question arises: "Are married deacons, though dispensed from the obligation of celibacy unless their wife dies, obliged to observe perfect and perpetual continence?"[4]

It can be argued that no exemption from continence is implied in the language of "in matrimonio viventibus" (living in marriage) used in *Lumen gentium* 29[5] and *Sacrum diaconatus ordinem* 26[6] to describe both married candidates

---

1 *Codex Iuris Canonici auctoritate Ioannis Pauli PP. II promulgatus* (Vatican City: Libreria Editrice Vaticana, 1983), c. 266 §1: "Per receptum diaconatum aliquis fit clericus et incardinatur Ecclesiae particulari vel praelaturae personali pro cuius servitio promotus est." Hereafter 83 *CIC*. English translation will be taken from *Code of Canon Law, Latin-English Edition: New English Translation* (Washington, DC: CLSA, 1998). All subsequent English translations of canons from this code will be taken from this source unless otherwise indicated.

2 83 *CIC*, c. 277 §1:"Clerici obligatione tenentur servandi perfectam perpetuamque propter Regnum caelorum continentiam, ideoque ad caelibatum adstringuntur...."

3 Paul VI, encyclical *Sacrum diaconatus ordinem*, June 18, 1967: *AAS* 59 (1967) 697-704. Hereafter *SDO*.

4 As will be evident in the course of this book, this specific issue cannot simply be ignored as illogical or inconsistent with the married state of certain deacons.

5 Vatican II, dogmatic constitution *Lumen gentium* 29, November 21, 1964: *AAS* 57 (1965) 36. Hereafter *LG*.

6 *SDO* 26.

to the diaconate and married deacons. Such terminology found in the code and in applicable Church documents may be read either as descriptive of the candidate simply or of the married state in which he is expected to continue. The 1983 code exempts permanent deacons from some obligations common to all clerics (see canon 288)[7] but canon 277 § 1 is not one of these. Such an exemption did exist in the revision process but was removed shortly before the code was promulgated.

The debate on the re-establishment of the permanent diaconate occurred in the midst of several currents: the restoration of the diaconate *per se*; the necessity of celibacy for deacons; the reservation of the topic of clerical celibacy to the pope alone and not for discussion by the council Fathers; and arguments for clerical continence even for married deacons. The above circumstances raise many questions: What is the distinction among continence, celibacy and chastity? Are married deacons in the Latin Church bound to observe continence? Was the exemption to the obligation of continence for permanent deacons removed during the revision process because it was obvious it did bind them or because it was obvious that it did not? Can continence be obliged of those who did not explicitly accept this obligation when they petitioned for ordination? If continence is an obligation for married deacons how should the Church prepare married men and their wives? Two ancillary issues concern the ordination of married men as priests in the Latin Church (the so-called pastoral provision) and also the Eastern Churches' tradition of married deacons and presbyters. These will be examined insofar as they illustrate the question before us.

Ultimately how one approaches the question of married deacons and conti-

---

7   83 *CIC*, c. 288: "Diaconi permanentes praescriptis canonum 284, 285 §§3 et 4, 286, 287 §2 non tenentur, nisi ius particulare aliud statuat."

nence will depend on how one understands the law of celibacy: (1) whether one believes that celibacy is of apostolic or ecclesiastical origin and (2) whether one accepts celibacy understood narrowly as a prohibition on marriage or broadly as the *lex continentiae,* no sexual relations *post ordinationem.*

The purpose of the study will be twofold: 1) to offer a broad overview of the development of the law of continence and celibacy for married deacons in the Latin Church; 2) to provide an interpretation of the law concerning continence and the obligation of permanent deacons and, consequent to such interpretation, practical implications of that law.

This book will have five chapters. Chapter one begins with a systematic treatment of the terminology fundamental to this book. Consideration will then be given to the question of the origins of the obligation of clerical celibacy which is so pivotal in determining not only how one approaches this subject but also the conclusions one reaches. Following this will be a general examination of certain significant pieces of ecclesiastical legislation and magisterial teaching concerning the obligation of chastity, continence and celibacy for clerics in the Latin Church from the Council of Elvira until the 1917 Code of Canon Law. This will allow us to place these obligations in their proper historical context. The chapter will end by offering some conclusions based on the material that was presented.

Chapter two will explore the canonical dispositions of chastity, continence and celibacy in the 1917 code. Particular examination will be given to canons 132 and 133 which obliged clergy in major orders to observe celibacy and chastity. These canons will be examined within their context in the code and in connection with the opinions of selected canonists. Interwoven throughout this examination consideration will be given to other pertinent canons, namely, the canons governing penalties for violations of these obligations; those governing dispensation from these obligations; and those that seek to protect and foster these obligations. Following this will be a brief treatment of significant magisterial teaching on celibacy from the promulgation of the code to the eve of the Second Vatican Council.

Chapter three will follow the discussions of the Fathers at the Second Vatican Council and post-conciliar norms concerning the restoration of the permanent diaconate in the Latin Church. It will also present the conciliar teaching on sexuality and marriage, with particular focus given to the compatibility of marriage and orders.

Chapter four will examine canon 277 §1 of the 1983 Code of Canon Law, with special attention given to the revision process. For the purposes of this chapter we will be concerned with the work of two *coetus* charged with revising the 1917 code: the *coetus de sacra hierarchia*, entrusted with the canons on clerics and the *coetus de matrimonio*, entrusted with canons on marriage. Of particular interest will be the *coetus de sacra hierarchia's* recommendations concerning clerical celibacy and the *coetus de matrimonio's* recommendations concerning orders as an impediment to marriage.

Chapter five will consider whether married deacons in the Latin Church are obliged to observe perfect and perpetual continence. Having already discerned two "schools" of thought in regard to the obligation of continence and married deacons, we will analyze the practical implications of their theses for the interpretation and implementation of the prescripts of canon 277 §1.

This book will contribute to canonical studies by offering a deeper understanding of the relationship between continence, chastity and celibacy. It will also contribute to the debate concerning whether or not married deacons are bound to observe perfect and perpetual continence by highlighting how this debate is influenced by two different understandings of the law of celibacy: celibacy understood as a prohibition on marriage; or celibacy understood as the *lex continentiae*, no sexual relations *post ordinationem.*

CHAPTER ONE

HISTORICAL OVERVIEW: ECCLESIASTICAL LEGISLATION AND MAGISTERIAL TEACHING CONCERNING CLERICAL CHASTITY, CONTINENCE AND CELIBACY FROM THE COUNCIL OF ELVIRA UNTIL THE 1917 CODE

Before we embark on an historical overview of ecclesiastical legislation and magisterial teaching concerning clerical chastity, continence and celibacy in the Latin Church, a number of clarifications and conceptual distinctions must be made.

This chapter will begin with a systematic treatment of the terminology fundamental to this book. Consideration will then be given to the question of the origins of the obligation of clerical celibacy which is so pivotal in determining not only how one approaches this subject but also the conclusions one reaches. Following this will be a general examination of certain significant pieces of ecclesiastical legislation and magisterial teaching concerning the obligation of chastity, continence and celibacy for clerics in the Latin Church from the Council of Elvira in 305 until the 1917 Code of Canon Law. This will allow us to place these obligations in their proper historical context. The chapter will end by offering some conclusions based on the material that was presented.

A. Fundamental Terminology

1. Cleric

The word 'cleric,' translated into Latin as 'clericus,' derives from the Greek word 'κλῆρος,' meaning 'lot.'[1] In the early centuries of Christianity the term 'cleric' was generally applied to all the Christian faithful.[2] From the third century onwards, 'cleric' came to be applied almost exclusively to those preparing for ordained ministry in the Church[3] and in the fourth century the term 'cleric' first appeared in ecclesiastical legislation.[4] By the end of the fifth century it had become common practice among the monastics that one became a cleric with the reception of 'tonsure,' having one's hair sheared.[5] Yet, the practice of tonsure differed from region to region, and more often than not, one was constituted a cleric with the reception of the first minor order. It was not until the twelfth

---

1   See F. Claeys-Bouuaert, "Clercs," in Dictionnaire de droit canonique, ed. Raoul Naz (Paris: Librairie Letouzey et Ané, 1935-1965) 3:828. Hereafter DDC. See also Petrus Tocanel, "Clerci," in Dictionarium Morale et Canonicum, ed. Pietro Palazzini (Rome: Officium Libri Catholici, 1962-1968) 1:705-706. Hereafter DMC. John A. Abbo and Jerome D. Hannan, The Sacred Canons: A Concise Presentation of the Current Disciplinary Norms of the Church (St. Louis, MO: B. Herder Book Co., 1952) 1:159-163.

2   DDC 3: 828.

3   Ibid., 828. There are shades of opinion as to how and when the clergy emerged as a distinct group. Alexander Faivre maintains that there was no lay/clerical distinction in the early church in Emergence of the Laity in the Early Church (New York, NY: Paulist Press, 1990). Another position holds that as a group the laity appeared somewhat sooner, though still without the hierarchical emphasis of a later time, as presented in an essay by Ignace de la Potterie, "L'origine et le sense primitive du mot 'Laïc,'" Nouvelle revue théologique 80 (1958) 840-853. Hereafter NRT. The middle position is maintained by Yves Congar in "Laïc et laïcat," Dictionnaire de spiritualité ascétique et mystique: doctrine et histoire, ed. Marcel Viller et al. (Paris: G. Beauchesne et fils, 1937-.) 9:79-108. Hereafter DSAM.

4   See the Apostolic Canons, in Sacrorum Conciliorum: Nova et Amplissma Collectio, ed. Ioannes Dominicus Mansi (Paris: Herbert Welter, 1902) 1:30. Hereafter Mansi.

5   See James McBride, Incardination and Excardination of Seculars: An Historical Synopsis and Commentary, Canon Law Studies 145 (Washington, DC: Catholic University of America, 1941) 30.

century that tonsure was established as a universal practice for admission to the clerical state.[6]

From the late third century until the twelfth century clerics were ordinarily divided into two categories: minor clerics, that is, those in minor orders (porter, exorcist, lector, acolyte, subdeacon; also known as 'lower clerics') and major clerics, those in major orders (deacon and presbyter; also known as 'higher clerics').[7] In the twelfth century the order of subdeacon was established as a major order after the Second Lateran Council, 1139[8] extended the prohibition on marriage to include subdeacons. Henceforth there were four minor orders and three major orders.[9] The 1917 Code of Canon Law retained these grades of orders.[10]

It is worth noting that prior to the Second Vatican Council, 1962-1965 the place of the episcopate within the grades of orders was disputed.[11] The common opinion of canonists was that the episcopate was included under the order of

---

6   *DDC* 3: 828-829.

7   Ibid.

8   See Second Lateran Council, c. 7. Decrees of the Ecumenical Councils, ed. Norman P. Tanner (London and Washington: Sheed and Ward and Georgetown University Press, 1990) 1:198. Hereafter Tanner.

9   See Kenan B. Osborne, *Priesthood: A History of Ordained Ministry in the Roman Catholic Church* (New York/Mahwah: Paulist Press, 1988) 202-204; Aidan Nichols, *Holy Order: The Apostolic Ministry from the New Testament to the Second Vatican Council* (Dublin: Veritas Publications, 1990) 73-74.

10   Codex Iuris Canonici Pii X Pontificis Maximi iussu digestus Benedicti Papae XV auctoritate promulgatus (Rome: Typis Polyglottis Vaticanis, 1917), c. 949: "In canonibus qui sequuntur, nomine ordinem maiorum vel sacrorum intelliguntur presbyteratus, diaconatus, subdiaconatus; minorum vero acolythatus, exorcistatus, lectoratus, ostiariatus." Hereafter 17 CIC.

11   For a fuller examination of this debate see Charles Journet, *The Church of the Word Incarnate* (London and New York: Sheed and Ward, 1955) 98-109.

presbyter.[12] It was only with the Second Vatican Council that the episcopate was explicitly recognised as an order distinct from the presbyterate.[13]

In 1967, in his motu proprio *Sacrum diaconatus ordinem*[14] Paul VI restored the diaconate as a permanent order in the Latin Church. Several years later, in his motu proprio *Ministeria quaedem,*[15] he abolished the division of the clergy into minor and major orders and replaced the four minor orders with two ministries, lector and acolyte. The pope further clarified that the sacrament of holy orders consisted of three grades: deacon, presbyter and bishop.[16] The pope also established that while previously one was constituted a cleric with the reception of tonsure[17] now one was constituted a cleric with the reception of diaconate.[18]

As demonstrated, the term 'cleric' has encompassed various realities at different times in the Church's history, giving rise to different obligations concerning chastity, continence and celibacy. These obligations were directly related to rank (minor or major cleric) and marital status (married, single, widowed). Though this book will address the situation of married deacons in the Latin Church, reference will also be made to clerics of the Eastern Churches insofar it illuminates the question before us. When the term 'cleric' is used in this book, the necessary distinctions will be made.

---

12   See T. Lincoln Bouscaren, Adam Ellis and Francis Korth, eds., Canon Law: A Text and Commentary (Milwaukee, WI: Bruce Publishing Company, 1946) 427; Matthaeus Conte a Coronata, Institutiones Iuris Canonici (Torino: Casa Editrice Marietti, 1936) 1:197; Heriberto P. Jone, Commentarium in Codicem Iuris Canonici (Paderborn: Ferdinand Schöningh, 1955) 2:173.
13   Vatican II, *Lumen gentium* 21, November 21, 1964 (Hereafter *LG*) in *Acta Apostolicae Sedis* 57 (1965) 24-25. Hereafter *AAS*. See Osborne, *Priesthood: A History of Ordained Ministry in the Roman Catholic Church,* 324-333.
14   Paul VI, motu proprio *Sacram diaconatus ordinem,* June 18, 1967: *AAS* 59 (1967) 697-704. Hereafter *SDO*.
15   Paul VI, motu proprio *Ministeria quaedam,* August 15, 1972: *AAS* 64 (1972) 529-534. Hereafter *MQ*.
16   See *LG* 18-29. *AAS* 57 (1965) 21-36.
17   17 CIC, c. 108: "Qui divinis ministeriis per primam saltem tonsuram mancipati sunt, clerici dicuntur."
18   *MQ* 1. *AAS* 64 (1972) 531.

2. Human Sexuality

Chastity, continence and celibacy are ultimately ways in which our human sexuality is lived. Thus any meaningful discussion of chastity, continence and celibacy can only begin within the context of the Church's teaching on human sexuality.

"God created man in his own image, male and female he created them."[19] Our understanding of sexuality depends primarily upon the way we view ourselves as human persons. In other words, it flows from our anthropology. Pope John Paul II emphasized that the Christian's understanding of sexuality necessarily flows from a Christian anthropology.[20] Concerning this "Christian anthropology" David Bohr in *Catholic Moral Tradition* states:

> A Christian anthropology has as its foundation the principal tenet that we have been created in the image and likeness of God, who is a Tri-unity of personal relationships. Person is thus the basic Christian value, and love the primary virtue. Through our misuse of God's gift of freedom, which alone allows us to stay in loving relationships and to remain whole, the human race from its beginning has come under the predominant influence of the sundering effects of sin.[21]

Man and woman are created in the image and likeness of God and are called into a personal relationship with him and with one another. God has graced hu-

---

19   Gen 1:27. In *The New American Bible* (Nashville: Catholic Bible Press, 1987). Hereafter *NAB*.

20   John Paul II, Original Unity of Man and Woman: Catechesis on the Book of Genesis. Addresses given to general audiences from September 5, 1979 through April 2, 1980 (Boston, MA: St. Paul Editions, 1981). See also John Paul II, Theology of the Body. Series of 129 lectures given at Wednesday audiences from September 5, 1979 and November 28, 1984. Published in Theology of the Body, trans. Michael Waldstein (Boston, MA: Pauline Books & Media, 2006). See also Benedict M. Guevin, Christian Anthropology and Sexual Ethics (Lanham, MD: University Press of America, 2002).

21   David Bohr, Catholic Moral Tradition (Eugene, OR: Wipf & Stock, 2006) 236.

manity with the gift of sexuality. Our maleness, our femaleness, our sexuality, our sexual appetite is sacred. However, due to the effects of original sin, our intellect is darkened and our will is constrained so that humanity, while essentially good, labors under a woundedness. Yet, even though our sexuality is a gift, it is not an ultimate end in itself. As Bohr reminds us:

> Throughout the New Testament human sexuality is always discussed within the perspective of the kingdom of God. Sex is perceived as a basic human good, a great gift of God, but it is certainly not the highest or greatest good. It is neither to be fled from nor worshipped.[22]

Accordingly, our sexuality, while 'a good,' is not the highest 'good.' Union with another person, though 'a good,' is not the same as 'union with God' which is a higher 'good.'

3. Chastity

The word 'chastity' derives from the Latin 'castitas,' meaning "purity in sexual matters."[23] Chastity falls under the virtue of temperance.[24] Aurelio Fernandez and James Socias define chastity as:

> The moral virtue which moves a person to moderate the use of the sexual powers out of love for God and a desire to please him by avoiding anything that would harm the dignity of other people. As such, chastity is another expression of the virtue of temperance....[25]

Chastity is the virtue which consists in moderating the sexual

22   Ibid., 245.
23   See Charlton T. Lewis and Charles Short eds., A Latin Dictionary (Oxford, England: Clarendon Press, 1962) 298. Hereafter Lewis and Short.
24   See Émile Jomart, "Chastité des clercs," in DDC 3:665-675; Pietro Palazzini, "Castitas," in DMC 1: 582-584.
25   Aurelio Fernandez and James Socias, Our Moral Life in Christ: A Basic Course on Moral Theology (Princeton, NJ: Scepter Press, 1997) 286.

appetite according to one's state in life. To live this virtue, one either abstains from all sexual relations or is moderate in its use, in conformity with the moral norms.[26]

Chastity as a Christian virtue is an integral part of our universal call to holiness, which we have received through faith and baptism.[27] The baptized are called to practice chastity as they live out their sexuality. Karol Wojtyla (later Pope John Paul II) spoke of chastity in these terms:

> Chastity is understood in the Church as the proper living of one's sexuality in accord with one's vocation. All human persons are sexual beings. Our sexuality is sacred and a gift from God. Like any gift our sexuality needs to be properly ordered. Chastity is the fundamental call to use the gift of our sexuality properly, according to our nature and condition in life. Chastity as a Christian virtue is an integral part of our universal call to holiness, which we received through faith and baptism. Chastity is not a "negative" virtue; "it is above all positive and creative."[28]

While all the baptized are called to chastity, married, unmarried, or celibate, the way this chastity is lived will differ depending on one's vocation. The 1975 Declaration of the Congregation for the Doctrine of the Faith, *Persona humana,* stated:

> Chastity is a virtue which should put its stamp on individuals according to their various states of life: on those who consecrate their virginity or celibacy to God as a privileged way of more easily giving themselves wholeheartedly to him alone, and on those who live according to the moral law set down for all, be they married or single. But, no matter

---

26   Ibid., 297.
27   See LG 39-40.
28   Karol Wojtyla, Love and Responsibility, trans. H. T. Willetts (San Francisco: Ignatius Press, 1993) 171.

what their state, chastity is not simply an external attitude; it must purify the heart, in accordance with the words of Christ: "You have heard the commandment, you shall not commit adultery. What I say to you is: anyone who looks lustfully at a woman has already committed adultery with her in his thoughts." (Mt. 5:28) Chastity is part of the continence St. Paul lists among the gifts of the Holy Spirit....[29]

The Church lists a number of offenses against the virtue of chastity: lust, masturbation, fornication, adultery, pornography, prostitution, homosexual acts and rape.[30]

In canonical tradition 'castitas' has had an even more specific meaning. The state of 'perfect chastity' is an expression often used to describe the chastity to be practiced by those who are living a dedicated or consecrated life in response to a specific calling from God.[31] The word 'perfect' does not connote a moral quality but rather a commitment which is total and complete.[32] This 'perfect chastity' always involves the renunciation of any and all sexual relations.

4. Continence

The word 'continence' derives from the Latin 'continentia,' meaning 'restraint.'[33] In Christian tradition continence is usually related to sexuality and to

---

[29]   Sacred Congregation for the Doctrine of the Faith, declaration Persona humana, Art. 11: AAS 68 (1976) 90: "Hac quidem virtute pro variis suae statibus homines ornari debent: alteri virginitatem aut caelibatum Deo sacram profitentes, qua quidem eminenti ratione ipsi facilius uni Deo vacare indivisio corde possunt; alteri vero vitam agentes ea forma, quae omnibus lege morali statuitur, prout matrimonio iunguntur aut sunt caelibes. Attamen, in quovis vitae statu castitas non circumscribitur solo externo corporis habitu; ipsum cor hominus purum efficere debet, secundum haec Christi verba: "Non moechaberis. Ego autem dico vobis, quia omnis qui viderit mulierem ad concupiscendum eam iam moechatus est in corde suo." Castitas includitur in ea continentia, quam S. Paulus donis Spiritus Sancti annumerat...." Hereafter PH. English translation from The Pope Speaks 21 (1976) 70. Hereafter TPS.

[30]   Ibid., 8-9.

[31]   See *DDC* 3: 665.

[32]   Ibid.

[33]   Lewis and Short, 448.

chastity in particular.[34] Continence is used to describe 'restraint' in one's sexual life. This restraint can be either relative, periodic (also known as 'temporary') or absolute (also known as 'perfect' or 'perpetual').[35]

Married persons are bound to have sexual relations only with their spouse. Therefore they must observe continence in regard to all persons except their spouse. The married person has a right to sexual relations with their spouse but not with anyone else. This is called relative continence. At times they may even abstain on a temporary basis from sexual relations with each other. Such abstinence may be motivated by reasons of religion, personal choice or circumstances and is called periodic continence.[36] A celibate cleric is bound to abstain totally from all sexual relations with anyone of either sex for life. This is called absolute continence and as such it is also a call to 'perfect chastity.'[37]

5. Celibacy

The word 'celibacy' derives from the Latin 'caelibatus,' meaning 'alone,' and is commonly translated as 'unmarried' or 'single.'[38] In a canonical sense it is applies to those who permanently renounce marriage in service to Christ and his gospel.[39] Such persons are said to be 'celibate.'

Presently 'celibacy' is understood to mean the renunciation of marriage as a primary condition for the reception of orders.[40] Yet this is rather an inadequate

---

34   Palazzani, "Continentia," in *DMC* 1: 944-945.

35   Ibid.

36   Roman Cholji, "Clerical Celibacy in the Western Church: Some Clarifications," *Priests and People* 3 (1989) 303.

37   Palazzani, "Continentia," in *DMC* 1: 944-945.

38   Lewis and Short, 262.

39   See Bonaventure Gangi, "Coelibatus," in *DMC* 1: 722-725 and Émile Jomart, "Célibat des clercs," in *DDC* 3: 132-145.

40   Alfons Maria Stickler, *The Case for Clerical Celibacy,* trans. Brian Ferme (San Francisco: Ignatius Press, 1995) 54; Christian Cochini, *Apostolic Origins of Priestly Celibacy* (San Francisco: Ignatius Press, 1990) 48.

notion when one considers that for much of the Church's history there was no law of celibacy as we presently understand it.[41] Both married and unmarried men were admitted to all ranks of the clergy. In fact no cleric in the Latin Church was obliged to be unmarried, until after the Council of Trent, though they had been prohibited from marrying after ordination.[42] This has led some to conclude that the obligation of celibacy was therefore a late innovation of the Latin Church.[43]

However, others argue that from the earliest times clerics in major orders, whether married or unmarried, were prohibited from marrying after ordination and were obliged to observe absolute continence (no sexual relations) from the day of their ordination.[44] These obligations bound married and unmarried clergy equally. Thus celibacy was understood more broadly in terms of the *lex continentiae,* the law of continence.[45]

It will be necessary to keep these distinctions in mind throughout this book. This author believes that understanding these distinctions is vital in comprehending the historical and theological development of the obligation of celibacy in the Latin Church and our present discussion.

6. Continence, Celibacy and the Story of Paphnutius

Allegedly, Paphnutius, a monk bishop from Egypt, addressed the Fathers

---

41   Stefan Heid, *Celibacy in the Early Church: The Beginnings of a Discipline of Obligatory Continence for Clerics in East and West* (San Francisco: Ignatius Press, 2000) 13; Cochini, *Apostolic Origins,* 48.

42   Heid, *Celibacy in the Early Church,* 15; Cochini, *Apostolic Origins,* 48.

43   Those who argue for the late innovation of celibacy include: Franz Funk, John Moehler, Ferdinand Probst, Elphège-Florent Vacandard, Henri Leclercq, Henri Deen, Jean Paul Audet, Edward Schillebeeckx, Roger Gryson, George Denzler, George Nedungatt, Peter L'Huillier and John P. McIntrye.

44   Those who argue for the apostolic origin of celibacy include: Gustav Bickell, Alfons Maria Stickler, Christian Cochini, Heinz Kruse, Roman Cholij, Thomas McGovern, Henri Crouzel, Stefan Heid and Donald J. Keefe.

45   See also Ludwig Hödl, "Lex Continentiae: A Study on the Problem of Celibacy," in *Priesthood and Celibacy,* ed. Joseph Coppens et al. (Milan: Editrice Ancora Milano, 1972) 693-727.

at the Council of Nicea in 325 as part of their discussions concerning the imposition of absolute continence upon married bishops, presbyters and deacons. He strongly opposed the imposition of absolute continence while at the same time favoring the retention of the prohibition of marriage after ordination. He urged the Fathers to keep the discipline the way it was, that is, as optional. The council Fathers, according to the story, agreed with Paphnutius and stated their opposition to any law that imposed absolute continence on married clergy as an obligation while retaining the prohibition on marriage after ordination. In the light of this intervention and the response of the council Fathers, canon three regarding the cohabitation of clerics with women not belonging to their families could not be interpreted as obliging absolute continence.[46]

The first reference to the story of Paphnutius is found in the fifth century writings of the Byzantine historian, Socrates, in the first book of his *Historia Ecclesiastica*.[47] It should be noted that Socrates wrote this work over one hundred years after the council had taken place and was unable to provide any sources for his information.[48] More telling is that the intervention of Paphnutius is not part of the authentic documents of the Council of Nicea.

Scholarly doubts about the intervention of Paphnutius date back to Bernold of Constance and Pope Gregory VII in the eleventh century.[49] In 1968, Professor Friedhelm Winkelmann, a Byzantine expert in East Berlin, demonstrated that

---

46   Canon three of the Council of Nicea will be examined in greater detail later in this chapter.

47   Socrates, *Historica Ecclesiastica,* ed. Jacques Paul Migne in *Patrologia Cursus Completus: Series Graeca* (Belgium: Brepols Press, 1857-1887) 67: 101b-104b. Hereafter *PG*.

48   Ibid.

49   "The first historical retrospective on the origins of priestly celibacy is written as a correspondence between two twelfth century clerics with regard to the Gregorian reform. Bernold of Constance, a papal theologian (1050-1100), embarks on a fierce polemic against a friend of his named Albonius, a canon. The main argument of Bernold is the basic incompatibility between canon 3 of Nicea regarding the cohabitation of clerics with women not belonging to their families and the story of the intervention of Paphnutius." Cochini, *The Apostolic Origins of Priestly Celibacy*, 18-19.

the Paphnutius episode was "the product of a progressive hagiographic confabulation."[50] Though his conclusions have been generally accepted in scholarly circles,[51] Winklemann's work does not seem to have entered into general knowledge. As a consequence, the Paphnutius' legend remains largely unchallenged.[52]

Through the centuries to the present day the story of Paphnutius has been used as evidence that a law of absolute continence did not exist during the first three centuries of the Church. It is contended that in making absolute continence an obligation for higher clerics the councils and roman pontiffs moved away from a tradition that had the highest antiquity in its favor. Therefore the practice of the Eastern Church in permitting conjugal relations to clergy below the rank of bishop is the more ancient practice.

If indeed the intervention of Paphnutius at Nicea is false, then an important piece of evidence for the late introduction of obligatory celibacy is called into question, and the entire subject is open to reevaluation. In the wake of Winklemann's refutation of the Paphnutius story, a number of respected scholars have produced studies reevaluating the Church's practice of clerical celibacy. Of the more noteworthy are Alfons Maria Stickler, Christian Cochini, Henri Kruse,

---

50   Friedhelm Winkelmann, "Paphnutios, der Bekenner und Bishof," in *Probleme der Koptischen Literatur* (Wittenburg: Institut für Byzantinsk der Martin Luther Universitat Halle-Wittenberg, 1968) 1: 145-153. See also Cochini, *The Apostolic Origins of Priestly Celibacy,* 197; Roman Cholij, *Clerical Celibacy in the East and the West* (Hereford, England: Fowler Wright Books, 1988) 92.

51   See Peter L'Huillier, "Book Review: Clerical Celibacy in the East and West by Roman Cholij," *Sobornost* 12 (1990) 182. L'Huillier states: "The episode of the intervention of Paphnutius during the Council of Nicea is rightly presented as spurious. Today, there is wide consensus among scholars on this point." See also Hans George Beck, *Byzantinische Zeitschrift* 62 (1969) 159; Wilhelm Gessel, "Besprechungen," *Annuarium Historiae Conciliorum* 2 (1970) 422-423 and George Denzler, *Das Papsttum und der Amtszölibat* (Stuttgart: Hiersemann, 1973-1976) 1:9-10.

52   Heid, *Celibacy in the Early Church,* 18, footnote 6: "It is particularly annoying when newer lexicons and reference works uncritically maintain a scholarly position that has long been outdated." See Jochen Eber, "Zölibat," in *Evangelisches Lexikon für Theologie und Gemeinde* (Wuppertal: Brockhaus, 1994) 3:2217.

The Obligation of Perfect and Perpetual Continence

Roman Cholij, and Stefan Heid.[53] Cardinal Stickler in his foreword to Cochini's work observes that:

Celibacy is not only, as most laymen tend to think, an interdict against marriage, but it is also continence, i.e., the relinquishing of the use of marital rights by those who had been married before ordination, which was very frequently, if not commonly, the case in the early Church.[54]

In the introduction to his book, *The Case for Clerical Celibacy,* Stickler makes the same distinction:

A reading of this text indicates a double obligation with respect to celibacy: not to marry and, if previously married, not to use the rights of marriage.[55]

Stefan Heid supports the conclusions of Stickler in this regard:

To understand the history of celibacy from today's perspective it is

---

53   Alfons Maria Stickler, "Evolution of the Discipline of Celibacy in the Western Church from the End of the Patristic Era to the Council of Trent," in Priesthood and Celibacy, ed. Joseph Coppens et al. (Milan: Editrice Ancora Milano, 1972) 503-597; Cochini, The Apostolic Origins of Priestly Celibacy; Heinz Kruse, "Eheverzicht im Neuen Testament und in der Frühkirche," Forum für Katholische Theologie 1 (1985) 94-116; Cholij, Clerical Celibacy in the East and West. Stickler authored a small volume in German (1993) that was translated into English in 1995, The Case for Clerical Celibacy. In this work Stickler regrets that a number of good contemporary works (he names a dozen) "have either not yet penetrated the general consciousness or they have been hushed up if they were capable of influencing that consciousness in undesirable ways." 8. Stefan Heid treated both the history and theology of the tradition of clerical continence and celibacy in Zölibat in der frühen Kirche die Anfänge einer Enthaltsamkeitspflicht für Kleriker in Ost und West (Paderborn: Ferdinand Schöningh, 1997). An English translation by Michael Miller appeared in 2000, Celibacy in the Early Church (San Francisco: Ignatius Press, 2000). These authors conclude that the obligation of continence was and remains the fundamental obligation of clergy married or unmarried. They further assert that the prohibition on future marriage only makes sense because of the continence obligation of the cleric. "While some critics have dismissed the conclusions of these works out of hand, as of this writing (2008) no opponent of their view has assembled a point-by-point refutation of their research into primary sources, their interpretation of those sources, or their conclusions concerning the ancient Church's practice of clerical continence." James Knapp, Celibate Chastity in the Life of the Priest in the Light of the Teaching of Karol Wojtyla/John Paul II. The Pontifical John Paul II Institute for Studies on Marriage and Family. STD dissertation. (Washington, DC: Catholic University of America, 1998) 44, see footnote 89.
54   Stickler in his foreword to Cochini, Apostolic Origins, xxii.
55   Stickler, The Case for Clerical Celibacy, 8.

necessary to realize that in the West, during the first millennium of the Church, a large number of bishops and priests were married men, something which today is quite exceptional. However, a precondition for married men to receive orders as deacons, priests and bishops was that after ordination they were required to live perpetual continence or the *lex continentiae*. They had, with the prior agreement of their spouses, to be prepared to forego conjugal life in the future.[56]

Stickler and others distinguish celibacy understood in the strict sense as "not married' and celibacy in the wider sense as "being married but freely foregoing use of the marital act."[57] This has important implications for the whole discussion on celibacy. As Stefan Heid observes:

> The broad outline of the last fifty years of celibacy scholarship shows that something has occurred that not infrequently causes misunderstanding in historical research: a one-sided formulation of the question has produced one-sided answers. Scholars took the present discipline of celibacy in the Roman Catholic Church as their point of departure and searched for a pattern of clerics in the unmarried state in the first centuries. This however, they did not find, at least not for all clerics. The question they should have asked is whether the early Church perhaps knew a different discipline of continence.[58]

While these scholars hold that there must have existed a *lex continentiae* there are still many others who argue that such a law did not exist as an obligation, and that celibacy was a later imposition of papal authority.

---

56   Thomas McGovern, Priestly Celibacy Today (Princeton, NJ: Scepter Publishers, 1998) 33.
57   The terms "law of celibacy in the strict sense," and "the law of celibacy–continence" are used by Cochini in his chapter on "Methodological Precisions" to distinguish unmarried celibacy from marital continence. Cochini, Apostolic Origins, 48-49. Cholij, Stickler and Heid have adopted similar terminology.
58   Heid, Celibacy in the Early Church, 14; See also Cochini, Clerical Celibacy in East and West, 32-38.

As we will discuss later in this chapter when examining the Council of Trullo, 692, many Eastern Church scholars including George Nedungatt, Peter L'Huillier, Constantin Pitsakis, Nicolae Dura and Vittorio Peri reject the thesis that there existed a law of absolute continence for married clergy. They assert that from the earliest times married clergy, without exceptions, were always free to make full use of their marital rights.[59] The only continence required of clerics was periodic. The law of absolute continence for married clergy was a later Western imposition.

B. The Origins of the Obligation of Clerical Celibacy: Bickell versus Funk

As previously noted in the Paphnutius story, the question of the origins of the obligation of celibacy is pivotal in determining not only how one approaches the subject but also the conclusions one reaches regarding the same. While the issue of clerical celibacy has had a long history accompanied by much debate, a particular debate took place at the end of the nineteenth century that is worth noting. The debate pitted two German scholars against each other, Professor Gustav Bickell, a priest-convert to Catholicism and an expert in Eastern Law, and Professor Franz X. Funk, also a priest and patristic scholar.[60]

Bickell claimed that the obligation of clerical celibacy had its origins in

---

59   Constantin G. Pitsakis, "Clergé marié et célibat dans la législation du Concile in Trullo: le point de vue Oriental," *The Council in Trullo Revisited,* Kanonika 6, eds. George Nedungatt & Michael Featherstone (Rome: Pontificio Istituto Orientale, 1995) 270-279.

60   Gustav Bickell and Franz Xavier Funk published a number of articles in defense of their own claims and to counter the claims of the other. Bickell, "Der Cölibat eine apostolische Anordnung," Zeitschrift für katholische Theologie 2 (1878) 26-64; Funk, "Der Cölibat keine apostolische Anordnung," Theologische Quartalschrift 61 (1879) 208-247; Bickell, "Der Cölibat dennoch eine apostolische Anordnung," Zeitschrift für katholische Theologie 3 (1879) 792-799; Funk, "Der Cölibat noch lange keine apostolische Anordnung," Theologische Quartalschrift 62 (1880) 202-221; Funk, "Cölibat und Priesterehe im christlichen Altertum," in Kirchengeschichtliche Abhandlungen und Untersuchungen (Paderborn, Ferdinand Schöningh, 1899) 121-155.

law derived from the apostles. No deacon, presbyter or bishop could marry. When a married man was ordained to any of these orders, he was required to abstain permanently from the use of marriage (no conjugal relations: *absolute continence*). Thus Bickell argued for the existence of celibacy understood in terms of the *lex continentiae*. The Council of Elvira, 305,[61] had simply reinforced in written legislation that which was already considered binding among the clergy.[62]

Funk countered that the obligation for a deacon, priest or bishop to be either celibate (no marriage after ordination) or else remain continent within his marriage dated only from the Council of Elvira and consequently, was not of apostolic origin. Before Elvira, clerics were commonly married and were permitted to continue conjugal relations. Funk cited the Paphnutius episode in support of this claim.[63] In this regard the Eastern law permitting married deacons and priests the right to conjugal relations was more authentic and represented the apostolic norm. Funk received the significant agreement of other leading scholars such as Elphège-Florent Vacandard and Henri Leclercq.[64] Funk's view of the matter became the *opinio communis* of many and even today it remains the most

---

61   Council of Elvira, c. 33. Mansi, 2:11. This was the first church council to legislate the obligation of continence for married deacons, presbyters and bishops.
62   Bickell, "Der Cölibat eine apostolische Anordnung," 26-64. Scholars such as Deen, Cochini, Heid, Heinz, Boni, Stickler, McGovern, Boni, Bonivento, agree with Bickell. See Henri Deen, *Le célibat des prêtres dans les premiers siècles de l'Église* (Paris: Éditions du Cèdre, 1969); Cholij (see footnote 52); Cochini (see footnote 52); Kruse (see footnote 52); Heid (see footnote 52); Andrea Boni, *Sacralità del celibato sacerdotale* (Genova, 1979); McGovern, *Priestly Celibacy Today;* Cesare Bonivento, *Priestly Celibacy: Ecclesiastical Institution or Apostolic Tradition* (Papua New Guinea: Vanimo, 2006) 37.
63   Funk, "Cölibat und Priesterehe im Christlichen Altertum," 121-122.
64   See Elphège-Florent Vacandard, "Les origines du célibat ecclésiastique," Études de critique et d'histoire religieuse 1(1905) 71-120; Henri Leclercq, "La législation conciliaire relative au célibat ecclésiastique," in Dictionnaire d'archéologie chrétienne et de liturgie 2 (1908) 2068-2088. Hereafter DACL.

widely accepted interpretation.[65]

Funk and Bickell did agree on two things. First, a *lex continentiae* did exist though they disagree on its origin: apostolic or ecclesiastical. Second, for much of the Church's history there was no obligation for a cleric to be unmarried. Now let us examine the first piece of ecclesiastical legislation to govern the sexual lives of deacons, priests and bishops.

C. Ecclesiastical Legislation from Elvira, 305 until Nicea, 325

1. Council of Elvira, 305[66]

The Council of Elvira was both the first church council to be held in Spain and the first council to promulgate disciplinary canons. It took place in the province of Betcia (present day Andalusia) around May 15, 305 A.D[67] and was at-

---

65   See John Adam Möhler, "Beleuchtung der Denkschrift für Die Aufhebung des Den Katholischen Geistlichen Vorgeschriebenen Cölibates. Mit drei Actenstucken," in *Gesammelte Schriften und Aufsatze* (Regensburg: Dollinger, 1839) 1:177-267; Ferdinand Probst, *Kirchliche Discipline in den drei ersten Christlichen Jahrhunderten* (Tübingen: H. Laupp, 1873); Bickell (see footnote 61); Elphège-Florent Vacandard, "Les origines du célibat ecclésiastique," Études de *critique et d'histoire religieuse* 1 (1905) 71-120; Henri Leclercq, "La législation conciliaire relative au célibat ecclésiastique," in *DACL* 2 (1908) 2068-2088; Jean Paul Audet, *Mariage et célibat dans le service pastorale de l'Église: Histoire et orientations* (Paris: Éditions de L'Orante, 1967); Edward Schillebeeckx, *Der Amtszölibat: Eine Kritische Besinnung* (Düsseldorf: Patmos, 1967); Roger Gryson, *Les origines du célibat ecclésiastique du premier au septième siècle* (Gembloux, J. Duculot, 1970); Georg Denzler, *Das Papsttum und der Amtszölibat* (Stuttgart, Hiersemann, 1973).

66   For a history of the council see Charles Joseph Hefele, "Concile d'Elvire," in *Histoire des conciles* (Paris: Letouzy et Ané, 1907) 1/1:212-264. See also Alfred William Winterslow Dale, *The Synod of Elvira and Christian Life in the Fourth Century* (London: Macmillan, 1882).

67   There is some disagreement concerning the date of this council because of the contention that some canons, including canon 33, may have been later added to the acts of the council. Hefele, Barionius, Binius and Mansi do not accept this and they date the canons of Elvira to around 306 AD. See Hefele, *Histoire Des Conciles,* 1/1:220. Those who argue that celibacy was a late invention of Rome postpone canon 33 to the end of the fourth century. See George Denzler, *Die Geschichte des Zölibats* (Freiburg: Herder, 1993) 25; Schillebeeckx, *Christliche Identität und kirchliches Amt* (Düsseldorf: Patmos Verlag, 1985) 289; Heinz-Jürgen Vogels, Priester dürfen heiraten: Biblische, geschichtliche und rechtliche Gründe gegen den Pflichtzölibat (Bonn: *Köllen*, 1992) 38-40. Yet even if a few canons had been added later to the acts of the council, there would be no evidence for assuming that canon 33 was among them. See also Eckhard Reichert, *Die Canones der Synode von Elvira: Einleitung und Kommentar* (Dissertation, University of Hamburg, 1990) 21-23, 49; Heid, *Celibacy in the Early Church,* 110.

tended by nineteen bishops, twenty-four priests and a certain number of deacons and lay persons.[68] Against the backdrop of a disintegrating Roman Empire, the Church in Spain sought to reclaim its unique identity by defining what it was to be a Christian in terms of sexual behavior with particular emphasis on the differentiation of clergy from laity.[69] The council dealt predominantly with matters related to sexuality and established sexual codes of conduct that bound laity strictly and clergy more strictly.[70]

The first instance of written legislation regulating the marriages of clergy was promulgated by this council.[71] Canon 33 under the title, "Concerning bishops and ministers of the altar who must live in abstinence with their wives," is particularly significant to our study. It stated:

> We have decreed a general prohibition for bishops, presbyters and deacons, that is all clerics who have been appointed to ministry, not to have sexual relations with their wives and procreate children. Whosoever

---

68   Hefele, "Concile d'Elvire," 1/1:214.

69   Samuel Laeuchli, *Power and Sexuality: The Emergence of Canon Law at the Synod of Elvira* (Philadelphia: Temple University Press, 1972) 88.

70   Ibid.

71   The Council of Elvira, c. 18: "Episcopi, presbyteres et diacones si in ministerio positi detecti fuerint quod sint moechati, placuit propter scandalum et propter profanum crimen nec in finem eos communionem accipere debere." Mansi, 2: 9; c. 27: "Episcopus, vel quilibet alius clericus, aut sororem, aut filiam virgenem dicatam Deo, tantum secum habeat; extraneam nequaquam habere placuit." Mansi, 2: 10; c. 65: "Si cuius clerici uxor fuerint maechata et scierit eam maritus suus moechari et non eam statim projecerit, nec in finem accipiat communionem, ne ab his qui exemplum bonae conversationis esse debent, ab eis videantur scelerum magisteria procedure." Mansi 2:16. When we examine other canons promulgated by Elvira that regulate the marriages of clergy, we also see reinforcement of the obligation of absolute continence. Canon 18 established penalties for a bishop, priest or deacon who committed adultery; Canon 27 prohibited women from living with bishops and other clerics, except for their sisters or their own daughters, such women had to also be virgins and consecrated to God; Canon 65 required a cleric to separate from an adulterous wife. A wife given to adultery may suggest that she had to look elsewhere for sexual relations because of the absolute continence lived by her cleric husband. Also there was the danger that such a woman could endanger the continence of her cleric husband. See Cochini, *Apostolic Origins of Priestly Celibacy,* 218-219.

shall do the same shall be expelled from the ranks of the clergy.[72]

The canon did not legislate for the celibacy of clerics as we presently under-stand it.[73] In fact the issue was not that clerics were married, but how they were to live their marriages. As incredible as this seems to our recent thinking, the higher ranks of clergy, deacons, presbyters and bishops, were all bound by the same obligation to refrain from sexual relations with their wives and to have no more children. As Fichter observes:

> Whether or not the decrees of the Council of Elvira received wide-spread notice they are a signal that changes were taking place in the tradition of clergy marriage.[74]

However, Maurice Meigne believes that the canon, far from prohibiting sexual relations, was in fact demanding marital intercourse in direct opposition to the ascetical Priscillianists.[75] Accordingly it was not a celibacy canon at all. The canon contained a double–negative, "prohibere…abstinere se," (to prohib-it…to abstain from) which caused Meigne to translate canon 33 in this way:

> We have decided to strictly prohibit bishops, presbyters and deacons, or all clerics appointed to serve in liturgical worship, to abstain from sexual intercourse with their wives and beget children. Anyone who does so will be deprived of his clerical status.[76]

---

72   Council of Elvira, c. 33: "Placuit in totum prohibere episcopis, presbyteris et diaconi-bus vel omnibus clericis positis in minsterio abstinere se a coniugibus suis et non generare filios. Quicumque vero fecerit, ab honore clericatus exterminetur." Mansi, 2:11. English translation from Cochini, The Apostolic Origins of Priestly Celibacy, 159.

73   Laeuchli, *Power and Sexuality,* 95.

74   Joseph H. Fichter, *Wives of Catholic Clergy* (Kansas City: Sheed and Ward, 1992) 6.

75   The heresy of Priscillianism originated in Spain in the fourth century and was derived from the Gnostic-Manichaean doctrines taught by Marcus, an Egyptian from Memphis. The Pris-cillianists were an Encratic group that demanded married adherents abstain from sexual relations.

76   Maurice Meigne, "Le concile d'Elvire et les origines du **célibat** ecclésiastique," *Revue d'histoire ecclésiastique* 70 (1975) 361-387.

Anthony McLaughlin

George Nedungatt agrees with Meigne:

According to the literal meaning, the canon is forbidding clerical refus-
al to render the *debitum coniugale* out of false piety, exactly what the
Synod of Gangres would do in the East; but canonical development in
Spain and in the West as a whole was in opposite sense.[77]

However, the hypothesis of Meigne, that the canon demanded conjugal relations, was challenged a year after his article was published, and the common
opinion is that the canon, while badly formulated, did oblige continence.[78]

While the canon obliged married deacons, presbyters and bishops to observe continence there was no obligation for such clerics to separate from their
wives and children. As Jean Paul Audet observes:

On analyzing it, however, it is clear that there was no intention of setting
the bishop, priest or deacon who was married free of his family cares....
Though obliged to continence, they remained in effect normally responsible for supporting and directing their households. From this point of
view, the obligation to continence in no way made the circumstances of
married clergy easier, it might indeed make it even more burdensome.[79]

The Paphnutius episode also has led some to interpret this obligation of

77   George Nedungatt, "Title 10:Clerics," *A Guide to the Eastern Code: A Commentary on the Code of Canons of The Eastern Churches*, Kanonika 10, ed. George Nedungatt (Rome: Pontificio Istituto Orientale, 2002) 296.

78   See Elie Griffe, "À propos du canon 33 du concile d'Elvire," *Bulletin de littérature ecclésiastique* 74 (1973) 142-145 and "Le concile d'Elvira et les origines du célibat ecclésiastique," *Bulletin de littérature ecclésiastique* 77 (1976) 123-127. Gryson agrees with Griffe, "Dix ans de recherches sur les origines de célibat ecclésiastique. Réflexion sur les publications des années, 1970-1979," *Revue théologique de Louvain* 11 (1980) 160-164.

"The original Latin has a double negative that causes the Spanish Fathers to say exactly the contrary of the obvious meaning. It is obvious that we are dealing with a clumsiness of style or an error on the part of the copiest." Cochini, *The Apostolic Origins of Priestly Celibacy,* 159, footnote 50. As will be demonstrated in this dissertation, the majority of scholars including Gryson, Audet, Schillebeeckx, Denzler, Vogels and Laeuchli, do not subscribe to Meigne's thesis.

79   Jean Paul Audet, *Structures of Christian Priesthood: A Study of Home, Marriage, and Celibacy in the Pastoral Service of the Church,* trans. Rosemary Sheed (New York: McMillan Company, 1967) 12.

continence in terms of only a periodic, ritual continence. The rationale being that if Nicea agreed with Paphnutius and rejected absolute continence for higher clergy and their wives, then Elvira could only have been speaking of periodic continence.[80] But with Winklemann's refutation of the Paphnutius episode, such an interpretation is considerably weakened.

By the fourth century married lay couples were exhorted, though not obliged, to observe temporary continence on the days when the Divine Liturgy was celebrated.[81] Canon 33 imposed continence as an obligation on married higher clergy along with the qualifier "and not to beget any children" (*et non generare filios*). A cleric who violated this obligation would be excluded from the ranks of the clergy. To fulfill the prescript that no children were to be conceived, it would seem that the continence obliged of clergy would have to be absolute. Laeuchli agrees that the major clergy were obliged to absolute and not periodic continence:

> In a somewhat awkward formulation all clerics were asked to abstain completely from their wives and not beget children.....The canon directed its force against the married clergy of Spain by insisting on a marital relationship without sexuality; it does not command celibacy, it prohibits the sexual act.[82]

Gerard Sloyan concludes that the use of Latin phrase "*in totum*" (in general) is an indication that clerical continence had a history. He observes that the periodic abstention from conjugal relations which existed prior to Elvira was now to be total.[83]

---

80   Heid, *Celibacy in the Early Church,* 159.
81   For a fuller treatment of the periodic continence for married lay persons see Cholij, *Clerical Celibacy in the East and West,* 144-178.
82   Laeuchli, *Power and Sexuality,* 95.
83   Gerard Sloyan, "Biblical and Patristic Motives for Celibacy of Church Ministers," *Concilium* 78 (1972) 26-27.

Heid argues that higher clergy were bound to continence not by the fact that they ministered at the altar but by the fact they were in the service of the ministry (*omnibus clericus positis in ministerio*). This is an important distinction.[84] Therefore, continence did not have a ritual basis at all, as though sexual relations made one impure and unfit for the Divine Liturgy.[85] Clerical continence was not limited to periodic ritual continence but was binding from the moment clerics took office, from the day of their ordination.[86] This is a disputed point. Some argue that, in fact, clerical continence did have a "cultic purity" dimension and was attached to an increased sacralization of the clergy.[87] As Galot remarks:

> There is much debate about the social and cultural evolution toward priestly celibacy. It is said that over the years the priesthood became "sacralized" and at the beginning of the third century sexuality was disavowed on the ground that it was considered defiling and was believed to impinge adversely upon the sacred.[88]

Roger Gryson also perceives in canon 33 the motive of ritual continence.[89] Jean Paul Audet contends that continence was obliged of higher clerics precisely because of their "ministerium," their service at the altar. He states:

> What constituted the Christian *ministerium* was thus actually the service of the *sacramenta* properly so-called, especially of course, the service of the supreme *Sacramentum,* the Eucharist. Ultimately, there-

84   Heid, *Celibacy in the Early Church,* 111.
85   Ibid.
86   Ibid., 112. See also Raymond Kottje, "Das Aufkommen der täglichen Eucharistiefeier in der Westkirche und die Zölibatsforderung," *Zeitschrift für Kirchengeschichte* 82 (1971) 226.
87   See Bernard Verkamp, "Cultic Purity and the Law of Celibacy," *Review for Religious* 30 (1971) 217. See also Gerard Sloyan, "Biblical and Patristic Motives for Celibacy of Church Ministers," *Concilium* 78 (1972) 13, 26-27; Jean Galot, *Theology of the Priesthood* (San Francisco: Ignatius Press, 1985) 240 and Henri Crouzel, "Celibacy in the Early Church," in *Priesthood and Celibacy,* 476.
88   Galot, *Theology of the Priesthood,* 240. See also John P. McIntrye, "Optional Priestly Celibacy," *Studia canonica* 29 (1995) 103.
89   Gryson, *Les origines du célibat ecclésiastique,* 39-40, 203.

fore, it was the direct service of the Eucharist, seen as *Sacramentum,* which determined the rule of married continence for the married bishop, priest, and deacon from the moment of entering on the function of their respective "ministries."[90]

Audet believes that the *ministerium* that was subject to continence was the *ministerium* that was in the service of the Eucharist. Therefore, married lower clerics were not bound to observe the continence required of higher clerics.

Cochini, Cholij, Stickler, Heid and Jaki see in this canon evidence that there must have existed in the Church a prior norm concerning continence for married clergy. In their view the canon did not introduce a new practice but merely reinforced an existing norm. The absence of any justification or exceptions indicates that the discipline obliged in canon 33 was neither novel nor controversial. These authors assert that this norm had its origin in the example and teaching of the apostles and was accepted as binding from the beginning.[91] Cochini asserts:

> When one reflects on the magnitude of the canon's demands, the silence of the legislators is easier to explain if they were repeating and confirming a practice already common than if it were the opposite case. One does not brutally impose on married people, even if they are clerics, the harsh asceticism of continence without first telling them why what had been permitted previously suddenly became forbidden. Though such comments do not amount to certainty, they suggest at least that one should not fall too easily into the temptation of making the origins of priestly celibacy coincide with the issuance of the first canonical document we happen to know.[92]

---

90   Audet, *Structures of Christian Priesthood,* 13.
91   This is a much disputed point that we will discuss later in this chapter.
92   Cochini, The Apostolic Origins of Priestly Celibacy, 77-78. Heid argues similarly in Celibacy in the Early Church, 77-78.

Cholij agrees:

The wording of this canon does not immediately suggest that an innovation is being introduced, and it would be an error in historical procedure to maintain *a priori* that such was the case. The seriousness of the
implications for the life of the clergy, the absence of justification for the
strictness of the discipline and the canonical penalty attached, would
suggest, on the contrary, that the Church authorities were concerned
with the maintenance and not the introduction of this rule. Convincing
testimonies to the normative nature of clerical continence in the fourth
century can be found in individual Western patristic authors such as
Ambrose, Augustine, Jerome.[93]

George Nedungatt counters that canon 33 was indeed an innovation:

The fact that celibacy was enforced with a law in the West presupposes
that a practice contrary to it existed. And to presume that such practice
was locally circumscribed or only by a minority (because written evidence is meager) is not good historical method.[94]

Stickler asserts that it is problematic to maintain that the official obligation
to celibacy first began only with the appearance of a specific written law. Stickler argues:

Every historian of law knows (as Hans Kelsen, one of the most authoritative legal theorists of this century, has clearly affirmed) that an identification between law in the general sense and norms (rules, statutes)
is mistaken, *ius et lex*. Law (*ius*) is any obligatory legal norm, whether
it be established orally or handed on by means of a custom or already
expressed in writing. A norm (*lex*), on the other hand, is any regulation established in written form and legitimately promulgated. It is a

---

93   Cholij, Clerical Celibacy in East and West, 36-37.
94   Nedungatt, "Title 10: Clerics," 296.

particular characteristic of law…that the origin of every legal system consists of oral traditions and in the transmission of customary norms which only slowly receive a fixed written form…..such obligations and regulations were handed on orally, particularly during the first three centuries of persecution, which made it difficult to fix them in writing.[95]

Scientific theory would then seem to suggest that the written law of Elvira had its roots in a previous observance.

Yet, there are many scholars who contend that Stickler's position is untenable. Gryson does not support the opinion that prior to Elvira there was any obligation for married higher clergy to surrender the use of their marriage. He aligns himself with the so-called "Funk School"[96] when he states:

There is no trace, before the fourth century, of a law which obliged clerics to celibacy or continence. One sees, on the contrary, that there are clerics who continued to have use of their marriage without reproach, along with clerics who freely choose continence or celibacy.[97]

Heid counters Gryson's claim in this way:

References to obligatory continence are found in the canonical contexts as well, which give expression, not to general exhortations or pious wishes, but rather to deliberate and definitive regulations. We should recall here the Syrian *Didascalia* and the Ecclesiastical Canons of the Holy Apostles. The pastoral letters already contained a legal provision with regard to clerical continence, which claims a validity allowing no

---

95 Stickler, The Case for Clerical Celibacy, 17-18.

96 The "Funk School" includes Möhler, Probst, Vacandard, Leclercq, Audet, Schillebeeckx, Gryson and Denzler. These scholars subscribe to the thesis of Franz Funk that the development of an obligation of continence for married clergy was a later imposition of ecclesiastical law.

97 Roger Gryson, *Les origines du célibat ecclésiastique du premier au septième siècle:* "On ne trouve pas trace, avant le IV siècle, d'une loi qui obligerait les clercs à garder le célibat ou la continence. On voit, au contraire, qu'il y a des clercs qui continuent à user du mariage, sans qu'on leur en fasse reproche, à côté de clercs qui optent librement pour la continence ou le célibat." 42.

exceptions. The ordination of bigamists was at least forbidden long before Elvira. And these regulations only make sense against a backdrop
of a continence discipline for clerics.[98]

Gryson further asserts that ecclesiastical legislation which caused a movement from optional continence to absolute is mostly due to the Church being
influenced by certain sects that discredited marriage and exalted virginity.[99]

L'Huillier argues that the apostolic origins of clerical continence have not
been proven, and he is very critical of the research and conclusions of Cholji,
Cochini and Stickler. He states the following concerning Cochini's research:

> One of the merits of Cochini's book is precisely to show how diffi-
> cult it is to make a genuine contribution to the completion of that task
> of legitimizing clerical continence. He himself seeks to contribute to
> that legitimization historically by contending that clerical continence
> is traceable to the teaching of the apostles. In my view, he does not
> manage to prove this.[100]

Robert McGarrity agrees with L'Huillier when he states:

> Before the fourth century, no extant written law forbids priests from
> marrying or prohibits married men from becoming priests. For the first
> three centuries, celibacy appears to have been a matter of personal and
> vocational choice for all bishops, priests and deacons. Some today

---

98   Heid, *Celibacy in the Early Church,* 114-115. Heid admits that he wrote this book to
'test the soundness of the Gryson and Cochini's theories," 22.

99   Gryson, *Les origines du célibat ecclésiastique du premier au septième siècle*: "Le mou-
vement en faveur du célibat ou de la continence des clercs s'est amorce au sein d'un climat
général de dépréciation du mariage et d'enthousiasme pour la virginité, qui tend à se répandre en
milieu chrétien, au troisième siècle, sous la pression de multiples influences convergentes : cer-
taines sectes juives, les hérésies encratites et gnostiques de douzième siècle." 43.

100   Peter L'Huillier, "The Apostolic Origins of Clerical Continence: A Critical Appraisal of
a New Book," *Theological Studies* 43 (1982) 705. Hereafter *TS.*

might wish it were otherwise. But there is simply no firm evidence that mandatory celibacy is of apostolic origins.[101]

As has been demonstrated there is much debate concerning the existence of a continence obligation prior to the Council of Elvira.

2. First Council of Arles, 314[102]

Certain traditions state that nearly six hundred bishops participated in this council at Arles in Gaul, modern day France, August 1, 314 AD.[103] Unlike El-vira which was a national assembly, "all the provinces of Constantine's empire were present at the council."[104] Constantine called the bishops together with the primary intention of definitively addressing the Donatist controversy.[105] Several of the bishops who attended were also present at the Council of Elvira.[106] The council did not limit itself to dealing with the Donatists, it also enacted various disciplinary decrees concerning the clergy. Canon 29 concerning the continence of clergy stated:

> Moreover, (concerned with) what is worthy, pure, and honest, we ex-
> hort our brothers (in the episcopate) to make sure that presbyters and

---

101   Robert M. McGarrity, "Spiritual and Canonical Values in Mandatory Priestly Celibacy," *Studia canonica* 27 (1993) 219.

102   Hefele, "Concile d'Arles dans les Gaules," 1/1:275-298. Yet, some have placed the num-ber of bishops who attended the council as low as thirty-three, see Hefele, "Concile d'Arles dans les Gaules," 1/1:275.

103   Mansi, 2: 469.

104   Hefele, "Concile d'Arles dans les Gaules," 1/1:276-277. Hefele refers to the Council of Arles as a "General Council of the West."

105   The Donatists were a schismatic sect of especially rigorous Christians in North Africa from the fourth to the seventh centuries. Donatism was essentially a response to alternating periods of persecution followed by toleration, culminating in the beginning of the fourth century by the for-mal legalization of Christianity by Constantine. The Donatists held that Christians who had given in to persecution were no longer fit to occupy positions of leadership in the Church, and, perhaps more importantly, had lost the grace of the Holy Spirit to effectively administer sacraments. See Hefele, "Origine du schisme des donatistes," 1/1: 265-272.

106   Hefele, "Concile d'Arles dans les Gaules," 1/1: 277.

levites (deacons) have no (sexual) relations with their wives, since they are serving the ministry every day. Whoever will act against this decision, will be deposed from the honor of the clergy.[107]

This canon was very similar to canon 33 of Elvira. The council Fathers urged the bishops to ensure that their priests and deacons did not have sexual relations with their wives. These clerics were obliged to continence on a daily basis which was directly related to the fact they were serving the ministry every day. A cleric who violated this obligation was to be deposed. As in Elvira, bishops and presbyters were grouped under the generic name *sacerdotes* and deacons under *levites*.

There is some debate concerning the authenticity of this canon as ascribed to the First Council of Arles. Cochini and Heid are satisfied that this canon is properly ascribed to First Arles and not to a later council based on the preponderance of evidence.[108] Yet others, such as Charles Joseph Hefele, Johannes Dominicus Mansi, and Friedrich Maassen, have argued that this canon was in fact the fruit of a later council in Arles.[109] If the canon is indeed from a later council this would seem to lend credence to the argument that clerical continence was a later imposition.

While Elvira and Arles were held in the West, we will now examine two councils held in the East that took place about the same time as Arles. They were those of Ancyra and Neocaesarea.

---

107   Council of Arles, c. 29: "Praeterea, quod dignum, pudicum, and honestum est, suademus fratribus ut sacredotes et levites cum uxoribus suis non coeant, quia ministerio quotidiano occupantur. Quicumque contra hanc constitutionem fecerit a clericatus honora deponatur." Mansi, 2:474. English translation from Cochini, 161.

108   Cochini, The Apostolic Origins of Priestly Celibacy, 161-169; Heid, Celibacy in the Early Church, 291.

109   Hefele-Leclercq, *Histoire des conciles d'après les documents originaux* (Paris: Letouzey et Ané, 1907-1931) 1/1:295; Mansi, 2:474; Friedrich Maasen, *Geschichte der Quellen und der Literatur des Canonischen Rechts im Abendlande bis zum Ausgange des Mittelalters* (Graz: Leuschner & Lubensky, 1870) 166.

3. Council of Ancyra, 314[110]

Twelve to eighteen bishops from Asia Minor and Syria participated in the Council of Ancyra in Asia Minor, modern day Turkey, around the fourth week of Easter, 314 AD. Though this council was primarily concerned with the issue of *lapsi,* it did also enact various decrees concerning clerical discipline.[111] Canon 10 concerned the testing of candidates for ordination to the diaconate and stated:

> Those who are promoted to deacons, if at the time of their promotion testify they must marry and if accordingly they marry, they may continue in their ministry, because the bishop gave them permission to marry; but if at the time of their ordination they were silent and received the imposition of hands and professed continence, and if later they marry, they ought to cease from ministry.[112]

At first sight this canon appears to stand in contradiction to the Western laws of Elvira, canon 33 and Arles, canon 29 and is interpreted by some as permission for deacons, in certain circumstances, to not only marry after ordination but to have sexual relations in order to consummate such a marriage.[113] Vacandard believes that canon 10 permitted deacons to marry after ordination, and that it had obvious implications for clerical continence. He states:

> Canon 10 of Ancrya obviously shows that if the Fathers of the council authorized the deacons to marry after their ordinations when they

---

110   Hefele, "Le Concile d'Ancyre," 1/1: 298-326.
111   Ibid., 299.
112   Council of Ancrya, c. 10: "Quicumque diaconi constituti, in ipsa constitutione testificati sunt et dixerunt, oportere se uxores ducere, cum non posset sic manere, ii si uxorem postea duxerint, sint in ministerio, eo quod hoc sit illis ab episcopo concessum. Si qui autem hoc silentio praeterito, et in ordinatione, ut ita manerent, suscepti sunt, postea autem ad matrimonium venerunt, ii a diaconactu cessent." Mansi, 2:518. English translation from Seven Ecumenical Councils of the Undivided Church, ed. Henry Percival (New York, NY: Charles Scribner's Sons, 1900) 67. Hereafter Percival.
113   Cochini, *The Apostolic Origins of Priestly Celibacy,* 170.

kept that right for themselves, all the more so did they grant to those who had already married the authorization to continue to use their conjugal rights.[114]

If this is correct, however, it would seem to mark a departure from the tradition of the Church in so far as a deacon could marry after ordination. According to Cochini:

> ….the exception they (council Fathers) make is an important one, and in this respect it can be said that this canon is very useful for the history of the origins of ecclesiastical celibacy.[115]

Cochini, Cholij and Heid all hold that this canon did not give deacons permission to marry nor did it give them license to have conjugal relations in marriage.[116] They point out that the Greek text of this canon distinguished clearly between the scrutinies at the time of promotion and the ordination ceremony. This canon dealt with the testing of unmarried candidates for the diaconate who still wished to marry. The desire to be married had to be expressed at the time the candidate was nominated for promotion. Up to this point the candidate, a lower order cleric, would not have been bound to renounce marriage or to live absolute continence within marriage. Since he was still a lower cleric an exception could be made for him to marry before ordination as a deacon. The bishop could still ordain such a candidate a few years after his marriage. However, with ordination to the diaconate, the unmarried candidate would be obliged to absolute continence, and his opportunity to choose marriage would have passed. The married candidate with the consent of his wife would promise absolute continence. Rather than giving

---

114 Elphège-Florent Vacandard, "Les origines du célibat ecclésiastique," Études de critique et d'histoire religieuse (Paris: Lecoffre, 1905) 92-93.

115 Cochini, The Apostolic Origins of Priestly Celibacy, 170.

116 Cochini, The Apostolic Origins of Priestly Celibacy, 169-176; Cholij, Clerical Celibacy in the East and the West, 28; Heid, Celibacy in the Early Church, 121-126.

permission to deacons to marry and have sexual relations with their wives this canon actually demonstrated the norm which was absolute continence after ordination both for the married and the unmarried. As Stefan Heid concludes:

> Canon 10 thus allows, not the marriage of deacons, but of deacon candidates and, therefore, in any case, of lower clerics. Lower clerics were obliged neither to practice continence nor to renounce marriage. This is also the reason why canon 10 speaks only about deacons. It would be erroneous to think that a concession was made, by way of exception for them to marry after ordination.[117]

Roger Gryson contends that canon 10 did in fact permit deacons to marry. He observes:

> The only thing that the text says about deacons who wanted to marry is that they may be in the diaconal service if they married later on.[118]

Petro B. T. Bilaniuk agrees with Gryson:

> …Ancrya decreed that clergy in major orders may not enter into marriage. Yet it made an exception of an unmarried deacon, who at the time of ordination reserved himself the right to future marriage. An unmarried deacon, who did not make this type of reservation, would lose office if he should marry.[119]

George Nedungatt argues that, in certain circumstances, deacons were permitted to marry after ordination, and that this is indirect evidence that there was no expectation of absolute continence. He states:

---

117 Heid, Celibacy in the Early Church, 125.

118 Gryson, Les origines du célibat ecclésiastique du premier au septième siècle, 84. See also, Cochini, The Apostolic Origins of Priestly Celibacy, 169-171; Cholij, Clerical Celibacy in the East and West, 75-78. Cochini and Cholij agree with Heid and Gryson in this regard.

119 Petro B. T. Bilaniuk, "Celibacy and Eastern Tradition," in *Celibacy: The Necessary Option,* ed. George H. Fein (New York: Herder and Herder, 1968) 39.

The canon providing for deacons to get married not only before but after ordination provided they declared their intention to marry since they could not observe perpetual continence, is indirect proof that they did not marry to live a spiritual marriage.[120]

L'Huillier adds that any attempt to interpret canon 10 as not granting deacons permission to marry after ordination is defective:

> Canon 10 of Ancrya is interpreted on the basis of a Latin translation made in the second part of the sixth century, one which was influenced by the existence of the Western law of clerical celibacy. The wording attested in the most reliable recensions is dismissed.[121]

The interpretation of canon 10 is subject to various conclusions none of which support either argument conclusively.

4. Council of Neocaesarea, 314-325[122]

Most of the bishops who participated in the Council of Ancrya were also present at the Council of Neocaesarea, including the council's president, Bishop Vitalis of Antioch.[123] The council was held in Neocaesarea of Cappadocia, a province of modern day Turkey. Of the fifteen canons promulgated, several concerned the sexual behavior of higher clergy.[124] One of these canons is most significant for our study. Canon 1 stated:

> If a presbyter marries, let him be removed from his order; but if he

---

120   Nedungatt, "Title 10: Clerics," 293.
121   L'Huillier, "Book Review," 182.
122   Hefele, "Concile de Neocaesaree," 1/1: 326-334. Though the exact year of the Council of Neocesarea is debated, most scholars agree that the council took place after Ancrya and before the Council of Nicea, 325.
123   Hefele, "Le Concile de Neocaesaree," 1/1: 326.
124   Council of Neoceasarae, cc. 1, 8, 9, 10. Mansi, 2: 546-550.

commits fornication or adultery, let him be altogether cast out from the Church and put to penance.[125]

Presbyters were prohibited from marrying, and one who violated this pre-script was subject to removal from the order. A presbyter who was guilty of forni-cation or adultery was to be excommunicated and subject to penance. Interesting-ly, Gryson observes that the penalty for a presbyter who committed fornication or adultery was more severe than that for a presbyter who had contracted marriage.[126]

One may wonder why Neocaesarea only prohibited presbyters from mar-rying. Was this an indication that deacons and bishops were permitted to mar-ry? And if so, is this evidence that canon 10 of Ancrya did permit deacons, in certain circumstances, to marry? Such an interpretation would seem to be rash when one considers the legislation of previous councils such as Elvira and Arles which prohibited deacons, presbyters and bishops from marrying. Perhaps the Fathers simply intended to address the specific abuse of some priests marrying after ordination and others committing fornication or adultery.

5. The First Ecumenical Council of Nicea, 325[127]

The Council of Nicea marked a turning point in the history of the Church. The persecution of the Christians had passed, and the same Church that had experienced persecution at the hands of successive emperors now experienced great favor at the hands of one of them, the Emperor Constantine.[128]

---

125   Council of Neocaesarea, c. 1: "Presbyter si uxorem duxerit, ab ordine suo illium deponi debere. Quod si fornicatus fuerit, vel adulterium commiserit, extra ecclesiam abjiciatur et poeni-tentiam." Mansi, 2: 546. English translation from Percival, 79.
126   Gryson, *Les origines du célibat ecclésiastique*, 86.
127   See Hefele, "Le premier concile oecuménique de Nicée," 1/1: 503-632. See also Edward Ingram Watkins, *The Church in Council* (New York: Sheed and Ward, 1960) 26-37 and Leo Donald Davis, *The First Seven Ecumenical Councils 325-787: Their History and Theology* (Collegeville: The Liturgical Press, 1990) 33-79.
128   Davis, *The First Seven Ecumenical Councils,* 27.

Anthony McLaughlin

In May 325, Constantine summoned the bishops to gather at Nicea in Bithynia, modern day Turkey, with the primary intention of addressing the heresy of Arianism.[129] While there had been other church councils, these concerned the Church in particular provinces, regions or areas, but this council was to have more 'universal' appeal. Anywhere from two hundred and fifty to three hundred and eighteen bishops (most of whom were from the East), as well as many priests, deacons and lay people, responded to the call of Constantine.[130] This council has rightly been called the "First Ecumenical Council of the Church."[131]

It is important to point out that while the Church underwent great change now that she was in essence the "official religion" of the empire, there is evidence of theological and disciplinary continuity that bridged the ante-Nicean and post-Nicean Church. Such continuity is especially evident in regards to clerical discipline.

The council promulgated a series of disciplinary canons governing the life of clerics. Virtually nothing was stated on the subject of celibacy. Canon 3 concerned 'women who live with clerics' and was the only canon which could be interpreted as having some relation to the obligation of clerical celibacy. It stated:

The great Synod has stringently forbidden any bishop, presbyter, deacon, or any one of the clergy whatever, to have a *subintroducta* dwell-

---

129   Arianism was a heresy disseminated by the monk Arius in the fourth century. It was one of the most widespread and divisive heresies in the history of Christianity. As a priest in Alexandria, Arius taught that God created, before all things, a Son who was the first creature, but who was neither equal to nor coeternal with the Father. According to Arius, Jesus was a supernatural creature not quite human and not quite divine. In essence Arius denied the divinity of Christ. See Hefele, "Arius," 1/1: 349-362.

130   Hefele, "Le premier concile oecuménique de Nicée," 509.

131   Charles Matson Odahl, *Constantine and the Christian Empire* (New York: Routledge, 2004) 196.

ing with him, except only a mother, or sister, or aunt, or such persons only as are beyond all suspicion.[132]

Prior to Nicea, the Council of Ancyra had rigorously condemned a particular type of cohabitation, the practice of "spiritual marriage," a celibate cleric or lay man cohabiting with a consecrated virgin.[133] Canon 3 of Nicea was directed only to clerics and applied to all cases of cohabitation (not just "spiritual marriage") with women.[134] The Council of Elvira had also legislated concerning women who could live with clerics.[135]

A *subintroducta* was any woman who was not the cleric's mother, sister, aunt or another who was beyond suspicion. It is noteworthy that 'wives' were not listed among those with whom a cleric cannot cohabit, and that no distinction was made between married and unmarried clergy. So the question arises as to whether married clergy were expected to separate from their wives or whether their wives were implicitly included among those who were "beyond suspicion."[136]

Gryson maintains that this canon has to be interpreted in light of the intervention of Paphnutius (which we examined earlier in this chapter) and therefore could only be addressed to unmarried clergy.[137] Others contend that the wives of clergy were included under those who were "beyond suspicion," because they shared the

---

132 Council of Nicea, c. 3: "Vetuit omnio magna synodus, ne liceat episcopo, nec presbytero, nec diaconio, nec illi penitus eorum qui funt in clero, introductam habere mulierem, praeterquam utique matrem vel sororem, vel amitam, vel eas solas personas, quae omnem suspicionem affugiunt." Mansi, 2:670. English translation from Percival, 11.

133 Council of Ancyra, c. 19. Mansi, 2:519.

134 Cholji, *Clerical Celibacy in the East and the West,* 79; Cochini, *The Apostolic Origins of Priestly Celibacy,* 185.

135 Council of Elvira, c. 27. This canon prohibits women from living with bishops and other clerics, except for their sisters or their own daughters; such women had to also be virgins and consecrated to God.

136 Cholji, *Clerical Celibacy in the East and the West,* 79.

137 Gryson, *Les origines du célibat ecclésiastique,* 91.

obligation of continence with their husbands.[138] Future Latin councils confirmed that "wives" were acceptable women to cohabit with clerics because they shared their husband's obligation of continence.[139] Yet even Cochini concedes that the text of canon 3 does not allow us to conclude much with certainty.[140]

D. Influence of Sects Antithetical to Sex, the Body and Marriage

As Heid aptly notes, "One cannot treat the subject of clerical continence without considering carefully the thesis that it was the product of early tenden-cies hostile to the body."[141] Already in the Church of the second century dualistic and pre-Gnostic tendencies were spreading against which the Pastoral Epistles protested: "These people who would forbid marriage and the use of particular food."[142] Later such theories would give rise to various schismatic and/or he-retical groups. Encratism ("*enkrateia*" meaning "continence") is the collective name for these rigorist tendencies and is also the proper name of such a sect.[143] Peter Brown describes the core values of Encratism:

> The Encratites declared that the Christian Church had to consist of men and women who were 'continent' in the strict sense: they had 'contained' the urge to have sexual intercourse with each other. It

---

138 Cholij, *Clerical Celibacy in the East and West,* 80; Cochini, *The Apostolic Origins of Priestly Celibacy,* 186-187.

139 The Second Council of Girona, 517, canons 6 and 7, authorized the wife of a cleric to re-main with her husband on condition that they live as 'brother and sister.' Mansi, 8:549. The Second Council of Arles (442-506) canon 4 permitted a 'converted' wife to live with her cleric husband. See Corpus Christianorum, Series Latina (Turnhout: Brepols Press, 1954-) 148:114. Hereafter CCL.

140 Cochini, *The Apostolic Origins of Priestly Celibacy,* 187.

141 Heid, *Celibacy in the Early Church,* 61-64.

142 NAB 1 Tim 4:1-5.

143 Henry Chadwick, "Enkrateia," in *Reallexikon für Antike und Christentum: Sachwörterbuch zur Auseinandersetzung des Christentums mit der Antiken Welt* 5 (1962) 343-365. Hereafter *RAC.* For a further treatment of Encratism see *Dictionnaire de théologie catholique,* ed. Alfred Vacant et al. (Paris: Letouzey et Ané, 1903-51) 5:4-13. Hereafter *DThC.* See also Joseph Cullen Ayer, *A Source Book for Ancient Church History* (NewYork, NY: Charles Scribner's Sons, 1913) 105-106.

made little difference whether baptized believers had remained virgins from birth, or whether they had decided to abstain from intercourse when already married. What mattered was that the rule of the demons over the human person had been replaced, at baptism, by the exclusive, intimate nurture of the Holy Spirit, which would henceforth admit no further sexual joining.[144]

At the core of these groups was the belief that the flesh was to be denied and the spirit exalted. It was natural that such a belief system would discredit the body, sex, marriage, and exult continence. The church Fathers, even the rigorist Jerome, forcefully opposed all forms of Encratism or other attitudes inimical to marriage.[145] Yet Fichter asserts:

In the fourth century a gradual change was introduced into the concept of marriage as a lower status than virginity or celibacy.[146]

The influence of Encratism on Christianity's view of marriage cannot be dismissed.

Towards the middle of the third century an Encratic group named the Manicheans arose.[147] This religious movement was characterized by a profound pessimism. The world was corrupt and inimical to God. Consequently strict continence and celibacy were required so as to guard the body from every dangerous taint of matter and ultimately to rescue the soul from the body. It was not long before all continence and especially the absolute continence of clergy was suspected as an expression of contempt for the body. As Sloyan observes:

---

144   Peter Brown, The *Body and Society: Men, Sex and the Body: Men, Women and Sexual Renunciation in Early Christianity* (New York, NY: Columbia University Press, 2008) 92-93.

145   Edward Schillebeeckx, Celibacy (New York, NY: Sheed & Ward, 1968) 29-30.

146   Fichter, *Wives of Catholic Clergy*, 7.

147   Manichaeism is the religion of Manes or Mani, which arose in Babylonia about the middle of the third century as one of the many sects classified under the name of Gnosticism. For a further treatment of Encratism see *DThC* 9:1841-1895.

The chief reason alleged in favor of clerical celibacy at the turn of the fourth century was the demeaning quality of sex and its capacity for rendering impure those who engaged in it. This impurity was not moral so much as ritual in the sense of "ill-befitting," "out of character." The increasingly poor view of marriage in Christian circles was the root cause of such an outlook.[148]

Even today celibacy is often interpreted as a vestige of Manichaean antipathy toward marriage. Such a claim presupposes that no celibacy discipline existed until the end of the fourth century.[149] Heid states:

> Such a claim presupposes that no celibacy discipline at all had developed until the end of the fourth century. For it was precisely in this period that the heyday of Manichaeism occurred. Nevertheless, this hypothesis cannot be correct, because clerical continence can be traced back much farther to the period well before Constantine. This discipline was upheld later, despite all suspicions of Manichaean influence. Already in the second century the continence discipline had become the subject of discussions, in which arguments antithetical to marriage and the body also played a role. Manichaeism was in part a revival and a transformation of the early Christian Encratite movement. Encratism had already been overcome successfully without in any way implicating clerical continence. Ambrosiaster confirms what was already clear in Clement: that the affirmation of marriage can go together very well with a discipline of continence within clerical marriage. Neither excludes the other.[150]

The obligation of continence predated the influence of Encratism and therefore could not have originated as a consequence of this heresy.

148 Sloyan, "Biblical and Patristic Motives for Celibacy of Church Ministers," 27.
149 Heinz-Jürgen Vogels, Priester dürfen heiraten: Biblische, geschichtliche und rechtliche Gründe gegen den Pflichtzölibat (Bonn: Köllen, 1992) 45.
150 Heid, Celibacy in the Early Church, 238-239.

The Obligation of Perfect and Perpetual Continence

In the early Church continence was considered as a form of Christian life to which special value was attributed. As Peter Brown states:

By the middle of the fifth century, the Christian Church stood out in the Roman world as an institution that gave pride of place to the continent.[151]

Continence was considered a gift from God and was prized as a moral virtue. In the early Church, continence was practiced by Christian couples:

It has also to be remembered that in the early Church, Christian couples practiced periodic marital continence in line with the St. Paul's counsel: "Do not refuse one another except perhaps by mutual agreement for a season, that you may devote yourself to prayer" (1 Cor. 7:5). It was expected that they would do so especially when it was time to celebrate the memorial of the Lord's Passion and Death. Conjugal abstinence was also recommended during the period of lent. Popes and Fathers of both the East and the West attest to the fact that periodic continence was regarded as normal practice for Christian couples.[152]

Fichter agrees:

There is no doubt that self-indulgence in the pleasures of the flesh and gratification of the senses, are extensive in Western Society. Yet, the virtues of self-control and continence are consciously practiced among both the celibate and the married.[153]

Continence was not simply the obligation of particular ranks of clerics but was also something that the lay faithful were exhorted to embrace periodically

---

151 Brown, The Body and Society, 428. Peter Brown examines sexual continence among clergy and laity from 40 A.D. thru 430 A.D. He demonstrates how early Christian society embraced both temporary and absolute continence for religious motives.

152 Thomas McGovern, Priestly Celibacy Today (Princeton, NJ: Scepter Publishers, 1998) 87-88.

153 Fichter, Wives of Catholic Clergy, 7.

"for the sake of prayer."[154] Even though the Church was exhorting the laity to temporary continence and obliging married clergy to absolute continence, it is incorrect to allege that the primary motivation for this was the influence of the Encratite sects. Schillebeeckx contends:

> Again in the third and fourth centuries, Encratic tendencies became prominent. But now they caused the great Church Fathers of the fourth century not only to begin a deeper theological reflection on religious celibacy but also to defend more emphatically the goodness of the married state. On the one hand, it cannot be denied that a patristic exposition of marriage more often supported the Christian advantages of complete continence than it presented a reflection on marriage itself. Time and time again one finds that marriage is good, but celibacy is better. A fundamental contempt for marriage is foreign to all orthodox Christian writers, even those like Tertullian or Jerome. On the other hand, people forget that the Father's positive achievements on the subject of marriage are the result of their hard struggle against the dualistic attitude of their times.[155]

The Church condemned the Encratites and taught favorably of sexuality and marriage. We can see evidence of this in the legislation of the Council of Gangres, 340.[156]

In the middle of the fourth century a council of thirteen bishops met in the city of Gangres in Paphlagonia (Asia Minor) to address the "evils of the Eusta-

---

154   *NAB* 1 Cor. 7:5. See Francis Martin, "Marriage in the New Testament Period," in *Christian Marriage: A Historical Study,* ed. Glenn W. Olsen (New York: The Crossroad Publishing Company, 2001) 80-82. Martin addresses the issue of St. Paul and his desire, not command, that married persons refrain from sexual relations to be freer for prayer. This is not an indication that sex rendered one impure for prayer but that it was a distraction.

155   Schillebeeckx, Celibacy, 29-30.

156   Council of Gangres, Mansi, 2:1102. See also Hefele, "Concilie de Ganges," 1/2: 1029-1045.

thians."[157] The Eustathians were another Encratic group. They rejected marriage in principle and demanded continence and marital separation for all Christians. Consonant with their beliefs they would only accept the Eucharist from presbyters who were unmarried or who had at least separated from their wives.[158] In response to these positions the council condemned those who rejected the goodness of marriage and conjugal relations. Canon 1 declared:

> If anyone despises wedlock, abhorring and blaming the woman who sleeps with her husband, even if she is a believer and devout, as if she could not enter the kingdom of God, let him be anathema.[159]

The Fathers also condemned a wife who would abandon her husband because she abhorred marriage:

> If a woman leaves her husband and separates herself, from abhorrence of the marriage, let her be anathema.[160]

Furthermore those who remained single because they had contempt for marriage were condemned:

> If anyone lives unmarried or in continence, avoiding marriage from contempt, and not because of the beauty and holiness of virginity, let him be anathema.[161]

---

157 Ibid., 1031.

158 Ibid., 1/ 2: 1031-1032.

159 Council of Gangres, c. 1: "Si quis matrimonium vituperet, et eam quae cum marito suo dormit quae est fidelis et, abhorreat et insimulet, tamquam quae no possit regnum Dei ingredi, sit anathema." Mansi, 2:1101. English translation in Hefele, *A History of the Councils of the Church,* 2: 327.

160 Council of Gangres, c. 14: "Si qua relinquit maritum et vult recedere, matrimonium abhorrens, sit anathema." Mansi, 2:1102-1103. English translation from Hefele, *A History of the Councils of the Church,* 332.

161 Council of Gangres, c. 9: "Si quis virgo sit, vel continens, a matrimonio tamquam abominando recedens, et non propter ipsam virginitatis pulchritudinem et sanctitatem, sit anathema." Mansi, 2:1102. English translation from Hefele, *A History of the Councils of the Church,* 330.

The council condemned those who would not receive Holy Communion or assist at a Mass offered by a married priest. Canon 4 declared:

> If anyone affirms that one should not receive Communion during the holy sacrifice celebrated by a priest who has taken a wife, let him be anathema.[162]

The Fathers resolutely defended the goodness of marriage and conjugal relations in the face of those who were antithetical to sex, the body and marriage. Additionally, the marriages of presbyters were also defended. It was not surprising that a church council would defend the marriages of presbyters. The Church had no difficulty with a presbyter being married. Yet did this also imply an acceptance of presbyters having conjugal relations? George Nedungatt argues that it did:

> Some early Christians refused to receive the Eucharist from married priests. The condemnation of the practice of these Christians implies that married priests were not obliged to observe perpetual sexual abstinence, the norm being periodic continence endorsed by St. Paul (1 Cor. 7:1-5)....The married priests were surely supposed to be using their marriage normally, only common sense is needed to infer that, although some writers seem to prefer to it their own thesis about universal clerical celibacy from apostolic times.[163]

---

162   Council of Gangres, c. 4: "Si quis de presbytero qui uxorem duxit, contendat, non oportere eo sacra celebrante oblatione communicare, sit anathema." Mansi, 2:1102. For a fuller treatment see Demetrios Constantelos, "Marriage and Celibacy of the Clergy in the Orthodox Church," *Concilium* 78 (1972) 30-38 and Christophores Knetes, "Ordination and Matrimony in the Eastern Orthodox Church," *Journal of Theological Studies* 11 (1910) 353.

163   Nedungatt, "Title 10: Clerics," 293, footnote 84, 289.

Yet, when one considers that several councils had already legislated for the daily continence of married presbyters, this remains an open question.[164]

E. Magisterial and Conciliar Teachings from Nicea to Leo the Great

1. Synod of Rome, 386[165] and Second Council of Carthage, 390[166]

At the end of the fourth century, the Synod of Rome, 386 and the Second Council of Carthage, 390 taught that the *lex continentiae* was an ancient discipline practiced from the beginning of the Church and could be related to the teaching of the apostles. The decrees of the Synod of Rome were made known by Pope Siricius in the letter, *Cum in unum,* which we will discuss later in this chapter.

The Second Council of Carthage decreed that married major clerics had to observe continence with their wives. The Fathers in their discussion of canon 2 'that the chastity of levites and presbyters be preserved' stated:

> Epigonius, bishop of Bulla Regia, said "As was established in a previous council with respect to continence and chastity, I demand that those three degrees which by ordination are strictly bound to chastity, that is, bishops, presbyters and deacons, be instructed again in detail to maintain purity."
>
> Bishop Genethlius said: "As was previously said, it is fitting that the holy bishops and presbyters of God, as well as the levites, that is the deacons, all those who are in the service of the divine sacraments, observe perfect continence, so that they may obtain in all simplicity

---

164   Some commentators contend that Gangres while defending the marriages of presbters, could not have also been defending their right to conjugal relations. They cite the legislation of prior church councils that bound married presbyters to continence. See Caesar Baronius, *Annales Ecclesiastici* (Paris: Barri-Ducis, 1864) 3:n. 5; Severin Binius, in Mansi, 2:1117. Gryson presumes that married presbyters were having conjugal relations, see *Les origines du célibat ecclésiastique,* 93-94.

165   Ibid., "Le Concile de Roma," 2/1:68-75.

166   Hefele, "Le Concile de Carthage," 2/1:75-78.

what they are asking from God; what the apostles taught and what antiquity itself observed, let us endeavor to keep."

The bishops declared unanimously: "It pleases us that bishops, presbyters and deacons, guardians of purity, abstain from conjugal intercourse with their wives, so that those who serve at the altar may keep a perfect chastity."[167]

The Fathers at Carthage continued the tradition of previous councils and obliged married deacons, presbyters and bishops to abstain from sexual relations with their wives so that their chastity would be perfect. This obligation arose from the reception of ordination and service at the altar. The African bishops further declared their belief that the law of continence was an ancient observance of the Church that had been taught by the apostles.

2. Third Council of Carthage, 401[168]

Eleven years after the Second Council of Carthage the bishops of Africa met again and addressed the situation of certain clerics not living continently with their wives. Canon 3 stated:

Furthermore, even if it is reported of some clerics that they do not live continently with their wives, nevertheless the bishops, priests and deacons, according to earlier statutes, still must refrain from relations with

---

167 Third Council of Carthage, c. 2: "Epigonius episcopus Bullensium Regirum dixit: 'Cum in praeterito concilio de continentiae et castitatis moderamine tractaretur, gradus isti tres, qui constrictione quadam castitati per consecrationes annexi sunt, episcopus, presbyter et diaconus, tractatu pleniore, ut pudicitam custodiant, doceantur." Genethluis episcopus dixit: 'Ut superimus dictum est, decet sacrosanctos antistes et Dei sacerdotes nec non et Levitas vel qui sacramentis Divinis inserviunt, continents esse in omnibus, quo possint simpliciter, quod a Deo postulant, impetrare, ut quod Apostoli docuerunt ei ipsa servavit antiquitas, nos quoque custodiamus.' Ab universis episcopis dictum est: 'Omnibus placet, ut episcope et diaconi, pudicitiae custodes etiam ab uxoribus se abstineant, ut in omnibus et ab omnibus pudicitia custodiatur, qui altari deserviunt.'" Mansi, 3:692-693. English translation from Heid, Celibacy in the Early Church, 206.

168 Hefele, "Le Concile de Carthage," 2:406-418.

their wives. If they do not, they are to be removed from ecclesiastical office. That other, lower clerics, though, are not compelled to do this, but each should observe the respective custom.[169]

Here the council Fathers were concerned with married bishops, priests and deacons. They again obliged these clerics to live continently in their marriages. They also exhorted 'lower clerics,' though not bound to celibacy-continence, to observe the local custom in their own regard.

We have seen that ecclesiastical legislation, beginning with the Council of Elvira, obliged married major clergy to live the *lex continentiae,* to refrain from sexual relations with their wives and to have no more children. Based on the research thus far we can state a number of things: 1) Married men were admitted to all grades of orders. 2) A married candidate for major orders had to be living in a first marriage. If he had been married more than once or had married a widow or a woman whose morals were questionable, he was not admitted to orders. 3) Married major clerics were obliged to observe continence, no sexual relations with their wives, and were to have no more children.[170] 4) An ordained man was prohibited from marrying. This prohibition was also extended for a time to the spouses of higher clerics.[171]

---

169 Third Council of Carthage, c. 3: "Praeterea cum de quorumdam clericorum quamuis erga uxores proprias incontinentia referretur, placuit episcopos, presbyteros et diaconos secundum priora statua etiam ab uxoribus continere. Quod nisi fecerint ab ecclesiastico removeantur officio. Ceteros autem clericos ad hoc non cogi, sed secundum uniuscuiusque consuetudinem obseruari debere." Mansi, 3:969. English translation from Heid, Celibacy in the Early Church, 213.

170 Nedungatt argues that the there was no continence obligation for clergy in the East until the Council of Trullo, 692. See Nedungatt, "Title 10: Clerics," 295.

171 In both the East and the West ordination has always been considered an impediment to marriage and remarriage for the cleric. The same was also true for the wife of a cleric. After the death of her cleric-husband she was prohibited from remarrying. The first written legislation on the impediment to second marriage for a cleric's widow is found in the First Council of Toledo 400, canon 18: "Si qua vidua episcopi vel presbyteri aut diaconi maritum acceperit, nullus clericus, nulla religiosa persona cum ea convivium sumsat, nunquam communicet; morienti tamen ei sacramenta subveniant." Herman Theodore Bruns, Canones Apostolorum et Conciliorum saeculorum: Saeculorum IV. V. VI. VII (Berlin: G. Reimeri, 1839) 2:206. Hereafter Bruns.

The obligation of continence for married clergy was not only legislated by various church councils in Spain, France, Italy, Africa, and Turkey, but as we shall see the popes themselves also became involved in the issue.

3. Papal Teaching

We will now examine the teaching of three popes who contributed in a significant way to the development of clerical celibacy: Popes Siricius, Innocent I, and Leo the Great. As Cesare Bonivento observes:

> Each pope was emphatic that clerical continence belonged to immemorial, even apostolic tradition. Patristic writings are often explicit in considering the apostles as models of priesthood. Yet those who might have been married were thought not to have lived other than in continence.[172]

These popes date from 385 to 604, and they provide us with a universal perspective on the discipline of clerical celibacy-continence.[173]

a. Pope Siricius: *Directa* and *Cum in unum* Decretals

In the fall of 384, the Spanish bishop Himerius, Metropolitan of the Province of Tarragona, wrote to Pope Damasus (366-384) asking him to address a number of specific questions. On February 10, 385, Pope Siricius (384-399) who had succeeded Damasus as bishop of Rome, responded to Himerius in the letter *Directa*.[174] This famous decretal was a milestone in the history of celibacy.

---

172   Cesare Bonivento, Priestly Celibacy, 37.
173   Stickler, The Case for Clerical Celibacy, 29-37.
174   Pope Siricius, Decreta, February 10, 385. PL. 13: 1131-1147. English translation from The See of Peter, ed. James T. Shotwell and Louise Ropes Loomis (New York, NY: Columbia University Press, 1991) 702-705.

The Obligation of Perfect and Perpetual Continence

Chapter seven of the *Directa* [175]addressed the situation that many married clerics in higher orders, bishops, priests and deacons, were having sexual relations with their wives and having children, and that they were justifying their behavior based on the temporary continence expected of ministers in the Old Testament. Siricius spoke against these violations and reiterated that married clerics, once they are admitted to major orders, may indeed live with their wives, but they were to observe continence. The pope clarified what type of continence such clergy were bound to observe. He stated that while the Old Testament law obliged the ministers of God to marry and beget children, their service in the temple was only periodic, thus only periodic continence was required. However, the priesthood of the New Testament is more perfect. The priestly service is a daily task. Therefore continence is to be observed absolutely.[176]

On January 6, 386, Pope Siricius held a synod at Rome attended by eighty bishops. He sent the canons enacted by this synod to the bishops of North Africa in his letter *Cum in unum*.[177] In this letter Siricius extolled the virtues of clerical continence. He wrote:

> Perhaps one believes that this is permitted for (priests and levites can have relations with their spouses) because it is written: "The husband of one wife" (1 Tim 3:2). But Paul was not talking about a man persisting in his desire to procreate; he spoke about the continence that one should observe. Paul did not accept those who were not beyond reproach and he said: "I should like everyone to be like me" (1 Cor 7:7). And he stated even more clearly: "People who are interested only in unspiritual things can never be pleasing to God. Your interests, however, are not in

---

175 *PL* 13: 1138-1141.
176 See *PL* 13: 1138a-39a.
177 Pope Siricius, *Epistola, Cum in unum*, January 6, 386. *PL* 13: 1155-1162.

the unspiritual, but in the spiritual" (Rom.8:8-9).[178]

For Siricius the continence expected of major clerics was to be absolute. He also offered an exegesis of the Pauline injunction "husband of one wife."[179] He argued that clerical monogamy was a guarantee of future continence, because St. Paul and indeed many in the Christian community considered remarriage as an inability to live continently. "To widows I have to say: it would be better if they remain as they are, even as I do myself; but if they cannot exercise self-control, they should marry. It is better to marry than to be on fire."[180] Cholji agrees with Siricius' interpretation:

> The parallelism between Paul's injunction for widows and that for clerics in 1 Tim 3:2 can be proffered as evidence to further the thesis that the Pauline injunction was a guarantee for future chastity by clerics who, once ordained, were to live as if they had no wife or as brother and sister (1 Tim 5:11-12). This thesis is supported by Cochini and Stickler. Supportive of this theory was the Church's praxis concerning the widow of the priest.[181]

Cochini, Cholij and Stickler hold that the impediment of *digamy* ("twice mar-

---

178   Pope Siricius, Epistola, Cum in unum, "Forte hoc creditur; quia scriptum est, *Unius uxoris virum* (1 Tim. 3: 2). Non permanentem in concupiscentia generandi dixit, sed propter continentiam futuram. Neque enim integros non admisit, qui ait: *Vellem autem omnes homines sic esse, sicuti et ego* (1 Cor. 7:7). Et apertius declarat dicens: *Qui autem in carne sunt, Deo placere non possunt. Vos autem jam non estis in carne, sed in spiritu* (Rom. 8:8)." PL 13:1160. English translation from Cholij, Clerical Celibacy in East and West, 20.

179   The meaning of the phrase 'husband of one wife' has been the subject of much dispute. See Knetes, "Ordination and Matrimony in the Eastern Orthodox Church," *Journal of Theological Studies* 11 (1910) 366-380.

180   *NAB,* 1 Cor 7:8-9.

181   Cholij, Clerical Celibacy in the East and West, 20-21.

ried," synonymous with "bigamy")[182] and the impediment of orders only make sense if the cleric and his wife were obliged to observe absolute continence.

Cholij contends that the impediment of orders did not flow from orders *per se*, but from the promise of absolute continence. The very *raison d'être* of the impediment of orders is absolute continence. He states:

> Once the law of absolute continence is abolished, the impediment to orders of digamy and the impediment to marriage of orders lose their *raison d'être*. Conversely, the practical reason for the impediment to orders of digamy and the prohibition of marriage after the reception of orders can only be on account of consecrated celibacy *propter continentiam futuram*.[183]

Nedungatt does not agree:

> Canon 10 of Ancrya, provided that deacons could marry after their ordination provided they declared this intention to the bishop at their ordination, which shows, first, that order is not theologically an impediment to marriage but only canonically; and secondly, that receiving ordination is not tantamount to assuming the obligation of celibacy, as some tendentious writers hold. Even if the Ancyran exception was limited in time and space (like Elvira legislation), the fact that later law forbade marriage after ordination to deacons does not change the nature of ordination theologically. Tertullian, for one, would forbid

---

182 "Bigamy, properly speaking, can only be successive. Canonists distinguish between 'true bigamy', which is a repetition of valid matrimony after the death of the first spouse or the annulment of the first marriage, and 'interpretative' bigamy which is a *fictio iuris* and involves illicit relations with a 'fictitious' wife, or relations with one's lawful wife given certain circumstances. To avoid possible confusion the term 'digamy' has been chosen to designate successive bigamy. " Cholji, *Clerical Celibacy in the East and West,* 12, footnote 41. See also Franz Wernz, *Ius Decretalium* (Rome: Ex Typographia Polyglotta S. C. de Propaganda Fide, 1901) 2/1 :180-183; D. Cummings, *The Rudder (Pedalion) of the Metaphorical Ship of the One Holy Catholic and Apostolic Church of Orthodox Christians* (Chicago, The Orthodox Christian Educational Society, 1957) 28-29.
183 Cholji, *Clerical Celibacy in the East and West,* 44.

marriage even to laypeople who once received the sacrament of marriage and became widowers or widows, in this view even marriage is an impediment to a future marriage....Just as the discipline regarding the digamy of widows does not imply any obligation to celibacy during the first marriage, so also the norm by which sacred ordination is an impediment to marriage does not imply the obligation to perpetual continence for married clerics, contrary to what some western writers have written recently.[184]

Nedungatt does not see any justification for holding that the impediments of digamy and orders are rooted in an obligation of absolute continence.

The first piece of canonical legislation concerning the impediment of digamy for the reception of orders comes to us in apostolic canon 17 which stated:

He who has been joined in two marriages after his baptism, or has had a concubine, cannot be a bishop or presbyter or deacon, nor in any way be a member of the clergy.[185]

The eighty-five canons known as the "Apostolic Canons" are found at the end of book eight of the "Apostolic Constitutions" which is said to have been compiled in Syria or Palestine anywhere from the late fourth to the early fifth century.[186] Canon 17 expressly stated that this impediment of digamy bound only the candidate who entered a second marriage after baptism. Yet the practice

---

184 Nedungatt, "Title 10: Clerics," footnote 99, 293-294. See also John H. Erikson, "The Council of Trullo: Issues Relating to the Marriage of Clergy," *The Greek Orthodox Theological Review* 40 (1995) 183-199.

185 Constitution of the Holy Apostles, c. 17: "Si quis post baptismum secundis fuerit nuptiis copulatus aut concubinam habuerit, non potest esse episcopus aut presbyter aut diaconus, nec prosus ex numero eorum qui ministerio sacro deserviunt." In Périclès-Pierre Joannou ed., *Discipline générale antique* (Grottaferrata, 1962) 1/2:16. Hereafter *Joannou*. English translation from *Ante-Nicene Fathers: The Writings of the Fathers down to A.D. 325*, eds., Alexander Roberts and James Donaldson (Peabody, MA: Hendrickson, 1994) 7:501.

186 Cochini, *The Apostolic Origins of Priestly Celibacy*, 310. See also Henri Leclercq, "Constitutiones Apostoliques," in *DCAL* 3: 2732-2748. Brundage gives 380 AD as the most probable date for the compilation of the *Apostolic Constitutions*; see Brundage, *Medieval Canon Law*, 10.

of the Latin Church was also to exclude candidates who had contracted their first marriage before receiving baptism.

The canon also excluded from the ranks of the clergy all those who had had concubines, because such men had demonstrated a lapse in morals. The Council of Elvira in canon 30 had also decreed that a man who had committed adultery or fornication after baptism would not be ordained to the subdiaconate because subdeacons were candidates for higher orders.[187] The exclusion of candidates from orders who had demonstrated incontinence seems to some to confirm the existence of an obligation of future continence.

b. Pope Innocent I: *Etsi tibi*, *Dominus inter* and *Consulenti tibi* Decretals

During his pontificate Innocent I (401-417) continued the work of his predecessors, and he continued to emphasize the scriptural and apostolic basis for the discipline of clerical celibacy. The pope issued three decrees concerning clerical continence: *Etsi tibi*,[188] *Dominus inter*[189] and *Consulenti tibi*.[190]

On February 15, 404, Innocent sent the decretal *Etsi tibi* to Victricius, Metropolitan of Rouen in Northern Gaul. In this decretal he repeated the injunction that bishops, priests and deacons were not to have sexual relations with their wives. Innocent referenced the periodic continence required of lay persons 'for the sake of prayer' and concluded that clergy for whom it is a constant duty to

---

187   Council of Elvira, c. 30: "Subdiaconos eos ordinari non debere, qui in adolescentia sus fuerint moechati; eo quod postmodum, per subreptionem: vel si qui sunt in praeteritum ordinari amoveantur." Mansi, 2:10.

188   Pope Innocent I, letter to Victricius *Etsi tibi*, February 15, 404, in *Epistolae Romanum Pontificum et Quae ad Eos Scriptae sunt: Clemente I usque Ad Inocentium III*, ed. Pierre Coustant (Braunsberg: Eduard Peter, 1868) 1:746-758. Hereafter Coustant.

189   Pope Innocent I, letter to Bishops of Gaul, Dominus inter. Coustant 1:686-700.

190   Pope Innocent I, letter to Exsuperius, *Consulenti tibi*, February 20, 405. Coustant 1:789-796.

pray and offer sacrifice were to be absolutely continent. Innocent further maintained that clerical continence has both scriptural and apostolic origins. He again asserted the understanding of Pope Siricius in relation to Paul's injunction, 'husband of one wife,' stating that monogamy was for the sake of future continence.

A year later in the decretal *Consulenti tibi,* Innocent I responded to Bishop Exsuperius of Toulouse, in southern Gaul. Exsuperius had written to Innocent seeking his counsel regarding some difficult situations in his diocese among which was the problem of incontinent clergy. Some of his deacons and priests were having children with their wives. Exsuperius wanted to know what should be done and what the appropriate penalties should be. Innocent I responded thus:

> You ask what is to be done about those who, while in the diaconal ministry or the priesthood, are proven to be or to have been incontinent, in that they have begotten children. About such clerics, the discipline of the divine laws is quite clear, and the plain admonitions of Bishop Siricius of blessed memory have been handed down, that incontinent men holding such offices must be deprived of all ecclesiastical dignity and must not be allowed to carry on a ministry that is fittingly performed only by those who practice continence.[191]

Innocent advised Exsuperius that if any clerics have acted out of ignorance of the discipline of continence they should be treated leniently provided that they immediately embrace absolute continence. Again the pope emphasized the scriptural and apostolic basis for clerical continence.

---

191   Pope Innocent I, Letter to Exsuperius, Consulenti tibi, February 20, 405: "Proposuisti, quid de his observari debeat, quos in diaconii ministeriis aut in officio presbyterii positosm incontinentes esse aut Suisse, geberati filii prodiderunt. De his et divinarum legum manifesta est disciplina, et beatae recordationis viri Siricii episcopi monita evidentia commearunt, ut incontinentes in officiis talibus positi, omni honore ecclesiastico priventur, nec admittantur accedere ad ministerium, quod sola continentia oportet impleri." Coustant 1:790-791. English translation from Heid, Celibacy in the Early Church, 265.

Finally, in a decretal generally attributed to Innocent I, *Dominus inter,*[192] the pontiff again stated the requirement of continence for bishops, presbyters and deacons. He repeated that clerical continence had its roots in scripture and apostolic tradition and spoke about the need for unity of faith and discipline among the bishops. The pope thus signaled that all bishops should ensure unity of faith and practice when it came to the observance of the discipline of clerical continence. Innocent was not asking for a new discipline to be imposed; he was simply asking that any violations be addressed.

From the fifth to the seventh centuries the obligation of clerical continence, as with other juridical institutions of the Church, became more finely tuned. Various councils issued more legislation reaffirming the discipline and correcting violations. There was a growing sense of a need to have canonical collections as well as a consciousness of legislating in conformity with a wider legal patrimony and ancient tradition.[193]

c. Pope Leo I

In the first year of Leo's pontificate the Council of Orange in 441 ruled that a married man could only be ordained a deacon if he promised continent chastity. Any cleric found guilty of incontinence would be removed from office.[194] Leo devoted himself to ensuring that absolute continence was observed by all bishops, priests and deacons. In 458, Bishop Rusticus of Narbonne wrote to

---

192 According to Stickler, this letter, Dominus inter, was first attributed to Pope Damasus and then to Pope Siricius. Stickler argues for Pope Innocent's authorship. The Case for Clerical Celibacy, 32. Cochini observes that the decree was in the papers of Siricius and believes that the synod met under Siricius, Damasus or Innocent I. Apostolic Origins of Priestly Celibacy, 14-15. Coustant attributes this letter to Innocent I, see Coustant 1:686.

193 Roman Cholij, "Priestly Celibacy in Patristics and in the History of the Church," in For Love Alone: Reflections on Priestly Celibacy (Maynooth, Ireland: St. Paul's Publications, 1993) 46.

194 McGarrity, "Spiritual and Canonical Values in Mandatory Priestly Celibacy," *Studia canonica* 27 (1993) 223. See also the Council of Orange, cc. 22, 23. *CCL* 148:84.

Pope Leo the Great (440-461) and posed the following question: "About those who serve at the altar and are married: is it permitted for them to have conjugal relations?" Leo responded:

> The law of continence is the same for ministers of the altar as for bishops and priests, who when they were laymen or readers could lawfully marry and have offspring. But when they reached the said ranks what was before lawful ceased to be so.[195]

Pope Leo the Great also decreed that such married clergy were not obligated to send their wives away but could live with them in continence. As Cholij states:

> One of the interesting features of legislation that appears throughout this period is the implicit or even explicit inclusion of a continent wife among that class of women that c. 3 of the First Ecumenical Council of Nicaea (325) had characterized as beyond suspicion: "The great council has absolutely forbidden bishops, priests and deacons — in other words, all the members of the clergy — to have with them a sister-companion with the exception of a mother, a sister, an aunt, or, lastly, only those persons who are beyond any suspicion." The wife, like the husband, was technically 'converted', conversio being the change of life that follows on the profession or public promise of continence. It is in mid-fifth century Gaul that an explicit public declaration of the commitment to continence first appears. This was to prevent excuses of ignorance of the obligation which previously had been implicit in the reception of orders. The wife (who in the Gallic Church was termed a presbytera, diaconissa, subdiaconissa or even episcopia according to the status of her husband) was to live as a 'sister' in a brother-sister

---

195 Pope Leo the Great, letter to Bishop Rusticus: "Lex continentiae eadem est ministris altaris quae episcopis atque presbyteris, qui cum essent laici sive lectores, licito et uxoris ducere et filios procreare potuerunt. Sed cum ad praedictos pervenerunt gradus, coepit eis non licere quod licuit." PL 54: 1204a. English translation from Cholij, Clerical Celibacy in the East and West, 37.

relationship. Her rights were protected as ordination could not go ahead without her agreement. Her promise to live in continence was also an impediment to future marriage.[196]

Councils and popes continued to concern themselves with the living arrangements of the clergy in order to protect their continence and to avoid scandal.[197] Even though the presence of the wife in the home of her cleric-husband was tolerated and was seen as "beyond suspicion," yet because of the ever-present possibilities of incontinence, there was already a move to encourage or in some cases insist on total separation.[198] "It was of course understood that the wife would not be left without means of livelihood, and to this end the husband could, if necessary, call on the resources of the Church."[199]

F. Continence and the Wives of Clergy

Thus far we have been discussing the continence of married clerics. While there is no reference to the cleric making an explicit promise of continence, it is clear from canon 33 of the Council of Elvira that deacons, priests and bishops were not to have sexual relations with their wives. Only with the Council of Orange, 441 in canon 21[200] was a cleric husband obliged to make an explicit promise of continence. But what about the wives of clergy who were obviously immediately affected by this decision? If there really was a continence discipline for clerics then would it not be reasonable to suppose that the wife of the candidate also be continent?

---

196   Cholij, Clerical Celibacy in the East and West, 60.
197   Council of Orléans (541), c. 17, CCL 148:136; Council of Tours (567), c. 20, CCL 148:180-181.
198   Council of Toledo (589), c. 5, Bruns 1: 214; Council of Lyons (583), c. 1, CCL 128: 232.
199   Stickler, "Celibacy from the Patristic Era to the Council of Trent," 504.
200   The Council of Orange, c. 21: "Sedit praeterea ut deinceps non ordinentur diacones coniugati nisi qui prius conversionis proposito professi fuerint castitatem.» CCL 148:84.

In the Syrian *Didascalia,* canon 4 required that the wife of one destined for major orders had to make a promise of continence.[201] Accordingly, with the wife also having consented to a promise of continence, the Church saw no difficulty with the cleric remaining under the same roof as his wife. She was now his "sister in the Lord."[202] The practice of clerics living with their wives was acceptable to the people because of the belief that both spouses would live the continence they had promised.

The First Council of Toledo, 400 established the prohibition of remarriage for the widows of deacons, priests and bishops.[203] A widow who remarried was subject to the penalty of excommunication. As Cholij observes:

> The reason for the impediment is clearly, in the tradition of the Western Church, the fact that the wife's promise or vow of perfect chastity which was made at the time of giving consent for her husband to be ordained. This requirement was an important act of justice, and a sine qua non for the husband's ordination, for otherwise the husband's continence would injure the marital rights of the wife. Thus, it was clerical celibacy that was the material cause of the impediment to the widow's remarriage. Her own free promise to live this discipline was the direct cause of the impediment.[204]

Cholji contends that the prohibition of remarriage for widows is the logical conclusion of the wives' promise of perfect chastity. Heid agrees with this observation.[205] Furthermore, the Council of Agde, 506 required not only the

---

201   Didascalia Apostolorum, trans. and ed. by R. Hugh Connolly (Oxford: Clarendon Press, 1929) 32.

202   Cholij, *Clerical Celibacy in the East and West,* 60.

203   First Council of Toledo, c. 18: "Si quia vidua episcopi vel presbyteri aut diaconi maritum acceperit, nullus clericus, nulla religiosa persona cum ea convivium sumsat, numquam communicet; morienti tamen ei sacramenta subveniant." Mansi, 3:1001.

204   Cholij, Clerical Celibacy in the East and West, 22-23.

205   Heid, Celibacy in the Early Church, 142-143.

profession of perfect continence of the ordinand, but the explicit consent of the spouse as well given through her promise of continence.[206] The evidence of a continence requirement for the wives of higher clergy supports the assertion that in the West higher clerics were obliged to live continently in their marriages.

G. Second Council of Trullo, 692[207]

The Second Council of Trullo promulgated seven canons (cc. 3, 6, 12, 13, 26, 30 and 48) which established the practice of clerical marriage and continence that would be binding for the East. These canons remain the fundamental legislation on these matters for the Eastern Churches. Faced with the perennial problem of some clergy's violation of the law of continence, canon 13, "About priests and deacons that they keep their wives," decreed:

> As we have learned that in the Church of Rome the rule was established that candidates, before receiving ordination as deacon or priest, make a public promise not to have relations any more with their wives; we, conforming ourselves to the ancient rule of strict observation and apostolic discipline, want the legitimate marriages of consecrated men to remain in effect even in the future, without dissolving the bond uniting these men to their wives, nor depriving them of mutual relations at the appropriate times...neither should it be demanded that he promise, at the time of his ordination, to abstain from legitimate relations with his own wife....

---

206   The Council of Agde, c. 16: "Episcopus vero benedictionem diaconatus minoribus a uiginti et quinque annorum penitus non committat. Sane si coniugati iuuenes consenserint ordinari, etiam uxorum uoluntas ita requirenda est, ut sequestrato mansionis cubiculo, religione praemissa, posteaquam pariter conuersi fuerint, ordinentur." CCL 148:201. See also, Cochini, The Apostolic Origins of Priestly Celibacy, 333-335.

207   See *The Council in Trullo Revisited,* Kanonika 6, eds. George Nedungatt & Michael Featherstone (Rome: Pontificio Istituto Orientale, 1995).

Anthony McLaughlin

We know that the Fathers gathered at Carthage, as a precautionary measure because of the seriousness of the morals of the ministers of the
altar, decided that "subdeacons, who touch the sacred mysteries, the
deacons and priests too, should abstain from their own wives during the
periods that are specifically assigned to them."[208]

The Fathers at Trullo interpreted the tradition of continence not as absolute
but as periodic, confined only to the time before the cleric's service at the altar
as required of the Old Testament priests.[209] They also stated that the custom of
periodic continence was an ancient and apostolic discipline. Canon 13 granted
to all married clerics of all ranks, with the exception of bishops, to have conjugal
relations save for the days when "they touch the holy things."

Cochini, Cholij, Stickler, Heid, and McGovern contend that this canon
marked a departure from the common legislative discipline which demonstrated

208   Council of Trullo 692, c. 13: "Quoniam in Romanum ecclesia pro canonis ordine traditum esse cognovimus, ut diaconi vel presbyteri, qui ut ordinentur digni existimati sunt, profiteantur
se non amplius suis uxoribus coniungendos, nos antiquum canonum apostolicae perfectionis ordinisque servantes, hominum qui sunt in sacris coniuga etiam ex hoc temporis momento firma et
stabilia esse volumus, nequaquam eorum cum uxoribus coniunctionem dissolventes vel eos mutual
tempore convenienti consuetudine privates....Scimus autem, quod et qui Carthagine convenerunt,
ministrorum gravitatis in vita curam gerentes dixerunt: 'Ut subdiaconi, qui sacra mysteria contrectant, et diaconi et presbyteri secundum easdem rationes a consortibus abstineant.'" Mansi, 11:
947. English translation from Percival, 371.
209   Canon 13 is foundational for the continence discipline of the Eastern Churches. Presently, nineteen of the twenty-one Eastern Catholic Churches permit all clergy below the rank of bishop
to be married and to have conjugal relations. All married clergy are bound to observe periodic
continence. The Syro-Malabar Church and the Syro-Malankara Church do not have married clergy.
Canon 13, while prescribing periodic continence for major clerics below the rank of bishop,
did not provide definite norms for periodic continence. It was not until the twelfth and thirteenth
centuries that clear norms for periodic continence were established. The general norm was abstinence for one day before celebrating Mass. Yet there was much variation between the Churches.
Some prescribed continence for three or five days before Mass, others one night before Mass.
Clerics were also to be continent during Lent and on certain holy days. Presently, though the prescriptions governing periodic continence differ. In the Eastern Churches there is still an obligation
of continence for major clerics before the celebrating Mass. It seems that this is left up to the con-
science of the cleric and not spelled out in particular law. For a fuller treatment see Cholji, *Clerical
Celibacy in the East and the West*, 106-118. Nedungatt, in his commentary on celibate and married
priests, makes no reference to the nature of the present obligation of periodic continence for major
clerics of the Eastern Churches. See Nedungatt, "Title 10: Clerics," 287-302.

that the East had adopted a much different interpretation concerning marital relations on the part of clergy lower than the rank of bishop who had married before being ordained. [210] As Cochini observes:

> It was the first time since 325, as far as we know, that a disciplinary tradition affirmed in a council interpreted explicitly the third canon of Nicea in a meaning that does not imply perfect continence for the clerics in question and their wives.[211]

They maintain that canon 13 of Trullo mistakenly claimed that the Council of Carthage obliged deacons and priests to observe temporary continence in connection with their liturgical service or in times of fasting. As Heid states:

> The canon (13) juxtaposes texts from two Carthaginian synods from 390 (canon 2) and 401 (canon 4). It abbreviates the texts and combines them in such a way that the result is the opposite of what they originally intended.[212]

They further assert that at no time since the first appearance of written law had the Church legislated that deacons and priests were obliged to temporary continence while bishops were obliged to absolute continence. In the history of celibacy-continence legislation the obligation bound all in major orders equally. There had never been a distinction between deacons and priests on the one hand and bishops on the other. Bishops, priests and deacons had been bound equally to absolute celibacy-continence after ordination.

Other scholars such as George Nedungatt, Peter L'Huillier, Constantin Pit-

---

210   Cochini, *The Apostolic Origins of Priestly Celibacy,* 194-195; Cholij, *Clerical Celibacy in the East and West,* 106-125; Heid, *Celibacy in the Early Church,* 311-315; Stickler, *The Case for Clerical Celibacy,* 69-81; McGovern, *Priestly Celibacy Today*, 58-68.
211   Cochini, *The Apostolic Origins of Priestly Celibacy,* 194.
212   Heid, Celibacy in the Early Church, 313.

sakis, and Nicolae Dura[213] strongly disagree that Trullo marked a departure from the common discipline concerning clerical continence. George Nedungatt argues forcefully against any consideration that Trullo marked such an innovation when he states:

> Cholij holds that celibacy was an obligation for the apostles and their successors and that the bishops, presbyters and deacons were canonically bound by celibacy. He tries to show that the Eastern Churches deviated from this apostolic tradition at the Council of Trullo, whereas the Latin Church has always preserved it; indeed, that celibacy is required by the very nature of priesthood itself, contrary to the conciliar teaching (PO 16). With scarce knowledge of the Greek sources, but relying on Latin polemists of the past, he charged Trullo with falsifying the canonical tradition. Cochini and Cholij won eminent Roman patronage and silent following, although their theses have generally been reviewed as critically inept and historically incompetent.[214]

Vittorio Peri in his introduction to the book, *Trullo Revisited,* asserts:

> The Trullan Council has safeguarded the common heritage of ecclesial Tradition in an orthodox manner.[215]

Nedungatt does admit that the obligation of absolute continence for bishops only was an imposition of civil law that was received into canon law. He explains:

213 Nedungatt, "Title 10: Clerics," footnote 92, 291; See also Peter L'Huillier's review of Cholij's book in Sobornost 12 (1990) 180-182 and his review of Cochini's book in Theological Studies 43 (1982) 693-705; Constantin G. Pitsakis, "Clergé marié et célibat dans la législation du concile in Trullo: le point du vue Oriental," The Council in Trullo Revisited, 263-306; Vittorio Peri, "Introduction," The Council in Trullo Revisited, 39; Nicolae Dura, "The Ecumenicity of the Council in Trullo: Witnesses of the Canonical Tradition in the East and the West," The Council in Trullo Revisited, 229-262.

214 Nedungatt, "Title 10: Clerics," 291-291.

215 Vittorio Peri, in The Council in Trullo Revisited: "Compreso in tale contest ecumenico garantito, il concilio Trullan ha salvaguardato in modo ortodosso la commune eredita della Tradizione ecclesiale." 39.

In the East, too, where the practice of virginity and celibacy was free and widespread as in the West, the law of obligatory celibacy emerged only later and was imposed selectively by Emperor Justinian I (483-565) on bishops as a safeguard against the loss of the temporal goods of the Church, which were canonically in the bishop's charge. Married bishops were occasionally tempted to divert the temporal goods of the Church in favor of their family and children. The imperial remedy for this abuse was a drastic law forbidding bishops to have family or children at all to care for. Later this "civil law" was received into canon law at the Council of Trullo, which forbade the ordaining of men to the episcopate who were not celibates or free from the marriage bond (c. 12) while establishing norms for the legal separation of the wife before ordination (c. 48). Thus the law of celibacy binding already all higher clerics in the West applied in the East only to bishops, albeit for quite a different reason. The other clerics could freely choose between celibacy and marriage, provided presbyters, deacons and subdeacons made the choice before their ordination (c. 13).[216]

Yet in spite of these diverging opinions, the East agrees with the West on the following points: (1) There must only be a single marriage contracted before ordination, and it cannot be with a widow or with other women excluded by law (those whose ability to be continent was questionable).[217] (2) To marry after or-

---

216   Nedungatt, "Title 10: Clerics," 297. Pitsakis agrees with Nedungatt that emperial legislation introduced celibacy for bishops into the canons, "Clergé marié et célibat dans la législation du concile in Trullo: le point du vue Oriental," in *The Council in Trullo Revisited,* 270-279. See also Nedungatt, "The Temporal Goods of the Church in the Legislation of the Ecumenical Councils," *Folia Canonica* 4 (2000) 117-133 and Spyros N. Troianos, "The Canons of the Trullan Council in the Novels of Leo VI," in *The Council in Trullo Revisited,* 189-198.

217   Council of Trullo, c. 3: "Eum qui secundis nuptiis post baptismum implicates sit, vel concubinam habuerit, non posse esse episcopum vel presbyterum vel diaconum vel omnino ex sacerdotali catalogo; Similiter et eum qui viduam acceperit vel dimissam vel meretricem vel servam vel scenicam non posse esse episcopum vel presbyterum vel diaconum vel omnino ex sacerdotali catalogo." Mansi, 11: 942-943.

dination was prohibited and therefore was not licit.[218] (3) Married bishops must be absolutely continent.[219] The East further insisted that the bishop's wife must depart and enter a monastery.[220] It is also interesting that the council Fathers did not reference the story of Paphnutius in support of their arguments for temporary continence.

The authority of Trullo was initially not accepted equally by the East and West. Pope Sergius I (687-701), who came from Syria, refused to recognize it. Later, Pope John VIII (872-882), a Roman, recognized those canons which were not contrary to the praxis of the Roman Church. The Council of Constantinople, 861, with papal legates present on behalf of Pope Nicholas I, considered Trullo's canons to be ecumenical and a legitimate expression of particular jurisdiction.[221] Dura states:

> This recognition by Rome of the ecumenicity of the Council of Trullo is acknowledged not only by the Roman Council assembled in 878 and presided over by Pope John VIII, who made express reference to 'regulas...a sexto synodo...editas,' but also by the Council of Unity (Constantinople 878-880) in which legates of the pope took part.[222]

---

218 Council of Trullo, c. 6: "Nos hoc servantes decernimus ne dehinc subdiacono vel diacono vel presbytero post peractam sui ordinationem coniugium inire ullo modo liceat; si autem hoc facere ausus fuerit, deponatur. Si quis autem eorum, qui in clerum veniunt, velit lege matrimonii mulieri coniungi, ante ordinationem subdiaconalem vel diaconalem vel presbyteralem, hoc faciat." Mansi, 11: 943.

219 Council of Trullo, c. 12: "Porro hoc quoque ad nos perlatum est, in Africa et in Libya et in aliis locis quosdam ex iis qui illic sunt dei amantissimi praesules cum propriis uxoribus, etiam post suam ordinationem, una habitare non recusare, ex eo offendiculum et scandalum populis afferentes. Cum itaque sollicitudo nostra eo magnopere tenderet, ut omnia ad gregis nobis traditi utilitatem efficerentur, visum est nihil eiusmodi dehinc ullo modo fieri. Si quis autem hoc agens deprehensus fuerit, deponatur. " Mansi, 11: 946-947.

220 Council of Trullo, c. 48: "Uxor eius qui ad episcopalem dignitatem promovetur, ex communi consensus a viro suo antea separata, post eius ordinationem episcopalem, in monasterium ingrediatur procul ab episcopi habitatione exstructum et episcopi providentia fruatur; sin autem digna visa fuerit, etiam ad diaconatus dignitatem provehatur. " Mansi, 11:966.

221 Dura, "The Ecumenicity of the Council in Trullo," 234.

222 Ibid., 246.

It is noteworthy that the Latin Church, especially since the Second Vatican Council, considers the Eastern Church's allowance for a married clergy to be a legitimate development.[223] From Trullo onwards the discipline of the East and the West became more distinctive. The West obliged celibate continence of all clergy. The East obliged celibate continence only of bishops and periodic continence of all other clergy.[224]

H. Magisterial and Conciliar Teachings from Gregory VII to Trent

1. Pope Gregory VII: The Gregorian Reform.

In the Gregorian reforms of the eleventh century, Pope Gregory VII (1073-1085) sought to eradicate various abuses within the Church.[225] Among them were the abuses of simony and incontinence of clergy.[226] At the Council of Rome in March 1074, Gregory directed that all incontinent clergy cease to exercise their ministry.[227] This directive gave rise to violent opposition from clergy, especially in France.[228]

There is also a common perception that the Church was determined to impose clerical celibacy as a way to stop the children of clergy from inheriting church property. However, James Knapp, S.J. does not agree:

Some think that the law of celibacy was an innovation, created out of whole cloth, and that the imposition of celibacy on the clergy was

---

223 This will be examined in more detail in chapter four of this book.
224 See McGarrity, "Spiritual and Canonical Values in Mandatory Priestly Celibacy," *Studia canonica* 27 (1993) 226; Jaroslav Pelikan, *The Spirit of Eastern Christendom: The Christian Tradition* (Chicago: University of Chicago Press, 1974) 2:134-137.
225 See Herbert Edward John Cowdrey, *Pope Gregory VII* (Oxford: Clarendon Press, 1998).
226 Ibid., 550-554.
227 See Council of Rome. Mansi 20:413-414.
228 See McGarrity, "Spiritual and Canonical Values in Mandatory Priestly Celibacy," *Studia canonica* 27 (1993) 231.

primarily a way to keep church property from being inherited by the children of a priest. The supposed motive for the law was the Church's desire to keep property which she claimed as her own. These characterizations are historically inaccurate. The discipline of celibacy was already a centuries old tradition when Hildebrand, a Benedictine monk of Cluny, was elected as Pope Gregory VII in 1073. Although the misuse of church property was only one of many problems facing the Church in Gregory's time, both ecclesiastical law and civil legislation had addressed the status of the children of priests and their property rights many years earlier.[229]

As part of a return to the general observance of celibacy, the number of married candidates that were accepted for ordination was gradually limited. This period also gave rise to many arguments for and against priestly celibacy. There was sustained opposition to the Latin Church's traditional interpretation of canon 3 of Nicea and to the discipline of celibacy. Those who wished to see the practice mitigated cited the story of Paphnutius and his intervention at Nicea to support their arguments. At the Roman Synod of 1077, Gregory VII condemned the story of Paphnutius "as a falsification of history."[230]

Gregory was a determined proponent of celibacy. He carried out his reform of this discipline mainly by means of regional synods presided over by his legates. Particular mention should be made here of the synods of Paris, Rouen,

---

229   Knapp, Celibate Chastity in the Life of the Priest in the Light of the Teaching of Karol Wojtyla/John Paul II, 85. The first chapter of this dissertation presents an historical overview of the obligation of celibacy. In it Knapp observes that in the West the Ninth Council of Toledo (655) and in the East, the laws of the Byzantine Emperor Justinian in 528, had sought to deal with such property issues concerning the children of priests. See also footnote 221.
230   See Cholij, Clerical Celibacy in the East and West, 89.

Poitiers, Mainz, Winchester, Lillebonne, Gerona[231] and the many letters written by Gregory that urged faithful and sincere observance of clerical celibacy. Gregory's successors followed in his footsteps.[232]

2. First Lateran Council, 1123[233]

Pope Callistus II (1119-1124) convoked the First Lateran Council primarily to address the issue of "lay investiture"[234] but the council also addressed the subject of clerical marriage.[235] The Fathers repeated previous legislation that any marriage entered into by a bishop, priest or deacon was illicit and that such clerics were subject to sanctions. Canons 7 and 21 of this same council stated:

> We absolutely prohibit presbyters, deacons, or subdeacons to live with concubines and wives, and to cohabit with other women, except those with whom the Council of Nicea permitted to dwell with them solely on account of necessity, namely a mother, sister, paternal or maternal aunt, or other such persons, about whom no suspicion could justly arise.
>
> We absolutely forbid priests, deacons, and subdeacons and monks to have concubines or to contract marriage. We decree in accordance with the definitions of the sacred canons, that marriages already contracted

---

231   See Mansi, 20:437-562. The Council of Winchester, 1076, established a formula for the profession of chastity before ordination to the subdiaconate, Mansi, 20:459: "Ego, N., promitto Deo omnibusque sanctis eius castitatem corporis mei, secundum canonum decreta et secundum ordinem mihi imponendum servari, Domino N. praesente."

232   Stickler, "Celibacy from the Patristic Era," 547.

233   Tanner, 1:188-194.

234   Lay investiture was the practice of civil authorities naming bishops, abbots and other church authorities. See *The Church in the Age of Feudalism: History of the Church,* ed. Friedrich Kempf et al. (New York: Seabury Press, 1980) 3: 398-403.

235   Hefele, "Neuvième concile general au Latran en 1123," 5/1: 631.

by such persons must be dissolved, and that the persons be condemned to do penance.[236]

Prior to the council, major clerics were permitted to cohabit with their lawful wives so long there was no suspicion of incontinence. But with the decline in clerical discipline, especially in the Middles Ages, total physical separation was insisted upon. Canon 7 now obliged such clerics to separate from their wives. This discipline already existed in the East long before it appeared in the West.[237] As for those major clerics who contracted marriage after ordination, they were subject to sanctions and obliged to dissolve the union. The canon bound only those in major orders, which now included subdeacons. Minor clerics could validly marry, but they fell *ipso iure* from the clerical state.

3. Second Lateran Council, 1139[238]

Council of Pisa, 1135 was the first council to explicitly declare that marriages contracted by bishops, priests and deacons were not only illicit but invalid. They were considered *matrimonium non esse* not "marriages."[239] The Second Lateran Council, convoked by Pope Innocent II (1130-1143) repeated the prescriptions of Pisa. Canon 7 stated:

---

236 First Lateran Council, c. 7: "Presbyteris, diaconibus vel subdiaconibus concubinarum et uxorum contubernio penitus interdicimus et aliarum mulierem cohabitationem, praeter quas synodus Nicaena propter solas necessitudinum causas habitare permisit, videlicet matrem sororem amitam vel materteram aut alias huiusmodi, de quibus nulla iuste valeat suspicio oriri." C. 21: "Presbyteris, diaconibus, subdiaconibus et monachis concubinas habere seu matrimonia contrahere penitus interdicimus, contracta quoque matrimonia ab huiusmodi personis disiungi et personas ad poenitentiam debere redigi, iuxta sacrorum canonum diffinitionem iudicamus." Tanner, 1:191.

237 As may be inferred from a letter of Pope Nicholas I to Boris I of Bulgaria (866): *PL* 119:1006d.

238 Tanner, 1:195-203.

239 Council of Pisa 1135: "Ut autem lex continentiae et Deo placens munditia in ecclesiasticis personis et sacris ordinibus dilatetur, statuimus quatenus episcopi presbyteri diaconi subdiaconi regulares canonici et monachi atque conversi professi, qui sanctum transgredientes propositum uxores sibi copulare praesumpserint, separentur. Huiusmodi namque copulationem, quam contra ecclesiasticam regulam constat esse contractam, matrimonium non esse sancimus. " Mansi, 21:489.

Adhering to the path trod by our predecessors, the roman pontiffs Gregory VII, Urban and Paschal, we prescribe that nobody is to hear the masses of those whom he knows to have wives or concubines. Indeed, that the law of continence and purity pleasing to God might be propagated among ecclesiastical persons and those in holy orders, we decree that where bishops, priests, deacons, subdeacons, canons regular, monks, and professed lay brothers have presumed to take wives and to transgress this holy precept, they are to be separated from their partners. For we do not deem there to be a marriage which, it is agreed, has been contracted against ecclesiastical law. Furthermore, when they have separated from each other, let them do a penance commensurate with such outrageous behavior.[240]

Marriages contracted by bishops, priests, deacons, subdeacons were *matrimonium non esse,* "not marriages." A cleric who had "married" was obligated to separate permanently from his "wife" and to undertake penance in accord with the gravity of his transgression. The marriages of clerics contracted before ordination remained unaffected by this legislation.

It is important to note that this canon did not exclude married men from orders. It merely declared marriages contracted after the reception of orders to be invalid. Married men were not impeded from the reception of orders. They continued to be ordained long after the Second Lateran Council. A married man could be ordained, but an ordained man in higher orders could marry neither

---

240   Second Lateran Council, c. 7: "Ad haec praedecessorum nostrorum Gregorii VII, Urbani et Paschalis Romanorum Pontificum vestigiis inhaerentes, praecipimus ut nullus missas eorum audiat, quos uxores vel concubinas habere cognoverit. Ut autem lex continentiae et Deo placens munditia in ecclesiasticis personis et sacris ordinibus dilatetur, statuimus quatenus episcopi presbyteri diaconi subdiaconi regulares canonici et monachi atque conversi professi, qui sanctum transgredientes propositum uxores sibi copulare praesumpserint, separentur. Huiusmodi namque copulationem, quam contra ecclesiasticam regulam constat esse contractam, matrimonium non esse censemus. Qui etiam ab invicem separati, pro tantis excessibus condignam poenitentiam agant." Tanner, 1:198.

licitly or validly. As we shall see the practice of ordaining only unmarried men arose only very gradually and without being formally instituted by any law. Despite the legislation of two Lateran councils, abuses remained in the course of the following centuries especially during the Renaissance period.

I. Gratian and the *Concordia Discordantium Canonum*

Soon after the Second Lateran Council the Camaldolese monk and Master of the School of Law of Bologna, Gratian, published a canon law textbook entitled *Harmony of Conflicting Canons* (*Concordia Discordantium Canonum*)[241] which came to be known simply as the *Gratian's Decree* (*Decretum Gratiani*). Gratian had gathered together in one collection various laws of the Church's first millennium, and he tried to present them in an orderly and consistent fashion. Despite the fact that this was a 'private collection,' the *Decretum Gratiani* became the foundational source for the study and development of canon law throughout the Latin Church.[242]

In his *Decretum*, Gratian treated the subject of clerical continence in the Pars Prima, distinctions 26-34 and 81-84.[243] From the Council of Elvira, 305 ecclesiastical legislation commonly used the term *lex continentiae* to speak of the obligation to be assumed by the cleric and his wife from the moment of his ordination.[244] The cleric and his wife made a promise to observe the *lex continentiae* by voluntarily renouncing sexual relations and the begetting of children

---

241   Gratian, Concordia Discordantium Canonum, in Corpus Iuris Canonici, ed. Emil Friedberg (Graz:Akademische Druck- u. Verlagsanstalt, 1959). All subsequent citations will be taken from this source. Hereafter Friedberg.

242   James A. Brundage, *Medieval Canon Law* (London and New York: Longman Group Limited, 1995) 44-69.

243   For a discussion on Gratian's treatment on celibacy and continence see Jean Gaudemet, "Gratien et le **célibat** ecclésiastique," *Studia Gratiana* 13 (1967) 341-369.

244   Hödl, "The Lex Continentiae: A Study on the Problem of Priestly Celibacy," 711. See also chapter one of this book: 14, 16-21.

within their marriage. Indeed, the *lex continentiae* implied a promise of perfect chastity. This promise was often called a profession or a vow.[245] Gratian developed the theory of the *votum continentiae* in several passages in his *Decretum*.[246] In the transition to distinction twenty-eight, he spoke of the "voto castitatis" to be taken by the one being ordained a subdeacon. By the thirteenth century, there was general agreement among canonists that the *lex continentiae* implied a vow of chastity.[247]

A married man who presented himself for ordination to higher orders was required to make a vow of absolute continence. He could only do so with the consent of his wife, because she had a right to sexual relations.[248] There was no ordination without the consent of the wife. Legislation in the *Corpus Iuris Canonici* dealt with this question. The wife had to consent to her husband taking a vow of perpetual continence, and she had to either take a vow of perpetual continence or enter religious life. If the wife agreed then her husband could be ordained. After ordination the wife could not marry again.[249]

Gratian accepted the story of the intervention of Paphnutius at Nicea as well as the ecumenicity of canon 13 of Trullo.[250] Cholij considers this to be problematic:

> In doing so Gratian presented the praxis of the East (only bishops obliged absolute continence) and the West (all bishops, priests and deacons obliged to absolute continence) as being different but equal and he and future generations of canonists sought to thoroughly accommodate

---

245   Ibid., 719.
246   Ibid.
247   Ibid.
248   Pars 1:D. 76 c. 6 : "...Sane si coniugati iuvenes consenserint ordinari, etiam uxorem voluntas ita requirenda est, ut sequestrato mansionis cubiculo, religione promissa, postquam pariter conversi fuerint, ordinentur.... "
249   Pars 1:D. 32 c. 14: "....Neque permittitur postea uxor iungi eidem marito suo carnaliter, nec cuiquam nubere in vita aut post mortem illius."
250   Cholij, Clerical Celibacy in the East and West, 63-65; Stickler, The Case for Clerical Celibacy, 45-49.

such a difference. Based on his uncritical acceptance of the Greek texts, Gratian made the assumption that the eastern practice concerning celibacy was the more ancient discipline and that the Latin Church came somehow to impose continence on married clerics at a later date.[251]

As noted earlier in this chapter, Nicolae Dura has argued that the ecumenicity of canon 13 had already been recognized by the Latin Church at the Council of Constantinople in 861. Therefore one could assert that Gratian's acceptance of the ecumenicity of this canon was based on the Church's acceptance of it and not on his erroneous conclusions.[252] It seemed that Gratian also felt a need to seek theological justification for the imposition of the law of celibacy on Western clerics. But Cholij comments on Gratian:

> Given that the discipline of continence was regarded generally as not being of apostolic origin, nor attached to the exercise of orders, the theological reasons in favor of celibacy could only be regarded, at most, as reasons of 'fittingness' or 'congruence.'[253]

Many of the Decretalists[254] adopted the opinions of Gratian without critically judging the Greek texts.[255] Some of these assumptions have remained the common opinion to this day.

---

251 Cholij, Clerical Celibacy in the East and West, 65.
252 Dura, "The Ecumenicity of the Council in Trullo," 229-262.
253 Cholij, Clerical Celibacy in the East and West, 67.
254 The "Decretalists" were those who studied and commented upon the law issued in "Decretals." See Brundage, *Medieval Canon Law,* 53.
255 Filippo Liotta, La continenza dei chierici nel pensiero canonistico classico da Graziano a Gregorio IX (Milan: Giuffre, 1971) 58.

J. From Trent until the 1917 Code

1. Council of Trent, 1545-1563[256]

From 1300 to the Council of Trent discussion concerning clerical celibacy continued. The majority of discussions concerned priests who contracted marriage or otherwise failed to observe continence. In England and Germany, just prior to the council, the Church sought to resolve the situation of such clerics. In many cases the pope granted a reduction to the lay state and sanated the marriages. If these clerics chose to remain married they were prohibited from ever exercising ministry again. In 1521, Martin Luther published his "Martin Luther's Judgment about Monastic Vows."[257] In this work he laid out his objections to the obligation of clerical celibacy. Luther rejected the authority of tradition and ecclesiastical law to establish celibacy. He had declared his own preference for optional priestly celibacy as early as 1520.[258] Concerning the pastor, Luther wrote:

> He should be quite free to marry, or not. At his side, he should have several priests or deacons, either married or not, as he prefers, to help him in ministering to the Church and the people at large with sermons and the sacraments....Such men should be granted permission by a Christian council to marry, in order to avoid temptation and sin. For, if God has not forbidden them, no man should or may do so....Anything to the contrary in canon law is pure fabrication and idle chatter.[259]

---

256 See Tanner, 2: 657-800.

257 Martin Luther, "Martin Luther's Judgment about Monastic Vows," in Luther's Works American Edition, eds. Jaroslav Pelikan and Helmut T. Lehmann (Augsburg: Augsburg Fortress, 1967) 44:245-400.

258 McGarrity, "Spiritual and Canonical Values in Mandatory Priestly Celibacy," *Studia canonica* 27 (1993) 233.

259 Martin Luther, "An Appeal to the Ruling Class of German Nationality as to the Amelioration of the State of Christendom," translated in *Martin Luther: Selections from His Writings,* ed. John Dillenberger (New York: Doubleday, 1961) 448-449.

Soon he was joined by other prominent reformers, Zwingli and Calvin, in his repudiation of celibacy.

In the face of this mounting criticism, the Council of Trent was forced to consider the question of celibacy at length, albeit in a polemical context. The council established a commission of seventeen experts to examine the objections of the reformers. This commission was to examine two propositions:[260]

1. Marriage should not be relegated to second rank: it is on the contrary, superior to chastity. God gives married couples a greater grace than other people.[261]
2. Western priests can marry licitly notwithstanding ecclesiastical vows or law; to affirm the contrary is nothing less than a condemnation of marriage.[262]

The discussions at Trent lasted for thirteen sessions. Cochini summarizes the expert's response to the criticism of the 'reformers' thus:

A distinction was made between the case of celibates who became priests and that of married men accepted for ordination. As far as the former were concerned, there had never been in the Church any exception to the prohibition of marriage: its origin was apostolic (Jean Peletier, Miguel of Medina, Jean Lubera, Jean de Ludenna, Francis Orantes, Didacus of Paivia). Some theologians went as far as to conclude that this was of divine law (Richard du Pre, Miguel of Medina, Francis

---

260 Cochini, The Apostolic Origins of Priestly Celibacy, 19-21.

261 Concilium Tridentinum Diariorum, Actorum, Epistularum, Tractum Nova Collectio. The Commission of Theologians of the Council of Trent, ed. Societas Goerresiana (Freiburg: Herder, 1901) 9: 6, 380-82: "Matrimonium non postponendum, sed anteferendum castitati, et Deum dare coniugibus maiorem gratiam quam aliis." Hereafter CDTA. English translation from Cochini, The Apostolic Origins of Priestly Celibacy, 19-20.

262 "Licite contrahere posse matrimonium sacredotes occidentales, non obstante voto vel lege ecclesiastica, et oppositum nihil aliud esse quam damnare matrimonium, posseque omnes contrahere matrimonium, qui non sentiunt se habere donum castitatis." CDTA 32. English translation from Cochini, The Apostolic Origins of Priestly Celibacy, 20.

Orantes), while others deemed that this was only a point of ecclesiastical law (Francis Ferrer, Didacus of Paiva). As to married men accepted for orders (an historical fact that no-one contested), Claude de Saintes argued that the obligation of perfect continence imposed on them from the moment of ordination was of apostolic origin; by that very fact it is *de iure divino primario*. More numerous were the theologians who saw in this obligation the result of an ecclesiastical decision (Miguel of Medina, Lucius Anguisciola, Didacus of Paivia). Lastly, it is notable, that all the advisors agreed that the apostles were married when Christ called them. Thereafter in conformity with their declaration: "We have left everything to follow you." (Mt 19:27). They practiced continence. If the apostles left everything to follow Christ, it is obvious that they gave up conjugal life with their wives.[263]

The deliberations led the Fathers to promulgate the following pertinent canons:

Canon 4: If anyone says the Church did not have the power to establish diriment impediments to marriage, or erred in doing so: let him be anathema.

Canon 9: If anyone says that clerics in holy orders, or regulars who have made solemn profession of chastity, may contract marriage, and that such a contract is valid, in spite of church law and the vow, and that the opposite view amounts to a condemnation of marriage; and that all can contract marriage who do not consider they have the gift of chastity (even if they have vowed it) let them be anathema. For God would not deny the gift to those who duly ask for it, nor allow us to be tempted beyond our strength.

Canon 10: If anyone says the married state is to be preferred to that of virginity or celibacy, and that it is no better or more blessed to

---

263   Cochini, The Apostolic Origins of Priestly Celibacy, 20.

persevere in virginity or celibacy than to be joined in marriage: let him be anathema.[264]

The council confirmed the legislation of earlier councils and declared anathema anyone who believed that clerics in sacred orders could contract a valid marriage. Yet the council did not exclude married men from orders. It merely repeated previous legislation that marriages contracted after the reception of orders were invalid and illicit. Furthermore, the council Fathers addressed Luther's claim that marriage was more grace-filled than chastity by formulating a hierarchy of states of life which was to be the prevailing mentality for centuries to come.

While the council did not exclude married men from the reception of orders the establishment of seminaries for the formation of priests was to *de facto* concretize the reality of an exclusively unmarried clergy. Canon 18 stated:

> ...the holy council decrees that all cathedral and metropolitan churches...shall be bound each according to its means, to educate in religion, and to train in ecclesiastical discipline, a certain number of boys...into this college shall be received such as are at least twelve years of age....[265]

---

264 Council of Trent, session 24, November 11, 1563, de matrimonio, c. 4: "Si quis dixerit, ecclesiam non potuisse constituere impedimenta matrimonium dirimentia, vel in iis constituendis errasse: anathema sit." C. 9: "Si quis dixerit, clericos in sacris ordinibus constitutos, vel regulares, castitatem solemniter professos, posse matrimonium contrahere, contractumque validum esse, non obstante lege ecclesiastica vel voto, et oppositum nil aliud esse, quam damnare matrimonium; posseque omnes contrahere matrimonium, qui non sentiunt se castitatis (etiam si eam voverint) habere donum: anathema sit. Cum Deus id recte petentibus non deneget, nec patiatur, nos supra id, quod possumus, tentari." C. 10: "Si quis dixerit, statum coniugalem anteponendum esse statui virginitatis vel coelibatus, et non esse melius ac beatius, maner in virginitate aut coelibatu, quam iungi matrimonio: anathema sit. " Tanner, 2:754-755.

265 Council of Trent, session 23, July 15, 1563, de sacramento ordinis, c. 18: "...sancta synodus statuit, ut singulae cathedrales, metropolitanae ecclesiae...alere ac religiose educare et ecclesiasticis disciplinis instituere teneantur...in hoc vero collegio recipiantur, qui ad minimum duodecim annos...." Tanner, 2:750.

The Obligation of Perfect and Perpetual Continence

This canon was primarily oriented towards the training of younger candidates, twelve years and older for major orders. The seminary system became the normal way in the West to form candidates for the priesthood. This had the effect that married men were generally no longer ordained. In fact, many of the Fathers at the council had expressed this wish.[266]

On the doctrinal and juridical level, the Council of Trent successfully withstood the concerted assault of the reformers on clerical celibacy. Though the council had spoken, the problem of clerical celibacy was far from settled in many Catholic areas. The Tridentine decrees long remained unpromulgated and ineffective in many countries well into the seventeenth century, largely because of political interference. The frontal attacks on the discipline of celibacy continued unabated, yet the official position of the Latin Church remained steadfast.[267]

From Trent onwards the concept of celibacy was understood in much narrower terms. Prior to Trent celibacy was understood as the renunciation of the use of marriage entered into before ordination (absolute continence) and the prohibition of a future marriage. In this sense it could rightly be called celibacy-continence. After Trent, clerical celibacy was commonly understood more narrowly only as a prohibition against marrying. The norms established by Trent were the guiding principles for all future decisions rendered by the Roman congregations.

---

266   Stickler, The Case for Clerical Celibacy, 53.
267   John Lynch, "Critique of the Law of Celibacy in the Catholic Church from the Period of the Reform Councils," in Celibacy in the Church, eds. William Bassett, Peter Huizing (New York, NY: Herder and Herder, 1972) 57-75.

2. Married Men and Irregularity for Tonsure

On January 23, 1610 the Sacred Congregation for the Council declared that a married man could not be admitted to tonsure.[268] Marriage was an irregularity *ex defectu libertatis,* preventing the reception of tonsure unless the necessary conditions for freedom had been established and safeguarded.[269] The irregularity arose from a valid marriage. If the marriage was annulled or if his spouse died, he could be admitted to first tonsure. The diocesan bishop could tonsure a married man and admit him to all orders only if he and his wife promised to refrain from sexual relations and have no more children. In the eighteenth century, Pope Benedict XIV (1740-1758) reserved the cases of young married men to himself.[270] Requests for the ordination of married men were to be directed to this same congregation. A dispensation would only be granted when certain conditions guaranteeing absolute continence were fulfilled. If the couple was young or there was a doubt concerning their ability to live in absolute continence each was expected to make a solemn vow of perpetual chastity before the husband's ordination.[271] If the couple was older and there was no doubt concerning their ability to live in absolute continence, the husband could be ordained without entering religious life. He and his wife would take a simple vow of perpetual chastity, which they could live in a religious community or in the world.[272] Among canonists there was much debate as to whether the wife's entry into reli-

---

268   Sacred Congregation for the Council, Tricaricen January 23, 1610, n. 2385: "Coniugatos, durante coniugio non posse ad primam tonsuram promoveri," in Codicis Iuris Canonici Fontes, ed. Pietro Gasparri (Rome: Typis Polyglottis Vaticanis, 1923-1939) 5:211. Hereafter Fontes.

269   Roman Cholji, "Clerical Celibacy in the Western Church: Some Clarifications," *Priests and People* 3 (1989) 308.

270   Benedict XIV, *Libri Octo de Synodo Diocesana* (Rome: Excudebant Nicolaus et Marcus Palearini, 1748) 13:12, nn. 14-15.

271   Franz Xavier Wernz, Ius Decretalium (Rome: Typographia Polygotta, 1989-1905) 5:175; Pietro Gasparri, Tractatus de Sacra Ordinatione (Paris: Delhomme & Briguet, 1893-94) 2: 3, n. 532.

272   Wernz, Ius Decretalium, 5:175; Gasparri, Tractatus de Sacra Ordinatione, 2: 3, 535-536.

gious life was an absolute requirement on her part. The Sacred Congregation for the Council responded in 1830 and declared that the wife did not have to enter religious life so long as she took a vow of perpetual continence and there was no fear of her endangering her continence in the world.

3. Dispensations: Exceptions Prove the Rule

The roman pontiff had the power to dispense clergy from their vow of celibacy. This is borne out in the various examples of dispensations granted to priests, especially in the cases of those who had attempted marriage. Benedict IX (1032-1044) permitted a religious priest to marry in order to propagate the family of Aragon which was threatened with extinction.[273] In 1548 after the reformation and at the insistence of Emperor Charles V, Pope Paul III (1534-1549) granted successive papal nuncios in Germany the faculty to sanate the marriages of secular priests.[274] In 1554 Julius III (1550-1555) granted Cardinal Reginald Pole the faculty to dispense priests who had married invalidly in the interval between the defection of Henry VIII and the accession of Queen Mary Tudor.[275] The dispensation was granted only with regard to the woman the cleric had married invalidly, and there was to be no other marriage after her death. Similarly, in 1801, Pius VII (1800-1833), upon signing the concordat with Napoleon, granted his legate the power to dispense priests and monks who had married during the French Revolution.[276] Five thousand priests and religious petitioned either for

---

273 Gasparri, *Tractatus Canonicus de Matrimonio* (Rome: Typis Polyglottis Vaticanis, 1932) 1: 373.

274 Pope Paul III, instructions to German bishops, in Augustino De Roskovány, *Caelibatus et Breviarum: Duo Gravissima Clericorum Officina, E Monumentis Omnium Seculorum Demonstrata* (Pestini: Typis Beimel et Basilii Kozma, 1861) 2: nn. 1289, 1290. Hereafter Roskovány.

275 Pope Julius III, papal bull to the papal legate to England, Cardinal Pole. Roskovány, 2: n. 1333.

276 Pius VII, papal bull to the papal legate to France, Cardinal Caprara. Roskovány, 3: 179-186. See also John A. Abbo, "The Problem of Lapsed Priests," *The Jurist* 23 (1963) 157-161.

reinstatement or for the regularization of their marriage. Of these 2,000 chose marriage.[277] It is important to note that if a priest's marriage was sanated, he was permanently excluded from exercising his ministry.

It was common that the dispensation was granted with various limitations. Sweeney observes:

> It should be indicated these dispensations were granted to priests who had already invalidly married, in regard only to the women whom the priest had married, and only for the period of her lifetime. After the death of his wife, the priest was forbidden to remarry.[278]

It is interesting to note that in a dispensation granted a certain French priest in 1802 the pope declared that any sin committed by this priest against the sixth commandment was also a sacrilege.[279]

Gasparri asserts that he did not know whether the Sacred Penitentiary had ever denied a dispensation when it was sought in cases where no scandal could arise as a consequence. Such would be the case if the sacerdotal condition of the priest was unknown to all, even to his "wife," in the place where he was now residing and no memory of him remained where he received his ordination.[280] Gasparri does not comment on whether such dispensations had the conditions similar to those observed by Sweeney.

As for bishops, there is at least one confirmed case of a bishop being reduced to the lay state. Until 2008 there was no evidence of a bishop ever having

---

277   See Simon Delacroix, La réorganisation de L'Église de France après la révolution 1801-1809 (Paris: Éditions du Vitrail, 1962) 1:363-370; John Lynch, "Marriage and Celibacy of the Clergy, The Discipline of the Western Church: An Historical-Canonical Synopsis," The Jurist 32 (1972) 210.

278   Sweeney, *The Reduction of Clerics to the Lay State*, 126. See also Roskovány, 3: nn. 1966-1967.

279   Roskovány, 3: nn. 1966, 1967.

280   Gasparri, *De Matrimonio,* 1: 373.

been dispensed from celibacy.[281] Charles Talleyrand was Bishop of Autun in France (1788-1791). He married civilly before the outbreak of the French Revolution. In 1802, he was reconciled to the Church and was reduced to the lay state, but he was not dispensed from the obligation of celibacy.[282] On June 30, 1802, Cardinal Consalvi communicated the denial to Talleyrand:

> I should have wished, truly, that Your Excellency's desires could have been entirely fulfilled and that the brief could have included permission to marry; but how was this to be when, in eighteen centuries of church history, there is not a single instance of such a concession? No consecrated bishop has ever been dispensed in order to marry. Not only is there no precedent in eighteen centuries but there are several instances in which this permission was consistently refused by the Holy See.[283]

In another case, John Butler had been the Bishop of Cork since 1763, and in 1786 with the death of his nephew he inherited the title of one of the most ancient peerages in Ireland, that of Lord Dunboyne.[284] He soon felt that he had an obligation to provide an heir so he petitioned Pope Pius VI for a dispensation from celibacy, which was denied June 9, 1787.[285] He renounced the Church, joined the Anglican Church and married his cousin, but could produce no heir.

---

281   On July 30, 2008, a statement signed by the Prefect of the Congregation for Bishops, Cardinal Giovanni Batista Re, made public a decree granting a dispensation from the clerical state for the Most Reverend Fernando Armindo Lugo Mendez, S.V.D., Bishop emeritus of San Pedro Bishop Lugo. The decree included a dispensation from the obligations of celibacy, c. 291. This would seem to be the first dispensation of its kind granted for a bishop. See *Origins* 38:12 (August 28, 2008) 196.

282   Roskovány, 3: n. 1970. See also Sweeney, *The Reduction of Clerics to the Lay State,* 125.

283   Françoise-Désiré Mathieu, *Le concordat de 1801: ses origines, son histoire d'après des documents inédits* (Paris: Perrin et Cie, 1903) 348. See also John A. Abbo, "The Problem of Lapsed Priests," *The Jurist* 23 (1963) 153-179.

284   Con Costello, *In Quest of an Heir: The Life and Times of John Butler Catholic Bishop of Cork Protestant Baron of Dunboyne* (Cork: Ireland: Tower Books of Cork, 1978) 18-19.

285   Ibid., 19.

On his deathbed, aged 84, he returned to the Church.[286] There are conflicting reports as to whether Dunboyne had been reduced to the lay state.

Even though various popes granted dispensations from celibacy these were the exception and not the rule. The popes continued to affirm the Church's discipline of clerical celibacy. Early in the nineteenth century an association was formed in Germany to advocate a change in the law of celibacy, but Gregory XVI (1831-1846) denounced this movement in his encyclicals *Mirari vos* and *Quo graviora*.[287] Pius IX (1846-1878) defended the discipline in his encyclical *Qui pluribus* and his apostolic letter *Multiplices inter.*[288]

In 1869 Pius IX convoked the First Vatican Council (1869-1870). There was a preparatory document recommending that the penalties imposed by Trent for violations of celibacy be retained and that diocesan bishops keep archival records concerning such violations. But the council ended abruptly with Victor Emmanuel's troops marching on Rome and no decree concerning clerical celibacy was promulgated.[289] At the beginning of the twentieth century, modernism provoked a new attack on the law of celibacy, but its effects were limited due largely to the decisive measures taken by St. Pius X (1903-1914).[290]

It is interesting to note that in the cases of different Eastern Churches re-

286 Ibid.

287 Gregory XVI, encyclical Mirari vos, August 15, 1832: Acta Gregorii Papae XIV (Rome: Ex Typographia Polyglotta, 1901) 1:169-174; encyclical Quo graviora, October 4, 1833: Acta Gregorii Papae XIV, 1:307-310.

288 Pius IX, encyclical *Qui pluribus,* November 9, 1846: *Pii IX Pontificis Maximi Acta* (Rome, 1856) 1/1: 4-24; apostolic letter *Multiplices inter,* June 10, 1851: Ibid., 1/1: 280-284. See also encyclical *Quanta cura,* Syllabus of Errors, December 8, 1864: *ASS* 3 (1864) 160-167.

289 See McGarrity, "Spiritual and Canonical Values in Mandatory Priestly Celibacy," *Studia canonica* 27 (1993) 235.

290 Pius X, encyclical Pascendi dominic gregis, September 8, 1907: ASS 40 (1907) 593-652. Pius condemned Modernism and observed that one of the goals of the movement was to suppress celibacy. See also, apostolic exhortation Harent animo, August 4, 1908: AAS 41 (1908) 555-577. In his apostolic exhortation on the priesthood, to mark the Golden Jubilee of his ordination, Pius referred to celibacy as 'the fairest jewel of our priesthood.'

turning to full communion with Rome from the fifteenth century onwards, the Latin Church respected their existing custom of periodic continence and did not oblige their married clergy to observe absolute continence as a condition for full communion.[291]

K. Conclusion

Presently 'celibacy' is understood narrowly to mean the renunciation of the right to enter marriage as a condition for the reception of orders. Yet for much of the Church's history there was no law of celibacy as we presently understand it. From the beginning married men were admitted to every degree of the hierarchy, both to minor and major orders. In fact no candidate for major orders in the Latin Church was obliged to be unmarried until after the Council of Trent.

From the fourth century ecclesiastical legislation in the Latin Church obliged absolute continence as a precondition for the ordination of married men to major orders. The cleric, with the consent of his wife, was obliged to observe the *lex continentiae*. He and his wife were to refrain from sexual relations and not to have any more children. All clerics married or unmarried were also prohibited from marrying after ordination. It would seem that the fundamental norm that bound all major clergy was absolute continence. Thus in the early centuries of the Church, celibacy was understood more broadly in terms of the *lex continentiae,* the law of continence.

By the seventh century, the East and West had developed distinctive legislative traditions for maintaining clerical chastity. The East obliged all married clerics, with the exception of bishops, to observe periodic continence. This remains the practice of the East to this day. The West obliged all major married

---

291   See Cholij, Clerical Celibacy in the East and West, 168-179.

clerics to observe absolute continence. In the West the insistence on absolute continence led to a steady decline in the number of married men chosen for ordination to major orders. Both East and West prohibited marriage after ordination.

With the institution of seminaries by the Council of Trent, the Latin Church had a steady flow of younger unmarried candidates for major orders. In 1610, the Sacred Congregation for the Council declared that a married man could not be admitted to tonsure.[292] The diocesan bishop could tonsure a married man and admit him to all orders only if he and his wife promised to refrain from sexual relations and have no more children. Cases involving younger married men were reserved the pope. In all cases the married man and his wife had to promise to refrain from sexual relations and to have no more children. Now we turn our attention to how the law of celibacy reached juridic expression in the 1917 Code of Canon Law.

---

292   Sacred Congregation for the Council, Tricaricen January 23, 1610, n. 2385: "Coniugatos, durante coniugio non posse ad primam tonsuram promoveri." Fontes 5:211.

CHAPTER TWO

CANONICAL DISPOSITIONS OF CLERICAL CHASTITY, CONTINENCE AND CELIBACY IN THE 1917 CODE

As part of the preparations for the First Vatican Council (1869-1870), a number of bishops called for a reform of the centuries' old *Corpus Iuris Canonici*.[1] This was mostly in response to the disordered collections of ecclesiastical laws which had given rise to legal uncertainty, obsolescence and lacunae.[2] Some bishops even requested a new and single collection of all ecclesiastical laws. Such a task had not been undertaken since Gratian's *Decretum* in the twelfth century.[3] However, the council ended abruptly, less than one year after it was convened without discussing the reform of canonical law.[4]

In 1904, Pius X responded to the requests of the bishops and announced the establishment of a commission of cardinals entrusted with the task of codifying

---

1   See *Postulatum* for Vatican I. In *Acta et Decreta Sacrorum Conciliorum Recentiorum Collectio Lacensis* (Freiburg: Herder, 1890) 6:889. See also John A. Alesandro, "General Introduction," in *The Code of Canon Law: A Text and Commentary,* ed. James A. Coriden et al. (New York/ Mahwah, NJ: Paulist Press, 1985) 4.

2   Stephen Findlay, *Canonical Norms Governing the Deposition and Degradation of Clerics: An Historical Synopsis and Commentary,* Canon Law Studies 130 (Washington, DC: Catholic University of America, 1941) 111.

3   Alesandro, "General Introduction," 4.

4   See Hubert Jedin, *Ecumenical Councils of the Catholic Church: An Historical Outline* (New York: Herder and Herder, 1960) 22-23. See also Roger Aubert, *Vatican I* (Paris: Éditions de l'Orante, 1964).

into one collection the laws of the Latin Church.[5] The resulting *Codex Iuris Canonici,* commonly known as 'the 1917 code,' was promulgated by his successor Benedict XV on May 27, 1917 and took effect on May 19, 1918.[6]

This chapter will explore the canonical dispositions of chastity, continence and celibacy in the 1917 code. Particular examination will be given to canons 132 and 133 which obliged clergy in major orders to observe celibacy and chastity. Interwoven throughout this examination consideration will be given to other pertinent canons, namely, the canons governing penalties for violations of these obligations; those governing dispensations from these obligations; and those that protect and foster these obligations. Following this will be a brief treatment of significant magisterial teaching on celibacy from the promulgation of the code up to the eve of the Second Vatican Council.

The term *lex caelibatus,* "law of celibacy," is rarely found in ecclesiastical legislation prior to the 1917 code.[7] The word 'celibacy,' though found in papal writing from the sixteenth century, is not found in any general council before the Council of Trent (1545-1563).[8] Before this time "the distinction made is usually *innupti, non-coniugati,* or *non-uxorati* (unmarried) and *coniugati,* or *uxorati* (married), but not between *celibate* and married."[9] As was demonstrated in chapter one for much of the Church's legislative history the terms continence, perfect continence, chastity and perfect chastity were more commonly used.

5   Pope Pius X, motu proprio *Arduum sane munus,* March 19, 1904: *Acta Sanctae Sedis* 36 (1904) 193-198. Hereafter *ASS.*
6   Pope Benedict XV, apostolic constitution *Providentissima Mater Ecclesia,* May 27, 1917: *AAS* 9 (1917) 2:5-7.
7   Roman Cholij, "Clerical Celibacy in the Western Church: Some Clarifications," *Priests and People* 3 (1989) 303.
8   Ibid.
9   Ibid.

The term *'caelibatus'* (celibacy) occurs explicitly in the 1917 code in two canons, 213 §2 and 214 §1 and implicitly in canon 132 §1 in the phrase "prevented from marrying."[10] The term *'castitatis'* (chastity) occurs on six occasions in canons 132 §1, 487, 1058 §1, 1309, 1990 and 2388 §1. The term *'continentia'* (continence) is not used explicitly in the code. However, continence is implicit in the obligation of clergy not to marry and in the chastity required of unmarried clergy.

Canons 132 and 133 are found in Book Two of the 1917 code, part one, section one, under title 3, "On the obligations of Clerics."

A. Canon 132 §1

Canon 132 §1 stated:

Clerics constituted in major orders are prohibited from marrying and are so bound to observe chastity that if they sin against it are also guilty of sacrilege, without prejudice to the provision of canon 214 §1.[11]

1. Clerics in Major Orders

The Church is by divine institution a hierarchical society. The Council of Trent decreed:

If anyone denies that there exists in the Catholic Church a hierarchy

---

10   Codex Iuris Canonici Pii X Pontificis Maximi iussu digestus Benedicti Papae XV auctoritate promulgatus (Rome: Typis Polyglottis Vaticanis, 1917), c. 132 §1: "... nuptiis arcentur ...." Hereafter 17 CIC. English translations from The 1917 Pio-Benedictine Code of Canon Law: In English Translation with Extensive Scholarly Apparatus, ed. Edward N. Peters (San Francisco, CA: Ignatius Press, 2001). All subsequent English translations of canons from this code will be taken from this source unless otherwise indicated.

11   17 CIC, c. 132 §1: "Clerici in maioribus ordinibus constitui a nuptiis arcentur et servandae castitatis obligatione ita tenetur, ut contra eandem peccantes sacriligii quoque rei sint, salvo praescripto c. 214 §1."

consisting of bishops, priests and ministers, instituted by divine appointment: let him be anathema.[12]

In the Church, there are those who have been constituted as *lay persons* and those who have been constituted as *clerics*. Canon 107 stated:

By divine constitution there are in the Church *clerics* distinct from *laity*, although not all clerics possess orders that are of divine institution; either of them can be *religious*.[13]

One is constituted a lay person by virtue of baptism validly received. Canon 87 stated:

By baptism a man is constituted a person in the Church of Christ with all of the rights and duties....[14]

From among the laity some are chosen to be clerics. A baptized male was constituted a cleric with the reception of first tonsure. Canon 108 §1 stated:

Those who are taken into divine ministries at least by the reception of first tonsure are called clerics.[15]

Tonsure was to be conferred only on those who intended to advance to the presbyterate.[16] Previously tonsure could be conferred on a candidate who

---

12   Council of Trent, session 23, July 15, 1563, de sacramento ordinis, c. 6: "Si quis dixerit, in ecclesia catholica non esse hierarchiam, divina ordinatione institutam, quae constat ex episcopis, presbyteris et ministris, anathema sit." Decrees of the Ecumenical Councils, ed. Norman T. Tanner (London and Washington: Sheed & Ward and Georgetown University Press, 1990) 2:744. Hereafter Tanner. The term 'ministris' included all orders below the rank of presbyter. See also Edward P. Echlin, The Deacon in the Church (Staten Island, NY: Alba House, 1971) 104.
13   17 CIC, c. 107: "Ex divina institutione sunt in Ecclesia clerici a laicis distincti, licet non omnes clerici sint divinae institutionis; utrique autem possunt esse religiosi."
14   17 CIC, c. 87: "Baptismate homo constituitur in Ecclesiae Christi persona cum omnibus christianorum iuribus et officiis...."
15   17 CIC, c. 108 § 1: "Qui divinis ministeriis per primam saltem tonsuram mancipati sunt, clerici dicunter."
16   17 *CIC*, c. 973 § 1:" Prima tonsura et ordines illis tantum conferendi sunt, qui propositum habeant ascendendi ad presbyteratum et quos merito coniicere liceat aliquando dignos futuros esse presbyteros. "

intended to serve the Church permanently in any of the orders. Since Trent it had become common practice for all to advance to the presbyterate unless some impediment prevented this.[17]

Tonsure was neither an order nor a sacrament.[18] However, according to canon 950, tonsure was included under the term *ordo*:

> In law the words: to ordain, order, ordination, sacred ordination encompass, besides episcopal consecration, those enumerated in canon 949 and first tonsure, unless it can be established otherwise by the nature of the thing or the context of the words.[19]

Tonsure was a sacramental and a legal requirement that disposed a person for the reception of orders, ecclesiastical benefices, pensions and jurisdictional power.[20]

The code did not explicitly state the age at which tonsure and minor orders could be received. Canon 976 required that the candidate must have begun his theological training before he received first tonsure. The code changed the former law established by Trent that required merely the use of reason for the reception of tonsure and the minor orders.[21]

The cleric was further set apart from the laity by ordination. Canon 948 stated:

> Ordination, by the institution of Christ, distinguishes clerics from laity for the governance of the faithful and the ministry of divine cult.[22]

---

17   Stanislaus Woywod, *A Practical Commentary on the Code of Canon Law.* Rev. by Callistus Smith (New York, NY: Wagner, 1962) 651.

18   Franz Wernz and Petri Vidal, *Ius Canonicum* (Rome: Apud Aedes Universitas Gregorianae, 1944) 4: n. 177.

19   17 *CIC,* c. 950: "In iure verba: ordinare, ordo, ordinatio, sacra ordinatio, comprehendunt, praeter consecrationem episcopalem, ordines enumeratos in can. 949 et ipsam primam tonsuram, nisi aliud ex natura rei vel ex contextu verborum eruatur." Canon 949 lists the minor and major orders.

20   Dominic M. Prümmer, *Handbook of Moral Theology.* Trans. by Gerald W. Shelton (Cork, Ireland: Mercier Press Ltd., 1956) 381.

21   See Council of Trent, session 23, July 15, 1563, de sacramento ordinis, c. 4. Tanner, 2:746.

22   17 CIC, c. 948: "Ordo ex Christi institutione clericos a laicis in Ecclesia distinguit ad fidelium regimen et cultos divini ministerium."

In addition canon 968 §1 stated:

Only a baptized male validly receives sacred ordination; for liciety,
however, he should be outstanding in qualities according to the norm
of the sacred canons, in the judgment of the proper ordinary, and not
detained by any irregularity or impediment.[23]

A cleric therefore was a baptized male called from the ranks of the laity
and entered the ranks of the clergy by the reception of first tonsure. The cleric
was further distinguished from the laity by subsequent ordinations to minor and
major orders. The Council of Trent decreed:

If anyone says that apart from the priesthood there do not exist other
orders in the Catholic Church, both major and minor, by which one
reaches the priesthood as by successive steps: let him be anathema.[24]

Among the clergy there was a hierarchy. Canon 108 §2 stated:

(Clerics) are not all of the same rank, but among them there is a sacred
hierarchy in which some are subordinated to others.[25]

Clerics were divided into two categories: 'minor clerics' and 'major clerics.'
Canon 949 stated:

....by the name of *major* orders or sacred orders are understood presbyterate, diaconate and subdiaconate; while *minor* orders are acolyte,
exorcist, lector and doorkeeper.[26]

---

23   17 *CIC*, c. 968 § 2: "Sacram ordinationem valide recipit solus vir baptizatus; licite
autem, qui ad normam sacrorum canonum debitis qualitatibus, iudicio proprii Ordinarii, praeditus
sit, neque ulla detineatur irregularitate aliove impedimento."
24   See Council of Trent, session 23, July 15, 1563, de sacramento ordinis, c. 2 :"Si quis
dixerit, praeter sacerdotium non esse in ecclesia catholica alios ordines, et maiores et minores, per
quos velut per gradus quosdam in sacerdotium : anathema sit." Tanner, 2:743.
25   17 *CIC*, c. 108 § 2: "Non sunt omnes in eodem gradu, sed inter eos sacra hierarchia est
in qua alii alliis subordinantur."
26   17 CIC, c. 949: "...nomine ordinum maiorem vel sacrorum intelligentur presbyteratus,
diaconatus, subdiaconatus: minorem vero acolythatus, exorcistatus, lectoratus, ostiariatus."

Minor clerics were those who had been ordained to the minor orders of porter, exorcist, lector, and acolyte. Major clerics were those who had been ordained to the major orders of subdeacon, deacon, and priesthood. Canonical commentators generally held that while the episcopate was not enumerated among the major orders it was included under the major order of the 'presbyterate'. The bishop is, after all, a priest and the episcopacy is the fullness of the priesthood.[27] As Bouscaren observed:

> The term *presbyterate* includes the episcopate as well as the simple priesthood.[28]

Canonists commonly pointed to canon 950 as establishing that the episcopacy was included in 'orders':

> In law the words: to ordain, order, ordination, sacred ordination encompass, besides episcopal consecration, those enumerated in canon 949 and first tonsure, unless it can be established otherwise by the nature of the thing or the context of the words.[29]

Therefore the term 'clerics in major orders' included bishops. A cleric in major orders was thus one who had been ordained a subdeacon, deacon, presbyter or bishop.

---

27   Kenan B. Osborne, *The Permanent Diaconate: Its History and Place in the Sacrament of Orders* (New York: Paulist Press, 2006) 65-72. Osborne discusses the common opinion beginning with Peter Lombard's *Liber IV Sententiarum,* "that there were two orders which belonged essentially to the Sacrament of Orders: Diaconate and Priesthood. The Episcopacy was an institutional office and an institutional dignity in the Church," 65-66. This was also the opinion of Thomas Aquinas, Bonaventure and John Duns Scotus. This remained the established wisdom until the teaching of the Second Vatican Council.

28   T. Lincoln Bouscaren, Adam Ellis, Francis Korth, Canon Law: A Text and Commentary (Milwaukee: Bruce Publishing Company, 1946) 427. See also Matthaeus A Coronata, Institutiones Iuris Canonici (Rome: Marietti, 1950) 1:197; Heriberto Jone, Commentarium in Codicem Iuris Canonici (Mainz: Paderborn, 1954) 1:173. These commentators are in agreement with Bouscaren.

29   17 *CIC,* c. 950: "In iure verba: ordinare, ordo, ordinatio, sacra ordinatio, comprehendunt, praeter consecrationem episcopalem, ordines enumeratos in can. 949 et ipsam primam tonsuram, nisi aliud ex natura rei vel ex contextu verborum eruatur."

Regarding the age at which a candidate could receive major orders, the Council of Trent decreed:

> Henceforth no one is to be advanced to the subdiaconate before his twenty-second, or to the diaconate before his twenty-third, or to the priesthood before his twenty-fifth year.[30]

In the 1917 code the age of ordination for the presbyterate was lowered to twenty-four. Canon 975 stated:

> Subdiaconate is not to be conferred before the completion of the twenty-first year of age; diaconate, before the completion of the twenty-second year; presbyterate, before the completion of the twenty-fourth year.[31]

Canon 331 stated that one being ordained to the episcopacy must be at least thirty years of age.[32]

2. Prohibition on Marriage: Obligation of Celibacy

Clerics in major orders were prohibited from marrying and were therefore bound to observe celibacy. According to canon 132, clerical celibacy implied a twofold obligation, celibacy (remaining unmarried, therefore obliged to absolute continence) and chastity (the living of one's sexuality in the continent state). At the time of the code, Latin Church candidates for major orders were ordinarily unmarried men so, while canon 132 does not make explicit reference to 'continence,' it is clear that an 'unmarried' cleric would be bound to absolute

---

30 Council of Trent, session 23, July 15, 1563, de ordinis, c. 12: "Nullus in posterum ad subdiaconatus ordinem ante vigesimum secundum, ad diaconatus ante vigesimum tertium, ad presbyteratus ante vigesimum quistum aetatis suae annum promoveatur." Tanner, 2:748.

31 17 CIC, c. 975: "Subdiaconatus ne conferatur ante annum vicesimum primum completum; diaconatus ante vicesimum secundum completum; presbyteratus ante vicesimum quartum completum."

32 17 *CIC*, c. 331: "Annos natus saltem triginta."

continence by natural law. A cleric was prohibited from marrying and could not engage in sexual relations as this is the privilege only of the married. Celibacy is the most perfect assurance of absolute continence.

The obligation of celibacy remained for the cleric in major orders even if he returned to the lay state. Canon 213 §2 stated:

> A major cleric, however, is bound by the obligation of celibacy, with due regard for the prescription of canon 214.[33]

A reduction to the lay state usually did not include a dispensation from the obligation of celibacy.

3. The Source of the Obligation of Celibacy

Did the obligation of celibacy arise from merely ecclesiastical law or from the nature of the vow implied in accepting the subdiaconate itself? This became an important question particularly because of its relationship to the impediment of orders for marriage. What exactly was it about orders that rendered the ordained man *inhabiles* for marriage? Was it the fact of being ordained, or was it the fact that he had professed absolute continence? According to Bouscaren, the more common opinion of Wernz, Lehmkuhl, Vermeersch and others was that:

> The immediate source of the obligation was the vow which, though no longer expressed, was implied in the ordination to the subdiaconate. If the ordinand expressly declines the vow he is bound by the law.[34]

This opinion was adopted in a decision of the Roman Rota, January 13, 1928,

---

33   17 *CIC*, c. 213 § 2: "Clericus tamen maior obligatione caelibatus tenetur, salvo prae-scripto can. 214." Canon 214 will be examined later in this chapter.
34   Bouscaren, Ellis & Korth, Canon Law: A Text and Commentary, 114.

coram Jullien.[35] For the East, the impediment of orders had to arise from the incompatibility of orders for marriage rather than from the vow of continence because clergy below the rank of bishop were not bound to absolute continence.[36] It followed that an incompatibility between orders and marriage must exist.

4. Penalties for the Violation of the Obligation of Celibacy

The Church enacted legislation to penalize those who violated their obligation of celibacy by attempting marriage. In cases of attempted marriage the cleric had to renounce the 'marriage' he had entered or seek a dispensation from celibacy so that his situation could be regularized. If he renounced his invalid marriage and separated permanently from his "wife" he could be readmitted to ministry. If he was granted a dispensation from celibacy and his marriage was subsequently validated, he would be permanently excluded from ministry. A dispensation from celibacy was always accompanied by a prohibition on the exercise of one's ministry.[37] The penalties for attempted marriage were excommunication, degradation, deprivation of office and, if a religious, dismissal from the congregation or order.

a. Excommunication

Those clerics in major orders who attempted marriage incurred excommunication.

---

35   Coram Jullien, January 13, 1928: S. Romanae Rotae Decisiones Seu Sententiae (Vatican City: Libreria Editrice Vaticana, 1909-) 20 (1928) 1-13. Hereafter RRDec. This case involved a priest who claimed that he simulated his intention to receive orders, and as a result was not bound to celibacy. The Rota stated that even if the priest did exclude the vow, he was still bound to celibacy by ecclesiastical law.

36   Roman Cholij, *Clerical Celibacy in the East and West* (Hereford, England: Fowler Wright Books, 1988) 63-68.

37   Ioannes Chelodi, *Ius canonicum de Matrimonio et de Iudiciis Matrimonialibus,* ed. Petri Ciprotti, 5th ed. (Vicenza: Società Anonima Tipografica Editrice, 1947).

Canon 2388 §1 stated:

Clerics constituted in sacred orders or regulars, or nuns after a solemn vow of chastity, and likewise all those who presume to contract even a civil marriage with any of the aforementioned persons incur automatic excommunication simply reserved to the Apostolic See.[38]

Canon 2257 §1 defined the nature of the penalty of excommunication:

Excommunication is a censure by which one is excluded from communion of the faithful with the effects that are enumerated in the canons that follow and that cannot be separated.[39]

Canons 2258-2267 detailed the effects of excommunication which included a prohibition on the reception and administration of the sacraments; a restriction on ecclesiastical burial; deprivation of certain spiritual benefits; deprivation of the right to exercise legal ecclesiastical acts, offices, functions, jurisdiction; and the right of appointment to ecclesiastical dignities, offices, benefices, and promotion to orders.[40]

b. Deprivation of Office

Canon 2388 §1 referenced canon 188, 5° which enacted:

Any office becomes vacant upon the fact and without any declaration

---

38   17 CIC, c. 2388: "Clerici in sacris constituti vel regulares aut moniales post votum sollemne castitatis, itemque omnes cum aliqua ex praedictis personis matrimonium etiam civiliter tantum contrahere praesumentes, incurrunt in excommunicationem latae sententiae Sedi Apostolicae simpliciter reservatum."

39   17 *CIC*, c. 2257 §1: "Excommunicatio est censura qua quis excluditur a communione fidelium cum effectibus qui in canonibus, qui sequuntur, enumerantur, quique separari nequeunt. "

40   See Stanislaus Woywod, *A Practical Commentary on the Code of Canon Law.* Revised by Callistus Smith (New York: Joseph F. Wagner, Inc., 1957) 2: 439-442; Franz Wernz, *Ius Canonicum* (Prati: Ex Officina Libraria Giachetti, 1911-1915) 7: 293-319; Émile Jomart, "Excommunication," in *Dictionnaire de droit canonique*, ed. Raoul Naz (Paris: Librairie Letouzey et Ané, 1935-1965) 5: 615-628. Hereafter *DDC.*

by tacit resignation recognized by the law itself if a cleric…contracts marriage even, merely civilly.[41]

A cleric who attempted marriage was by that fact deprived of every and all ecclesiastical offices that he held.

c. Degradation

Canon 2388 §1 also stated:

Clerics moreover, having been warned, if they do not come back to their senses within a time defined by the ordinary according to the diversity of circumstances will be degraded.[42]

Degradation was a penalty applied only to clerics, canon 2298, 12°.[43] Concerning the effects of degradation of the offending cleric canon 2305 §1 stated:

Degradation contains within itself deposition, the perpetual privation of ecclesiastical habit, and the reduction of the cleric to the lay state.[44]

Degradation was the only canonical penalty whereby a cleric in major orders was reduced to the lay state.[45] A degraded cleric, though no longer obliged to the recitation of the Divine Office, was still bound to the obligation of celibacy.[46] Being thus bound, any sin committed against chastity by such a degraded

---

41   17 CIC, c. 188, 5°: "Ob tactitam renuntiationem ab ipso iure admissam quaelibet officia vacant ipso facto et sine ulla declaratione, si clericus…matrimonium etiam civile tantum, ut aiunt, contraxerit."
42   17 CIC, c. 2388 § 1: "Clerici praeterea, si moniti, tempore ab ordinario pro adiunctorum diversitate praefinito, non resipuerint, degradentur, firmo praescripto can. 188, n. 5."
43   17 *CIC*, c. 2298, 12°: "Poenae vindicativae quae clericis tantum applicantur, sunt: Degradatio."
44   17 *CIC*, c. 2305 § 1: "Degradatio in se continet depositionem, perpetuam privationem habitus ecclesiastici et reductionem clerici ad statum laicalem." See also c. 211.
45   Findlay, *Canonical Norms Governing the Deposition and Degradation of Clerics,* 245.
46   17 *CIC*, c. 211 § 1 : " Etsi sacra ordinatio, semel valide recepta, nunquam irrita fiat, clericus tamen maior ad statum laicalem redigitur rescripto Sanctae Sedis, decreto vel sententia ad normam can. 214, demum poena degradationis."

cleric would be a sacrilege and he was *inhabiles* to enter a valid marriage.[47] However, the obligation of celibacy did cease for the degraded cleric who was expressly dispensed.[48]

5. Irregularity

A cleric who attempted marriage was also irregular for the reception of further orders. Canon 985, 3° stated:

> The following are irregular by delict: Those who attempt marriage, even civilly, or who dare to place the act of consent, while themselves bound by the marriage bond or by sacred orders, or by religious vows, even if simple and temporary, or with a woman bound by the same vows or already joined in valid marriage.[49]

The dispensation from the irregularity of attempted marriage and the censure attached to the violation were reserved to the Apostolic See, and "it was scarcely to be expected that it would be granted, for such a cleric cannot be regarded as a worthy candidate for promotion to higher orders."[50]

6. Dispensation from the Obligation of Celibacy

According to canon 211 §1 a major cleric could be 'reduced to the lay state' by a rescript from the Holy See, by a decree or sentence according to canon 214,

---

47   Findlay, Canonical Norms Governing the Deposition and Degradation of Clerics, 212-213.
48   Ibid.
49   17 CIC, c. 985, 3°: "Sunt irregulares ex delicto: "Qui matrimonium attentare aut civilem tantum actum ponere aussi sunt, vel ipsimet vinculo matrimoniali aut ordine sacro aut votis religiosi etiam simplicibus ac temporariis ligati, vel cum muliere iisdem votis adstricta aut matrimonio valido coniuncta. "
50   Woywod, A Practical Commentary on the Code of Canon Law, 651. See also Jone, Commentarium in Codicem Iuris Canonici, 1:141-142.

or by the penalty of degradation.[51] Generally, the authorities of the Roman Curia competent to issue a rescript of this nature were the Sacred Congregation for the Sacraments[52] and the Sacred Congregation of the Council[53] for secular clerics, and the Sacred Congregation for the Sacraments and the Sacred Congregation for Religious[54] for religious clerics. In certain cases pertaining to the internal forum, the Tribunal of the Sacred Penitentiary had been named the competent authority.[55]

The reduction of a cleric in major orders to the lay state usually did not include a dispensation from the obligation of celibacy.[56] Thus the code stated that a major cleric who has been reduced to the lay state was still obliged to the law of celibacy. An exception was made for those clerics who were ordained through grave force or fear.[57] Therefore, for a cleric reduced to the lay state a dispensation from the obligation of celibacy was also required. It was possible to receive a dispensation, but such was rarely given. As Cappello observes:

> The faculty of dispensing is the competence of the roman pontiff, who

---

51   17 *CIC*, c. 211 §1: "Etsi sacra ordinatio, semel valide recepta, nunquam irrita fiat, clericus tamen maior ad statum laicalem redigitur rescripto Sanctae Sedis, decreto vel sententia ad normam can. 214, demum poena degradationis."

52   17 *CIC*, c. 249 §3: "Ipsa cognoscit quoque et exclusive de facto inconsummationis matrimonii et de exsistentia causarum ad dispensationem concedendam, nec non de iis omnibus, quae cum his sunt connexa. Potest tamen cognitionem horum omnium, si id expedire iudicaverit, ad Sacram Romanam Rotam remittere. Pariter ad eam deferri possunt quaestiones de validitate matrimonii, quas tamen, si accuratiorem disquisitionem aut investigationem exigant, ad tribunal competens remittat. Eodem modo ad ipsam pertinet videre de obligationibus ordinibus maioribus adnexis, atque examinare quaestiones de ipsa validitate sacrae ordinationis, aut eas ad tribunal competens remittere. Et ita porro de aliis Sacramentis."

53   17 *CIC*, c. 250 §1: "Congregationi Concilii ea pars negotiorum est commissa, quae ad universam disciplinam cleri saecularis populique christiani refertur."

54   17 *CIC*, c. 251 §3: "Huic denique Congregationi reservatur concessio dispensationum a iure communi pro sodalibus religiosis, firmo praescripto can. 247, §5."

55   17 *CIC*, c. 258 §1: "Sacrae Poenitentiariae praeficitur Cardinalis Poenitentiarius Maior. Huius tribunalis iurisdictio coarctatur ad ea quae forum internum, etiam non sacramentale, respiciunt; quare hoc tribunal pro solo foro interno gratias largitur, absolutiones, dispensationes, commutationes, sanationes, condonationes; excutit praeterea quaestiones conscientiae easque dirimit."

56   Francis Sweeney, *The Reduction of Clerics to the Lay State: An Historical Synopsis and Commentary*, Canon Law Studies 223 (Washington, DC: Catholic University of America, 1945) 127.

57   17 CIC, c. 213 § 2: "Clericus tamen maior obligatione caelibatus tenetur, salvo praescripto can. 214."

never uses this (faculty) with Bishops, most rarely with priests, more rarely with deacons, and rarely with subdeacons by means of the lesser rigor which is granted in ancient discipline.[58]

The Sacred Penitentiary in *Lex Sacri Caelibatus,* April 18, 1936,[59] and in a subsequent declaration on May 4, 1937[60] reiterated the gravity of the crime of attempted marriage. In this decree, the Sacred Penitentiary stated the following concerning the granting of dispensations:

> The law of sacred celibacy for the Latin clergy has always been and is now so treasured by the Church that, in the cases of priests' dispensation from it, in past times, was hardly ever granted, and according to present discipline is never given, not even in danger of death.[61]

The decree also outlined the conditions under which absolution from the excommunication and reduction to the lay state would be granted for a priest for whom separation from the one he attempted marriage with was impossible. However, the priest had to promise to observe absolute and perfect continence forever afterward.[62]

It seems that the dispensation would not admit of the possibility of the priest marrying according to canonical form. The promise of continence that

---

58   Felix Cappello, "De Matrimonio," in Tractatus Canonico-Moralis De Sacramentis (Rome, Italy: Officina Libraria Mariette, 1939) n. 442: "Dispensandi facultas competit Romani Pontifici, qui ea nunquam utitur cum Episcopis, rarissime cum presbyteris, rarius cum diaconis, et raro cum subdiaconis minore cum rigore quam in antiqua disciplina conceditur."

59   Sacred Apostolic Penitentiary, decree Lex Sacri Caelibatus, April 18, 1936: AAS 28 (1936) 242-243. Hereafter LSC.

60   Sacred Apostolic Penitentiary, declaration, May 4, 1937: AAS 29 (1936) 283-284.

61   LSC, AAS 28 (1936) 242: "Lex sacri caelibatus inter Latinos adeo Sanctae Ecclesiae curae semper fuit atque est ut, si agatur de sacerdotibus, fere nunquam super ea retroactis temporibus dispensatum fuerit, nunquam prorsus, ne in mortis quidem periculo, in praesenti disciplina dispensetur." English translation from CLD 2: 579.

62   LSC, AAS 28 (1936) 242: "...data fide de absoluta perfectaque in posterium continentia perpetuo servanda..." ("...given faith as regards observing absolute and perfect continence afterwards in perpetuity..." CLD 2: 579.

he was expected to make as a condition for the granting of such a dispensation would have surely precluded this as he would not be able to consummate his marriage. The priest and his civil wife, living as brother and sister, would then be able to receive the sacraments in the manner of lay people.

In the case of a priest who attempted marriage but had repented and wished to return to priestly ministry, if children had been born of this union, a dispensation would rarely be granted for his return. If there were no children from his union, a real separation and departure from his partner was required along with true repentance and conversion of life.[63] Then an absolution from the excommunication along with a dispensation from the irregularity would be granted, and the priest permitted to return to priestly ministry in limited fashion.[64] The Sacred Congregation for the Sacraments also declared that the violation of the law of celibacy was a violation of the oath taken by clerics before the reception of major orders.[65]

a. Dispensation for Subdeacons and Deacons

In the case of subdeacons and deacons, the Holy See would grant a reduction to the lay state along with a dispensation from celibacy if it could be shown that these orders were received by persons who were unfit or unwilling to be promoted to higher orders.[66] The customary *praxis curae* in such cases was to include in the rescript the phrase: "*sine spe readmissionis ad statum clericalem,*" that is "without hope of being readmitted to the clerical state." This indicated the reluc-

---

63 Francis Moriarty, *The Extraordinary Absolution from Censures*, Canon Law Studies 113 (Washington, DC: Catholic University of America, 1945) 279-290.

64 Ibid.

65 Sacred Congregation for the Sacraments, decree *Quam ingens,* December 27, 1930: *AAS* 23 (1931) 127.

66 Ibid., 126. See also 17 *CIC*, cc. 1043-1045.

tance of the Holy See to re-admit such a person to the clerical state. Further, if a deacon or subdeacon attempted marriage the Holy See would ordinarily grant a dispensation from celibacy and effect the reduction to the lay state. Finally, in danger of death subdeacons and deacons could be dispensed from celibacy. This dispensation also effected the reduction to the clerical state.[67]

b. Dispensation for Priests and Bishops

As for presbyters and bishops ordinarily a reduction to the lay state did not include a dispensation from celibacy.[68] Indeed up until 2008, there was no evidence that a dispensation from celibacy was ever granted for bishops.[69] Even in danger of death, recourse was necessary to the Holy See. However, there were cases in the past when presbyters were granted a reduction to the lay state along with a dispensation from the obligation of celibacy. We know that such dispensations, though rare, were given for especially grave reasons.[70]

7. The Power of the Ordinary to Dispense from the Obligation of Celibacy

A question arose concerning the interpretation of canon 81 and the ordinary's power, in special circumstances, to grant a dispensation from the obligation of celibacy. Canon 81 stated:

> Ordinaries below the roman pontiff cannot dispense from the general
> laws of the Church, even in a specific case, unless this power has been
> explicitly or implicitly granted to them, or unless recourse to the Holy

---

67   Sweeney, *The Reduction of Clerics to the Lay State*, 173.
68   Ibid., 127.
69   See chapter one, footnote 282.
70   See chapter one, 85-88, for a fuller treatment of the history of such dispensations for presbyters and bishops.

See is difficult and there is also grave danger of harm in delay and the dispensation concerns a matter from which the Apostolic See is wont to dispense.[71]

The code commission was asked: (1) whether the words of canon 81, "*a generalibus ecclesiae legibus*" included vows reserved to the Holy See; (2) whether, in virtue of canon 81 and under the clauses there contained, ordinaries could dispense subdeacons and deacons from the obligation of observing sacred celibacy. The code commission responded in the negative to both.[72]

However, in danger of death, the local ordinaries could dispense from the form of marriage as well as any and all impediments of ecclesiastical law, public and occult, including the impediments arising from subdiaconate and diaconate. Canon 1043 stated:

> In urgent danger of death, local Ordinaries, for the consolation of con-
> sciences and, if there is cause, for the legitimization of children, can
> dispense their subjects wherever they are and all those actually in their
> territory both from the (canonical) form to be observed in the celebra-
> tion of marriage and from each and every impediment of ecclesiastical
> law, whether public or occult, even if multiplied, except for those im-
> pediments coming from sacred ordination to the presbyterate or affin-
> ity in the direct line, the marriage having been consummated, scandal

---

71   17 *CIC*, c. 81: "A generalibus Ecclesiae legibus Ordinarii infra Romanum Pontificem dispensare nequeunt, ne in casu quidem peculiari, nisi haec potestas eisdem fuerit explicite vel implicite concessa, aut nisi difficilis sit recursus ad Sanctam Sedem et simul in mora sit periculum gravis damni, et de dispensatione agatur quae a Sede Apostolica concedi solet."

72   Pontifical Commission for the Authentic Interpretation of Canon Law, *Responsa ad Proposita Dubia*, January 26, 1949: "Dubium (1) An sub verbis canon 81 'a generalibus Ecclesiae legibus' comprehendantur vota Sedi Apostolicae reservata; Dubium (2) An Ordinarii, vi canon 81 et sub clausulis in eo recensitis, valeant dispensare subdiaconos et diaconos ab obligatione servandi sacrum caelibatum. Responsa: Negative ad utrumque." *AAS* 41 (1949) 158. *CLD* 3: 56.

being removed and, if dispensation is granted from disparity of cult or mixed religion, with the usual precautions.[73]

The power to dispense was also extended to a pastor, the priest who assisted at the marriage and the confessor in the event that the local ordinary could not be contacted.[74] The faculties could be used even though the party on whose side alone the impediment lies was not in danger of death and even though the parties were not living together.[75]

8. The Obligation of Chastity

Clerics also had the obligation to observe chastity, an obligation which was shared by all the baptized. Coronata in his commentary on canon 132 stated that there are three types of chastity: virginal chastity, celibate chastity and married chastity.[76] "For clerics, both internal and external sins against chastity would assume the special malice of sacrilege."[77] All acts of impurity which are forbidden by divine law to unmarried persons were in turn forbidden to the cleric; i.e., *interior* acts by the ninth commandment, *exterior* acts by the sixth.

Canon 743 obliged the bishop to confer orders only on those he was certain

---

73   17 *CIC*, c. 1043: "Urgente mortis periculo, locorum Ordinarii, ad consulendum conscientiae et, si casus ferat, legitimationi prolis, possunt tum super forma in matrimonii celebratione servanda, tum super omnibus et singulis impedimentis iuris ecclesiastici, sive publicis sive occultis, etiam multiplicibus, exceptis impedimentis provenientibus ex sacro presbyteratus ordine et ex affinitate in linea recta, consummato matrimonio, dispensare proprios subditos ubique commorantes et omnes in proprio territorio actu degentes, remoto scandalo, et, si dispensatio concedatur super cultus disparitate aut mixta religione, praestitis consuetis cautionibus."

74   17 *CIC*, c. 1044: "In eisdem rerum adiunctis de quibus in can. 1043 et solum pro casibus in quibus ne loci quidem Ordinarius adiri possit, eadem dispensandi facultate pollet tum parochus, tum sacerdos qui matrimonio, ad normam can. 1098, n. 2, assistit, tum confessarius, sed hic pro foro interno in actu sacramentalis confessionis tantum."

75   See Sacred Congregation of the Roman and Universal Inquisition, *Litterae ad Ordinarios locorum quoad dispensationes matrimonialis,* February 20, 1888: *ASS* 20 (1888) 543-544; Sacred Congregation for the Sacraments, decree *Venetiarum,* August 16, 1909: *AAS* 1 (1909) 656.

76   Coronata, Institutiones Iuris Canonici, 1: 218.

77   Abbo-Hannan, The Sacred Canons, 1:189-190.

were canonically suitable. The bishop was to judge the candidate's moral suitability. Canon 974 §1, 2° stated the following concerning the requirements for the licit reception of orders:

> In order to be licitly ordained, there is required: Morals congruent with the order being received.[78]

The candidate had to have the morals congruent with the order being received. In the case of those receiving major orders this necessarily required that the candidate commit himself to being permanently unmarried and to the chastity-continence that would follow from this state.

9. Sacrilege and the Obligation of Chastity

There was no doubt that even interior acts of impurity committed by a cleric were sacrilegious, for the canon makes no distinction between the interior and exterior acts, simply declaring them all sacrilegious. Regarding this point there was much agreement.[79]

The common opinion of moralists concerning the definition of sacrilege was enunciated by Edwin Healy:

> Sacrilege is the violation of a sacred (1) person, (2) place or (3) thing. *Sacred* means *publicly dedicated to God.* A priest is sacred through ordination, a nun through her vows, a chalice through its consecration by a bishop.[80]

---

78   17 *CIC*, c. 974 §1, 2°: "Ut quis licite ordinari possit, requiruntur: Mores ordini recipiendo congruentes."

79   Cappello, Summa Iuris Canonici, 1: nn. 234, 235; Cappello, De Matrimonio, nn. 432, 433; Augustino Lehmkuhl, Theologiae Moralis (Freiburg: Herder, 1898) 1: nn. 378-384; Arthur Vermeersch, Theologiae Moralis Principia: De Personis, De Sacramentis, De Legibus Ecclesiae et Censuris (Rome: Universitatis Gregorianae, 1923) 3: n. 30.

80   Edwin Healy, *Moral Guidance* (Chicago, IL: Loyola University Press, 1943) 99.

The Obligation of Perfect and Perpetual Continence

A cleric who violated his obligation of chastity would commit the sin of sacrilege, because being a *sacred person by virtue of ordination* he had violated himself. Canon 2325 stated that one who has committed a sacrilege was to be punished by the ordinary:

> Whoever excites superstition or perpetrates a sacrilege is to be punished by the ordinary according to the gravity of the fault, with due regard for the penalties established by law against such superstitions or sacrilegious acts.[81]

However, a cleric who had been reduced to the lay state due to ordination under duress or grave fear would not be guilty of sacrilege if he sinned against chastity. Canon 214 stated:

> § 1: A cleric who, coerced by grave fear, receives ordination, and does not later, once the fear has passed, ratify that ordination at least tacitly by the exercise of orders, (and) wanting by such an act to subject himself to clerical obligations, is returned to the lay state by sentence of a judge, upon legitimate proof of coercion and lack of ratification, (by which sentence) all obligations of celibacy and canonical hours cease.
> § 2: The coercion and lack of ratification must be proved according to the norms of canons 1993-1998.[82]

This canon spoke of a cleric who had been returned to the lay state by a judicial or administrative decree issued by the competent congregation, namely, the

---

81   17 *CIC*, c. 2235: "Qui superstitionem exercuerit vel sacrilegium perpetraverit, pro gravitate culpae ab Ordinario puniatur, salvis poenis iure statutis contra aliquos actus superstitiosos vel sacrilegia."

    82   17 *CIC*, c. 214: "§1: Clericus qui metu gravi coactus ordinem sacrum recepit nec postea, remoto metu, eandem ordinationem ratam habuit saltem tacite per orainis exercitium, volens tamen per talem actum obligationibus clericalibus se subiicere ad statum laicalem, legitime probata coactione et ratihabitionis defectu, sententia iudicis redigatur sine ullis caelibatus ac horarum canonicarum obligationibus. §2. Coactio autem et defectus ratihabitionis probari debent ad normam can. 1993-1998."

Sacred Congregation for the Sacraments.[83] Such a person, while still in essence sharing in major orders, was no longer a cleric and as such, his sins against chastity, though morally culpable, did not constitute the additional sin of sacrilege. The cleric must have proved the presence of grave fear and the absence of ratification according to canons 1993-1998. The effect of a favorable judgment was to dispense the cleric from the obligation of celibacy and the recitation of the breviary.

On December 27, 1930, the Sacred Congregation for the Sacraments[84] and later on December 1, 1931, the Sacred Congregation for Religious[85] both issued special instructions governing how to assure the freedom of the candidate to assume major orders. A major cleric who had been removed from the clerical state could be readmitted to that state only with the permission of the Holy See.[86]

10. Penalties for Violation of the Obligation of Chastity

Clerics who had violated their obligation of chastity were subject to certain penalties depending on the nature and gravity of the offense. Canon 2359 stated:

§1: Concubinious clerics in sacred orders, whether secular or religious, previous warnings not being heeded, are to be coerced into giving up their illicit relationship and to repair scandal by being suspended from divine things and the loss of the benefits of office, benefices, and dignities, the prescriptions of canons 2176-81 being observed.

§2: If they (clerics in sacred orders) engage in a delict against the sixth precept of the Decalogue with a minor below the age of sixteen, or

---

83   The Sacred Congregation for the Sacraments, decree *Regulae Servandae in Processibus Super Nullitate Sacrae Ordinationis,* June 9, 1931: *AAS* 23 (1931) 457-492. *CLD* 1: 812-833.

84   *AAS* 23 (1930) 120-129.

85   AAS 24 (1931) 74-81.

86   17 CIC, c. 212 §2: "Clericus vero maior qui ad statum laicalem rediit, ut inter clericos denuo admittatur, indiget Sanctae Sedis licentia."

engage in adultery, debauchery, bestiality, sodomy, pandering, incest with blood relatives or affines in the first degree, they are suspended, declared infamous, and are deprived of any office, benefice, dignity, responsibility, if they have such, whatsoever, and in more serious cases, they are to be deposed.

§3: If they have transgressed against the sixth commandment in another way, they shall be corrected with appropriate penalties proportionate to the gravity, even deprivation of office, or benefice, especially if they have the care of souls. [87]

This canon stated a number of violations against chastity: concubinage, impure acts with a minor and other sins of impurity against the sixth commandment.

Concubinage was taken to mean illict and habitual sexual intercourse with the same woman; the fact that she did not live under the same roof was immaterial.[88] The crime of concubinage always involved a violation of the cleric's obligation to observe chastity but was not to be confused with "attempted marriage." The cleric was liable to the penalties for concubinage not only when actual concubinage was proven but also when there was the suspicion of concubinage and the cleric had ignored the warning of his ordinary.[89]

---

87   17 *CIC*, c. 2359 §1: "Clerici in sacris sive saeculares sive religiosi concubinarii, monitione inutiliter praemissa, cogantur ab illicito contubernio recedere et scandalum reparare suspensione a divinis, privatione fructuum officii, beneficii, dignitatis, servato praescripto can. 2176-2181. §2: Si delictum admiserint contra sextum decalogi praeceptum cum minoribus infra aetatem sexdecim annorum, vel adulterium, stuprum, bestialitatem, sodomiam, lenocinium, incestum cum consanguineis aut affinibus in primo gradu exercuerint, suspendantur, infames declarentur, quolibet officio, beneficio, dignitate, munere, si quod habeant, priventur, et in casibus gravioribus deponantur. §3: Si aliter contra sextum decalogi praeceptum deliquerint, congruis poenis secundum casus gravitatem coerceantur, non excepta officii vel beneficii privatione, maxime si curam animarum gerant." English translation of 2359 §3 is my own. For a definition of the terms used in canon 2359 see Wernz-Vidal, *Ius Decretalium,* 7: 494.

88   Anacletus Reiffenstuel, Ius Canonicum Universum: Complectens Tractatum de Regulis Iuris (Paris: Ludovicum Vivès, 1864-1870) 3:395.

89   17 *CIC*, c. 2176: "Ordinarius clericum qui contra praescriptum can.133 mulierem suspectam secum habeat aut quoquo modo frequentet, moneat ut eam dimittat vel ab eadem frequentanda sese abstineat, comminatis poenis in clericos concubinarios can. 2359 statutis."

A cleric who engaged in a crime against the sixth commandment with a male or female who had not completed their sixteenth year, or who had committed adultery, rape, bestiality, sodomy, pandering, incest with blood relatives or legal relatives in the first degree,[90] was to be suspended, declared infamous and suffer deprivation of office, benefice, dignity, responsibility, and in more serious cases they were to be removed from the clerical state.[91] A cleric who had committed other transgressions against the sixth commandment was to be punished depending on the nature and the gravity of the offense.

A cleric who solicited a penitent to commit an act of unchastity in the context of confession would also be subject to severe penalties not excluding degradation. Canon 2368 §1 stated:

> Whoever commits the crime of solicitation mentioned in canon 904 (hearing confession) is suspended from the celebration of Mass and from hearing sacramental confessions and even, for the gravity of the delict, is declared incapable of receiving them, is deprived of all benefices, dignities, active and passive voice, and is for all these declared incapable, and in more serious cases is also subject to degradation.[92]

Solicitation, according to Augustine, was:

> An external and grievously culpable provocation to sin against the sixth commandment, perpetrated in the confessional, or in the act of confession, even though the confessor has no jurisdiction or does not impart

---

90   That is to say: with mother, daughter, step-mother, step-daughter, sister, step-sister or sister-in-law.

91   For a definition of the terms used in canon 2359 see Wernz, *Ius Decretalium*, 6: 494.

92   17 *CIC*, c. 2368 §1: "Qui sollicitationis crimen de quo in can. 904, commiserit, suspendatur a celebratione Missae et ab audiendis sacramentalibus confessionibus vel etiam pro delicti gravitate inhabilis ad ipsas excipiendas declaretur, privetur omnibus beneficiis, dignitatibus, voce activa et passiva, et inhabilis ad ea omnia declaretur, et in casibus gravioribus degradationi quoque subiiciatur."

absolution, and even though the provocation may not be effective. Solicitation may be made to a person of either sex.[93]

The absolution of an accomplice in a sin against the sixth commandment was punishable by various penalties including degradation.[94] The penitent who was solicited in this fashion had a legal and moral duty to denounce the cleric.[95] If a penitent falsely accused a confessor of the crime of solicitation, he incurred an excommunication the dispensation of which was reserved to the Holy See.[96]

11. Canonical Dispositions to Protect and Foster the Obligation of Chastity

As the Church obliged clerics in major orders to observe chastity in the celibate-continent state, canon law also legislated for the protection of this ob-

---

93   Charles Augustine Bachofen, *A Commentary on Canon Law* (London: B. Herder Book Co., 1920) 4:318.

94   17 *CIC*, 2367: "§1. Absolvens vel fingens absolvere complicem in peccato turpi incurrit ipso facto in excommunicationem specialissimo modo Sedi Apostolicae reservatam; idque etiam in mortis articulo, si alius sacerdos, licet non approbatus ad confessiones, sine gravi aliqua exoritura infamia et scandalo, possit excipere morientis confessionem, excepto casu quo moribundus recuset alii confiteri. §2. Eandem excommunicationem non effugit absolvens vel fingens absolvere complicem qui peccatum quidem complicitatis, a quo nondum est absolutus, non confitetur, sed ideo ita se gerit, quia ad id a complice confessario sive directe sive indirecte inductus est."

95   17 *CIC*, c. 904: "Ad normam constitutionum apostolicarum et nominatim constitutionis Benedicti XIV Sacramentum Poenitentiae, 1 Iun. 1741, debet poenitens sacerdotem, reum delicti sollicitationis in confessione, intra mensem denuntiare loci Ordinario, vel Sacrae Congregationi S. Officii; et confessarius debet, graviter onerata eius conscientia, de hoc onere poenitentem monere."

96   17 *CIC*, c. 894: "Unicum peccatum ratione sui reservatum Sanctae Sedi est falsa delatio, qua sacerdos innocens accusatur de crimine sollicitationis apud iudices ecclesiasticos." And c. 2363 : "Si quis per seipsum vel per alios confessarium de sollicitationis crimine apud Superiores falso denuntiaverit, ipso facto incurrit in excommunicationem speciali modo Sedi Apostolicae reservatam, a qua nequit ullo in casu absolvi, nisi falsam denuntiationem formaliter retractaverit, et damna, si qua inde secuta sint, pro viribus reparaverit; imposita insuper gravi ac diuturna poenitentia, firmo praescripto can. 894."

ligation. Canon 133[97] forbade cohabitation with certain women. Canon 909[98] obliged the use of the grille for the hearing of confessions. Canon 140[99] prohibited the cleric's attendance at particular shows, dances and spectacles. Canons 138[100] and 139[101] prohibited the cleric from certain professions and places that might distract him from his priestly duties.

There were also certain canons that reinforced the necessity of the cleric nurturing a spiritual life which was essential if the chastity required of celibate living was to be realized. Canon 135[102] obliged the recitation of the breviary.

---

97   17 *CIC*, c. 133: "§1. Caveant clerici ne mulieres, de quibus suspicio esse possit, apud se retineant aut quoquo modo frequentent. §2. Eisdem licet cum illis tantum mulieribus cohabitare in quibus naturale foedus nihil mali permittit suspicari, quales sunt mater, soror, amita et huiusmodi, aut a quibus spectata morum honestas, cum provectiore aetate coniuncta, omnem suspicionem amoveat. §3. Iudicium an retinere vel frequentare mulieres, etiam illas in quas communiter suspicio non cadit, in peculiari aliquo casu scandalo esse possit aut incontinentiae aferre periculum, ad Ordinarium loci pertinet, cuius est clericos ab hac retentione vel frequentatione prohibere. §4. Contumaces praesumuntur concubinarii."

98   17 *CIC*, c. 909: "§1. Sedes confessionalis ad audiendas mulierum confessiones semper collocetur in loco patenti et conspicuo, et generatim in ecclesia vel oratorio publico aut semi-publico mulieribus destinato. §2. Sedes confessionalis crate fixa ac tenuiter perforata inter poenitentem et confessarium sit instructa."

99   17 *CIC*, c. 140: "Spectaculis, choreis et pompis quae eos dedecent, vel quibus clericos interesse scandalo sit, praesertim in publicis theatris, ne intersint." See also Eduardus F. Regatillo, *Institutiones Iuris Canonici* (Santander: Sal Terrae, 1946) 1: n. 252.

100   17 *CIC*, c. 138: "Clerici ab iis omnibus quae statum suum dedecent, prorsus abstineant: indecoras artes ne exerceant; aleatoriis ludis, pecunia exposita, ne vacent; arma ne gestent, nisi quando iusta timendi causa subsit; venationi ne indulgeant, clamorosant antem nunquam exerceant; tabernas aliaque similia loca sine necessitate aut alia iusta causa ab Ordinario loci probata ne ingrediantur."

101   17 *CIC*, c. 139: "§1. Ea etiam quae, licet non indecora a clericali tamen statu aliena sunt, vitent. §2. Sine apostolico indulto medicinam vel chirurgiam ne exerceant; tabelliones seu publicos notarios nisi in Curia ecclesiastica, ne agant; officia publica, quae exercitium laicalis iurisdictionis vel administrationis secumferunt, ne assumant. §3. Sine licentia sui Ordinarii ne ineant gestiones bonorum ad laicos pertinentium aut officia saecularia quae secumferant onus reddendarum rationum; procuratoris aut advocati munus ne exerceant, nisi in tribunali ecclesiastico, aut in civili quando agitur de causa propria aut suae ecclesiae; in laicali iudicio criminali, gravem personalem poenam prosequente, nullam partem habeant, ne testimonium quidem sine necessitate ferentes. §4. Senatorum aut oratorum legibus ferendis quos deputatos vocant munus ne sollicitent neve accepent sine licentia Sanctae Sedis in locis ubi pontificia prohibitio intercesserit; idem ne attentent aliis in locis sine licentia tum sui Ordinarii, tum Ordinarii loci in quo electio facienda est."

102   17 *CIC*, c. 135: "Clerici, in maioribus ordinibus constituti, exceptis iis de quibus in can. 213, 214, tenentur obligatione quotidie horas canonicas integre recitandi secundum proprios et probatos liturgicos libros." See also Regatillo, *Institutiones Iuris Canonici*, 1: n. 247; Coronata, *Institutiones Iuris Canonici*, 1: n. 194.

The Obligation of Perfect and Perpetual Continence

Canon 125[103] obliged frequent confession, mental prayer and a devotional life. Canon 126[104] obliged a spiritual retreat. Canons 130[105] and 131[106] required ongoing formation. Canon 136 §1[107] obliged the wearing of the clerical habit. All of these measures were intended to encourage external and internal observance of celibacy.

12. Post 1917 Code Legislation Concerning Formation in Chastity

In the years after the code, the Church issued complementary legislation aimed at ensuring that candidates for the religious life and priesthood were pre-

---

103   17 *CIC*, c. 125: "Curent locorum Ordinarii: 1° Ut clerici omnes poenitentiae sacramento frequenter conscientiae maculas eluant; 2° Ut iidem quotidie orationi mentali per aliquod tempus incumbant, sanctissimum Sacramentum visitent, Deiparam Virginem mariano rosario colant, conscientiam suam discutiant." See also Alberto Blat, *Commentarium Textus Codicis Iuris Canonici* (Rome: Apud Angelicum, 1921-1938) 1: n. 62; Jone, *Commentarium in Codicis Iuris Canonici,* 1: 134.

104   17 *CIC*, c. 126: "Omnes sacerdotes saeculares debent tertio saltem quoque anno spiritualibus exercitiis, per tempus a proprio Ordinario determinandum, in pia aliqua religiosave domo ab eodem designata vacare; neque ab eis quisquam eximatur, nisi in casu particulari, iusta de causa ac de expressa eiusdem Ordinarii licentia." See also Charles Patterson, *The Obligation of Spiritual Retreats for Secular Clergy according to Canon 126.* JCD Dissertation. (Rome: Pontifical University of St. Thomas, 1956-1957); Blat, *Commentarium Textus Codicis Iuris Canonici,* 1: n. 63.

105   17 *CIC*, c. 130: "§1. Expleto studiorum curriculo, sacerdotes omnes, etsi beneficium paroeciale aut canonicale consecuti, nisi ab Ordinario loci ob iustam causam fuerint exempti, examen singulis annis saltem per integrum triennium in diversis sacrarum scientiarum disciplinis, antea opportune designatis, subeant secundum modum ab eodem Ordinario determinandum. §2. In collatione officiorum et beneficiorum ecclesiasticorum ratio habeatur eorum, qui, ceteris paribus, in memoratis periculis magis praestiterunt." See also Jone, *Commentarium in Codicis Iuris Canonici,* 1: 137-138.

106   17 *CIC*, c. 131: "§1. In civitate episcopali et in singulis vicariatibus foraneis saepius in anno, diebus arbitrio Ordinarii loci praestituendis, conventus habeantur quos collationes seu conferentias vocant, de re morali et liturgica; quibus addi possunt aliae exercitationes quas Ordinarius opportunas iudicaverit ad scientiam et pietatem clericorum promovendam. §2. Si conventus haberi difficile sit, resolutae quaestiones scriptae mittantur, secundum normas ab Ordinario statuendas. §3. Conventui interesse, aut, deficiente conventu scriptam casuum solutionem mittere debent, nisi a loci Ordinario exemptionem antea expresse obtinuerint tum omnes sacerdotes saeculares, tum religiosi licet exempti curam animarum habentes et etiam, si collatio in eorum domibus non habeatur, alii religiosi qui facultatem audiendi confessiones ab Ordinario obtinuerunt." See also Blat, *Commentarium Textus Codicis Iuris Canonici,* 1: n. 68; Émile Jombart, *Manuel de droit canon: conforme au Code de 1917 et aux plus récentes décisions du Saint-Siège* (Paris: Beauchesne et Ses Fils, 1949) n. 96.

107   17 *CIC*, c. 136 §1: "Omnes clerici decentem habitum ecclesiasticum, secundum legitimas locorum consuetudines et Ordinarii loci praescripta, deferant, tonsuram seu coronam clericalem, nisi recepti populorum mores aliter ferant, gestent, et capillorum simplicem cultum adhibeant." See also Regatillo, *Institutiones iuris canonici,* 1, n. 248.

pared adequately to undertake the chastity necessary in celibate living. The Sacred Congregation for the Sacraments issued the instruction, *On the testing of candidates before they are promoted to Orders,* December 27, 1930.[108] Section 1 was entitled: "The Duty of Ordinaries to Test Carefully the Morals of Candidates Before Their Ordination." Section 3 outlined the tests to be undertaken before clerics were advanced to major orders. The instruction placed emphasis on determining the candidate's willingness and capacity to live chastity:

It is always important to inquire into the candidate's character and moral qualities as shown in his seminary life and in his progress in studies.[109]

The instruction also contained a list of questions to be asked of the candidates. Some of these questions are directly related to the candidates' suitability for the chastity required of one in major orders.[110]

A parallel instruction was issued by the Sacred Congregation for Religious, *Quantum Religiones,*[111] December 1, 1931. The Sacred Congregation for Religious instructed the superiors general of religious communities and clerical societies on the proper religious and clerical training of their subjects and on the investigation to be undertaken before profession and the reception of sacred orders. Special attention was to be paid to the candidate's capacity and suitability to embrace the chastity required by profession and sacred orders.

Twenty-five years after the instruction *On the testing of candidates before they are promoted to Orders*, the same congregation issued a private letter to all

---

108   The Sacred Congregation for the Sacraments, instruction *De Ordinariorum Munere Sedulo Scrutandi Mores Candidatorum Ante Ordinationem,* December 27, 1930: *AAS* 23 (1930) 120-127. Hereafter *De Ordinariorum.* English translation in *CLD* 1: 463-473.

109   *De Ordinariorum:* Section 3, n.1: "Interest vero semper inquirere de alumni moribus eiusque moralibus qualitatibus, quomodo nempe istae se exhibuerint ex vita in seminario acta, atque ex profectu in studiis."

110   *De Ordinariorum:* Form I & II, 127-129. *CLD* 1:472-473.

111   The Sacred Congregation for Religious, instruction *Quantum Religiones,* December 1, 1931: *AAS* 24 (1932) 74-81. English translation in *CLD* 1: 473-482.

local ordinaries on December 27, 1955.[112] This letter again urged these ordinaries to undertake a thorough examination of candidates for orders with special attention to the candidates' freedom and motivation and their ability to live the chastity that would be required of them. The tone of the letter was determined and strong. In part, it stated:

> 4. The canonical fitness of the candidate must be supported by positive proofs (C. 973). Evidence of it must be had from all the requisites and qualities, which come under the title of the gifts of nature and of grace, among which stands out the virtue of chastity.[113]

> 8. With regard to proof of the virtue of chastity in seminarians, this should be held as a general principle: a student is well able to stand out chaste and pure if he is physically and psychologically normal, and, as a result, is of such character as to be able to respond to the divine grace of vocation with full vigor in both physical and psychic orders. To put it briefly it is very necessary for the candidate for Orders to have soundness of both soul and body.[114]

> 9. If, then, it is discovered that a student has a habit of masturbation and has been morally corrupt since youth, especially by reason of disgraceful relations with adults or girls, if he has not mended his ways and has not given consistent and lasting proof of his amendment, i.e., tested chastity, in proportion, that is, to the gravity and duration of the

---

112 The Sacred Congregation for the Sacraments in a private circular letter sent to all local ordinaries, strongly emphasizing a thorough examination of candidates for orders, December 27, 1955. The letter addressed the necessity to assure the candidates' freedom from all external pressure to receive orders and the requirement of proven capacity to live the chastity that would be required of them. Canon 198 defined local ordinaries as: "In addition to the roman pontiff, a residential bishop in his own territory, an abbot or prelate of no-one and his vicar general, administrator, vicar or prefect apostolic, and those who take the place of any of these."
113 *CLD* 4: 310.
114 *CLD* 4: 311.

base habit contracted, which in every case is not less than at least a year, he must be dismissed from the clerical ranks.[115]

The previously cited instructions and circular letter demonstrate the seriousness with which the Church approached formation in chastity for those preparing for orders. The chastity required of those in major orders was not that required of laymen. The cleric in major orders was to live chastity in the celibate-continent state for the whole of his life.

B. Canon 132 §2

Canon 132 §2 stated:

Minor clerics can contract marriage, but, unless the marriage is null because of force or fear applied to them, they fall *ipso iure* from the clerical state.[116]

1. Minor Clerics and Marriage

Minor clerics were those who had received tonsure and had been ordained into the minor orders of porter, exorcist, lector, and acolyte. Canon 949 stated: "....*minor* orders are acolyte, exorcist, lector and doorkeeper."[117] Since only major clerics were bound to celibacy, minor clerics could marry validly and licitly. Under the 1917 code, however, a minor cleric who entered a valid marriage would by that fact lose the clerical state. The exception was a minor cleric whose marriage was invalid because of force or fear. Yet the force or fear could not be presumed; it had to be proven.[118]

---

115   *CLD* 4: 311-312.
116   17 CIC, c. 132 §2: "Clerici minores possunt quidem nuptias inire, sed, nisi matrimonium fuerit nullum vi aut metu incusso, ipso iure e statu clericali decidunt."
117   17 CIC, c. 949: "... minorem vero acolythatus, exorcistatus, lectoratus, ostiariatus."
118   17 *CIC*, cc. 1993-1998 outline the process to be followed to prove force or fear.

The Obligation of Perfect and Perpetual Continence

This change reflected the Latin Church's preference for the ordination of unmarried men. The Church was now choosing priests from unmarried candidates, so when a minor cleric married he necessarily ceased to be a candidate for major orders. Therefore, it made sense that he would lose the clerical state, because he could not ordinarily be advanced to major orders.[119] A cleric in minor orders who wished to be readmitted to the clerical state would require the consent of the ordinary of the diocese of incardination.[120] Ordinarily he would have to renounce his marriage. Those in minor orders, like all the baptized, were obliged to observe chastity, yet a violation of chastity did not rise to the level of a sacrilege. They were also obliged to continence with regards to all persons because they were unmarried.

C. Canon 132 §3

Canon 132 §3 stated:

A married man who without apostolic dispensation receives major orders, even in good faith, is forbidden to exercise those orders.[121]

---

119   A minor cleric would also lose the clerical state automatically for various other offenses, c. 136 §3: "Clerici minores qui propria auctoritate sine legitima causa habitum ecclesiasticum et tonsuram dimiserint, nec, ab Ordinario moniti, sese intra mensem emendaverint, ipso iure e statu clericali decidunt." C. 141 §2: "Clericus minor qui contra praescriptum §1 sponte sua militiae nomen dederit, ipso iure e statu clericali decidit." C. 648: "Religiosus dimissus ad normam can. 647 ipso facto solvitur ab omnibus votis religiosis, salvis oneribus ordini maiori adnexis, si sit in sacris, et firmo praescripto can. 641, §1, 642; clericus autem in minoribus ordinibus constitutus eo ipso redactus est in statum laicalem." C. 669: "Professus qui vota perpetua emisit, a religione dimissus, votis religiosis manet adstrictus, salvis constitutionibus aut Sedis Apostolicae indultis quae aliud ferant. §2. Si clericus est in minoribus ordinibus constitutus, eo ipso reducitur ad statum laicalem."

120   17 CIC, c. 212 §1: "Qui in minoribus ordinibus constitutus ad statum laicalem quavis de causa regressus est, ut inter clericos denuo admittatur, requiritur licentia Ordinarii dioecesis cui incardinatus fuit per ordinationem, non concedenda, nisi post diligens examen super vita et moribus, et congruum, iudicio ipsius Ordinarii, experimentum."

121   17 CIC, c. 132 §3: "Coniugatus qui sine dispensatione apostolica ordines maiores, licet bona fide, suscepit, ab eorundem ordinum exercitio prohibetur."

129

Anthony McLaughlin

1. The Impediment of Marriage for the Reception and Exercise of Orders

The impediment of marriage for the reception of orders received juridic expression in the 1917 code. Canon 987, 2° stated:

The following are simply impeded (from the reception of orders):
Men having wives.[122]

The impediment of marriage arose from a valid marriage and existed as long as the wife was alive. The impediment was "simple" not "perpetual." It could cease with the death of a spouse, by a declaration of nullity, by dissolution of the marriage or by solemn religious profession. The Congregation for the Sacraments was competent to grant these dispensations.[123] Yet a dispensation permitting the reception of orders by a married man could be granted, but only by the Holy See and only for very grave reasons. According to Cappello, such dispensations were very rare and were never granted without the expressed or tacit consent of the wife and always included the obligation of absolute continence on the part of both spouses.[124]

It seemed advisable, though the law did not strictly oblige this, to seek a dispensation for a married man to a enter a seminary. With a dispensation, a married man could be ordained, but he was prohibited to use the rights of his marriage. He and his wife were bound to observe absolute continence. In addition, any children born after the married man had received major orders were considered illegitimate. Canon 1114 stated:

---

122   17 *CIC*, c. 987, 2°: "Sunt simpliciter impediti: Viri uxorem habentes."
123   17 *CIC*, c. 249 §1: "Congregationi de disciplina Sacramentorum proposita est universa legislatio circa disciplinam septem Sacramentorum, incolumi iure Congregationis S. Officii circa ea quae in can. 247 statuta sunt, et Sacrorum Rituum Congregationis circa ritus et caeremonias quae in Sacramentis conficiendis, ministrandis et recipiendis servari debent."
124   Felix Cappello, *De Sacra Ordinatione* (Rome: Mariette Press, 1935) 2: 3, n. 520.

Those children are legitimate who are conceived or born of a valid or putative marriage unless the parents, because of a solemn religious profession or the taking up of sacred orders, had been at the time of conception, prohibited from using the marriage contracted earlier.[125]

It is clear from this canon that a married man who was dispensed from the impediment of marriage to receive major orders was at the same time obliged to absolute continence in his marriage.[126] It was precisely because he was forbidden the use of his marriage, as a condition of his ordination, that children born to him after ordination were considered to be illegitimate.[127]

According to Cappello, dispensations from the impediment of marriage were very rare. He presents a list of circumstances in which the congregation occasionally dispensed a married man to receive major orders:

(1) If a man leaves his wife because of her sin of adultery and she has obtained a civil divorce and also has contracted a civil marriage with another man; (2) If it is at least probable that one of the spouses has become affected with impotence which arose only after the marriage was validly contracted; (3) If the wife has lost her mind and the mental illness on her part has been declared permanent by qualified doctors; (4) If the wife has been given a life-term prison sentence because of a very grave crime; (5) If the wife has obtained a civil divorce from her innocent husband and now lives in an adulterous union with another

---

125   17 *CIC*, c. 1114: "Legitimi sunt filii concepti aut nati ex matrimonio valido vel putativo, nisi parentibus ob sollemnem professionem religiosam vel susceptum ordinem sacrum prohibitus tempore conceptionis fuerit usus matrimonii antea contracti."

126   This is also the conclusion of Henry Vogelpohl, *The Simple Impediments to Holy Orders: An Historical Synopsis and Commentary,* Canon Law Studies 224 (Washington, DC: Catholic University of America, 1945) 24-25.

127   See also Woywod, *A Practical Commentary on the Code of Canon Law,* 868; Heriberto Jone, *Commentarium in Codicem Iuris Canonici,* 2:353; Gilbert Joseph McDevitt, *Legitimacy and Legitimation: An Historical Synopsis and Commentary*, Canon Law Studies 138 (Washington, DC: Catholic University of America, 1941) 88-96.

man; (6) If both spouses, by mutual free consent, wish to live a more holy life in a higher state of perfection.[128]

It was more common that a deacon or priest would be dispensed from celibacy in order to marry than a married man would be dispensed to be ordained.

2. Prohibition on Bigamy

Candidates for the reception of orders were irregular by defect if they had been married more than once. This irregularity was also called "digamy" in previous legislation.[129] An irregularity by defect was one which arose from a *lack of some quality* required for the reception of an order or for its lawful exercise.[130] Canonical bigamy implied two things:

> That there were two or more successive marriages, and that they were valid marriages. To incur the irregularity it is not necessary that the marriages be consummated. The irregularity is also incurred by a man married twice before baptism, or once before and once after baptism.[131]

Concerning the admittance of candidates who had been married at least twice the Council of Trent decreed:

> And if there are not enough celibate clerics to carry out the functions of the four minor orders, there can be added married clerics of worthy life,

---

128 Cappello, De Sacra Ordinatione, 2: 3, 520: "(1) Si uxor adulterium commiserit, et a fortiori si virum dereliquerit et civile cum alio viro contraxerit; (2) Si coniuges impotentia dubia laborent vel impotentia certa sed superveniente matrimonio iam contracto; (3) Si uxor lapsa sit in amentiam quae a peritis perpetua declarata fuerit ; (4) Si uxor ob gravissimum delictum poena carceris perpetui condemnata fuerit; (5) Si, contra virum innocentem, uxor seperationem obtinuerit a civili magistratu et coniugaliter vivat cum alio viro; (6) Si ambo coniuges, mutuo et libero plane consensu, velint caste vivere et sanctiorem vitam ducere." English translation from Vogelpohl, Simple Impediments to Holy Orders, 40-41.

129 See chapter one, 55-58. "Digamy" and "Bigamy" are synonymous.

130 Bouscaren, Ellis and Korth, *Canon Law: A Text and Commentary,* 441.

131 Ibid., 444.

as long as they have not married twice, who fulfil these tasks and wear the tonsure and clerical dress in the Church.[132]

Trent upheld the ancient law that those who had married a second time would not be admitted to orders, even minor orders. In the 1917 code, the impediment of "bigamy" was listed among those things that make a candidate for orders irregular by defect:

The following are irregular by defect: Bigamists, namely, those who have contracted two or more valid marriages successively.[133]

The reason for the irregularity of bigamy was stated in canon 1142:

Although chaste widowhood is more honorable, nevertheless, second and subsequent marriages are valid and licit, with due regard for the prescription of canon 1069 §2.[134]

It seemed that a higher degree of perfection was attributed to honorable widowhood.[135] In fact regarding the form of the celebration of the second marriage, canon 1143, even forbade a woman who married a second time from receiving the solemn nuptial blessing again.

3. The Latin Church and Married Eastern Clergy

While the Latin Church firmly held to the discipline of celibacy, it is interesting to note the attitude of the Latin Church towards the orthodox and previ-

---

132   Council of Trent, session 23, July 15, 1563, de ordinis, c. 17: "Quodsi ministeriis quatuor minorum ordinum exercendis clerici caelibes praesto non erunt, suffice possint etiam coniugati vitae probatae, dummodo non bigamy, ad ea munia obeunda idonei, et qui tonsuram et habitum clericalem in ecclesia in ecclesia gestent." Tanner, 2:750.

133   17 *CIC*, c. 984, 4°: "Sunt irregulares ex defectu: Bigami, qui nempe duo vel plura matrimonia valida successive contraxerunt." See also Woywod, *A Practical Commentary on the Code of Canon Law,* 665.

134   17 *CIC*, c. 1142: " Licet casta viduitas honorabilior sit, secundae tamen et ulteriores nuptiae validae et licitae sunt, firmo praescripto can. 1069, §2."

135   Bachofen, *Commentary on Canon Law,* 397-399.

ously called "uniate" churches. The majority of these churches have the practice of married clergy below the rank of bishop who are not bound to absolute continence within their marriage.

Yet the East agrees with the West on the following points: (1) There must only be a single marriage contracted before ordination, and it cannot be with a widow or with other women excluded by law (those whose ability to be continent was questionable).[136] (2) To marry after ordination is prohibited.[137] (3) Married bishops must be absolutely continent.[138] The East further insists that the bishop's wife must depart and enter a monastery.[139] In both the East and the West continence is still obliged for married clergy. In the West this continence is absolute, in the East it is periodic.

---

136   See Council of Trullo, c. 3: "Eum qui secundis nuptiis post baptismum implicates sit, vel concubinam habuerit, non posse esse episcopum vel presbyterum vel diaconum vel omnino ex sacerdotali catalogo ; Similiter et eum qui viduam acceperit vel dimissam vel meretricem vel servam vel scenicam non posse esse episcopum vel presbyterum vel diaconum vel omnino ex sacerdotali catalogo." Mansi, 11: 942
943. See also Constantin Pitsakis, "Clergé marié et célibat dans la législation du Concile in Trullo: le point de vue Oriental," *The Council in Trullo Revisited,* Kanonika 6, eds. George Nedungatt & Michael Featherstone (Rome: Pontificio Istituto Orientale, 1995) 263-306; Pitsakis, "Le droit matrimonial dans les canons du concile in Trullo," *Annuarium historiae conciliorum: Internationale Zeitschrift für Konziliengeschichtsforschung* 24 (1992) 158-185. Hereafter *AHC.*
137   Council of Trullo, c. 6: "Nos hoc servantes decernimus ne dehinc subdiacono vel diacono vel presbytero post peractam sui ordinationem coniugium inire ullo modo liceat; si autem hoc facere ausus fueri, deponatur. Si quis autem eorum, qui in clerum veniunt, velit lege matrimonii mulieri coniungi, ante ordinationem subdiaconalem vel diaconalem vel presbyteralem, hoc faciat." Mansi, 11: 943. See also Pitsakis, "Clergé marié et célibat dans la législation du Concile in Trullo: le point de vue Oriental," 263-306; Cholij, "Married Clergy and Ecclesiastical Continence in Light of The Council of Trullo," *AHC* 19 (1987) 71-230, 241-299.
138   Council of Trullo, c. 12 : "Porro hoc quoque ad nos perlatum est, in Africa et in Libya et in aliis locis quosdam ex iis qui illic sunt dei amantissimi praesules cum propriis uxoribus, etiam post suam ordinationem, una habitare non recusare, ex eo offendiculum et scandalum populis afferentes. Cum itaque solliticitudo nostra eo magnopere tenderet, ut omnia ad gregis nobis traditi utilitatem efficerentur, visum est nihil eiusmodi dehinc ullo modo fieri. Si quis autem hoc agens deprehensus fuerit, deponatur. " Mansi, 11:946-947. See also Peter L'Huillier, "Episcopal Celibacy in the Orthodox Tradition," St. Vladimir's Theological Quarterly, 35 (1991) 271-300.
139   Council of Trullo, c. 48: "Uxor eius qui ad episcopalem dignitatem promovetur, ex communi consensus a viro suo antea separata, post eius ordinationem episcopalem, in monasterium ingrediatur procul ab episcopi habitatione exstructum et episcopi providentia fruatur ; sin autem digna visa fuerit, etiam ad diaconatus dignitatem provehatur." Mansi, 11:966. See also L'Huillier, "Episcopal Celibacy in the Orthodox Tradition," 271-300; Knetes, "Ordination and Matrimony in Eastern Church," *Journal of Theological Studies* 11 (1910) 348-400 and 481-509.

At the turn of the first millennium, for a variety of reasons, the Churches in the East and West were divided. Over the centuries there have been various attempts at reunification. While the Latin Church continued to oblige absolute continence for its married clergy in major orders, she accepted reunification with Eastern Churches without insisting that married Eastern clergy also live absolute continence in their marriage in order to continue exercising their ministry. Yet, the Latin Church was keen to enact legislation for the Eastern Churches in order to ensure that periodic continence of their clergy was observed faithfully.[140]

4. Prohibition on Ministry of Married Eastern Clergy

While the Latin Church acknowledged the particular law of various Eastern Churches that did not oblige absolute continence of clergy below the rank of bishop, the Church legislated to ensure that at least the necessary periodic continence was observed, and at the same time restricted the ministry of married Eastern priests in the United States where the Latin Church was in the majority.

In the 1880's Greek Ruthenian Catholics from West Ukraine and the Carpathian regions started to immigrate the United States in very large numbers.[141] The predominantly Latin hierarchy did not always receive them well, and they were particularly disturbed at what they saw as the innovation, for the United States, of a married Catholic clergy.[142] At their request, the Sacred Congregation

---

140   Cholij, *Clerical Celibacy in the East and the West,* 179-189. Cholij details the various 'acts of union' between the Latin Church and various Eastern Orthodox Churches. The marriage discipline of Eastern clerics was not judged to be an obstacle to union. He also examines various pieces of ecclesiastical legislation enacted by the Latin Church aimed at defining the parameters for temporary continence. See also Benedict XIV, constitution *Eo quamvis tempore,* May 4, 1745 in *Iuris Pontificii De Propaganda Fide* (Rome: Ex Typographia Polyglotta S. C. de Propaganda Fide, 1888-1909) 3:227. Hereafter *PPF.* Benedict renewed the regulation of Clement VIII on temporary continence for Eastern clergy; Benedict XIV, constitution *Allatae sunt,* June 26, 1755 in *PPF* 3: 606. Benedict urged the Eastern clergy to observe continence.

141   *A Guide to the Eastern Code: A Commentary on the Code of the Canons of the Eastern Churches,* Kanonika 10, ed. George Nedungatt (Rome: Pontificio Istituto Orientale, 2002) 302.

142   Ibid.

for the Propagation of the Faith issued the decree, *Romana Ecclesia*,[143] which applied legislation already set out in a letter of 2 May 1890 to François-Marie-Benjamin Richard, the Archbishop of Paris.[144] This legislation stated that only celibates or widowed priests coming without their children would be permitted in the United States.[145] This legislation was restated with special reference to secular clerics of the Ruthenian Church[146] who sought to minister in the United States of America in the March 1, 1929 decree, *Cum data fuerit*,[147] issued by the Sacred Congregation for the Oriental Church. Article 12 stated:

In the meantime, as has already several times been provided, priests of the Greek-Ruthenian rite who wish to go to the United States of North America and stay there must be celibates.[148]

On December 23, 1929, the same congregation issued another decree, *Graeci-Rutheni Ritus*,[149] regulating the presence of the Greek Ruthenians in Canada even going as far as obliging celibacy for such clergy. Article 12 stated in part:

But they (Greek-Ruthenians) may not admit to the seminary any but

---

143 Sacred Congregation for the Propagation of the Faith, decree *Romanae Ecclesiae*, May 1, 1897: *ASS* 30 (1897-1898) 635-636. Hereafter *RE*.

144 *ASS* 24 (1891-1892) 390-391.

145 *RE* Art. 3; *ASS* 30 (1887-1898) 636: "In provinciis ecclesiasticis Americae Septentrionalis, in quibus multi sunt fidelis Rutheni ritus, Archiepiscopus cuiuscumque Provinciae, initis consiliis cum suis suffraganeis, sacerdotem Ruthenum caelibatu et idoneitate commendabilem deputet, et huius defectu sacredotem Latinii ritus Ruthenis benevisum, qui super populum et clerum dicti ritus vigilantiam et directionem exerceat, sub omnimoda tamen dependentia Ordinarii loci, qui pro suo arbitrio, facultates ei tribat, quas in Domino expedire iuducaverit."

146 Constantin Simon, "The First Years of Ruthenian Church Life in America," *Orientalia Christiana Periodica* 60 (1994) 187-232.

147 Sacred Congregation for Eastern Church, decree *Cum data fuerit*, March 1, 1929: *AAS* 21 (1929) 152-159. For a fuller treatment of this document see Walter Paska, *Sources of Particular Law for the Ukrainian Church in the United States,* Canon Law Studies 485 (Washington, DC: The Catholic University of America, 1975) 132-133. See also Roman Cholij, "An Eastern Catholic Married Clergy in North America," *Studia canonica* 31 (1997) 311-339.

148 *Cum data fuerit*, art. 12, *AAS* 21 (1929) 155: "Interim, sicut iam pluries statutum est, sacredotes ritus graeco-rutheni, qui in Status Foederatos Americae septemtrionalis proficisci et commari cupiunt, debent esse caelibes." English translation in *CLD* 1: 10.

149 Sacred Congregation for the Oriental Church, decree *Graeci-Rutheni Ritus*, December 23, 1929: *AAS* 22 (1930) 346-354.

those who shall promise before the ordinary to preserve perpetual celibacy; and only celibates may be promoted to sacred orders.[150]

Regarding the ministry of clerics from all other Eastern Churches on May 24, 1930, the Sacred Congregation for the Oriental Church issued a decree, *Qua sollerti alacritate.*[151] Article 6 stated:

Secular priests who have a wife shall not be admitted to exercise the sacred ministry in these countries, but only celibate priests or widowers. Widowers may, however, for just cause, be excluded by this Sacred Congregation from those dioceses and places in which they may have children living or in any way present; and the same is true of the adjoining localities.[152]

The congregation also restricted the ability of oriental priests to minister freely in any place other than their own patriarchates or countries.[153] In essence, Eastern rite clergy who ministered outside of their own patriarchate or country were to resemble Latin clergy in being either celibate or widowers. As late as 1932, the Sacred Congregation for the Oriental Church wrote to the Ruthenian Bishop of Pittsburgh, Basil Takach, reiterating article 12 of the decree, *Cum data fuerit,* of March 1, 1929, which prohibited the ministry of married clergy in America.[154]

---

150 *Graeci-Rutheni Ritus,* art. 6, *AAS* 22 (1930) 348: "Sed non nisi qui se caelibatum perpetuo servaturos *coram* Ordinario promiserint, in seminarium admittere licebit, et non nisi caelibes ad sacros Ordines promoveri potuerunt." English translation in *CLD* 1: 32.

151 *AAS* 22 (1930) 346-354.

152 Sacred Congregation for the Oriental Church, decree *Qua sollerti* 6, May 24, 1930: *AAS* 22 (1930) 102-103: "Ad sacrum ministerium exercendum in praefatis regionibus non admittantur sacerdotes saeculares uxorem habentes, sed solum sacrdotes caelibes, aut vidui. Vidui tamen iustis de causis ab hac Sacra Congregatione excludi poterunt ab iis dioecesibus et locis, in quibus eorum proles forte degat aut quocumque modo inveniatur, pariterque si in viciniis eorundem locorum." English translation in *CLD* 1: 20-21.

153 Sacred Congregation for the Oriental Church, decree *Quo faciliter,* September 26, 1932: *AAS* 24 (1932) 344-346.

154 Sacred Congregation for the Oriental Churches, letter to Bishop Basil Takech, April 16, 1932. Archdiocesan Archives of Pittsburgh, prot. No. 572/30.

D. Canon 133 §1

Canon 133 §1 stated:

Clerics should take care not to retain or in other ways to frequent women upon whom suspicion can fall.[155]

1. Clerics and Forbidden Cohabitation with Women

The term 'clerics' was used in this canon without any qualifying clause. It would seem that "clerics" in this canon referred to all clerics, both minor and major. Ordinarily only unmarried men were admitted to the clerical state in preparation for the promise of celibacy. In order to protect them from themselves and from others, the law legislated for the prudence of all clerics in their relations with women. It is interesting that the cleric was not presumed to be under suspicion. The presumption was that he was determined to remain faithful to the promises he made to observe celibacy (no marriage) and therefore to observe continence (no sexual relations) and to live chastely. By no means were all women to be suspected, but only those upon whom 'suspicion' could fall. Though the canon speaks only of "women," it would follow that the cleric was to avoid anyone, male or female, who might endanger his chastity.

In addition to not "retaining, frequenting or cohabiting" with women upon whom suspicion could fall, clerics were also obliged to avoid places and things that could also compromise their chastity or at least give rise to the suspicion of unchastity. Canons 138, 139 and 140 are of particular interest in this regard. These canons had a twofold purpose of safeguarding the decorum of the clerical state and preserving clerics from troublesome distractions. Canon 138 stated:

---

155   17 CIC, c. 133 §1: "Caveant clerici ne mulieres, de quibus suspicio esse possit, apud se retineant aut quoquo modo frequentent."

Clerics shall entirely abstain from all those things that are indecent to their state; they shall not engage in indecorous arts; they shall abstain from gambling games with risks of money; they shall not carry arms, except when there is just cause for fearing; hunting should not be indulged, and (then) never with clamor; taverns and similar places should not be entered without necessity or another just cause approved by the local ordinary.[156]

Clerics were to abstain from "those things that are indecent." One could reasonably assume that 'those things that are indecent' would also include those things that would offend against chastity. The canon then continued by listing a number of very specific activities to be avoided. According to Bachofen, the examples of things unbecoming to the clerical state was not meant to be an exhaustive list.[157]

From the earliest days, ecclesiastical legislation has been eager to ensure that clergy remain aloof from unbecoming professions, persons and practices. Ecclesiastical legislation sought to safeguard the cleric in three areas, profession, people, and places. The first evidence of such ecclesiastical legislation is found in the fourth and fifth canons of the Council of Arles, 314.[158] Over the centuries various ecclesiastical laws sought to legislate in like manner.[159]

The Council of Trent did not legislate explicitly concerning unbecoming professions for clerics. As Thomas Donovan observes:

This is satisfactorily explained when one realizes that the council did not change the extant law on clerical obligations, but rather furnished

---

156 17 *CIC*, c. 138: "Clerici ab iis omnibus quae statum suum dedecent, prorsus abstineant: indecoras artes ne exerceant; aleatoriis ludis, pecunia exposita, ne vacent; arma ne gestent, nisi quando iusta timendi causa subsit; venationi ne indulgeant, clamorosant antem nunquam exerceant; tabernas aliaque similia loca sine necessitate aut alia iusta causa ab Ordinario loci probata ne ingrediantur."

157 Bachofen, *Commentary on Canon Law,* 2: 87.

158 Council of Arles, canons 4 & 5 prohibited clerics from being members of theatrical groups and from becoming charioteers. Mansi, 2: 471.

159 John Thomas Donovan, The Clerical Obligations of Canons 138 and 140, Canon Law Studies 272 (Washington, DC: Catholic University of America, 1948) 21-27.

added importance, new force, and supplementary direction to the body of clerical law which had been handed down from the earliest centuries.[160]

Continuing in the same vein, canon 139 §1 stated:

> They (clerics) should avoid those things that, while not indecent, are still alien to the clerical state.[161]

Here again, one could reasonably assume that such a prohibition included those things that would offend against the chastity expected of the cleric. Canon 140 further obliged the cleric:

> Where there is danger of scandal, especially in public theaters, clerics should avoid shows, dances and spectacles.[162]

Historically, such spectacles had a reputation for lewdness that could endanger the cleric's chastity and give rise to the suspicion of his acting in an unchaste manner.[163]

E. Canon 133 §2

Canon 133 §2 stated:

> It is permitted to them to cohabit only with the sort of women whose natural bond places them above suspicion, such as a mother, sister, aunt, and others of this kind, or others whose upright way of life in view of maturity of years removes suspicion.[164]

---

160   Ibid., 27.
161   17 *CIC*, c. 139 §1: "Ea etiam quae, licet non indecora a clericali tamen statu aliena sunt, vitent."
162   17 *CIC*, c. 140: "Spectaculis, choreis et pompis quae eos dedecent, vel quibus clericos interesse scandalo sit, praesertim in publicis theatris, ne intersint."
163   Donovan, *The Clerical Obligations of Canons 138 and 140*, 138-170.
164   *CIC*, c. 133 §2: "Eisdem licet cum illis tantum mulieribus cohabitare in quibus naturale foedus nihil mali permittit suspicari, quales sunt mater, soror, amita et huiusmodi, aut a quibus spectata morum honestas, cum provectiore aetate coniuncta, omnem suspicionem amoveat."

The Obligation of Perfect and Perpetual Continence

1. Clerics and Permission to Cohabit with Women

From the Council of Nicea (325), the Church was eager to legislate concerning those with whom a cleric could cohabit.[165] Bouscaren and Ellis in their commentary on canon 133 stated the following:

> Cohabitation in the wide sense meant to live in the same house with, or to frequent a person, that is, frequently to visit or to receive visits from him or her. The reasons for the prohibition to clerics of such relations with women are obviously:
> 1. To safeguard the chastity to which the priest is dedicated.
> 2. To guard against even the appearance of evil.[166]

It is interesting to note that such a prohibition did not extend to correspondence by mail, telegraph, telephone, or messenger though when such correspondence was accompanied by visits to the female the cleric could fall under the canon.[167] Ordinarily near relatives were considered, because of their close familial relationship to the cleric, to be free from all suspicion. The kinship that may be considered justifying a common dwelling shared by a cleric and a woman should be restricted, according to canonists, within the second degree of consanguinity or affinity, e.g., the cleric's mother, sister or aunt. In other cases, the combination of two qualities made the proximity of a woman relatively free from scandal or danger, namely, an irreproachable character and a rather advanced age. What constituted "advanced age" has changed at various times, but at the time of the 1917 code it was considered to be between thirty-five and forty.[168]

---

165   Council of Nicea, c. 3. Mansi, 2: 670.
166   Bouscaren, Ellis & Korth, Canon Law: A Text and Commentary, 115.
167   Ibid., 116.
168   See Bachofen, A Commentary on the New Code of Canon Law, 1: c. 133; Blat, Commentarium Codicis Iuris, 2: n. 70.

The Plenary Councils of Baltimore (1852, 1866, 1884), even though they did not specify a determined age, also required maturity in domestic staff employed by clerics as well as untarnished reputation. They especially prohibited the habitual presence in the rectory of the families of the priest's relatives and of young women who may be related to the assistant priest of the parish.

F. Canon 133 §3

Canon 133 §3 stated:

The judgment about retaining or frequenting women, even those who commonly fall under no suspicion, in particular cases where scandal is possible or where there is given a danger of incontinence, belongs to the local ordinary, who can prohibit clerics from retaining or frequenting (such women).[169]

1. The Local Ordinary and the Cohabitation of Clerics

The decision as to the propriety of cohabitation in all cases, even where the woman was by natural standards and according to this canon above suspicion, belonged entirely to the ordinary.[170] The ordinary was empowered to act to preserve the chastity and continence of the celibate cleric. He could do so even when the woman in question was ordinarily beyond suspicion if there was the danger of scandal or if the cleric's continence might be endangered. The ordinary could prohibit the cleric from having any contact with such women. The

---

169   17 *CIC*, c. 133 §3: "Iudicium an retinere vel frequentare mulieres, etiam illas in quas communiter suspicio non cadit, in peculiari aliquo casu scandalo esse posit aut incontinentiae afferre periculum, ad Ordinarium loci pertinet, cuius est clericos ab hac retentione vel frequentatione prohibere."

170   John A. Abbo and Jerome D. Hannan, *The Sacred Canons: A Concise Presentation of the Current Disciplinary Norms of the Church,* 2nd ed. (St. Louis, MO: B. Herder Book Company, 1960) 1:192.

cleric was not only to do the "right thing," but he needed to be seen to do the "right thing." In canon 132 §1 there was reference to the 'cleric's chastity'. In canon 133 §3 there was reference made to the cleric's "continence." The cleric, like all others, was obliged to chastity, that is, the proper living out of his sexuality in accord with his condition. As an unmarried man, the cleric was obliged to practice the chastity obliged for unmarried persons. As an unmarried person, who had committed himself to celibacy he was obliged to continence by natural law and by ecclesiastical positive law. Again, we see how these three concepts of chastity, continence and celibacy are closely linked in the life of the cleric.

G. Canon 133 §4

Canon 133 §4 stated:

Clerics who are contumacious in this regard are presumed to be guilty of concubinage.[171]

1. Presumption of Concubinage

Contumacious clerics were those who stubbornly refused to obey their ordinary in these matters. Such clerics were presumed to be the guilty of the grave crime of concubinage and were subject to penalties.[172] Canons 2176-2181 detailed the manner of proceeding against concubinious clerics.[173] The crime of concubinage has already been dealt with in much detail earlier in this chapter.[174] These canons are an example of how much the Church desired to promote clerical celibacy and to protect against its violation.

---

171   17 *CIC*, c. 133 §4 : "Contumaces praesumuntur concubinarii."
172   17 CIC, cc. 2176-2181; 2359.
173   17 CIC, c. 2242 §2.
174   See pages 113-115.

H. Post 1917 Code Magisterial teaching on Celibacy

1. Benedict XV

In 1920 Pope Benedict XV (1914-1922) reprimanded certain priests of Bohemia who had fomented agitation against clerical celibacy. He declared that the Latin Church would never abrogate this law nor mitigate it. He highly praised clerical celibacy in the Latin Church and added this impressive declaration: "We solemnly testify that the Holy See will never in any way mitigate, much less abolish, this most sacred and salutary law."[175] We know, however, that popes had in the past granted dispensations from celibacy, and that they would continue to do so.

2. Pius XI

Nearly seventeen years after the promulgation of the code, in articles 40 and 74 of his encyclical on the Catholic priesthood *Ad catholici sacerdotii* Pope Pius XI (1922-1939) declared:

> It is impossible to treat of the piety of a Catholic priest without being drawn on to speak, too, of another most precious treasure of the Catholic priesthood, that is, of chastity; for from piety springs the meaning and the beauty of chastity. Clerics of the Latin Church in higher Orders are bound by a grave obligation of chastity; so grave is the obligation in them of its perfect and total observance that a transgression involves the added guilt of sacrilege. In short, let all canonic prescriptions be carefully obeyed, and let everyone put into practice the wise rules on

---

175 Benedict XV, allocution Cum multa hoc, December 16, 1920: AAS 12 (1920) 585: "...sollemniter affirmatque testamur, fore numquam ut haec Apostolica Sedes sanctissimam eam maximeque salutarem legem caelibatus ecclesiastici aliqua ex parte extenuando mitiget, nedum aboleat." Hereafter CM. English translation in CLD 1:121. The pope addressed the difficulties experienced on the foreign missions, the schism of priests in Bohemia and reiterated the reasons for celibacy.

this subject, thus will the Church be saved much grief and the faithful much scandal.[176]

Yet as anxious as the Church was to legislate for mandatory clerical celibacy, the Church was also willing in certain circumstances to make exceptions to the rule by granting dispensations.

3. Pius XII

Pius XII's (1939-1958) apostolic exhortation to the clergy of the world, *Menti Nostrae,*[177] was an instruction on holiness in the life of the priest. The theme of the document is union with Christ. In his reflection on the life of virtue, the pope gave particular attention to chastity "because the choice of the priestly state and perseverance in it depend in great part on this virtue."[178] He directed that young seminarians should be taught about the importance of this obligation and given instruction on the means of persevering in it. As for seminarians who, after trial, were not able to live a chaste celibate life, "it is absolutely necessary to dismiss them from the seminary before they receive Holy Orders."[179]

Pius XII's encyclical *Sacra virginitas,* "On Sacred Virginity," affirmed the importance of chastity in the lives of ordained ministers:

> It is that they may acquire this spiritual liberty of body and soul, and
> that they may be freed from temporal cares, that the Latin Church de-

---

176 Pius XI, encyclical Ad catholici sacerdotii, December 20, 1935: AAS 28 (1936) 390-395. Hereafter AC.

177 Pius XII, apostolic exhortation Menti nostrae, September 23, 1950: AAS 42 (1950) 657-702. Hereafter MN.

178 *MN* 3; *AAS* 42 (1950) 690: "…quippe in qua sit magnam partem positum quod eiusmodi vitae genus iidem sibi constituant, in eoque permaneant." English translation from *Catholic Documents* 4 (1951) 20. Hereafter *CDoc.*

179 *MN* 3; *AAS* 42 (1950) 691: "…is erit utique e seminario exigendus, antequam sacris ordinibus initietur." English translation from *CDoc.* 4 (1951) 20.

mands of her sacred ministers that they voluntarily oblige themselves to preserve perfect chastity.[180]

Pope Pius XII further concluded that the doctrine of the excellence of virginity and of celibacy and of their superiority over the married state was revealed by Our Lord. He stated:

This doctrine of the excellence of virginity and of celibacy and of their superiority over the married state was, as We have already said, revealed by our Divine Redeemer and by the Apostle of the Gentiles; so too, it was solemnly defined as a dogma of divine faith by the holy Council of Trent, and explained in the same way by all the holy Fathers and Doctors of the Church. Finally, We and Our Predecessors have often expounded it and earnestly advocated it whenever occasion offered. But recent attacks on this traditional doctrine of the Church, the danger they constitute, and the harm they do to the souls of the faithful lead Us, in fulfillment of the duties of Our charge, to take up the matter once again in this Encyclical Letter, and to reprove these errors which are so often propounded under a specious appearance of truth.[181]

---

180   Pius XII, encyclical Sacra virginitas, March 25, 1954. N. 22: "Quam quidem spiritualem corporis animique libertatem ut sacrorum administri adipiscantur, utque terrenis negotiis ne implicentur, Latina Ecclesia ab iisdem postulat ut volentes libentesque perfectae castitatis obligationi pareant." Hereafter SC. AAS 46 (1954) 169. English translation from The Pope Speaks 1 (1954) 107.

181   SC 32, AAS 46 (1954) 174: "Haec doctrina, qua statuitur virginitatem et caelibatum omnino excellere ac matrimonio praestare, iam a Divino Redemptore et a genitum Apostolo, ut diximus, patefacta fuit; itemque in sancrosanta Tridentia synodo sollemniter fuit ut divinae fidei dogma definite, et Sanctis Patribus Ecclesiaeque Doctoribus concordi semper sentential declarata. Praeterea ut Decesores Nostri, ita Nosmet ipsi, quotiescumque occasion data est, eam etiam atque etiam explanavimus ac valde commendavimus. Verumtamen, cum recens non defuerint qui hanc eandem doctrinam a maioribus Ecclesiae traditum impugnarent non sine gravi christifidelium periculo ac detriment, nos pro officii nostri conscientia opportunum duximus rem iterum per encyclicas has litteras resumere, et eiusmodi errores, qui saepenumero sub fucata veri specie proponuntur, detegere ac reprobare." English translation from The Pope Speaks 1 (1954) 111. The Council of Trent, in canon 10 on marriage, affirmed the excellence of virginity and chaste celibacy when it condemned those who taught marriage was superior. Council of Trent, session 24, November 11, 1563, de matrimonio, c. 10: "Si quis dixerit, statum, coniugalem anteponendum esse statui virginitatis vel coelibatus, et non esse melius ac beatius, manere in virginitate aut coelibatu, quam iungi matrimonio." Tanner, 2:755. Trent did not explicitly say that virginity and chaste celibacy were superior to marriage. Yet this was how Pope Pius interpreted canon 10.

During the 1950's, Pius XII authorized a number of married former Luther-an ministers in Germany who had entered full communion with the Church to be ordained Catholic priests. There were also similar cases in Denmark and Swe-den.[182] The law required that such dispensations were never granted without the consent of the wife and always included the obligation of absolute continence on the part of both spouses.[183] However, Ralph Wiltgen insists that Pius XII permitted the former Lutheran pastors who were ordained priests in Germany to retain the use of their marriages.[184] Fichter also asserts that a number of married former Protestant clergymen were ordained Catholic priests in the 1950's and 1960's, and that they were not asked to relinquish their marital relations with their spouses.[185]

J. Conclusion

Under the 1917 code, clerics in major orders- subdeacons, deacons, priests and bishops- were bound by the obligation of celibacy and chastity. This obliga-tion was assumed with ordination to the subdiaconate. The cleric was prohibited from having sexual relations with anyone and was rendered incapable of enter-ing marriage. The pope was the only authority competent to dispense a cleric from these obligations. Dispensations were rare and ordinarily only granted to a cleric who was already living in a merely civil marriage. Though a dispensation

182   William Woestman, The Sacrament of Orders and the Clerical State, 3rd ed. (Ottawa: Saint Paul University, 2001) 182.
183   Vogelpohl, The Simple Impediments to Holy Orders, 24-25; Cappello, De Sacra Ordina-tione, 2: 3, 520.
184   Ralph Wiltgen, The Rhine Flows into the Tiber: The Unknown Council (New York: Haw-thorn Books, Inc., 1967) 265. However, Wiltgen does not offer any sources for his assertion that these former Lutheran ministers continued to have conjugal relations after their ordination as priests.
185   Joseph H. Fichter, Wives of Catholic Clergy (Kansas City, MO: Sheed and Ward, 1992) 97. See also Rudolf Goethe, "Die offene Tur," in Bekenntnis zur Katholische Kirche (Würzburg: Echter-Verl, 1956) 117-165. Goethe was a married former Lutheran minister who was ordained a Catholic priest in 1951, on his seventy-fifth birthday. In his book there is no suggestion that he was asked to live continently with his wife after ordination.

made it possible for such a cleric to marry according to canonical form, he was subsequently prohibited from contracting any future marriage and permanently excluded from ministry.

It did remain possible for a married man to be admitted to tonsure and receive major orders. A dispensation from the impediment of marriage was necessary and was granted on condition that the married man, with the consent of his wife, observe the *lex continentiae*. The promise of absolute continence had to be made before the reception of tonsure. This reflected the consistent canonical tradition of the Latin Church from the fourth century. Yet, even though the ordination of a married man was possible, it rarely happened.

The canonical dispositions of the 1917 code concerning chastity, continence and celibacy remained in harmony with much of the canonical legislation in the West from the Council of Elvira, 305. Continence was the fundamental norm for all clergy in major orders, married, unmarried or widowed. The most notable difference with regard to prior legislation was that candidates for major orders were almost exclusively chosen from among unmarried men.

Now let us explore the effect the Second Vatican Council and the revision of the code had on the canonical dispositions of chastity, continence and celibacy.

CHAPTER THREE

CONCILIAR AND POST CONCILIAR TEACHING CONCERNING CELIBACY AND THE RESTORATION OF THE PERMANENT DIACONATE

On the feast of the conversion of St. Paul, January 25, 1959, Pope John XXIII announced his intention to convoke a synod for Rome and an ecumenical council for the universal Church.[1] In turn, he believed that these would lead to "the desired and long awaited modernization of the Code of Canon Law."[2]

Several months later on the feast of Pentecost, the pontiff established an antepreparatory commission[3] and appointed Cardinal Domenico Tardini as its president. This commission was charged with the organization of the council and with determining the topics to be treated by it. Letters were sent to all cardinals, archbishops, bishops, Roman congregations and pontifical universities asking for suggestions and proposals. On October 11, 1962, after nearly three

---

1   John XXIII, allocution *Questa festiva ricorrenza,* January 25, 1959: *Acta Apostolicae Sedis* 51(1959) 65-69. Hereafter *AAS.*
2   Ibid: "Esse condurrano felicemente all'auspicato e atteso aggiornamento del Codice di Diritto Canonico...." *AAS* 51 (1959) 68. English translation from *The Pope Speaks* 5 (1958-1959) 400.
3   Vatican Council II, *Acta et Documenta Concilio Oecumenico Vaticano II Apparando, Series 1 Antepraeparatoria* (Vatican City: Typis Polyglottis Vaticanis, 1960) 1:22-23. Hereafter *ADA.*

years of preparations, John XXIII presided at the opening session of the Second Vatican Council at St. Peter's Basilica, Rome.[4]

The work of the council was divided into four periods, each one lasting approximately ten weeks during successive autumns.[5] It is estimated that a total of two thousand, eight hundred and sixty-five bishops participated in the council, which was the twenty-first ecumenical council of the Church.[6] John XXIII died on June 3, 1963, and with the election of Pope Paul VI less than two weeks later the work of the council continued unabated until its conclusion on October 28, 1965.[7]

This chapter will examine key conciliar and post-conciliar teaching concerning clerical celibacy and the restoration of the permanent diaconate from the time of the council until the promulgation of the 1983 code. With the admission of married men to the permanent diaconate, this chapter will also include an examination of other significant conciliar and post conciliar teaching regarding the nature both of marriage and of conjugal life and their compatibility with holy orders. This is important when one recalls that for much of the Latin Church's history married men were ordinarily only admitted to orders on condition that conjugal life cease. The chapter will conclude with certain summary conclusions.

A. The Second Vatican Council (1962-1965)[8]

The Second Vatican Council issued sixteen documents. Five of these docu-

---

4   Gregory Baum, *The Teachings of the Second Vatican Council* (Westminster, MD: The Newman Press, 1966) 608.

5   Norman T. Tanner, ed., *Decrees of the Ecumenical Councils* (London and Washington: Sheed & Ward and Georgetown University Press, 1990) 2: 818. Hereafter Tanner.

6   Ibid., 2:817.

7   Baum, *The Teachings of the Second Vatican Council,* 611.

8   For a detailed history of the Council see Giuseppe Alberigo and Joseph Komonchak, eds., *History of Vatican II* (Leuven: Peeters; Maryknoll, New York: Orbis Books, 1995-2006) and *The Documents of Vatican II,* ed. Walter M. Abbott (New York: Herder and Herder, 1966).

ments are particularly important for this study: *Lumen gentium,*[9] the Dogmatic Constitution on the Church; *Perfectae caritatis,*[10] the Decree on Renewal of Religious Life; *Optatam totius,*[11] the Decree on the Training of Priests; *Presbyterorum Ordinis,*[12] the Decree on the Ministry and Life of Priests; and *Gaudium et spes,*[13] the Pastoral Constitution on the Church in the Modern World. These documents will be treated in the order in which they were promulgated.

1. *Lumen gentium:* The Dogmatic Constitution on the Church

The First Vatican Council (1869-1870) had intended to promulgate a document on the nature of Church,[14] but its deliberations were cut short by the Franco-Prussian war and the invasion of the Papal States by the Piedmontese armies.[15] Following Vatican I, two landmark encyclicals focused attention on the nature of the Church and ultimately prepared the way for the Vatican II decree *Lumen gentium.*[16] In *Satis cognitum* (1896)[17] Pope Leo XIII sought to re-focus the attention of the faithful on this topic. Pius XII in his encyclical *Mys-*

---

9   Vatican II, dogmatic constitution *Lumen gentium*, November 21, 1964: *AAS* 57 (1965) 5-67. Hereafter *LG.*
10   Vatican II, decree *Perfectae caritatis*, October 28, 1965: *AAS* 58 (1966) 702-712. Hereafter *PC.*
11   Vatican II, decree *Optatam totius,* October 28, 1965: *AAS* 58 (1966) 713-727. Hereafter *OT.*
12   Vatican II, decree *Presbyterorum Ordinis,* December 7, 1965: *AAS* 58 (1966) 991-1024. Hereafter *PO.*
13   Vatican II, pastoral constitution *Gaudium et spes*, December 7, 1965: *AAS* 58 (1966) 1025-1115. Hereafter *GS.*
14   *Prima Schema Constitutionis Dogmaticae de Ecclesia Christi Patrum Examini Propositum* in *Sacrorum Conciliorum: Nova et Amplissma Collectio*, ed. Ioannes Dominicus Mansi (Paris: Herbert Welter, 1901-1927) 51:539-553. Hereafter Mansi. See also *Schema Constitutionis Dogmaticae Secundae de Ecclesia Christi Secundum Reverendissimorum Patrum Animadversiones Reformatum.* Mansi, 53: 308-317.
15   Avery Dulles, "The Church," in *The Documents of Vatican II,* 9.
16   Ibid.
17   Leo XIII, encyclical *Satis cognitum,* June 29, 1896: *ASS* 28 (1895-96) 708-739. Hereafter *SCo.*

tici Corporis (1943)[18] provided a more profound treatment of the same theme. The Fathers of the Second Vatican Council wanted to develop this work more fully in the dogmatic constitution on the Church, *Lumen gentium.* This was to be one of only two constitutions issued by the council, the second being *Dei verbum,*[19] on Divine Revelation. *Lumen gentium* has been hailed as the most momentous achievement of the council, both because of its content and its central place among the conciliar documents.

The constitution enunciates the nature and organization of the Church and as such all other conciliar decrees must be read in the light of this constitution.[20] This is especially true when it comes to an understanding of the theology of the priesthood. As Kenan B. Osborne observes:

> Since a theology of the priest can be understood only in the light of a theology of the Church, and since the formation of priests can be accomplished only in the light of a theology of the Church, the ecclesiology of *Lumen gentium* is foundational. One cannot lose sight of the fact that ecclesiology determines the meaning and role of the ordained person in the Church. The theology of the ordained person does not determine ecclesiology.[21]

According to Osborne, *Lumen gentium* established five major developments regarding institutional church ministry:

(1) The establishment of the mission and ministry of all the bap-

---

18   Pius XII, encyclical *Mystici Corporis,* July 24, 1943: *AAS* 35 (1943) 193-248. Hereafter *MC.*
19   Vatican II, dogmatic constitution *Dei verbum,* November 18, 1965: *AAS* 58 (1966) 817-830. Hereafter *DV.*
20   Gerard Philips, "Dogmatic Constitution on the Church," in *Commentary on the Documents of Vatican II,* ed. Herbert Vorgrimler (New York: Herder and Herder, 1967) 1:105.
21   Kenan B. Osborne, "Priestly Formation," in *From Trent to Vatican II: Historical and Theological Investigations,* ed. Raymond F. Bulman et al. (Oxford, NY: Oxford University Press, 2006) 127.

tized-confirmed Christians as a foundation of institutional church ministry. (2) The re-establishment of the episcopacy as an official part of the sacrament of orders. (3) The redefinition of priesthood on the basis of the *tria munera.* (4) The re-establishment of the permanent diaconate. (5) The official expansion of lay ministry into the ecclesial dimensions of the *tria munera.*[22]

For the purposes of this chapter, particular focus will be given to the implications of *Lumen gentium* concerning the obligation of celibacy and the restoration of the diaconate. This will be situated within the context of the constitution's teaching on baptism as the foundational sacrament for ministry in the Church.

Lumen gentium describes the Church as the "People of God."[23] This community of believers is hierarchically ordered with the laity being full members of the Church.[24] *Lumen gentium* declared that in the Church all the baptized have a share in the one priesthood of Christ. The baptized share in the "common priesthood," and the ordained in "the ministerial priesthood:"

> The common priesthood of the faithful and the ministerial or hierarchical priesthood, though they differ in essence and not simply in degree, are nevertheless interrelated: each in its own particular way shares in the one priesthood of Christ. On the one hand, the ministerial priest, through the sacred power that he enjoys, forms and governs the priestly people; in the person of Christ he brings about the Eucharistic sacrifice and offers this to God in the name of the whole people. The faithful, on the other hand, by virtue of their royal priesthood, join in the offering

---

22   Kenan B. Osborne, *The Permanent Diaconate: Its History and Place in the Sacrament of Orders* (New York: Paulist Press, 2006) 40.

23   *LG* 39.

24   *LG* 18-28. For an earlier effort to develop a theology of the laity, see Yves Congar, *Jalons pour une théologie du laïcat* (Paris: Éditions du Cerf, 1954).

of the Eucharist, and they exercise their priesthood in receiving the sacraments, in prayer and thanksgiving, through the witness of a holy life,
by self-denial and active charity.[25]

This was the first time a church council had spoken in such detail concerning the significance of the common priesthood.[26] The council declared that
the common priesthood of the faithful and the ministerial priesthood of the ordained, though they are interrelated, differ in essence. Each is equipped to minister in different ways.

No matter the way in which one participates in the priesthood of Christ, all
are called to holiness of life. The call to holiness is not reserved to the ordained
or to those in religious life. The call to holiness is a universal one.

> For this reason everyone in the Church is called to holiness, whether he
> belongs to the hierarchy or is cared for by the hierarchy, according to
> the saying of the apostle: "For this is the will of God, your sanctifica-
> tion." (1 Th 4:3; Eph 1:4).[27]

Laypersons, whether married, widowed or single, are called to strive for
the holiness and perfection proper to their own state in life. *Lumen gentium*
expresses this thinking:

> All the faithful are, therefore, invited and bound to strive towards ho-

---

25   *LG* 10, *AAS* 57 (1965)14-15: "Sacerdotium autem commune fidelium et sacerdotium mi-
nisteriale seu hierarchicum, licet essentia et non gradu tantum differant, ad invicem tamen ordinantur; unum enim et alterum suo peculiari modo de uno Christi sacerdotio participant. Sacerdos quidem ministerialis, potestate sacra qua gaudet, populum sacerdotalem efformat ac regit, sacrificium
eucharisticum in persona Christi conficit illudque nomine totius populi Deo offert; fideles vero, vi
regalis sui sacerdotii, in oblationem Eucharistiae concurrunt, illudque in sacramentis suscipiendis,
in oratione et gratiarum actione, testimonio vitae sanctae, abnegatione et actuosa caritate exercent."
Tanner, 2:857.
26   Philips in Vorgrimler, 1:120.
27   *LG* 39, *AAS* 57 (1965) 44: "Ideo in Ecclesia omnes, sive ad Hierarchiam pertinent sive
ab ea pascuntur, ad sanctitatem vocantur, iuxta illud Apostoli: 'Haec est enim voluntas Dei, sancti-
ficatio vestra.'" (1Thess 4,3; Eph 1,4). Tanner, 2:880.

liness and the perfection of their particular state of life. Consequently all must be careful to keep due control over their emotions, so as not to be held back from the pursuit of perfect charity by using this world's goods and being attached to riches in a way that is against the spirit of evangelical poverty; as the apostle warns us: "Those who deal with the world must not be attached to it, for the form of this world is passing away" (1 Cor 7:31).[28]

The emphasis on the universal call to holiness for all the baptized has the effect of dignifying further all vocations within the Church.

Within this universal call to holiness shared by all the baptized, some are called to embrace virginity or celibacy for the sake of the kingdom of God.

The holiness of the Church is also nourished in a special way by the manifold counsels the observance of which the Lord in the Gospel commends to his disciples. Outstanding among these is that precious gift of divine grace which is granted to some by the Father (Mt 19:11:1; 1 Cor 7:7), that in the state of virginity or celibacy they may more easily devote themselves to God alone with an undivided heart (1 Cor 7:32-34). This perfect continence for the sake of the kingdom of Heaven has always been held in particular esteem by the Church as a sign and a stimulus of charity and as a singular source of spiritual fruitfulness in the world.[29]

---

28   *LG* 42, *AAS* 57 (1965) 49: "Omnes igitur christifideles ad sanctitatem et proprii status perfectionem prosequendam invitantur et tenentur. Attendant igitur omnes, ut affectus suos recte dirigant, ne usu rerum mundanarum et adhaesione ad divitias contra spiritum paupertatis evangelicae a caritate perfecta prosequenda impediantur, monente Apostolo: Qui utuntur hoc mundo, in eo ne sistant: praeterit enim figura huius mundi (cf. 1 Cor 7:31). Tanner, 2:884.

29   *LG* 42, *AAS* 57 (1965) 42: "Sanctitas Ecclesiae item speciali modo fovetur multiplicibus consiliis, quae Dominus in Evangelio discipulis suis observanda proponit. Inter quae eminet pretiosum gratiae divinae donum, quod a Patre quibusdam datur (Mt 19, 11 :1; 1 Cor 7:7), ut in virginitate vel coelibatu facilius indiviso corde (1Cor 7:32-34). Deo soli se devoveant. Haec perfecta propter Regnum coelorum continentia semper in honore praecipuo ab Ecclesia habita est, tamquam signum et stimulus caritatis, ac quidam peculiaris fons spiritualis foecunditatis in mundo." Tanner, 2:883-884.

The Fathers stated that virginity and celibacy are outstanding among the evangelical counsels.

2. The Restoration of the Permanent Diaconate

Three conciliar texts contain references to the restoration of the permanent diaconate: *Lumen gentium* 29, *Ad gentes* 16 and *Orientalium Ecclesiarum* 17.[30] The most important text for our study is that found in *Lumen gentium.*

Prior to the council, the diaconate had not existed in the Church as a permanent order for nearly twelve hundred years.[31] Indeed the diaconate itself remained transitory and subordinate to the presbyterate. The office of deacon had been present in the Church from its earliest days and developed gradually, in response to circumstances and needs.[32] Though the New Testament referred to all Christian ministry as *diakonia,* certain men were designated as *diakonoi* in a special sense.[33] St. Paul's letter to Timothy enumerated the qualities to be expected of these *diakoni.*[34] In the Acts of the Apostles the word *diakonia* was used in the technical sense to refer to the ecclesiastical office to which the apostles appointed seven men, laying hands on them and entrusting them with the service of the Christian community of Jerusalem.[35] The *Didache,* compiled around 150 A.D., mentioned

---

30   William T. Ditewig, *The Emerging Diaconate: Servant Leaders in a Servant Church* (New York: Paulist Press, 2007) 102. The diaconate is also referred to in the Constitution on the Sacred Liturgy, *Sacrosanctum Concilium* 35 and the Dogmatic Constitution on Divine Revelation, *Dei Verbum* 25.

31   Osborne, *The Permanent Diaconate,* 93. A 'transitional' diaconate had continued to exist during this period of time.

32   Robert Nowell, *The Ministry of Service: Deacons in the Contemporary Church* (New York, NY: Herder and Herder, 1968) 40-41.

33   Edward P. Echlin, *The Deacon in the Church: Past and Future* (New York, NY: Alba House, 1971) 5.

34   1 Tim 3:8-13. In *The New American Bible* (Nashville: Catholic Bible Press, 1987). Hereafter *NAB.*

35   *NAB* Acts 6:1-7. See also José L. Casañas Medina, *The Law for the Restoration of the Permanent Diaconate: A Canonical Commentary,* Canon Law Studies 460 (Washington, DC: Catholic University of America, 1968) 5-6.

the office of deacon.[36] Both St. Clement of Rome[37] and St. Ignatius of Antioch[38] testified to the presence of deacons in the Church in the late first century.

From the time of St. Ignatius of Antioch to the Council of Nicea (325) the diaconate entered a so-called golden age.[39] As Edward P. Echlin states:

In the two centuries from Ignatius of Antioch to Nicea permanent deacons were vitally important ministers of the Church. Their ministry was as much a part of Church order as was the ministry of bishops and presbyters. They were taken for granted by people and council alike. But with the developing sacralization of presbyters, the seeds of the decline were planted.[40]

In the pre-Nicene Church the diaconate was conceived of as a permanent vocation. Deacons could become presbyters but usually did not.[41]

Following Nicea the diaconate began to decline into a largely ceremonial and transitional form.[42] By the eighth century the permanent diaconate had, for a series of reasons, all but been extinguished in the life of the Church. As James Barnett observes:

Sixth century inscriptions on towers and some literary references record that deacons died in Gaul at sixty, seventy or eighty years. Alcin,

---

36   Echlin, *The Deacon in the Church,* 16. According to Echlin, the *Didache* is the most important document of the subapostolic period and the oldest source of ecclesiastical law.

37   Clement of Rome, "The First Epistle to the Corinthians," in *The Epistles of St. Clement of Rome and St. Ignatius of Antioch,* ed. James Kleist (Westminster, MD: The Newman Bookshop, 1949) 33. Clement was the third successor of St. Peter in Rome from 92 AD-101 AD. "His letter to the Corinthians is among the most important documents of subapostolic times, the earliest piece of Christian literature outside the New Testament for which name, position and date of author are historically attested." Johannes Quasten, *Patrology* (Westminster, MD: The Newman Press, 1951-1960) 42-43. Hereafter Patrology.

38   Ignatius of Antioch, *Trallians* 3:1, in *Early Christian Fathers,* ed. Cyril C. Richardson (New York: Collier Books, 1970) 99. Ignatius was the second bishop of Antioch from 98 AD-117 AD. See also Patrology, 63.

39   Ditewig, *The Emerging Diaconate,* 61.

40   Echlin, *The Deacon in the Church,* 29.

41   See James Monroe Barnett, *The Diaconate: A Full and Equal Order* (Valley Forge, PA: Trinity Press International, 1995) 83.

42   Ibid., 61.

who had been ordained deacon about thirty-five years old and who died in the year 804 at about seventy-five, was never ordained a priest. But such men increasingly became the exception.[43]

There is no historical data indicating that there was an official edict revoking the permanent diaconate. Historical data simply indicated that a permanent diaconal ministry from 800 A.D. onwards became the exception and eventually disappeared.[44] While many factors contributed to the decline of the diaconate, including its gradual subordination to the presbyterate, Barnett is convinced that the overarching factor was the idea of the *cursus honorum*.[45] William T. Ditewig agrees with Barnett:

> During the fourth century, Christian life underwent significant transformation. Partly as a result of Christianity's new relationship with the empire, Christian public life gradually took on the trappings and structures of the state. It is during this time that the minor orders appeared, along with supraepiscopal offices such as 'metropolitan.' Such a structure easily gives rise to the idea of a succession of grades onto which one moves from lower to higher, traditionally called *cursus honorum*.[46]

The *cursus honorum* had a profound effect on ordained ministry, especially the diaconate. First, it led to a diminishing of the role of the deacon as subordinate to the presbyter and mainly ceremonial. Second, it led to the extinguishing of the diaconate as a permanent order.[47]

By the eighth century the permanent diaconate had become a rare exception.

---

43   Barnett, *The Diaconate,* 110.
44   See Osborne, *The Permanent Diaconate,* 94.
45   See Barnett, *Diaconate,* 104.
46   See Ditewig, *The Emerging Diaconate,* 75. See also Barnett, *Diaconate,* 156. For a full treatment of the *Cursus Honorum* see John St. H. Gibaut, *The Cursus Honorum: A Study of the Origins and the Evolution of Sequential Ordination* (New York, NY: Peter Lang Publishing, 2000).
47   See Echlin, *The Deacon in the Church,* 94; Ditewig, *The Emerging Diaconate,* 75-78.

Yet it never wholly vanished in the Latin West. There were rare instances of clerics serving as deacons for many years.[48] St. Francis of Assisi is probably among the most famous of permanent deacons. He was a cleric for sixteen years and was never ordained a priest.[49] Cardinal Piccolomini administered the diocese of Siena for forty years as a deacon until his election as pope in 1503.[50] Cardinal Reginald Pole, who was one of the three presidents of Trent, was a deacon and remained so until being ordained a bishop many years after being named a cardinal.[51] Cardinal Giacomo Antonelli, Secretary of State for the Vatican (1858-1876) remained a deacon until his death. He was the last deacon to be created a cardinal before Pope Benedict XV decreed in 1918 that all cardinals must be ordained priests.[52]

The diaconate that was practiced in the Church at the time of the Council of Trent was "temporary, subordinate, and mainly ceremonial."[53] The council sought to revive the order of deacon and the other orders below the presbyterate, though it did not speak directly of reestablishing the diaconate as a permanent state.[54] On July 15, 1563 the council decreed in part:

> The functions of holy orders from deacon to doorkeeper have been commendably accepted in the Church since apostolic times, and though lapsing for a time in some places are now being brought back to use according to the sacred canons....[55]

---

48   Ibid., 80.
49   See Johannes Jörgensen, *St. Francis of Assisi: A Biography* (New York, NY: Longmans Press, 1913) 97-98.
50   See Norbert Brockman, *Ordained to Service: A Theology of the Permanent Diaconate* (Hickville, NY: Exposition Press, 1976) 30.
51   Ibid.
52   See Carlo Falconi, *Il Cardinale Antonelli: Vita e carriera del Richelieu italiano nella chiesa di Pio IX* (Milan: Mondadori, 1983) 13.
53   See Echlin, *The Deacon in the Church,* 93.
54   See Medina, *The Law for the Restoration of the Permanent Diaconate,* 15.
55   Council of Trent, session 23, July 15, 1563, *de sacramento ordinis,* c. 17: "Ut sanctorum ordinum a diaconatu ad ostiariatum functiones, ab apostolorum temporibus in ecclesia laudabiliter receptae, et pluribus in locis aliquamdiu intermissae, in usum iuxta sacros canones...." Tanner, 2:750.

Unfortunately this decree was never implemented.[56] Yet the fact that Trent had discussed the diaconate at all became an influential factor for some bishops at the Second Vatican Council.[57]

Trent continued to legislate for the transitory nature of the diaconate. It decreed that deacons were to be ordained to the priesthood after they had served at least a year in this office unless the bishop judged otherwise.[58] The transitory, subordinate and mainly ceremonial role of the deacon in the post-Tridentine Church was finally codified in the 1917 Code of Canon Law.

Canon 973 §1 stated that only those who had the intention of being ordained to the priesthood could be admitted to tonsure; thus the discipline of the Church seemed settled: the diaconate was a transitory order.[59] The period between ordination to the diaconate and the priesthood was reduced to at least three months[60] but in reality this period may only have been a matter of days.[61] The ordination rite for deacons made clear that the order was preparatory to the higher grade of the priesthood.[62] Ecclesiastical legislation continued to subordinate the diacon-

---

56   See Echlin, *The Deacon in the Church,* 105; Barnett, *The Diaconate,* 145.

57   See Ditewig, *The Emerging Diaconate,* 88.

58   Council of Trent, session 23, July 15, 1563, *de sacramento ordinis,* c. 11: "Bonum habeant testimonium, et hi sint, qui non modo in diaconatu ad minus annum integrum, nisi ob ecclesiae utilitatem ac necessitatem aliud episcopo videretur." Tanner, 2:749.

59   *Codex Iuris Canonici Pii X Pontificis Maximi iussu digestus Benedicti Papae XV auctoritate promulgatus* (Rome: Typis Polyglottis Vaticanis, 1917), c. 973 §1: "Prima tonsura et ordines illis tantum conferendi sunt, qui propositum habeant ascendendi ad presbyteratum et quos merito coniicere liceat aliquando dignos futuros esse presbyteros." Hereafter 17 *CIC.* English translations from *The 1917 Pio-Benedictine Code of Canon Law: In English Translation with Extensive Scholarly Apparatus,* ed. Edward N. Peters (San Francisco, CA: Ignatius Press, 2001). All subsequent English translations of canons from this code will be taken from this source unless otherwise indicated.

60   17 *CIC,* c. 978 §2: "Interstitia primam tonsuram inter et ostiariatum vel inter singulos ordines minores prudenti Episcopi iudicio committuntur; acolythus vero ad subdiaconatum, subdiaconus ad diaconatum, diaconus ad presbyteratum ne antea promoveantur, quam acolythus unum saltem annum, subdiaconus et diaconus tres saltem menses in suo quisque ordine fuerint versati, nisi necessitas aut utilitas Ecclesiae, iudicio Episcopi, aliud exposcat."

61   See Echlin, *The Deacon in the Church,* 106.

62   See Aurelius Stehle, "De Ordinatione Diaconi," in *Manuale Ordinandorum: According to the Roman Pontifical* (Latrobe, PA: Archabbey Press, 1917) 48-58.

ate to the presbyterate: while the faculty of preaching was granted to deacons,[63] in practice few deacons ever preached regularly.[64] The deacon, an extraordinary minister of baptism[65] and Holy Communion,[66] needed the permission of the pastor or the ordinary to baptize and distribute Holy Communion. The dispositions of the 1917 code concerning the diaconate remained in place until the Second Vatican Council.

3. The Movement towards a Restoration of the Permanent Diaconate[67]

In 1963 a German lawyer, Dr. Joseph Hornef, authored a book entitled *The New Vocation*, in which he argued for the restoration of the diaconate as a permanent order.[68] In the preface to his book, Hornef stated that he had been influenced by an earlier article written by Father Otto Pies, S.J. In his article Pies referenced the discussions of priests imprisoned in Dachau concerning a revival of the diaconate. Hornef was an enthusiastic proponent of the restoration of the diaconate and had written several articles on the subject before and after the publication of his book.[69]

In 1953, as Hornef was publishing his articles on the restoration of the di-

---

63   17 *CIC*, c. 1342 §1: "Concionandi facultas solis sacerdotibus vel diaconis fiat, non vero ceteris clericis, nisi rationabili de causa, iudicio Ordinarii et in casibus singularibus."

64   See Echlin, *The Deacon in the Church,* 106.

65   17 *CIC,* c. 741: "Extraordinarius baptismi sollemnis minister est diaconus; qui tamen sua potestate ne utatur sine loci Ordinarii vel parochi licentia, iusta de causa concedenda, quae, ubi necessitas urgeat, legitime praesumitur. "

66   17 *CIC*, 845 §2. Extraordinarius est diaconus, de Ordinarii loci vel parochi licentia, gravi de causa concedenda, quae in casu necessitatis legitime praesumitur."

67   For an excellent treatment of this movement from the 1917 Code to the council see Medina, *The Law for the Restoration of the Permanent Diaconate,* 35-63; Ditewig, *The Emerging Diaconate,* 94-122; and Echlin, *The Deacon in the Church,* 95-124.

68   Joseph Hornef, *The New Vocation* (Techny, IL: Divine Word Publications, 1963).

69   See Joseph Hornef, "The Deacon in the Parish," *Life of the Spirit* 14 (1959) 161-167; Also "Rebirth of the Diaconate in the Roman Catholic Church," *Dominicana* 47 (1962) 20-31; Paul Winniger and Joseph Hornef, "Le Renouveau du Diaconat: Situation Présent de la Controverse," *Nouvelle revue théologique* 83 (1961) 337-366. Hereafter *NRT.*

aconate, Father Wilhelm Schamoni, a priest of Paberborn, Germany who had been in Dachau along with Father Pies, authored a book entitled *Married Men as Ordained Deacons.*[70] In it he advocated the restoration of the permanent diaconate and the admission of married men to this order.

Interest in the diaconate spread beyond Germany and three years later, at the First International Congress for Pastoral Liturgy in Assisi, Bishop Wilhelm van Bekkum, the vicar apostolic of Ruteng Island, Indonesia, joined the chorus calling for a revival of the diaconate and the admission of married men to the order.[71] This was the first time a bishop had spoken publicly calling for a restoration of the diaconate.[72]

In 1957, Father Michel Epagneul, founder of the Frères Missionaires des Campagnes, penned an article in which he also called for a restoration of the permanent diaconate.[73] He believed that permanent deacons could be of great pastoral assistance to missionary priests. Epagneul forwarded a copy of his article to Pius XII who in turn wrote to the author and expressed his interest in the matter.[74]

In October 1957, at the World Congress of the Lay Apostolate in Rome, Pius XII became "the first pontiff to speak publically about the restoration of the diaconate."[75] He declared:

> We know that thought is being given at present to the introduction of
> a diaconate conceived as an ecclesiastical office independent of the

---

70   Wilhelm Schamoni, *Married Men as Ordained Deacons* (London: Burns & Oates, 1955).
71   See Wilhelm van Bekkum, "Le renouveau liturgie au services des missions," in *La Maison Dieu : revue de pastorale liturgique* 45 (1956) 174-190. Hereafter *LMD.*
72   See John Hofinger, "The Case for Permanent Deacons," *Catholic Mind* 57 (1959) 116.
73   See Michel Dominique Epagneul, "Du rôle des diacres dans L'Église d'aujourd'hui," *NRT* 79 (1957) 153-168.
74   See Paul Winninger, *Vers un renouveau du diaconat* (Paris: Desclée de Brouwer, 1958) 13; Medina, *The Law for the Restoration of the Permanent Diaconate,* 37.
75   Medina, *The Law for the Restoration of the Permanent Diaconate,* 38.

priesthood. Today, at least, the idea is not ready for application. Should it someday become so, what we just said would still hold true and this diaconate would take its place with the priesthood in the distinctions we have just drawn.[76]

The pope believed that the time was not right for the restoration of the diaconate, but he did not rule it out. In the same allocution the pontiff agreed with the common theological opinion of the day that the diaconate was part of the hierarchy of the Church.[77] Two years later in the Netherlands, Archbishop D'Souza proposed that the married diaconate be established in all Christian countries.[78] According to Ditewig these many arguments for re-establishing the permanent diaconate- the early German experience, the Dachau experience, the growth of the proposal in mission and catechetical fields, and the interventions of Pius XII- all converged on January 25, 1959, when Pope John XXIII declared his intention to convene the Second Vatican Council.[79]

During the pre-preparatory phase for the council, the ante-preparatory commission received many comments from bishops and others who favored the restoration of the permanent diaconate and the admission of married men to this order.[80] It seemed that the restoration of the permanent diaconate was an

---

76   Pius XII, allocution to World Congress of the Lay Apostolate in Rome, *Six ans se sont,* October 5, 1957: *AAS* 49 (1957) 925: "Nous savons qu'on pense actuellement à introduire un ordre du diaconat conçu comme fonction ecclésiastique indépendante du sacerdoce. L'idée, aujourd'hui du moins, n'est pas encore mure. Si elle le devenait un jour, rien ne changerait a ce que nous venons de dire sinon que diaconat prendrait place avec le sacerdoce dans les distinctions que nous avons indiquées." English translation from *TPS* 4 (1957-1958) 122.

77   Ibid. 924-925. Since Trent there had been a debate about the identity of the lower 'ministeri' within the hierarchy. Pius XII stated that the 'ministeri' which included the diaconate was part of the hierarchy. See also Echlin, *The Deacon in the Church,* 109.

78   Echlin, *The Deacon in the Church,* 109.

79   Ditewig, *The Emerging Diaconate,* 102.

80   For some examples see: *ADA* Series 1, Vol. 2, Pars 1: 128-130; 186; 236; 370; 462; Series 1, Vol. 2, Pars 5: 23; 40; 58; 78; 132; 162; 231; 345; Series 1, Vol. 2, Pars 6, 57; 108; 223; 347. See also Medina, *The Law for the Restoration of the Permanent Diaconate,* 39-43.

almost universal desire among the hierarchy of the Church.[81] In 1962, a group of eighty-two persons including Yves Congar, Karl Rahner and Bernard Haring, sent a document to all the bishops outlining their position in favor of the restoration of the permanent diaconate.[82] Yet, despite movement towards a restoration of the permanent diaconate, the first draft of the Constitution on the Church *De Ecclesia* contained no mention of the diaconate.[83]

The second draft, now known as *Lumen gentium,* mentioned the possibility of restoring the permanent diaconate.[84] The proposal came to the floor of the council during the second session, October 4-16, 1963[85] and was debated at length by the Fathers. Countless opinions were raised for and against the restoration.[86] Much of the debate centered on celibacy. Should the permanent diaconate be restored with or without the obligation of celibacy? As Medina observes:

> The opinions of the Fathers ranged from those who would not accept any exception to this law to those who saw no difficulty at all in dispensing from it. Some of the Fathers approved of the married diaconate, but made a distinction between younger and older candidates. Very few were in favor of relaxing the law of celibacy for young candidates who were not yet married. Even Fathers who originally accepted the possibility of married deacons had envisioned candidates who were already married: 'patres familias, homines iam conjugates, viros probates et uxorates' and so forth.[87]

---

81 Medina, *The Law for the Restoration of the Permanent Diaconate,* 43.

82 These studies and discussions were published in *Diaconi in Christo,* eds., Karl Rahner and Herbert Vorgrimler (Freiberg: Herder Verlag, 1962).

83 See Vatican Council II, *Acta Synodalia Sacrosancti Concilii Oecumenici Vaticani II.* Vol. 1, pars 4 (Vatican City: Typis Polyglottis Vaticanis, 1970-78) 23-24. Hereafter *AS.*

84 *AS* 2/1: 235.

85 See Echlin, *The Deacon in the Church,* 110.

86 For a fuller treatment of some of the arguments for and against the proposal see Medina, *The Law for the Restoration of the Permanent Diaconate,* 46-50 and Ditewig, *The Emerging Diaconate,* 111-116.

87 Medina, *The Law for the Restoration of the Permanent Diaconate,* 50.

The Obligation of Perfect and Perpetual Continence

Those who opposed the restoration of the diaconate feared that the approval of a married diaconate would result in a de-emphasis of the value of celibacy and endanger future vocations to the priesthood.[88] These discussions in part led to the crafting of a third draft of *Lumen gentium*. On September 29, 1963, the Fathers overwhelmingly approved paragraph 29. The last section stated:

> …According to the current discipline of the Latin Church, the diaconate can for the future be restored as a proper and permanent grade of the hierarchy. It is, however, the responsibility of the competent territorial conferences of bishops, which are of different kinds, to decide with the approval of the supreme pontiff himself whether and where it is opportune for such deacons to be appointed for the care of souls. With the consent of the roman pontiff it will be possible to confer this diaconate on men of more mature age, even upon those living in the married state, and also on suitable young men for whom, however, the law of celibacy must remain in force. [89]

Interestingly the council did not make the restoration of the permanent diaconate obligatory.[90] They opted instead to leave it up to the respective bishop's conferences with the approval of the roman pontiff.

---

88   For a fuller treatment of these discussions see Medina, *The Law for the Restoration of the Permanent Diaconate,* 50-53 and Herbert Vorgrimler, "The Hierarchical Structure of the Church, with Special Reference to the Episcopate," in Vorgrimler, 1:226-230.

89   *LG* 29, *AAS* 57 (1965) 36: "In disciplina Ecclesiae latinae hodie vigenti in pluribus regionibus adimpleri difficulter possint, Diaconatus in futurum tamquam proprius ac permanens gradus hierarchiae restitui poterit. Ad competentes autem varii generis territoriales Episcoporum *coetus*, approbante ipso Summo Pontifice, spectat decernere, utrum et ubinam pro cura animarum huiusmodi diaconos institui opportunum sit. De consensu Romani Pontificis hic diaconatus viris maturioris aetatis etiam in matrimonio viventibus conferri poterit, necnon iuvenibus idoneis, pro quibus tamen lex coelibatus firma remanere debet. " Tanner, 2:874.

90   In the Decree on the Eastern Churches, *Orientalium Ecclesiarum,* November 21, 1964, the Fathers strongly urged the restoration of the permanent diaconate in the Eastern Churches. Art. 17, *AAS* 57 (1965) 81-82: "Ut antiqua sacramenti Ordinis disciplina in Ecclesiis Orientalibus iterum vigeat, exoptat haec Sancta Synodus, ut institutum diaconatus permanentis, ubi in desuetudinem venerit, instauretur. Quoad subdiaconatum vero et Ordines inferiores eorumque iura et obligationes, provideat Auctoritas legislativa uniuscuiusque Ecclesiae particularis."

One year later in the decree on the missionary activity of the Church, *Ad gentes,*[91] the council again stated that the permanent diaconate could be restored according the norms of *Lumen gentium,* and that those men already performing diaconal services could be ordained as deacons. *Ad gentes* 16 stated:

> Where it seems opportune to episcopal conferences, the order of the diaconate, as a permanent state of life, should be restored in accordance with the norms of the Constitution on the Church. It would be helpful to those men who are exercising what is in fact the ministry of a deacon, either by preaching the word of God as catechists, or by taking charge of scattered Christian communities in the name of the parish priest and the bishop, or by practicing charity in social or charitable works, to be strengthened and bound more closely to the altar, by the imposition of hands which has come down from the Apostles, so that they may be able to carry out their ministry more effectively through the sacramental grace of the diaconate.[92]

These documents do not contain any reference to the ancient discipline of continence for Latin married clergy in major orders. *Lumen gentium* and *Ad gentes* make no reference to either the absolute continence required in the West or the temporary continence required in the East. There is also no mention of the ancient prohibition of remarriage for those in major orders. Further, the Fathers did not offer any norms or guidelines governing how such a restoration would

---

91 Vatican II, decree *Ad gentes,* December 7, 1965: *AAS* 58 (1966) 947-990. Hereafter *AG*.

92 *AG* 16, *AAS* 58 (1966) 967: "Ubi Conferentiis Episcoporum opportunum apparuerit, ordo diaconatus ut status vitae permanens restauretur ad normam Constitutionis De Ecclesia. Iuvat enim viros, qui ministerio vere diaconali fungantur, vel verbum divinum tanquam catechistae praedicantes, vel nomine parochi et episcopi dissitas communitates christianas moderantes, vel caritatem exercentes in operibus socialibus seu caritativis, per impositionem manuum inde ab Apostolis traditam corroborari et altari arctius coniungi, ut ministerium suum per gratiam sacramentalem diaconatus efficacius expleant." Tanner, 2:1026.

be realized. The Fathers' discussions concerning celibacy for deacons focused exclusively on celibacy understood narrowly as a prohibition on marriage after ordination and not on celibacy understood broadly as a prohibition on marriage after ordination and an obligation of "absolute continence" for those who were already married.

In 1964, as momentum to restore the diaconate as a permanent order increased, Alfons Cardinal Stickler, canonist and a *peritus* at the council, wrote an article in a leading Roman journal entitled "La continenza dei diaconi specialmente nel primo millennio della chiesa."[93] In it Stickler discussed the importance of understanding celibacy not only in the sense of prohibiting clerics from marrying but also in the sense of perfect (absolute) continence for those already married.[94] He examined ecclesiastical legislation and magisterial teaching from the fourth century and concluded that it was the uninterrupted tradition of the Church that all clergy in major orders-married or unmarried-were obliged to absolute continence.[95] In addition, Stickler asserted that to permit married deacons the use of their marriages would rupture the unity of the celibacy-continence obligation that had bound all grades of major clerics equally.[96] In other words, if an exception was going to be made for deacons

---

93   *Salesianum* 26 (1964) 275-302. Stickler also published several further articles all of which he argued that from the beginning continence was the fundamental norm for all major clergy, married or unmarried, and that this obliged all grades equally. See his articles "Tratti salenti nella storia del celibato," *Sacra Doctrina* 15 (1970) 585-620; "Historical Note on the Celibacy of Clerics in Major Orders," *Osservatore Romano*, March 19, 1970 and "The Evolution of the Discipline of Celibacy in the Western Church from the End of the Patristic Era to the Council of Trent," *Priesthood and Celibacy*, ed. Joseph Coppens et al. (Milan: Editrice Ancora Milano, 1972) 503-597.
94   Stickler, "La continenza dei diaconi specialmente nel primo millennio della chiesa," *Salesianum* 26 (1964) 301: "Attualita della questione non solo del celibate nel senso di divieto di sposarsi ma anche nel senso della Continenza perfetta per gli sposati precedentemente."
95   Ibid.
96   Ibid., 298: "Il trinomio costante che sin dall'inizio associa sempre vescovi, sacerdoti e diaconi quando si parla dell'obbligo della Continenza, è inoltre una delle prove più chiare, ma nella letteratura contemporanea meno avvertita, della motivazione spirituale di questo obbligo come inerente alla natura intrinseca di ogni ministero sacro."

then why continue to oblige priests and bishops? As we noted in chapter one, Stickler's conclusions and assertions are not shared by many scholars.[97]

From October 22-25, 1965, the first international congress on the diaconate was held in Rome. The congress discussed the theology of the diaconate, the formation of deacons, the mission of deacons today, deacons working in missionary countries, deacons in religious orders and deacons in Latin America.[98] The obligation of absolute continence for married deacons was not raised. The discussions instead focused again on celibacy as a prohibition not to marry.[99]

It was not until June 18, 1967 that norms governing the restoration of the diaconate were promulgated by Paul VI in his motu proprio *Sacrum diaconatus ordinem.*[100] Additional legislation was promulgated in the motu proprios *Ad pascendum*[101] and *Ministeria quaedam,*[102]August 15, 1972. These will be examined in more detail later in this chapter.

4. *Perfectae caritatis*: Decree on the Adaptation of Religious Life

The Decree on Religious Life, *Perfectae caritatis,* had as its primary goal the updating and renewal of religious life in the Church. It was a reaffirmation of the consecrated life and the evangelical counsels. According to *Lumen gentium,* all the baptized are called to perfection by embracing the evangelical counsels

---

97   See chapter one, 20-21.
98   The main contributions were published in *Le diacre dans l'Église et le Monde d'Aujourd'hui,* ed. Paul Winniger et al. (Paris: Éditions du Cerf, 1966) along with several essays from *Diaconia in Christo.*
99   See Karl Rahner, "L'enseignement de Vatican II sur le diaconat et sa restauration, " in *Le diacre dans l'Église,* 3: 228.
100   Paul VI, encyclical *Sacrum diaconatus ordinem,* June 18, 1967: *AAS* 59 (1967) 697-704. Hereafter *SDO.*
101   Paul VI, motu proprio *Ad pascendum,* August 15, 1972: *AAS* 64 (1972) 534-540. Hereafter *AP.*
102   Paul VI, motu proprio *Ministeria quaedam,* August 15, 1972: *AAS* 64 (1972) 529-534. Hereafter *MQ.*

of poverty, chastity and obedience, according to their vocation.[103] Among the baptized some are called to embrace these counsels in a more intense way.[104] These baptized are numbered among those who bear the name "religious."[105]

The decree's teaching on chastity, celibacy and continence is applicable not only to consecrated religious but also to secular clergy. Article 12 stated:

> The commitment to chastity accepted by religious 'for the sake of the kingdom of heaven' (Mt 19:12) is a remarkable gift of grace. It wonderfully frees the affections (1 Cor 7:32-35) for a more fervent love of God and all humanity. It is a special manifestation of divine favor and the authentic way by which religious commit themselves, ready for God's service and apostolic work. Religious chastity demonstrates to all Christians an astonishing alliance, initiated by God himself, to be completed in the world to come, when the church has Christ alone for her spouse.
>
> Religious must, therefore, strive to keep their vow intact by taking the teaching of Christ to heart: they must rely on the grace of God, in the practice of asceticism and restraint of sensuality, in doubt of their own strength of will. They must not despise the ordinary ways towards health of mind and body. They must reject the specious teaching that absolute continence is impossible, or at least inimical to human maturity; they must repudiate intuitively anything which threatens the chaste life. All religious, especially superiors, must believe that the community experience of truly personal regard is a great safeguard to chastity. The practice of absolute celibacy touches the deep, intimate longings of humankind. Aspirants, therefore, must neither take, nor be allowed to take, this vow without adequate preparation and the presence of both emotional maturity and psychological balance. They must not just be

---

103   See *LG* chapters 5 and 6.
104   *PC* 2.
105   Ibid.

Anthony McLaughlin

warned about threats to the chaste life, but led to integrate religious celibacy into the wholeness of a balanced personality.[106]

The Fathers repeated much of what has already been taught by the council in relation to celibacy, and they again specifically mention and connect chastity, continence and celibacy. Responding to psychological theories of the time that attacked celibacy/continence as unhealthy,[107] the decree stated that religious should be properly instructed to appreciate their celibacy as something that ultimately is beneficial to their whole personality.[108] This is a very important point and one that will be repeated in later documents. Chastity, absolute continence and celibacy, rather than harming the human person, can lead to a truly balanced life.

5. *Optatam totius:* Decree on the Formation of Priests

The council Fathers were particularly aware of the significance of the for-

---

106 *PC* 12, *AAS* 58 (1966) 707-708: "Castitas 'propter regnum caelorum' (Mt. 19 : 12), quam religiosi profitentur, tamquam eximium gratiae donum aestimanda est. Cor enim hominis singulari modo liberat (I Cor. 7 : 32-35), ut magis accendatur caritate erga Deum et homines universos, ideoque est peculiare signum bonorum caelestium necnon medium aptissimum quo religiosi alacriter servitio divino operibusque apostolatus sese dedicent. Sic ipsi coram omnibus Christifidelibus mirabile illud evocant connubium a Deo conditum et in futuro saeculo plene manifestandum quo Ecclesia unicum sponsum Christum habet. Oportet ergo ut religiosi, professionem suam fideliter servare studentes, verbis Domini credant et, Dei auxilio confisi, de propriis viribus ne praesumant, mortificationem sensuumque custodiam adhibeant. Media quoque naturalia ne omittant, quae mentis et corporis sanitati favent. Ita fit ut falsis doctrinis, quae continentiam perfectam tamquam impossibilem vel humano profectui nocivam ostentant, non moveantur, et omnia quae castitatem in periculum adducunt, instinctu quodam spirituali, respuant. Meminerint insuper omnes, praesertim Superiores, castitatem securius servari cum inter sodales vera dilectio fraterna in vita communi viget. Cum observantia continentiae perfectae profundiores naturae humanae inclinationes intime attingat, candidati ad professionem castitatis ne accedant neve admittantur, nisi post probationem vere sufficientem et cum debita maturitate psychologica et affectiva. Ipsi non solum de periculis castitati occurrentibus moneantur, sed ita instruantur ut coelibatum Deo dicatum etiam in bonum integrae personae assumant. " Tanner, 2:943.

107 James Knapp, *Celibate Chastity in the Life of the Priest in the Light of the Teaching of Karol Wojtyla/John Paul II.* S.T.D. dissertation. The Pontifical John Paul II Institute for Studies on Marriage and Family (Washington, DC: Catholic University of America, 1998) 134.

108 *PC* 12.

mation of priests for the renewal of the Church. In the introduction to the decree they stated:

> This Holy Synod is well aware that the desired renewal of the whole Church depends to a great extent on a priestly ministry animated with the spirit of Christ. It proclaims the supreme importance of priestly formation....[109]

Nearly four hundred years before, the Council of Trent had established the seminary system as the normative method for the formation of priests.[110] During the third session of the council on December 3, 1963, a ceremony was held in St. Peter's to mark the four hundredth anniversary of this decree.[111] Any reform of the formation of priests had to have this decree of Trent as its starting point.[112]

Optatam totius established general regulations regarding the preparation of candidates for the priesthood. Significant for the purposes of this study is article 10 of the decree where the Fathers decreed that all candidates for the priesthood should be adequately prepared to embrace the commitment of celibacy.

Although clerical celibacy was not one of the major themes of the council, "and even though not much was said officially on the subject, in all phases of the council it formed a topic for the most heated discussion."[113] At a press conference on April 17, 1961, Archbishop Felici stated that the question of celibacy

---

109   *OT* introduction, *AAS* 58 (1966) 713: "Optatam totius Ecclesiae renovationem probe noscens Sancta Synodus a sacerdotum ministerio, Christi spiritu animato, magna ex parte pendere gravissimum institutionis sacerdotalis momentum proclamat, eiusque primaria quaedam principia declarat...." Tanner, 2:947.

110   Council of Trent, session 23, July 15, 1563, *de sacramento ordinis,* c. 18. Tanner, 2:750.

111   Josef Neuner, "Decree of Priestly Formation," in Vorgrimler, 2: 371.

112   Ibid. See also the conclusion of this decree where the Fathers declared that they had finished the work begun by Trent. Tanner, 2:958-959.

113   See Friedrich Wulf, "Commentary on the Decree Presbyterorum ordinis," in Vorgrimler, 4: 279. Though Wulf makes this general observation concerning celibacy as part of his commentary on *Presbyterorum ordinis,* it holds true for the discussion of celibacy by the Fathers at all stages of the council.

would certainly not be discussed at the council.[114] Yet, during the council a series of public statements, exaggerated by the press, had revealed that a number of the Fathers were opposed to the continuance of the law of celibacy.[115] This coupled with the council's decision to admit married men to the diaconate, fueled public rumors that the Church was moving towards abolishing celibacy.[116] Precisely because of this, the council found itself having to address the issue in several documents.

On October 11, 1965, Paul VI intervened dramatically during voting on the final *schema* of *Optatam totius*. Cardinal Tisserant, dean of the praesidium of the council, read a letter to the Fathers from the pope in which he stated that it had come to his attention that some of the council Fathers intended to raise the question of the celibacy of Latin clergy for discussion on the council floor.[117] He declared that public debate on the matter was inopportune as the whole subject demanded profound prudence.[118] The pope made known his intention not simply to maintain the law of celibacy but to reinforce its observance for Latin priests. He stated:

> Not only to maintain this ancient, sacred and providential law, in so far
> as it falls to us to do so, but to strengthen its observance by remind-
> ing the priests of the Latin Church of the reasons and causes, for the
> supreme suitability of this law, to which priests owe their capacity to

---

114 Ibid., 4:280.

115 Mauro Velari, "Completing the Conciliar Agenda," in *History of Vatican II*, 4:231-232.

116 Ralph Wiltgen, *The Rhine Flows into the Tiber: The Unknown Council* (New York, NY: Hawthorn Books Inc., 1967) 262.

117 Letter of Paul VI to Cardinal Tisserant, October 10, 1965: "Certiores facti sumus, non-nullis Patribus Concilaribus id in animo esse, ut in proximis Concilii coetibus quaestionem de caelibatu clericorum Ecclesiae Latinae ponant, utrum scilicet lex illa servanda sit necne, quae caelibatum cum sacerdotio quodammodo coniungit." *AS* 4/1:40.

118 Ibid: "Nos in ea esse opinione, nequaquam expedire, publicam habere disceptationem circa rem, quae et tantum postulat prudentiam et tanti ponderis est." English translation from *Documentation Catholique* 47 (1965) 1461.

direct all their love to Christ and to devote themselves completely and magnanimously to the service of the Church and of souls.[119]

The pontiff also requested those Fathers who wished to express views on the subject to do so in writing, and these would be passed on to him for consideration. The intervention

of Paul VI effectively ended any debate regarding celibacy.[120] The pope promised to address priestly celibacy after the council's conclusion.[121]   \

In the light of the intervention of Paul VI, the Fathers voted overwhelming[122] to approve article 10 of *Optatam totius* which stated:

Students who follow the venerable tradition of priestly celibacy, according to the holy and firm rules of their own rite, must be diligently trained up to this state. In it they give up marriage for the sake of the kingdom (Mt. 19:12); they hold fast to the Lord with undivided love which is deeply in harmony with the new covenant; they bear witness to the resurrection in the world to come (Lk 20:36) and receive the best possible help to the lasting achievement of that perfect charity by which they can become all things to all people in the priestly ministry. They must become deeply convinced how eagerly that state ought to be undertaken, not just as laid down as ecclesiastical law, but as a precious gift to be sought from God with humility, a gift which

---

119   Ibid: "Itemque Nobis esse propositum, quantum in Nobis erit, non tamen huiusmodi legem antiquam, sacram, providamque servare, sed eius etiam corroborare observantiam, sacerdotes Ecclesiae Latinae ad conscientiam revocantes causarum rationque, quae hodie, immo hodie quam maxime, efficient, ut lex ipsa ab omnibus tamquam perapta significatio habeatur, et plene seipos Christo eiusque solius amori sacravisse." English translation from *Documentation Catholique* 47 (1965) 1461.

120   This was not the first time Paul VI had intervened at the council removing certain topics from discussion. He had done so in regard to mixed marriages, indulgences, forms of penance adapted to times, birth control, celibacy, the reform of the curia, the establishment of the episcopal synod, and other sensitive subjects. See Giacomo Lercaro, *Lettere dal concilio,* ed. Giuseppe Battelli (Bologna: Edizione Dehoniane Bologna, 1980) 346.

121   Letter of Paul VI to Cardinal Tisserant, October 10, 1965. *AS* 4/1:40.

122   See Neuner in Vorgrimler, 2:377. 1989 votes were cast, 1971 in favor, 16 against, 2 were invalid.

they must freely and generously respond to, with the inspiration and assistance of the grace of the Holy Spirit. Students should acquire a right understanding of the duties and dignity of Christian marriage, as representing the love between Christ and His Church (Eph 5:22-33). They should realize, however, the greater excellence of virginity consecrated to Christ, so that by maturely considered and magnanimous free choice they may consecrate themselves to the Lord by an entire dedication of body and mind.

They are to be warned of the dangers that their chastity will encounter especially in present day society. They should learn how, with suitable safeguards both human and divine, to integrate their giving up of marriage, so that their life and work will not only suffer no disadvantage from celibacy, but rather that they may acquire a deeper mastery of mind and body, grow in fuller maturity and receive more perfectly the blessedness promised in the gospel.[123]

This statement of the council went far beyond a merely juridical attitude to

---

123   *OT* 10, *AAS* 58 (1966) 719-720: "Alumni qui secundum proprii ritus sanctas firmasque leges venerandam coelibatus sacerdotalis traditionem sequuntur, diligenti cura educentur ad hunc statum, in quo societati coniugali propter regnum coelorum renuntiantes (Mat. 19: 12), Domino adhaerent amore indiviso novo Foederi intime congruente, futuri saeculi resurrectionis testimonium exhibent (Lk 20: 36) et aptissimum consequuntur auxilium ad eam perfectam caritatem continuo exercendam, qua in ministerio sacerdotali omnia omnibus fieri valeant. Alte persentiant quam grato animo ille status suscipi debeat non quidem solum ut lege ecclesiastica praeceptus, sed ut pretiosum donum Dei humiliter impetrandum, cui gratia Spiritus Sancti excitante et adiuvante, libere et generose respondere properent. Officia et dignitatem christiani matrimonii, quod amorem inter Christum et Ecclesiam repraesentat (Eph. 5: 22-33), alumni debite cognoscant; perspiciant autem virginitatis Christo consecratae praecellentiam, ita ut optione mature deliberata ac magnanimi, integra corporis et animi deditione Domino se devoveant. De periculis quae eorum castitati maxime in praesentis temporis societate occurrunt, moneantur; aptis praesidiis divinis humanisque adiuti, matrimonii renuntiationem ita integrare addiscant ut ipsorum vita et operositas ex coelibatu non modo ullum patiatur detrimentum, sed potius ipsi altius animi corporisque dominium pleniorisque maturitatis profectum acquirant atque Evangelii beatitudinem perfectius percipiant.Alumni qui secundum proprii ritus sanctas firmasque leges venerandam coelibatus sacerdotalis traditionem sequuntur, diligenti cura educentur ad hunc statum, in quo societati coniugali propter regnum coelorum renuntiantes, Domino adhaerent amore indiviso novo Foederi intime congruente, futuri saeculi resurrectionis testimonium exhibent et aptissimum consequuntur auxilium ad eam perfectam caritatem continuo exercendam, qua in ministerio sacerdotali omnia omnibus fieri valeant. Alte persentiant quam grato animo ille status suscipi debeat non quidem solum ut lege ecclesiastica praeceptus, sed ut pretiosum donum Dei humiliter impetrandum, cui gratia Spiritus Sancti excitante et adiuvante, libere et generose respondere properent." Tanner, 2:953.

celibacy as a prerequisite for priestly ordination or a prohibition of marriage. While the council affirmed the connection between celibacy and the preparation for ordination, the commitment of celibacy is presented positively as a free, mature choice, the setting aside of one 'good' and the embracing of another 'good.' The vocation to celibacy is a grace and as such must be sought, gratefully received and freely and generously made one's own.[124]

The core of article 10 is the eschatological nature of celibacy. Celibacy is to be embraced "for the sake of the kingdom." It is a sign of how we shall all live our eternity where there will be no-one given or taken in marriage.[125] The celibate state is a call to love God and neighbor in a most radical and singular way. Following these fundamental considerations the Fathers offered practical directives for those preparing for this commitment. Seminarians are to understand that the value of celibacy is never found in the devaluation of marriage. They are to have a deep appreciation for marriage. Yet they must also know of the greater excellence of virginity consecrated to Christ.[126] There also needs to be a realistic understanding of the challenges to such a commitment. It is most important that celibacy be integrated into the priest's personality and activity. All issues in this regard need to be worked out so that celibacy will not lead to an impoverishment of the person but to full maturity.

6. *Presbyterorum ordinis:* Decree on the Ministry and Life of Priests

The decree *Presbyterorum ordinis* had its roots in the questionnaire sent to all the bishops by John XXIII immediately after he announced his decision to

---

124   See Neuner in Vorgrimler, 2:389.
125   *NAB,* Mt 22:29-30.
126   Pius XII in *Sacra virginitas,* article 32, *AAS* 46 (1954) 174. He also stated that virginity and celibacy are superior to marriage.

convoke a council on January 25, 1959.[127] The responses revealed a common concern among the bishops for the spiritual life of the clergy and the fruitfulness of their ministry.[128] It has also been asserted that this decree is a consequence of the inadequate treatment of the ministerial priesthood in *Lumen gentium* and the desire of the bishops that a fuller treatment be given to the topic.[129] Several years after the council, Father Joseph Ratzinger, who had been a peritus at the council, wrote the following concerning the emphasis of this decree:

> The emphasis of the entire document is clearly on the second chapter, on the question of the true nature of the priestly office. The prime concern of the first chapter is to situate the question within the total pattern of Christology and theology. The fundamental proposition here states that the origin of priestly office is to be found in the mystery of Easter, that the meaning of the priesthood can be grasped only in unity with the Christian realities in the light of this central mystery.[130]

Again in *Presbyterorum ordinis* the Church's commitment to celibacy was affirmed and expounded upon after considerable discussion. The first section of article 16 states:

> The perfect and perpetual continence for the sake of the kingdom of heaven that was commended by Christ the Lord (Mt 19:12), has been willingly freely accepted and admirably observed by many of the faithful throughout the ages, as in our own day. It has always been held of the greatest value in the Church in a special way for the priestly life: it is at once a sign of and a stimulus for pastoral love and a special source

---

127 Joseph Lécuyer, "Decree on the Ministry and Life of Priests: History of the Decree," in Vorgrimler, 4:183.

128 See *ADA* 2/1: 255-335.

129 Richard Gaillardetz, *The Church in the Making* (New York/Mahwah, NJ Paulist Press, 2006) 181-183.

130 Joseph Ratzinger, "Priestly Ministry: A Search for its Meaning," *Emmanuel* 76 (1970) 490.

of spiritual fruitfulness in the world. It is not of course required by the very nature of priesthood, as is clear from the practice of the early church and the tradition of the eastern churches: in these there are admirable married priests side by side with those who, together with all the bishops, have the grace of choosing to observe celibacy. This synod, while commending ecclesiastical celibacy, has no intention of changing that different discipline which lawfully flourishes in eastern churches, and in a loving spirit exhorts all who have received the priesthood in the married state to persevere in their holy vocation, and continue to spend themselves fully and freely on the flock entrusted to them.[131]

In this section the Fathers repeat much of what had been stated in earlier conciliar documents, (e.g., *Lumen gentium* 42; *Perfectae caritatis* 12 and *Optatam totius* 10) concerning celibacy, namely that celibacy is recommended by the Lord, that it is a sign and stimulus for pastoral love and that it is to be embraced willingly for the sake of the kingdom of heaven. Rather than focus on celibacy as a purely legal obligation the council continued to focus on celibacy for the sake of the kingdom. As Wulf observes:

> The article proceeds from the assumption that celibacy is fulfilled not in the realization, however honorable and perfect, of an ecclesiastical precept, but signifies that gift of grace mentioned in Mt 19:11f. and 1 Cor 7:25f. It presumes the knowledge that this celibacy, for the sake

---

131   *PO* 16, *AAS 58* (1966) 1015: "Perfecta et perpetua propter Regnum coelorum continentia a Christo Domino commendata, per decursum temporum et etiam nostris diebus a non paucis christifidelibus libenter accepta et laudabiliter observata, ab Ecclesia speciali modo pro vita sacerdotali semper permagni habita est. Est enim signum simul et stimulus caritatis pastoralis atque peculiaris fons spiritualis foecunditatis in mundo. Non exigitur quidem a sacerdotio suapte natura, uti apparet ex praxi Ecclesiae primaevae et ex traditione Ecclesiarum Orientalium, ubi praeter illos qui cum omnibus Episcopis ex dono gratiae coelibatum eligunt servandum, sunt etiam optime meriti Presbyteri coniugati: dum vero ecclesiasticum coelibatum commendat, Sacrosancta haec Synodus nullo modo absimilem illam disciplinam immutare intendit, quae in Orientalibus Ecclesiis legitime viget, omnesque illos peramanter hortatur, qui in matrimonio presbyteratum receperunt, ut, in sancta vocatione perseverantes, plene et generose vitam suam gregi sibi commisso impendere pergant." Tanner, 2:1062. *PO* 16 is listed among the sources for canon 277 §1 of the 1983 Code.

of the kingdom of heaven, has been mostly highly esteemed in the Church since the earliest times and that it has found its deepest basis in spiritual experience.[132]

Celibacy cannot be fully explained purely theoretically. In the end it is a matter of faith and spiritual experience, otherwise it cannot be fully lived out. This article is unique in the statement by the Fathers that celibacy is not demanded by the nature of priesthood.[133]

Reference is made to the practice of married clergy both in the early Church and in the Eastern Churches as testimony to this truth. Yet the Fathers did not offer a definition of what is meant by the *nature* of the priesthood. All that is said of priestly ministry is that there is no essential incompatibility between priesthood and marriage. The article further confirmed the practice that a married man may indeed be ordained, but that a ordained man could not marry. Nothing further was said about the lifestyle of married priests, and the entire article focused primarily on celibate priests. The accent seems to be placed upon the fact that 'this synod' recommends celibacy while acknowledging the contribution of "admirable married priests."[134] According to the council there seems to be something more appropriate about priesthood and celibacy than priesthood and marriage. Article 16 continues:

> Celibacy is in very many ways appropriate to the priesthood. For the whole mission of the priest is a dedication to the service of the new humanity, which Christ who triumphed over death brings into being in the world by his Spirit, and draws its origin "not of blood nor of the will of the flesh nor of the will of man, but of God" (Jn 1:13). Through virginity or celibacy persevered for the sake of the kingdom of heaven, priests

---

132 Wulf in Vorgrimler, 4:283.
133 In light of the research offered in chapter one in relation to celibacy understood in terms of the *lex continentiae,* this statement by the Fathers invites the question: "While celibacy is not demanded by the nature of priesthood, is continence?"
134 Schmaus in Vorgrimler, 4: 285.

are consecrated to Christ in a new and exalted manner, and more easily cleave to him with singleness of heart; in him and through him they devote themselves with greater freedom to the service of God and people; they are more untrammeled in serving his kingdom and his work of heavenly regeneration; and thus they are more equipped to accept a wider fatherhood in Christ. By this state they make an open profession to people that they desire to devote themselves with undivided loyalty to the task entrusted to them, namely to betroth the faithful to one husband and present them as a pure bride to Christ, and so they appeal to that mysterious marriage, brought into being by God and to be openly revealed in time to come, in which the Church has Christ as her only husband. They become, indeed, a living sign that the world to come, in which the children of the resurrection will neither marry nor be given in marriage is already present among us through faith and love.[135]

Even though celibacy is not demanded by the nature of priesthood, the council spoke of the interconnectedness of celibacy and priesthood. The council offered theological and spiritual reasons for the appropriateness of priestly celibacy as Wulf observes:

Celibacy and priesthood are both connected with *mission* and with a special *consecration* of the priest. First in respect of mission, the priest is entrusted with a ministry of supernatural life, of the redemption of men,

---

135 *PO* 16, *AAS 58* (1966) 1015-1016: "Coelibatus vero multimodam convenientiam cum sacerdotio habet. Missio enim sacerdotis integra dedicatur servitio novae humanitatis, quam Christus, victor mortis, per Spiritum suum in mundo suscitat, quaeque originem suam «non ex sanguinibus, neque ex voluntate carnis, neque ex voluntate viri, sed ex Deo habet. Per virginitatem autem vel coelibatum propter Regnum coelorum servatum, Presbyteri nova et eximia ratione Christo consecrantur, Ei facilius indiviso corde adhaerent, liberius in Ipso et per Ipsum servitio Dei et hominum sese dedicant, Eius Regno ac operi regenerationis supernae expeditius ministrant, et sic aptiores fiunt qui paternitatem in Christo latius accipiant. Hoc ergo modo, coram hominibus profitentur se velle indivise muneri sibi commisso dedicari, fideles scilicet despondendi uni viro, illosque exhibendi virginem castam Christo, et sic arcanum illud evocant connubium a Deo conditum et in futuro plene manifestandum quo Ecclesia unicum Sponsum Christum habet. Signum insuper vivum efficiuntur illius mundi futuri, per fidem et caritatem iam praesentis, in quo filii resurrectionis neque nubent neque ducent uxores." Tanner, 2:1062-1063.

the originator and mediator of which Christ is, who through the spirit, becomes operative in men. Therefore it is fitting that he should have no family of his own. Second in respect of consecration, what is meant here is not the sacramental consecration arising from holy orders but that connected with the vow of celibacy for the sake of Jesus and his gospel.[136]

As in previous conciliar decrees, the Fathers again spoke of celibacy as an "eschatological sign." Celibacy points to the reality of life with Christ in eternity, when we will not be taken or given in marriage and the Lord will be our only spouse. This section followed very closely the arguments from Pope Pius XII's exhortation on the subject of priestly chastity, *Menti Nostrae*.[137] Commenting on the betrothal language of this section, James Knapp observes:

His work is to betroth/espouse the people of God to one spouse, Jesus Christ. The priest's own celibacy is a sign of his single-hearted dedication to his mission. As we have seen, Paul's principle of "unius uxoris vir' in the Pastoral Epistles was the basis for a later use of spousal imagery to describe the bond of a bishop and his diocese, and a motive for continence of married priests as well. Since the cleric is "married" to the Church, his relations with his earthly wife cease.[138]

Article 16 concludes:

For these reasons which are rooted in the mystery of Christ and his mission, celibacy was at first commended to priests, and was later imposed by law in the Latin Church on all who were to be advanced to holy orders. As regards those destined for the priesthood, this synod once more approves and confirms that law, trusting to the Spirit that gift of

---

136   Wulf in Vorgrimler, 4:285. Also, on the 'consecration' that comes through vowing the evangelical counsels see *LG* 44 and *PC* 5.

137   Pius XII, apostolic exhortation *Menti nostrae,* September 23, 1950: *AAS 42* (1950) 663.

138   Knapp, *Celibate Chastity in the Life of the Priest in the Light of the Teaching of Karol Wojtyla/John Paul II,* 136.

celibacy, so fitting as it is to the priesthood of the new covenant, will be generously given by the Father, as long as those who share in the priesthood of Christ by the sacrament of order, and indeed the whole church, humbly and earnestly ask for it. Further the synod exhorts all priests, who in reliance on God's grace have freely accepted celibacy after the example of Christ, to hold to it with greatness and fullness of spirit, to persevere faithfully in this state, to acknowledge the outstanding gift given them by the Father and so openly extolled by the Lord, and keep ever in mind the great mysteries that are symbolized and fulfilled in it. The more that perfect continence is regarded as impossible by many people in today's world, the more will priests together with the church humbly and perseveringly beg for the grace of fidelity, never denied to those who ask, while at the same time they avail themselves of all the readily accessible supports, both natural and supernatural. In particular, they should not fail to observe the rules of ascetical practice which have been tested by the experience of the church, and which are no less necessary in the modern world. The synod asks not only priests but all the faithful to cherish this precious gift of priestly celibacy, and to beg of God that he will ever lavishly bestow it upon his church.[139]

---

139 *PO* 16, *AAS* 58 (1966) 1016-1017: "His rationibus in mysterio Christi Eiusque missione fundatis, coelibatus, qui prius sacerdotibus commendabatur, postea in Ecclesia Latina omnibus ad Ordinem sacrum promovendis lege impositus est. Quam legislationem, ad eos qui ad Presbyteratum destinantur quod attinet, Sacrosancta haec Synodus iterum comprobat et confirmat, confidens in Spiritu donum coelibatus, sacerdotio Novi Testamenti tam congruum, liberaliter a Patre dari, dummodo qui sacerdotium Christi per Sacramentum Ordinis participant, immo et universa Ecclesia, humiliter et enixe illud expetant. Exhortatur etiam haec Sacra Synodus omnes Presbyteros, qui sacrum coelibatum gratia Dei confisi libera voluntate secundum exemplum Christi acceperunt ut, illi magno animo et toto corde inhaerentes, atque in hoc statu fideliter perseverantes, agnoscant praeclarum illud donum, quod a Patre sibi datum est quodque a Domino tam aperte extollitur, necnon prae oculis habeant magna mysteria, quae in eo significantur atque adimplentur. Quo magis autem perfecta continentia in mundo huius temporis a non paucis hominibus impossibilis reputatur, eo humilius et perseverantius Presbyteri gratiam fidelitatis, numquam petentibus denegatam, una cum Ecclesia expostulabunt, cuncta subsidia supernaturalia et naturalia insimul adhibentes, quae omnibus praesto sunt. Normas praesertim asceticas quae ab experientia Ecclesiae probantur et quae in mundo hodierno haud minus necessariae sunt, sequi ne omittant. Rogat itaque haec Sacrosancta Synodus non solum sacerdotes, sed et omnes fideles, ut eis hoc pretiosum donum coelibatus sacerdotalis cordi sit, petantque omnes a Deo, ut Ipse illud donum Ecclesiae suae semper abundanter largiatur." Tanner, 2:1063.

The decisive part of this article is this third and last section of article 16. The teaching of *Lumen gentium* 42 and *Optatam totius* 10 is repeated concerning celibacy as a "gift" and an "eschatological sign." Unique to this section, however, is the Fathers' answer to the long posed question, "If celibacy is a 'gift,' a special 'grace,' how can it be made obligatory?"

The answer was as simple as it was profound. The Fathers believed that God the Father would freely grant the gift of celibacy to those called to the priesthood if they and the people would urgently pray for it. The reason for this belief is also given. As Michael Schmaus observes:

> Celibacy is so appropriate to the priesthood of the New Covenant and is so consonant with Christ's priesthood that God will not deny to those whom he calls to the priesthood, this other grace also.[140]

Later in his encyclical *Sacerdotalis caelibatus* Paul VI would continue to affirm the appropriateness of celibacy for the priesthood.[141]

The council Fathers encouraged all those who have accepted the call to celibacy to live that call more faithfully, and urged the faithful to respect this calling and to pray that God would continue to pour this gift upon his Church. As can be seen in these conciliar documents, *Lumen gentium, Perfectae caritatis, Optatam totius* and *Presbyterorum ordinis,* the Latin Church continued to affirm the necessity of celibacy for priests and unmarried deacons while admitting the possibility of ordaining married men to the diaconate. While it was clear that celibacy was not demanded by the nature of priesthood, was continence?

---

140   Schmaus in Vorgrimler, 4:287.
141   Paul VI, encyclical *Sacerdotalis caelibatus* 14-15, June 24, 1967: *AAS* 59 (1967) 662-663. Hereafter *SCa.*

7. The Relation of Sexuality and Marriage to Holy Orders.

Previous chapters have spoken in detail concerning the ordination of married men to major orders in the Latin Church and the corresponding obligation that the cleric and his wife surrender the "use of their marriage" by committing themselves to absolute continence from the moment of ordination. The fundamental norm for all those in ordained ministry was absolute continence whether they were married, unmarried or widowed. This was the common practice of the Latin Church from the Council of Elvira in the fourth century up to the 1917 code. Admittedly the trend to ordain married men declined. Since the Council of Trent and the introduction of the seminary system that encouraged younger unmarried candidates, the Latin Church began to ordain unmarried men almost exclusively.

In *Lumen gentium* and *Ad gentes* the council stated that the diaconate as a permanent order could be restored in the future with the option of admitting married men to this order. There was no mention of the obligation of absolute continence or a prohibition on marriage after ordination. Alongside this willingness to admit married men to the diaconate the council also declared that unmarried candidates to the diaconate would be obliged to celibacy, and that priestly celibacy would remain the norm. The Fathers declared that virginity and celibacy were "outstanding among the counsels."[142] In *Perfectae caritatis,* chastity for the sake of the kingdom was described as "a remarkable gift of grace."[143] In *Optatam totius* marriage was to be given up for the sake of the kingdom.[144] In *Presbyterorum ordinis* virginity and celibacy were described as having "greater excellence" and being "most appropriate to the priesthood and always held in

---

142   See *LG* 29 and 42.
143   See *PC* 12.
144   See *OT* 10.

esteem."[145] While the Fathers stated that celibacy is not demanded by the nature of priesthood, they also stated that celibacy is appropriate to the priesthood.[146]

With the restoration of the permanent diaconate and the admission of married men to this order, the question remains whether such men were still bound to observe absolute continence. Now we must weigh this long standing practice of the Church with the conciliar teachings on marriage and sexuality.

8. The Notion of Conjugal Relations and Marriage Prior to the Council

Many commentators argue that in the light of the Second Vatican Council's teaching on conjugal relations and marriage that to oblige a married man to observe absolute continence, as a condition for ordination, is tautological. It offends against the rights and obligations of the spouses and may even offend against the nature of marriage itself.[147] It is therefore important for this study that we examine the Church's teaching concerning conjugal relations and marriage both before and after the council to discern whether the obligation of continence can be obliged of a married cleric for major orders.

Prior to the council the Church's teaching on marriage, while acknowledging the importance of the personal aspects and values of marriage, continued to emphasize the primacy of procreation.[148] The 1917 code understood the primary end of marriage to be the procreation and education of children, and the second-

---

145   See *PO* 16.
146   Ibid.
147   See for example, James H. Provost, "Permanent Deacons in the 1983 Code," *CLSA Proceedings* 46 (1985) 186; Joseph H. Pokusa, "The Diaconate: A History of Law Following Practice," *The Jurist* 45 (1985) 125-126 and *A Canonical-Historical Study of the Diaconate in the Western Church,* Canon Law Studies 495 (Washington, DC: Catholic University of America, 1979); Robert M. Garrity, "Spiritual and Canonical Values in Mandatory Priestly Celibacy," *Studia canonica* 27 (1993) 241.
148   David E. Fellhauer, "The *Consortium Omnis Vitae* as a Juridical Element in Marriage," *Studia canonica* 13 (1979) 82-83.

ary end to be mutual assistance and the allaying of concupiscence.[149] Therefore, marriage consisted basically in the giving and receiving of the *ius in corpus*.[150]

In the 1920's and 1930's some German theologians challenged the Church to come to a broader understanding of the nature of marriage.[151] Principle among them were Dietrich von Hildebrand, who taught that marriage was a community of love[152] and Herbert Doms, who taught that marriage was a community of life.[153] Yet Pius XI in *Casti connubii*[154] reaffirmed the teaching of the code concerning the primary and secondary ends of marriage. He stated that the primary blessing of marriage was the procreation of children and that the education of children completed this first blessing.[155] The pope also praised the role of marital love and declared conjugal love to be among the secondary ends of marriage.[156]

Subsequently, Pope Pius XII in an address to the Roman Rota on October 31, 1941,[157] stated that the primary purpose of marriage was procreation. He also stated that, though the secondary end was subordinate to the primary end, it must not be disregarded.[158] Again in various addresses to newlyweds in 1942,

---

149   See 17 *CIC*, cc. 1013 §1; 1081 §2; 1082 § 1 and 1086 §2. Commentators on the code held that procreation was the primary end of marriage. See Pio Fedele, "Ancora sulla definizione del matrimonio in diritto canonico," *Ephemerides Iuris Canonici* 33 (1977) 54; Pietro Gasparri, *Tractatus Canonicus de Matrimonio* (Vatican City: Typis Polyglottis Vaticanis, 1932) 2:15-16; Felix M. Cappello, *Tracatus Canonico-Moralis de Sacramentis* (Rome: Marietti, 1939) 3:1, 6; Francis X. Wernz and Petri Vidal, *Ius Canonicum* (Rome: Universitas Gregoriana, 1946) 4:43-44.

150   John Anthony Renken, *The Contemporary Understanding of Marriage: An Historico-Critical Study of Gaudium et spes, 47-52, and its Influence Upon the Revision of the Codex Iuris Canonici.* JCD Dissertation. (Rome: Pontifical University of St. Thomas, 1981) 41.

151   See William Roberts, "Christian Marriage," in *From Trent to Vatican II: Historical and Theological Investigations,* ed. Raymond F. Bulman et al., 210.

152   See Dietrich von Hildebrand, *Die Ehe* (München: Ars Sacra, 1929).

153   See Herbert Doms, *Vom Sinn und der Ehe* (Breslau: Ostdeutsche Verlagsanstalt, 1935).

154   Pius XI, encyclical *Cast connubii,* December 31, 1930: *AAS* 22 (1930) 539-592. Hereafter *CC.*

155   *CC* 543-546.

156   Ibid., 561. See also John C. Ford, "Marriage: Its Meaning and Purposes," *Theological Studies* 3 (1942) 372.

157   Pius XII, allocution to Roman Rota, *Gia per la terza volta,* October 31, 1941: *AAS* 33 (1941) 421-426. Hereafter *Gia* .

158   *Gia* 423.

Pius XII reiterated that the essential and primary end of marriage was procreation.[159] Throughout his pontificate, Pius XII continued to place emphasis on procreation as the primary end of marriage. Yet the pontiff also consistently emphasized the importance of the personal aspects of marriage in relation to the primary end although these personal aspects of marriage had practically no juridic value.[160] Concerning the magisterium of Pius XII in the area of marriage, Theodore Mackin observes:

> No magisterial voice in the history of the Church can compare with that of Pius XII in its abundance of statements about marriage and about the family, despite his never writing an encyclical on the subject.[161]

In January 1944, a rotal decision *coram* Wynen stressed the personal values of marriage.[162] Yet these personal values remained subordinate to the primary end of marriage which was procreation. Following this rotal decision on April 1, 1944, the Sacred Congregation of the Holy Office issued a decree condemning those who argued for a broader understanding of the ends of marriage:[163]

> Question: Whether the opinion of certain modern writers can be admitted, who either deny that the primary end of marriage is the generation of children, or teach that the secondary ends are not essentially subordinate to the primary end, but are equally principle and independent.

---

159   Pius XII, address to newlyweds, *Un giogo,* March 18, 1942. In *Discorsi e Radiomessagi de Sua Santità Pio XII* (Vatican City: Tipografia Poliglotta Vaticana, 1955-1959) 4 (1942-1943) 5. Hereafter Discorsi. Also address to newlyweds, *A un alto concetti,* April 22, 1942. Discorsi, 4 (1942-1943) 46.

160   Renken, *Contemporary Understanding of Marriage,* 42-43.

161   Theodore Mackin, "Conjugal Love in the Magisterium," *The Jurist* 36 (1976) 275.

162   *Coram* Wynen, January 22, 1944. In *Sacrae Romanae Rotae decisiones seu sententiae* 36 (1944) 55-79. Hereafter *RRDec.* This decision also appeared in *AAS* 36 (1944) 179-200.

163   See Fellhauer, "The *Consortium Omnis Vitae* as a Juridical Element in Marriage," 93. Fellhauer believes that this decree was directed primarily against Herbert Doms.

Reply: In the negative.[164]

According to Francis J. Connell, the answer given by the sacred congregation in this decree was definitive:

> The direct and absolute form in which this decision was rendered is worthy of note....As far as the Holy Office is concerned, the question is settled definitively and conclusively. The primary end of marriage is the procreation and education of children; no other end is of equal importance with this or of greater importance, nor are the other ends independent of this primary end of conjugal union.[165]

Yet in spite of this decree, Mackin, insists that "personalists" such as Von Hildebrand and Doms did accept the traditional teaching of the Church on the hierarchy of ends in marriage. He states:

> They did not counter claim, as the Church's Congregation of the Holy Office protested when condemning their thesis in 1944, that procreation and nurture are not the primary ends of marriage, but its secondary or even lesser end. Indeed, they accepted the traditional hierarchy of ends in marriage. What they did claim was that marriage is not to be understood primarily according to its ends, that is ends are not its first intelligible element. Marriage is not an instrument reality, they insisted. It is not for anyone or anything outside itself.[166]

The teaching of the Church concerning the primacy of procreation and the

---

164   Sacred Congregation of the Holy Office, decree *De finibus matrimonii,* April 1, 1944: *AAS* 36 (1944) 103: "Proposito sibi dubio: An admitti possit quorumdam recentiorum sententia, qui vel negant finem primarium matrimonii esse prolis generationem et educationem, vel docent fines secundarios fini primario non esse essentialiter subordinatos, sed esse aeque principales et independens. Respondentum decreverunt: Negative." English translation from *CLD* 3:401-402. Hereafter *CLD.*

165   Francis J. Connell, "The Catholic Doctrine of the Ends of Marriage," in *The Catholic Theological Society of America: Proceedings of the Foundation Meeting* (New York, NY: The Catholic Theological Society of America, 1946) 34-35.

166   Theodore Mackin, *The Marital Sacrament* (New York: Paulist Press, 1989) 598. See also Roberts, "Christian Marriage," 212.

subordination of the secondary ends of marriage such as love and personal values remained the predominant teaching of the Church up until the council.[167]

9. The Dignity of Marriage and Family: *Gaudium et spes*

The pastoral constitution on the Church in the modern world, *Gaudium et
spes,* makes no mention of priestly celibacy or the permanent diaconate. Yet, it
is significant to our study primarily because of its teaching concerning marriage
and sexuality.

With the restoration of the permanent diaconate and the admission of married men to this order, it is important to place the conciliar teaching on the permanent diaconate alongside its teaching on the nature of marriage, the primacy
of procreation and the compatibility of marriage and holy orders. This is all the
more necessary when one considers that for much of the Latin Church's history
married men were ordinarily only admitted to orders on condition that conjugal
life cease.

Gaudium et spes is primarily concerned with how the Church relates to the
modern world. Indeed the council Fathers declare their audience to be all humanity, believer and non-believer:

...the Second Vatican Council now immediately addresses itself not just
to the church's own daughters and sons and all who call on the name
of Christ but to people everywhere, in its desire to explain to all how it
understands the church's presence and activity in today's world.[168]

The nature of Christian marriage is treated in part one of chapter two of

---

167   Renken, *Contemporary Understanding of Marriage,* 43.
168   *GS* 2, *AAS* 58 (1966) 1026: "...iam non ad solos Ecclesiae filios omnesque Christi nomen invocantes, sed ad universos homines incunctanter sermonem convertit, omnibus expone-
re cupiens quomodo Ecclesiae praesentiam ac navitatem in mundo hodierno concipiat." Tanner,
2:1069.

The Obligation of Perfect and Perpetual Continence

Gaudium et spes under the title, "The Dignity of Marriage and the Family," articles 48-52. This entire section falls under the general rubric of "Urgent Problems." As the Fathers stated:

> Having outlined the dignity of the human person and the individual and social task which he and she is called to fulfill in the world as a whole, the council now draws attention in the light of the gospel and of human experience to certain urgent contemporary needs which particularly affect human race.[169]

Any teaching on marriage and human sexuality must be understood in the light of the council's teaching on the dignity of the human person. The chapter continued with a statement of purpose:

> Accordingly, by highlighting some major features of the church's teaching, the council aims to enlighten and encourage Christians and all people who are working for the protection and fostering of the inherent dignity and the noble and sacred significance of the state of matrimony.[170]

Much time and effort was spent by the council Fathers discussing how the Church's teaching on marriage should be presented in *Gaudium et spes*.[171] Some of the Fathers believed that marriage should be presented with a particular emphasis on its "procreative" dimension, others, that marriage should presented in a more "personalistic" way with particular emphasis on the role of love in marriage.[172]

---

169 *GS* 46, *AAS* 58 (1966) 1066: "Concilium, postquam exposuit cuiusnam dignitatis sit persona hominis necnon ad quodnam munus, sive individuale sive sociale, in universo mundo adimplendum sit vocata, sub luce Evangelii et humanae experientiae omnium nunc animos ad quasdam urgentiores huius temporis necessitates convertit, quae maxime genus humanum afficiunt." Tanner, 2:1099-1100.

170 *GS* 47, *AAS* 58 (1966) 1067: "Quapropter Concilium, quaedam doctrinae Ecclesiae capita in clariorem lucem ponendo, christianos hominesque universos illuminare et confortare intendit, qui nativam status matrimonialis dignitatem eiusque eximium valorem sacrum tueri et promovere conantur." Tanner, 2:1100.

171 Renken, *The Contemporary Understanding of Marriage,* 1.

172 Ibid.

Gaudium et spes contains no formal definition of marriage,[173] and yet the Fathers clearly sought to present a fresh description of marriage.[174] The pre-conciliar tendency was to define marriage in terms of its "ends," the primary end being the procreation and education of children and the secondary end being the couple's mutual help and the allaying of concupiscence. The council chose not to use hierarchical terminology in regard to the purpose or ends of marriage. It also moved away from the negative definition that had reduced sexual relations in marriage to an "allaying of concupiscence." Instead the Fathers chose to place marriage within the much broader framework of "an intimate partnership of life and love."[175]

The main teaching of *Gaudium et spes* on the nature of marriage can be summarized as follows: Marriage is an intimate partnership of life and love between a man and a woman. It has its origins in the will of God and was raised to the dignity of a sacrament between the baptized by Christ the Lord. Marriage is brought into existence by the free consent of the spouses and its nature is an indissoluble covenant. Marriage is a vocation and a means of holiness. Sexual intimacy is proper to marriage. The fruit of sexual relations gives rise to family which is described as the domestic church.[176]

At this point, it must be stated that it is beyond the scope of this book to examine every aspect of the council's teaching on marriage. This work is particularly oriented towards the question of absolute continence for married clerics within their marriage. Therefore we will focus on the council's teaching concerning the role of sexual relations in marriage. This is important as some maintain that it is a tautology to bind married clerics to absolute continence, because

---

173   Theodore Mackin, *What is Marriage?* (New York, NY: Paulist Press, 1982) 15.
174   Ibid.
175   *GS* 48, *AAS* 58 (1966) 1067: "Intima communitas vitae et amoris coniugalis...." Tanner 2: 1100.
176   Roberts, "Christian Marriage," 212-217.

in some way continence offends against the nature of marriage and therefore cannot and should not be imposed.[177]

Concerning sexual relations within marriage the council stated:

This devoted love finds its unique expression and development in the behavior which is proper to marriage. The acts by which married couples are intimately and chastely united are honorable and respectable, and when they are carried out in a truly human way they express and encourage a mutual giving in which a couple gladly and gratefully enrich each other.[178]

The council reaffirmed that marriage and marital love are by nature ordered to the procreation and education of children:

Of their nature marriage and married love are directed towards the begetting and bringing up of children. Children are the supreme good of marriage and they contribute greatly to the good of their parents.... Thus the practice of marital love and the whole dimension of family life which results from it, without prejudice to the other purposes of marriage, point towards married couples being courageously prepared to cooperate with love of the creator and savior who is daily increasing and enriching his family through them.[179]

The council is careful to situate the procreation and education of children in the context of the total meaning of marriage:

177 See footnote 143.

178 *GS* 49, *AAS* 58 (1966) 1070: "Haec dilectio proprio matrimonii opere singulariter exprimitur et perficitur. Actus proinde, quibus coniuges intime et caste inter se uniuntur, honesti ac digni sunt et, modo vere humano exerciti, donationem mutuam significant et fovent, qua sese invicem laeto gratoque animo locupletant." Tanner, 2:1102.

179 *GS* 50, *AAS* 58 (1966) 1070-1071: "Matrimonium et amor coniugalis indole sua ad prolem procreandam et educandam ordinantur. Filii sane sunt praestantissimum matrimonii donum et ad ipsorum parentum bonum maxime conferunt.... Unde verus amoris coniugalis cultus totaque vitae familiaris ratio inde oriens, non posthabitis ceteris matrimonii finibus, eo tendunt ut coniuges forti animo dispositi sint ad cooperandum cum amore Creatoris atque Salvatoris, qui per eos Suam familiam in dies dilatat et ditat." Tanner, 2:1103.

Marriage, however, was not instituted just for procreation; the very nature of an unbreakable covenant between persons and the good of the children also demand that the mutual love of the partners should be rightly expressed and should develop and mature. And therefore even if children, often longed for, are not forthcoming, marriage remains as a sharing and communion for the whole of life and retains its goodness and indissolubility.[180]

It is obvious that sexual relations are proper to marriage and that they are oriented towards the procreation of children. Prior to the Second Vatican Council, though a personalist approach to marriage was not primary, it was not entirely absent either.[181] Nonetheless, since the fourth century the Latin Church felt free to oblige a married man who was ordained to major orders, with the consent of his wife, to observe absolute continence.

B. Paul VI and Post-Conciliar Teaching on Celibacy

1. *Sacrum Diaconatus Ordinem:* Norms Governing the Restoration of the Permanent Diaconate

In the Dogmatic Constitution on the Church, *Lumen gentium,* the council stated that "the diaconate can in the future be restored as a proper and permanent rank in the hierarchy."[182] To implement this restoration it was necessary to establish certain norms and guidelines. This was indeed a daunting task because the diaconate as a fuller and permanent order had not existed in the Church for

---

180   *GS* 50, *AAS* 58 (1966) 1071-1072: "Matrimonium vero, non est tantum ad procreationem institutum; sed ipsa indoles foederis inter personas indissolubilis atque bonum prolis exigunt, ut mutuus etiam coniugum amor recto ordine exhibeatur, proficiat et maturescat. Ideo etsi proles, saepius tam optata, deficit, matrimonium ut totius vitae consuetudo et communio perseverat, suumque valorem atque indissolubilitatem servat." Tanner, 2:1103.

181   *Gia* 423. See also David E. Fellhauer, "The *Consortium Omnis Vitae* as a Juridical Element in Marriage," *Studia canonica* 13 (1979) 82-83.

182   *LG* 29, *AAS* 57 (1965) 36: "....diaconatus in futuram tamquam proprius ac permanens gradus hierarchiae restitui poterit." Tanner, 2: 874.

nearly 1,200 years. Faced with these realities, Paul VI established an international commission on the diaconate to advise him.[183]

On June 18, 1967 Paul VI issued the motu proprio *Sacrum diaconatus ordinem* which contained "certain and definite norms"[184] for the restoration of the permanent diaconate. The motu proprio consisted of an introduction and eight sections which were divided into thirty-six articles. These thirty-six articles contained the legislation that would govern the restoration. For our purposes we will address the document's legislation concerning celibacy for deacons.[185]

In the introduction to *Sacrum diaconatus ordinem,* the pope stated that the law governing the rights and obligations of deacons was still the *ius vigens,* unless the contrary was established.[186] It is important to note that under the *ius vigens* a married man could be ordained only with a dispensation from the Holy See.[187] This was only granted on condition that he and his wife observed absolute continence.[188] No commentator on the 1917 code held licit the use of marriage by men in major orders.[189]

---

183   See Echlin, *The Deacon in the Church,* 121.

184   *SDO* Introduction, *AAS* 59 (1967) 698: "…ut certae ac definitae hac de re normae edantur ad eam…." English translation from *TPS* 12 (1967) 238.

185   It is beyond the scope of this book to address every aspect of this document. The document dealt with the authority for the restoration, the qualifications and requirements of the candidate, the rights, obligations and functions of the permanent deacon.

186   See *SDO* Introduction, *AAS* 59 (1967) 698. According to Medina: "Rights and obligations for all clerics are found in Book 2 of the 1917 Code, Titles 1 & 2. Some of these rights and obligations are applicable to all clerics: cc. 118, 123 and 125. Some are applicable to clerics in major orders: cc. 132 and 135. Some are applicable only to priests: cc. 126 and 130. Elsewhere in the code law referring to clerics in general and to deacons in particular was also applicable to permanent deacons unless the law of the motu proprio declared otherwise. Laws for the reception of orders: cc. 955, 968; seminary formation, c. 972; with the proper modifications of the new law, in canon 975 regarding age, canon 976 §2, regarding the study of theology are likewise to be applied to the permanent deacon. The norms of the council concerning clerics were also applicable to the permanent deacon." Medina, *The Law for the Restoration of the Permanent Diaconate,* 65-66.

187   17 *CIC,* c. 987, 2°: "Sunt simpliciter impediti: Viri uxorem habentes."

188   According to Cappello, such dispensations were very rare and were never granted without the consent of the wife and always included the obligation of absolute continence on the part of both spouses. Cappello, *De Sacra Ordinatione* (Rome: Mariette Press, 1935) 2: 3, n. 520. See also chapter two of this book 23-25.

189   See Peters, "Canonical Considerations on Diaconal Continence," 159.

Anthony McLaughlin

While the motu proprio promulgated some new laws, much of it simply modified the existing law.[190] In the case of doubt concerning whether the old law had been abrogated, the former law is presumed to be in force.[191] The law governing the restoration of the permanent diaconate concerned only the Latin Church. The restoration of the permanent diaconate was not obligatory and need not be restored throughout the entire Latin Church.[192] The law of the motu proprio becomes applicable only when the permanent diaconate is established by the respective episcopal conferences.[193]

The motu proprio made a number of important distinctions between young and older candidates to the permanent diaconate. It is evident that young candidates were unmarried men, while older candidates were either married or unmarried. There are certain qualifications demanded of each group in addition to the requirements specified for both.

The permanent diaconate was not to be conferred on a young candidate (unmarried) before he had completed his twenty-fifth year.[194] A period of preparation of at least three years was established.[195] Young candidates who received ordination to the diaconate were bound to observe celibacy. Article 4 stated:

On the basis of Church law, with the approval of the Ecumenical Council, young men called to the diaconate are bound by the law of celibacy.[196]

According to the 1917 Code of Canon Law such deacons were prohibited

---

190 See *SDO* 21: Support of married deacons is a new law.
191 17 *CIC*, c. 23: In dubio revocatio legis praeexsistentis non praesumitur, sed leges posteriores ad priores trahendae sunt his, quantum fieri possit conciliandae."
192 See *SDO* 1.
193 See *SDO* 1-3.
194 See *SDO* 5. For transitional deacons the minimum age was twenty-two, see 17 *CIC*, c. 975.
195 See *SDO* 7.
196 *SDO* 4, *AAS* 59 (1967) 699: "Ex Ecclesiae instituto, ipso Oecumenico Concilio comprobante, ii, qui ad diaconatum iuvenes vocantur, lege caelibatus servandi astringunter." English translation from *TPS* 12 (1967) 239.

194

from marrying, and such marriages would be invalid. Those deacons who attempted marriage would be subject to penalties.[197] The new rite of ordination for deacons, promulgated one year later, had a commitment to celibacy for unmarried candidates to the diaconate inserted after the homily.[198]

The permanent diaconate was not to be conferred on an older candidate (married or unmarried) before he had completed his thirty-fifth year.[199] Married candidates could be married only once[200] and were to have lived as married men for a number of years and proven themselves to be good fathers. Their wives and children should lead good Christian lives, and they should have good reputations.[201] There was to be a period of preparation for older candidates though no definite length of time was established.[202]

While the motu proprio did not expressly state that older unmarried candidates were obliged to celibacy it did reaffirm the ancient practice of the Church that prohibited marriage after ordination. Article 16 stated:

> Once they received the order of deacon, even those who have been promoted at a more mature age, cannot contract marriage by virtue of the traditional discipline of the church.[203]

In this way all older unmarried candidates were obliged to remain in the celibate state, and they and the married deacons could not enter marriage validly or licitly.

---

197   17 *CIC*, cc. 1072; 2388; 985.
198   Paul VI, apostolic constitution *Pontificalis Romani Recognitio,* June 17, 1968: *AAS* 60 (1968) 369-373.
199   *SDO* 11.
200   17 *CIC*, c. 984, n.4: "Sunt irregulares ex defectu: Bigami, qui nempe duo vel plura matrimonia valida successive contraxerunt."
201   See *SDO* 13.
202   See *SDO* 14.
203   *SDO* 16, *AAS* 59 (1967) 701: "Post ordinem receptum diaconi, grandiore etiam aetate promote, ex tradita ecclesiae disciplina ad ineundum matrimonium inhabiles sunt." English translation from *TPS* 12 (1967) 240.

Furthermore, the wives of married candidates had to consent to the ordination of their husbands and have the necessary moral character that would not hinder their husband's ministry nor be out of keeping with it.[204] These requirements are very significant. For most of the Church's history, the consent of the wife and her moral qualities were directly related to the promise of absolute continence and the surrendering of the use of marriage from the day of ordination onwards.[205] Yet, the motu proprio is silent on how married deacons are to live their married lives. Again as in *Lumen gentium* 29 so in the motu proprio, the ordination of married men as deacons is discussed without reference to the ancient discipline of continence for married clergy in major orders, either the absolute continence required in the West or the temporary continence as is the practice in the East. It is interesting to note that in 1968 the French ritual for the ordination of deacons called for the bishop to ask the ordinand's wife whether she accepted "what this ordination will entail for her conjugal and familial life."[206]

2. *Ad pascendum:* Clarifying the Role of Deacons

Five years after *Sacrum diaconatus ordinem* on August 15, 1972, Paul VI promulgated further norms governing the permanent diaconate in his motu proprio *Ad pascendum.* On the same day the pope issued another motu proprio *Ministeria quaedam* in which he abolished the division of clergy into minor and major orders. He also established that while previously one was constituted

---

204　See *SDO* 11.

205　The research presented in chapter one demonstrated that the consent of the wife and her moral qualities were directly related to the promise of absolute continence expected of both spouses after the husband's ordination.

206　Pierre Jounel, "Ordinations," *The Church at Prayer: An Introduction to the Liturgy,* ed. Aimé Georges Martimort (Collegeville, Minnesota: The Liturgical Press, 1987) 3:178. See also Matthieu Cnudde, "L'ordination des diacres," *LMD* 98 (1969) 88-89.

a cleric with the reception of tonsure,[207] now one was constituted a cleric with the reception of diaconate.[208] It was to clarify what this motu proprio meant for deacons that he issued *Ad pascendum.*

Concerning celibacy and deacons, the pontiff repeated the legislation of *Sacrum diaconatus ordinem* namely, that unmarried candidates would be obliged to celibacy and married candidates were prohibited from entering a new marriage.[209]

3. *Sacerdotalis caelibatus:* On Priestly Celibacy

The post-conciliar period was marked by several landmark documents that further developed the Church's teaching on celibacy. Among these post-conciliar documents the 1967 encyclical letter on priestly celibacy, *Sacerdotalis caelibatus,* is especially pertinent.[210] Though this encyclical made little mention of the diaconate, what it said concerning celibacy, the ordination of married former Protestant ministers as priests and the Eastern tradition of a married clergy is of particular interest to this study.

In his intervention during the conciliar discussions on celibacy, Paul VI had stated his intention to affirm this discipline, and he promised the Fathers that he would address the subject of celibacy in more detail after the council.[211] Nearly two years later he fulfilled this promise in an elaborate and heartfelt encyclical that set forth at some length the arguments for and against celibacy. Borrowing heavily from *Presbyterorum ordinis,* Pope Paul VI declared:

Priestly celibacy has been guarded by the Church for centuries as a brilliant jewel, and retains its value undiminished even in our time

---

207   17 *CIC,* c. 108: "Qui divinis ministeriis per primam saltem tonsuram mancipati sunt, clerici dicuntur."

208   See *MQ* 1, *AAS* 64 (1972) 531.

209   See *AP* 5.

210   Paul VI, encyclical *Sacerdotalis caelibatus,* June 24, 1967: *AAS* 59 (1967) 657-697.

211   See footnote 73.

when the outlook of men and the state of the world have undergone such profound changes. Amid the modern stirrings of opinion, a tendency has also been manifested, and even a desire expressed, to ask the Church to re-examine this characteristic institution. It is said that in the world of our time the observance of celibacy has come to be difficult or even impossible.

This state of affairs is troubling consciences, perplexing some priests and young aspirants to the priesthood; it is a cause for alarm in many of the faithful and constrains us to fulfill the promise we made to the council Fathers. We told them that it was our intention to give new luster and strength to priestly celibacy in the world of today. Since saying this we have, over a considerable period of time earnestly implored the enlightenment and assistance of the Holy Spirit and have examined before God opinions and petitions which have come to Us from all over the world, notably from many pastors of God's Church.[212]

One of the very interesting elements of this encyclical is the fact that Paul VI acknowledged that some serious questions had been raised regarding celibacy. In articles three and four he proceeded to outline what he described as 'some serious questions':

---

212 *SCa* 1, *AAS* 59, 657-658: "Sacerdotalis caelibatus, quem Ecclesia quasi quandam nitentem suae coronae gemmam tutatur, in summa laude et aestimatione nostris etiam diebus est, cum sive hominum sensus sive corporearum rerum condiciones sunt fere penitus immutata. Sed in nova huiuscemodi animorum aestuatione quorundam simul erupit proclivitas vel, ut verius dicamus, significata voluntas Christi Ecclesiam ad id impellendi, ut hoc proprium ac suum institutum recognoscat, cuius conservationem, ut eorum fert opinio, et nostro tempora et nostri mores difficilem vel potius impossibilem efficient. 2: Quapropter huius generis rerum statu, quo cum nonnullorum sacerdotum et sacerdotii candidatorum conscientia commovetur in diversumque trahitur, tum multorum fidelium animi perturbantur, Nobis veluti adigi ipsi videmur, ut, omni cunctatione discussa, quod Venerabilibus Patribus Concilii promisimus teneamus, quibus esse Nobis propositum diximus, ut in hac temporum ratione novum decus novamque firmitatem sacerdotali caelibatui adderemus. Quo interim spatio, non solum diu ferventerque Spiritum Paracletum ad necessaria lumina atque auxilia devocavimus, sed consilia etiam flagitationesque ante Dei oculos momentis suis ponderavimus, ad Nos undique, in primis vero a multis Ecclesia Dei Pastoribus, delata." English translation from *Vatican Council II: More Postconciliar Documents,* ed. Austin Flannery (Collegeville: The Liturgical Press, 1982) 2:285. Hereafter Flannery.

The Obligation of Perfect and Perpetual Continence

The great question concerning the sacred celibacy of the clergy in the Church has long been before our mind in its deep seriousness: must that grave, ennobling obligation remain today for those who have the intention of receiving major orders? Is it possible and appropriate nowadays to observe such an obligation? Has the time not come to break the bond linking celibacy with the priesthood in the Church? Could the difficult observance of it not be made optional? Would this not be a way to help the priestly ministry and facilitate ecumenical approaches? And if the golden law of sacred celibacy is to remain, what reasons are there to show that it is holy and fitting? What means are to be taken to observe it, and how can it be changed from a burden to a help for the priestly life?

Our attention has rested particularly on the objections which have been and are still made in various forms against the retention of sacred celibacy. In virtue of our apostolic office We are obliged by the importance, and indeed the complexity, of the subject to give faithful consideration to the facts and the problems they involve, at the same time bringing to them—as it is our duty and our mission to do—the light of truth which is Christ. Our intention is to do in all things the will of Him who has called us to this office and to show what we are in the Church: the servant of the servants of God.[213]

---

213   *SCa* 3, *AAS* 59 (1967) 658: "Equidem fatemur magnam hanc quaestionem, quae in Ecclesia de sacro cleri caelibatu est, longum tempus pro sua amplitudine et gravitate in animo Nostro versatam esse. Etiamne nunc ita Nobiscum quaerebamus severa illa et nobilitante sponsione obligentur, qui sacris maioribus ordinibus initiari cupiant? Sitne hodie huic sponsioni et possibilis et consentanea obtemperatio? Tempusne advenisse putemus, cum vinculum dissolvatur, quo in Ecclesia caelibatus cum sacerdotio conectatur? Curnam integrum cuilibet potius non sit arduam hanc legem servare? Fructumne exinde sacerdotale munus capiat, et facilior fiat ad nos incatholicorum aditus? Quodsi praeclara sacri caelibatus lex in posterum etiam est servandae, quibusnam hodie rationibus eam esse sanctam et opportunam probemus? Quo posito, quibusnam modis lex eadem colenda, et ex onere in vitae Sacerdotalis adiumentum convertenda? 4 :Quae omnia dum meditaremur, ea maxime animum Nostrum subibant, quae variis argumentis contra sacri caelibatus custodiam et allatae sunt et afferuntur. Etenim tam gravi implicataque materia quasi cogi videmur, ut pro apostolico, quo fungimur, ministerio cum rem ipsam tum in ea insitas quaestiones fideliter perpendamus, et, quemadmodum sive iniunctum officium sive creditum munus a Nobis postulant, eam demissa a Christo luce illustremus; eo nempe spectantes, ut non modo illius voluntati omnio obediamus et pareamus, qui Nobis has detulit partes, sed ut Nos etiam *servos servorum Dei,* quales ab Ecclesia putamur, reapse praestemus." Flannery, 2: 285-286.

Paul VI then proceeded to systematically deal with these serious questions by outlining the constant understanding of the Church regarding clerical celibacy. His examination of the debate was not one sided. He faced the issues directly and offered the Church's perspective on each. The pope acknowledged the confusion of some about the discipline of celibacy, and he expressed his heartfelt regret at the number of priests who had left the ministry.[214] He then addressed a number of questions and objections that some had advanced in opposition to the Church's discipline of celibacy.[215] He did this by basically summarizing the Church's constant tradition in this regard. Paul VI outlined the evolution of clerical celibacy, its long history, its biblical basis, the teaching of church councils, the teaching of the popes, its solemnization with the Council of Trent and how this reached juridic expression in the 1917 code. Paul VI did, however, uphold celibacy as a condition of ordination even in the midst of the difficulties it had given rise to and criticism it had drawn. He stated:

> Hence we consider that the present law of celibacy should today continue to be linked to the ecclesiastical ministry. This law should support the minister in his exclusive, definitive and total choice of the unique and supreme love of Christ; it should uphold him in the entire dedication of himself to the public worship of God and to the service of the Church; it should distinguish his state of life both among the faithful and in the world at large.
>
> The gift of the priestly vocation dedicated to the divine worship and to the religious and pastoral service of the People of God, is undoubtedly distinct from that which leads a person to choose celibacy as a state of consecrated life. But the priestly vocation, although inspired by God, does not become definitive or operative without having been tested and

---

214 See *SCa* 85.
215 See *SCa* 7-12. Paul VI listed the classical arguments against celibacy. In *SCa* 17-59, the pope answered these arguments and expounded the reasons for the Church's discipline.

accepted by those in the Church who hold power and bear responsibility for the ministry serving the ecclesial community. It is, therefore, the task of those who hold authority in the Church to determine, in accordance with the varying conditions of time and place, who in actual practice are to be considered suitable candidates for the religious and pastoral service of the Church, and what should be required of them. [216]

Paul VI expressed his esteem for all the clergy of the Eastern Churches and also acknowledged their tradition, established by the Council of Trullo, 692, which permits the ordination of married men to all orders except the episcopacy. This discipline had also been recognized by the council.[217] Paul VI attributed this different discipline to "the different historical background of that most noble part of the Church, a situation which the Holy Spirit has providentially and supernaturally influenced."[218] He also noted the Eastern Church's esteem for virginity and celibacy. The pope referenced the Eastern Church's practice of only ordaining celibate men to the episcopacy and the prohibition against marriage for anyone in major orders. He concluded, therefore, that there existed in the Eastern Churches the principle of a celibate priesthood which demonstrated

---

216   *SCa* 14: "Legem igitur vigentum sacri caelibatus nunc etiam cum sacerdotali munere esse conectendam censemus; eaque fulciri oportere sacerdotem, cum constituit praeterquam se totum, se in perpetuum, se uni tantummodo summo Christi amori dicare, operam quoque suam Dei religioni, Ecclesiaeque commodes navare. Ea insuper caelibatus lege status et condicio sacerdotis opus est distinguatur, sive ad fidelium sive ad profanorum hominum convictum quod spectat. 15: Concedimus sane, donum supernae invitationis ad sacerdotium, ad cultum Deo adhibendum et ad religiosa bona christiana Populo ministranda spectans, a dono differre, quo quis ad caelibatum, uti vitae condicionem Deo sacratum, eligendum movetur. Attamen superna, quam diximus, ad sacerdotium invitatione nihil sane efficitur, nihil absolvitur, nisi is illiam periclitatus fuerit et probaverit, penes quem ministerii populi christiani est onus et potestas. Quam ob causam in rationem ecclesiasticae auctoritatis cadit, pro locis et temporibus, decernere quibus reapse numeris et virtutibus eos ornari deceat, quibus opportune animorum et Ecclesiae sint utilitates concredendae." *AAS* 59 (1967) 662-663. Flannery, 2:289.

217   *PO* 16.

218   *SCa* 38, *AAS* 59 (1967) 673: "…aliis id certe rerum locorumque adiunctis, ad electissimam hanc partem catholicae ecclesiae pertinentibus, est tribuendum, quibus sane omnibus Sanctum Spiritum provido supernoque auxilio suo praefuisse credimus." Flannery, 2:296.

the appropriateness of celibacy for the priesthood.[219] However, the Church of the West would not weaken her faithful observance of her own tradition.[220] Significantly, Paul VI recognized that the council's affirmation on the dignity and goodness of marriage may have given rise to uncertainty about the role of celibacy. He stated:

> In fact, it might seem that celibacy conflicts with the solemn recognition of human values by the Church in the recent council. And yet a more careful consideration reveals that the sacrifice of human love as experienced in a family and as offered by the priest for the love of Christ is really a singular tribute paid to that superior love. Indeed, it is universally recognized that man has always offered to God what is worthy of both the giver and the receiver.[221]

Yet while he affirmed the Latin Church's commitment to celibacy the pontiff also admitted the possibility, in particular circumstances, of ordaining married men to the priesthood and the diaconate.[222] Any reference to the ancient discipline of continence for married clergy in major orders, either the absolute continence required in the West or the temporary continence as is the practice in the East, is absent from the encyclical.

The second half of the encyclical addressed the admission and formation of candidates for the priesthood. The pope described the characteristics of one fit for ordination including his biological and psychological state, and he cau-

---

219   *SCa* 40.

220   *SCa* 41.

221   *SCa* 50, *AAS* 59 (1967) 677: "Videatur enim caelibatus haud congruere cum amplo illo ac praeclaro laudis praeconio, quod ecclesia inter Oecumenicum Concilium Vatican II humanitatis bonis tribuit. Sed si res attentius consideratur, patet sacerdotes, qui Christi caritate ducti amorem priocere dicantur, quo ceteri homines coniugio devincti in sua cuiusque familia fruuntur, re vera ad hunc amorem magnum decus conferre. Nam inter omnes constat, homines munera Deo semper obtulisse, sive iis digna, qui donarent, sive eo, qui eadem susciperit." Flannery, 2:299.

222   *SCa* 42. See also *Sacrum diaconatus ordinem,* in which Paul VI, only several weeks before issuing *Sacredotalis caelibatus* promulgated norms for the restoration of the diaconate and the admission of married men to this order.

tioned against ordaining candidates with psychological and moral issues.[223] The pontiff emphasized that the commitment to celibacy, though clearly added to the priesthood by the Church, is ultimately a free choice not an imposition. The Church respects the liberty of the human person. The candidate is always free not to embrace this commitment and therefore not to pursue ordination. From the document one gets a sense that the pontiff considered that the call to celibacy accompanies and confirms the call to ordination.

Finally the pope addressed the issue of dispensations from celibacy. Throughout the history of the Church there have been instances of priests leaving the ministry. While the Church always affirmed her commitment to celibacy, popes had dispensed certain priests from this commitment. As we demonstrated in chapter two, such dispensations from celibacy were rarely granted before the council. Paul VI signaled a willingness to examine the cases of priests who petitioned for a dispensation and in certain circumstances to grant their requests in order that "love conquers sorrow."[224] He stated that such dispensations are granted for the sake of the salvation of the individual, to safeguard the commitment of celibacy, to protect the faithful from further scandal, to demonstrate mercy and only as a last measure when the person's priesthood cannot be saved.[225]

4. *Ultimis temporibus:* On the Ministerial Priesthood[226]

Four years after his encyclical *Sacerdotalis caelibatus,* Paul VI con-

---

223   *SCa* 61-64.
224   *SCa* 88: "…potiorem habens amorem quam dolorem....." Flannery, 2: 309.
225   See *SCa* 84-90.
226   For an indepth treatment of the doctrinal significance of *Sacerdotalis caelibatus* see Donald Wuerl, *The Priesthood : The Doctrine of the Third Synod of Bishops and Recent Theological Conclusions.* S.T.D. dissertation. (Rome: Pontifical University of St. Thomas Aquinas, 1974).

vened the second session of the 1971 Synod of Bishops. One of the areas addressed by the synod was the ministerial priesthood and the commitment of celibacy in particular. The bishops spoke about the basis of celibacy, the reasons for the discipline, the importance of celibacy in the Latin Church and the conditions conducive for a life of faithful celibacy. When the synod was completed a special commission was set up to prepare a document summarizing the synodal discussions. The document, *Ultimis temporibus*,[227] was subsequently made public through a papal rescript dated November 30, 1971. This document is of particular interest to this study because of its teaching on celibacy, the Eastern tradition of married clergy and the ordination of married men in the Latin Church. It is also listed among the sources to canon 277 §1 of the 1983 code which obliges clerics to observe perfect and perpetual continence.

Ultimis temporibus repeated much of the earlier conciliar teaching concerning celibacy. The bishops spoke of the appropriateness of celibacy for the priesthood in the Latin Church and of its intense sign value:

> Celibacy for priests is in full accord with the vocation to the apostolic following of Christ as well as with the unconditional response of a man who has been called and who takes up pastoral service. Through celibacy the priest, following his Lord, demonstrates in a fuller way that he is prompt and ready and, setting out on the way of the cross, he desires with a paschal joy to be consumed somewhat as the Eucharist. If, however, celibacy is lived in the spirit of the gospel, in prayer and watchfulness, with poverty, joyfulness, contempt of honors, brotherly love, it is a sign which cannot long be hidden but which effectively proclaims Christ to men even of our age. For today words are scarcely valued but

---

227 Synod of Bishops, decree on the ministerial priesthood *Ultimis temporibus,* November 30, 1971: *AAS* 63 (1971) 898-922. Hereafter *UT.* English translation in Flannery, 2:672-694.

the witness of a life which shows the *radicalism* of the Gospel has the power to attract vehemently.[228]

While again recognizing the traditions of the Eastern Churches the bishops reaffirmed the Latin Church's commitment to celibacy:

The traditions of the Eastern Churches shall remain unchanged, as they are now in force in the various territories.

The Church has the right and duty to determine the concrete form of the priestly ministry and therefore to select more suitable candidates, endowed with certain human and supernatural qualities. When the Latin Church demands celibacy as an indispensable condition for undertaking the priesthood she does not do this because she thinks that this style of life is the only path of holiness. She does it while sedulously considering the concrete form of exercising the ministry in the community for the upbuilding of the Church.

Because of the intimate and multiform connection between the pastoral function and the celibate life, the current law is upheld, for one who freely wishes *total disposability*, which is the distinctive note of this function, also freely takes on celibacy.[229]

---

228   *UT* Part 2, Section 1, 4a, *AAS* 63 (1971) 915: "Caelibatus sacerdotum plene concordat cum vocatione ad apostolicam sequelam Christi necnon cum responso, omnis exceptionis nescio, hominis vocati, qui servitium pastorale assumit. Per caelibatum sacerdos Dominum suum sequens, se pleniore modo promptum et paratum demonstrat et, viam cruces aggrediens, cum gaudio paschali quodammodo eucharistice consummari cupit. Si autem caelibatus in spiritu Evangelii, in oratione et vigilantia, cum paupertate, laetitia, honorum despectu, amore fraterno vivitur, signum est, quod diu latere non potest, sed efficaciter Christum hominibus etiam nostrae aetatis proclamat. Nam verba hodie vix aestimantur, sed vitae testimonium, radicalismum evangelicam ostendens, virtutem habet vehementer trahendi." Flannery, 2: 687.

229   *UT* Part 2, Section 1, 4c, *AAS* 63 (1971) 916-917: "Ecclesia ius habet et officium determinandi formam concretam ministerii Sacerdotalis et proinde etiam seligendi candidates aptiores, certis qualitatibus humanis et supernaturalibus insignitos. Cum Ecclesia Latina caelibatum ut condicionem sine qua non ad sacerdotium suscipiendum exigit, hoc non facit propterea quod putet hunc vitae modum esse unicam viam ad sanctificationem assequendam. Id facit sedulo considerans formam concretam ministerium exercendi in communitate ad aedificationem Ecclesiae. Propter intimam et multiformem cohaerentiam inter munus pastorale et vitam caelibem, lex vigens sustinetur: qui enim libere vult disponibilitatem totalem, quae est nota distinctiva huius muneris, libere etiam suscipit caelibem vitam." Flannery, 2: 688-689.

The synod affirmed the eschatological sign value of celibacy alongside the sign value of marriage:

> While the value of the sign and holiness of Christian marriage is fully recognized, celibacy for the sake of the kingdom nevertheless more clearly displays that spiritual fruitfulness or generative power of the new law, by which the apostle knows that in Christ he is the father and mother of his communities.[230]

The synod repeated the need for proper formation for seminarians so that they can freely and maturely embrace celibacy.[231] The situation of priests who left the ministry was also addressed with the bishops urging that such priests receive just and fraternal care. Such priests were not to exercise priestly ministry in the Church.

At the end of the synod, the bishops were asked to vote on how the Church should address the discipline of celibacy. In the first vote they were presented with the following proposition:

A) The law of celibacy. The current law of celibacy for priests in the Latin Church must be kept in its entirety.[232]

B) Ordination of married men. Two formulae were proposed for the vote of the Fathers:

Formula A: Always without prejudice to the right of the supreme pontiff, the ordination of married men as priests is not admitted, not even in special cases.

Formula B: It belongs to the supreme pontiff alone, in special cases, because of pastoral needs and in view of the good of the universal

---

230   *UT* Part 2, Section 1, 4b, *AAS* 63 (1971) 916: "Plene agnito valore signi et sanctitatis matrimonii christiani, caelibatus propter regnum clarius ostendit illam pneumaticam fecunditatem seu virtutem generatricem Novae Legis, qua apostolus se in Christo patrem et matrem suarum communitatum esse novit." Flannery, 2: 688.

231   *UT* Part 2, Section 1, 4d.

232   *UT* Part 2, Section 1, 4e, *AAS* 63 (1971) 917: "Lex caelibatus: Lex caelibatus sacerdotalis in Ecclesia Latin vigens integer servari debet." Results of the vote: *Placet* 168; *Non placet* 10; *Placet iuxta modum* 21; *abstentiones* 3. Flannery, 2:689.

Church, to allow ordination as priests to married men who, however, are of rather advanced age and of upright life.[233]

The bishops voted overwhelmingly that the current law of celibacy should be observed in the Church and that in general the ordination of married men as priests should be restricted. Again it is striking that any reference to the ancient discipline of continence for married clergy in major orders, either the absolute continence required in the West or the temporary continence as is the practice in the East, is absent from synodal discussions.

C. John Paul II: Celibacy and Marriage

With the death of Pope Paul VI on August 6, 1978[234] the College of Cardinals elected John Paul I as his successor.[235] Tragically, John Paul I died only thirty-three days into his pontificate.[236] On October 16, 1978, he was succeeded by Pope John Paul II.[237] During his pontificate John Paul II wrote extensively on the priesthood, celibacy, sexuality, marriage and the family. We will now examine several significant documents issued by John Paul II that are particularly germane to this study. They address the rationale for celibacy and the relationship between marriage and celibacy.

---

233 *UT* Part 2, Section 1, 4f, *AAS* 63 (1971) 918: "De ordinatione virorum matrimonio iunctorum. Duae formulae propositae sunt suffragationibus Patrum: Formula A: Salvo semper Summi Pontificis iure, ordinatio presbyteralis virorum matrimonio iunctorum non admittitur ne in casibus quidem particularibus. Formula B: Solius Summi Pontificis est, in casibus particularibus, ob necessitates pastorales, attento bono universalis Ecclesiae, concedere ordinationem presbyteralem virorum matrimonio iunctorum provectioris tamen aetatis et probatae vitae." In accord with the directives given by the president, the votes were not taken by *placet* or *non placet*, but through the choice of the one or the other formula. Formula A received 107 votes and Formula B received 87. There were 2 abstentions and 2 null votes. Flannery, 2: 689-690.
234 *AAS* 70 (1978) 545.
235 *AAS* 70 (1978) 676.
236 *AAS* 70 (1978) 797.
237 *AAS* 70 (1978) 905.

Anthony McLaughlin

1. *Redemptor hominis*: Encyclical on the Mystery of Redemption

Within six months of taking office Pope John Paul II published his first encyclical *Redemptor hominis.*[238] While the encyclical concentrated on the mystery of redemption, it also touched upon many other topics and themes. In chapter four the Holy Father spoke of fidelity to one's vocation whatever that may be. He said this about the fidelity asked of the Church's priests:

> Priests must be distinguished for a similar fidelity to their vocation (same fidelity as married people have to their vocation of marriage) in view of the indelible character that the sacrament of orders stamps on their souls. In receiving this sacrament, we in the Latin Church knowingly and freely commit ourselves to live in celibacy, and each one of us must therefore do all he can, with God's grace, to be thankful for this gift and faithful to the bond that he has accepted forever.[239]

The pope called on priests to live their commitment to celibacy with greater fidelity. He repeated the assertion of the council that celibacy is a gift and as such cannot be imposed on the individual. Celibacy is a commitment that is knowingly and freely undertaken by the fact that one presents oneself for ordination.

2. *Novo incipiente*: Holy Thursday Letter to Priests

On the occasion of the Lord's Supper, Holy Thursday, 1979, the pope wrote to the priests of the whole world concerning the question of celibacy. He stated:

---

238   John Paul II, encyclical *Redemptor hominis,* March 4, 1979: *AAS* 71 (1979) 257-324. Hereafter *RH.*

239   *RH* 21.4, *AAS* 71 (1979) 319: "Similiter eminere decet sacerdotes pari fidelitate erga propriam vocationem; id quod poscit character indelebilis, quem Sacramentum Ordinis in ipsorum animis figit. Nam hoc Sacramentum cum recipimus, obstringimus nos, in Ecclesia Latina, conscii ac liberi officio vivendi in caelibatu; quocirca unusquisque nostrum debet, quantum sane in eo situm est, efficere, ut Dei gratia sustentatus, gratias de hoc dono sit ac semper fidelis officio, quo in omne tempus se obligavit." English translation from *Origins* 8 (March 22, 1979) 642.

The Obligation of Perfect and Perpetual Continence

Allow me at this point to touch on the question of celibacy. I shall deal with it briefly, since it was treated fully and in depth at the council, in the encyclical *Sacerdotalis caelibatus*, and at the 1971 synod of bishops. [240]

He admitted that on this question he would have nothing new to add to what the council, the synod or Paul VI had to say. His letter, however, would be an attempt to move the discussion of celibacy to an even deeper level.

Such reflection was deemed necessary in the interests of a fuller presentation of the issue and to provide a deeper understanding of the decision taken by the Latin Church took so many centuries ago, a decision which endeavored to abide by and which it wishes to continue to abide in the future.[241]

The pope continued towards the end of his letter:

The essential, proper and adequate reason (for celibacy) is contained in the truth which Christ proclaimed when he spoke of the renunciation of marriage for the sake of the kingdom of heaven and which St. Paul proclaimed when he wrote that each person in the church has his or her own gifts. Celibacy is precisely a gift of the spirit.[242]

John Paul II emphasized that celibacy is not assumed by the cleric for natural reasons but for a supernatural one. The raison d'être for priestly celibacy is found in Christ's call to renounce marriage for the sake of the kingdom.

---

240   John Paul II, letter *Novo incipiente* 8, April 8, 1979: *AAS* 71 (1979) 405-406: "Sinite Nos hoc loco Sacerdotalis caelibatus quaestionem attingere. Quam summatim tantum perstringemus, quippe quae iam alte absoluteque pertracta sit in Concilio ac deinde in Litteris Encyclicis *Sacerdotalis caelibatus* et postremo in ordinaria sessione Synodi Episcoporum anno MCMLXXI celebratae." Hereafter *NI.* Flannery, 2: 354.

241   *NI* 8, *AAS* 71 (1979) 406: "Tum ut certioribus etiam rationibus confirmaretur ipse sensus illius voluntatis quam Ecclesia Latina tot ante saeculis susceperat cuique fidelis esse contendit et cui posthac pariter vult fidelitatem praestare." Flannery, 2: 354.

242   *NI* 8, *AAS* 71 (1979) 407: "Ratio, contra, essentialis, propria, congruens continetur in veritate illa quam Christus aperuit, cum de matrimonii renuntiatione propter Regnum caelorum est locutus quamque Sanctus Paulus protulit, cum scripsit unumquemque proprium habere donum ex Deo. Caelibatus autem ipsum nominatim est 'donum Spiritus'." Flannery, 2: 355.

3. *Familiaris consortio*:

Apostolic Exhortation on Marriage and the Family

The 1980 Synod on the Family was the first assembly at which John Paul II presided as pope. Less than one year later, the pope synthesized the deliberations and proposals of the synod in his apostolic exhortation *Familiaris consortio*.[243]

John Paul II spoke of the complimentarity of celibacy and marriage. Both vocations were expressions of profound love of God and neighbor. Each vocation comes from God and each is oriented towards God. The idea that in some way marriage and celibacy share a certain complementary seemed to be a contradiction in terms. Yet the pontiff presented this in a most profound way in *Familiaris consortio* when he stated at length:

> Virginity or celibacy for the sake of the Kingdom of God not only does not contradict the dignity of marriage but presupposes it and confirms it. Marriage and virginity or celibacy are two ways of expressing and living the one mystery of the covenant of God with His people. When marriage is not esteemed, neither can consecrated virginity or celibacy exist; when human sexuality is not regarded as a great value given by the Creator, the renunciation of it for the sake of the Kingdom of Heaven loses its meaning.
>
> Rightly indeed does St. John Chrysostom say: "Whoever denigrates marriage also diminishes the glory of virginity. Whoever praises it makes virginity more admirable and resplendent. What appears good only in comparison with evil would not be particularly good. It is something better than what is admitted to be good that is the most excellent good."

---

[243]   John Paul II, apostolic exhortation *Familiaris consortio,* November 22, 1981: *AAS* 74 (1982) 81-191. Hereafter *FC.*

The Obligation of Perfect and Perpetual Continence

In virginity or celibacy, the human being is awaiting, also in a bodily way, the eschatological marriage of Christ with the Church, giving himself or herself completely to the Church in the hope that Christ may give Himself to the Church in the full truth of eternal life. The celibate person thus anticipates in his or her flesh the new world of the future resurrection.

By virtue of this witness, virginity or celibacy keeps alive in the Church a consciousness of the mystery of marriage and defends it from any reduction and impoverishment.

Virginity or celibacy, by liberating the human heart in a unique way, "so as to make it burn with greater love for God and all humanity," bears witness that the Kingdom of God and His justice is that pearl of great price which is preferred to every other value no matter how great, and hence must be sought as the only definitive value. It is for this reason that the Church, throughout her history, has always defended the superiority of this charism to that of marriage, by reason of the wholly singular link which it has with the Kingdom of God.

In spite of having renounced physical fecundity, the celibate person becomes spiritually fruitful, the father and mother of many, cooperating in the realization of the family according to God's plan.

Christian couples therefore have the right to expect from celibate persons a good example and a witness of fidelity to their vocation until death. Just as fidelity at times becomes difficult for married people and requires sacrifice, mortification and self-denial, the same can happen to celibate persons, and their fidelity, even in the trials that may occur, should strengthen the fidelity of married couples.

These reflections on virginity or celibacy can enlighten and help those who, for reasons independent of their own will, have been unable to marry and have then accepted their situation in a spirit of service.[244]

According to John Paul II, marriage and virginity or celibacy are both undertaken for the sake of the kingdom. They are two ways of expressing and living the mystery of God's covenant with his people. Each calling is fruitful and life giving.

D. Conclusion

This chapter examined conciliar and post conciliar teaching concerning the obligation of clerical celibacy, the restoration of the permanent diaconate, the nature of sexuality and its intrinsic relationship to marriage. While these teach-

---

244 *FC* 16, *AAS* 74 (1982) 98-99: "Virginitas et caelibatus propter Regnum Dei non solum non adversantur matrimonii dignitati, sed eam prius poscunt atque confirmant. Matrimonium ac virginitas duae rationes sunt exprimendi unicum mysterium Foederis Dei cum Populo Eius ex eoque vivendi. Quoties magni non aestimatur matrimonium, ne virginitas quidem Deo consecrata exsistere potest; quoties sexualitas humana non iudicatur bonum praestans a Creatore concessum, renuntiatio eius propter Regnum caelorum vim omnen amittit. Aequissime quidem loquitur Sanctus Ioannes Chrysostomus: 'Qui matrimonium damnat, is virginitatis etiam gloriam carpit; qui laudat, is virginitatem admirabiliorem augustioremque reddit. Nam quod deterioris comparatione bonum videtur, id haud sane admodum bonum est; quod autem omnium sententia bonis melius, id excellens bonum est.' In ipsa virginitate homo exspectat, etiam corpore, nuptias eschatologicas Christi cum Ecclesia, dum se totum Ecclesiae tradit sperans Christum quoque se Ecclesiae daturum in plena vitae aeternae veritate. Persona virgo ita in carne sua novum resurrectionis futurae mundum antecapit. Vi huius matrimonii testificationis virginitas vivam in Ecclesia servat conscientiam mysterii matrimonii illudque tuetur adversus omnem imminutionem et extenuationem. Hominis corde singulariter ita liberato, 'ut magnis accendatur Dei Regnum eiusque iustitiam esse illiam magni pretii margaritam, quae omni alii anteponenda sit bono quantumvis magno quaeque immo conquirenda sit ut unicum bonum certum ac perenne. Hac de causa Ecclesia progrediente toto rerum suarum cursu semper defendit huius doni praestantiam prae gratia matrimonii, propter ipsum singulare omnio vinculum, quod habet cum Dei Regno. Virgo, quamvis fecunditati corporis renuntiaverit, persona spiritaliter redditur fecunda, multorum pater ac mater, et sic operam confert ad perficiendam familiam secundum Dei consilium. Christianis itaque coniugibus ius est a personis virginibus bonum exemplum exspectandi necnon testimonium fidelitatis erga earum vocationem usque ad mortem. Quemadmodum coniugibus nonnumquam difficilis accidit fidelitas ac se devovendi studium deposcit et mortificationem et sui abnegationem, sic pariter personis virginibus potest evenire. Earum enim fidelitas, etiam in temptatione, si qua fuerit, debet illorum coniugum fidelitatem sustentare. Hae considerationes de virginitate illuminare valent et adiuvare eos qui ob causas a sua voluntate alienas contrahere matrimonium non potuerunt ac deinde statum suum in serviendi spiritu acceperunt." Flannery, 2: 826-827.

ings offer a fresh understanding certain questions remain, particularly in the area of the compatibility of marriage and holy orders. What remains certain is that a married man can be ordained, but an ordained man cannot marry.

In the Latin Church the fundamental obligation for all clergy in major orders was absolute continence. This bound all major clergy equally, married, unmarried or widowed. While the council permitted married men to be ordained to the permanent diaconate, there was little indication given as to how these deacons were to live their married lives after ordination. There was no reference in conciliar or post-conciliar documents to the ancient discipline of continence for married clergy in major orders, either the absolute continence required in the West or the temporary continence as is the practiced in the East. Nor was there any comment on whether the discipline that had bound all major clerics equally was now changed, if indeed a change was intended. The issue was posed in exclusive terms, "celibacy versus married clergy." In many ways this muddied the waters and mooted any discussion on the law of continence.

In *Sacrum diaconatus ordinem* Pope Paul VI required the consent of the candidate's wife to his ordination, and he stated that the wife needed to have the necessary moral qualifications. This is interesting when one notes that in the past the consent of the wife and her moral qualities were directly related to the promise of absolute continence and the surrendering of the use of marriage from the day of ordination onwards.[245] In the introduction to *Sacrum diaconatus ordinem,* the pope stated that the law governing the rights and obligations of deacons

---

245 The research presented in chapter one demonstrated that the consent of the wife and her moral qualities were directly related to the promise of absolute continence expected of both spouses after the husband's ordination.

was still the *ius vigens,* unless the contrary was established.[246] It is important to note that under the *ius vigens* a married man could be ordained only with a dispensation from the Holy See.[247] This was only granted on condition that he and his wife observed absolute continence.[248] Alongside these questions there is also the fresh conciliar understanding of baptism, sexuality and marriage as given in *Lumen gentium* and *Gaudium et spes.* This in turn raises further questions concerning the compatibility of marriage and orders. As Roberts observes:

> If we really believe that married couples are signs of Christ and sacraments of Christ's love, not despite, but precisely because of their intimate sexual relationship, then what is the theological incompatibility between marriage and orders? If the married couple is called through their baptism to share in the priestly, prophetic, and kingly mission of Christ, not despite, but precisely in terms of, their marital state, then what is the theological incompatibility between their marital ministry and the ministry of the ordained? If the married couple is called through baptism to the fullness of holiness, the perfection of love, not despite, but precisely in terms of their marriage, then what is the theological incompatibility between the holiness required of marriage and of the sacrament of orders.[249]

---

246   See *SDO* Introduction, *AAS* 59 (1967) 698. According to Medina: "Rights and obligations for all clerics are found in Book 2 of the 1917 Code, Titles 1 & 2. Some of these rights and obligations are applicable to all clerics: cc. 118, 123 and 125. Some are applicable to clerics in major orders: cc. 132 and 135. Some are applicable only to priests: cc. 126 and 130. Elsewhere in the code law referring to clerics in general and to deacons in particular was also applicable to permanent deacons unless the law of the motu proprio declared otherwise. Laws for the reception of orders: cc. 955, 968; seminary formation, c. 972; with the proper modifications of the new law, in canon 975 regarding age, canon 976 §2, regarding the study of theology are likewise to be applied to the permanent deacon. The norms of the council concerning clerics were also applicable to the permanent deacon." Medina, *The Law for the Restoration of the Permanent Diaconate,* 65-66.

247   17 *CIC,* c. 987, 2°: "Sunt simpliciter impediti: Viri uxorem habentes."

248   According to Cappello, such dispensations were very rare and were never granted without the consent of the wife and always included the obligation of absolute continence on the part of both spouses. Cappello, *De Sacra Ordinatione* (Rome: Mariette Press, 1935) 2: 3, n. 520. See also chapter two of this book 23-25.

249   Roberts, *From Trent to Vatican II,* 223.

The Obligation of Perfect and Perpetual Continence

Perhaps the silence on how married deacons are to live their married lives is because it should be obvious that absolute continence is still to be observed because that's what the Church did for centuries? Or is it because it is obvious that a married person should not be bound to continence based on the understanding of sexuality and marriage as taught by the council? Also if married deacons are not bound to observe continence, why are unmarried deacons obliged to celibacy? Why is continence obliged of one and not the other? Was the unity of the discipline of celibacy-continence that bound all grades of major orders equally changed? These are the many questions that we must return to in chapter five of this book.

Now we turn our attention to how these conciliar and post-conciliar teachings effected the revision of canons 132 and 133 of the 1917 code, and how they found juridic expression in the 1983 Code of Canon Law, namely, in canon 277 §1 and the obligation of clerics to observe perfect and perpetual continence for the sake of the kingdom.

CHAPTER FOUR

THE 1983 CODE AND THE OBLIGATION OF CLERICAL CHASTITY, CONTINENCE AND CELIBACY

Several weeks before the conclusion of the Second Vatican Council, Pope Paul VI inaugurated the work of the Pontifical Commission for the Revision of the Code of Canon Law. In his allocution, the pope emphasized that the revision process must be informed and guided by the teachings of the council. He stated:

> Now, however, with changed conditions, life seems to move along with greater speed, we must recognize with due prudence that canon law must be adapted to the new mentality of the Second Vatican Ecumenical Council from which great contributions are being made to pastoral duties and the new needs of the People of God.[1]

By January 1966, the consultors of the commission had been organized into ten study groups (*coetus studiorum*), with each group being responsible for the revision of a certain section of the code.[2] The various *coetus* then prepared re-

---

1   Paul VI, allocution *Singulari cum animi,* November 20, 1965: *AAS* 57 (1965) 988: "Nunc admodum mutatis rerum condicionibus, cursus enim vitae celerius ferri videtur, ius canonicum, prudentia adhibitia, est recognoscendum; scilicet accommodari debet novo mentis habitui, Concilii Oecumenici Vaticani Secundi proprio, ex quo curae pastorali plurimum tribuitur, et novis neccesitatibus populi Dei." English translation from "Allocution to the Commission for the Revision of the Code of Canon Law," *The Jurist* 26 (1966) 39.
2   Pontificia Commissionis Codici Iuris Canonici Recognoscendo, *Communicationes* 1 (1969) 44. Hereafter *Communicationes.*

vision drafts (*schemata*) of these sections. The following year ten revision principles were approved by the Synod of Bishops that would guide the process.[3]
One of the main purposes of the revision principles was to ensure a harmony
between the Church's revised law and the conciliar documents.[4]

The revision of the 1917 code underwent four major stages:[5] the 1972-1977
primae versiones, the 1980 *Schema Codicis*, the 1982 *Schema Codicis* and finally
the 1983 code.[6] For the purposes of this chapter we will be concerned with the
work of two of these *coetus*: the *coetus de sacra hierarchia*, which was entrusted
with the canons on clerics and the *coetus de matrimonio*, which was entrusted
with canons on marriage. Of particular interest will be the *coetus de sacra hierarchia's* recommendations concerning clerical celibacy and the *coetus de matrimonio's* recommendations concerning sacred orders as an impediment to marriage.

A. The Revision Process

1. *Coetus Studiorum de Sacra Hierarchia*

The *coetus studiorum de clericis,* later renamed *coetus studiorum de sacra
hierarchia,*[7] conducted the first of its eighteen sessions on October 24-28, 1966.[8]
In its initial discussions on clerical celibacy in 1972, the *coetus* affirmed the
Church's commitment to perfect and perpetual continence and therefore cel-

---

3   *Communicationes* 1 (1969) 78-85.
4   John A. Alesandro, "The Revision of the *Code of Canon Law:* A Background Study,"
Studia canonica 24 (1990) 106.
5   According to Edward Peters, a "stage may be considered 'major' when a complete set
of canons, usually covering what will be an entire book of the new code, is published in mono-
graph form and sent for comment beyond the confines of the *coetus* charged with its drafting to
various episcopal conferences, Roman dicasteries, religious superiors and ecclesiastical faculties."
In *Incrementa in Progressu 1983 Codicis Iuris Canonici,* ed. Edward Peters (Montréal: Wilson &
Lafleur, 2005) xii. Hereafter *Incrementa.*
6   Ibid.
7   *Communicationes* 3 (1971) 187: "*Coetus studiorum,* qui prius vocatus est *de Clericis,*
postae vero appellatus est *De Sacra Hierarchia....*"
8   *Communicationes* 1 (1969) 47.

ibacy for all candidates aspiring to the priesthood. This obligation was to be assumed with ordination to the diaconate. Married deacons, however, would be exempt from this obligation.[9]

2. 1977 *Schema Canonum Libri II de Populo Dei:* Canons 135 and 136

In 1977, the *coetus de sacra hierarchia* with the *coetus de laicis deque associationibus fidelium* published the *Schema Canonum Libri II de Populo Dei.*[10] This *schema* was the culmination of nearly five years of *primae versiones,* earlier versions of proposed canons.[11] The *schema* contained revisions of canons 132 and 133 of the 1917 code that obliged clerical celibacy. Strictly speaking, the revisions contained in the various *schemata* prior to the promulgation of the 1983 code, though they are referred to as "canons," are not "canons" but rather "proposed canons."[12] It is important to bear this in mind when the word canon is used in the context of the various *schemata.*

Canons 132 and 133 of the 1917 code were revised as canons 135 and 136 respectively. Canon 135 stated the following concerning the obligation of clerical celibacy:

---

9   *Communicationes* 3 (1971) 193: "Ad obligationem coelibatus quod attinet, norma in *schema*ta proposita convenit cum doctrina et praescripto, quae in eodem decreto *Presbyterorum ordinis,* 16, enuntiantur, et proponit ut haec obligatio, scilicet obligationem ad perfectam continentiam ideoque et ad coelibatum, pro clericis ad sacerdotium aspirantibus, initium sumat recepto diaconatus ordine. Expresse autem affirmatur hac obligatione non teneri viros maturioris aetatis in matrimonio viventes qui, iuxta decreta competentis Episcoporum Conferentiae a Summo Pontifice adprobata, ad diaconatum stabilem promoventur. Clerici itaque qui diaconatus ordinem non iam receperunt possunt nuptias inire, sed, nisi sint viri maturioris aetatis ad diaconatum stabilem destinati, nuptias contrahendo ipso iure a statu clericali decidunt, nisi quidem eorum matrimonium fuerit nullum vi metu eisdem incusso." See chapter three of this book for a fuller treatment of the exemption of married deacons from celibacy.

10   *Incrementa,* XVI. It had previously been decided by the revision commission that the canons on clergy would be included in the *schema* on *The People of God.*

11   For a detailed examination of these *primae versiones* see *Communicationes* 28 (1996) 191-236.

12   The Holy See warned against premature attempts to accept these 'proposed canons' as law. See *Communicationes* 7 (1975) 149.

§1: Clerics are bound by the obligation to observe perfect and perpetual continence for the sake of the kingdom of heaven and they are, therefore, held to celibacy.

§2: Men of more mature age, who are living in a married life and have been promoted to the permanent diaconate are not held to the prescript of §1; nevertheless these men also, if they have lost their wife, are held to observe celibacy.[13]

This *schema* had taken into account the changes made by Paul VI in his motu proprio *Ministeria quaedem*.[14] Therefore in the 1977 *Schema* any reference to minor or major clerics was omitted. The term "cleric" now referred only to deacons, presbyters and bishops. The obligation of perfect continence and therefore celibacy was now assumed with ordination to the diaconate and entry into the clerical state. Canon 135 also contained the qualifying clause "for the sake of the kingdom of heaven" (*"propter regnum caelorum"*), a phrase that was taken directly from conciliar documents.[15] There was also no mention, as in the former code, of the violation of clerical chastity constituting a sacrilege.

Paragraph two of the canon expressly stated that married deacons, though clerics, are not bound to the obligation of perfect and perpetual continence and

---

13   Pontificia Commissio Codici Iuris Canonici Recognoscendo, *Schema Canonum Libri II De Populo Dei* (Vatican City: Typis Polyglottis Vaticanis, 1977), c. 135: "§1. Clerici obligatione tenentur servandi perfectam perpetuamque propter Regnum caelorum ideoque ad caelibatum adstringuntur. §2. Praescripto §1 non tenetur viri maturioris aetatis in matrimonio viventes qui ad diaconatum stabilem promoti sunt; qui tamen et ipsi, amissa uxore, ad caelibatum servandum tenetur." Hereafter *Schema de Populo Dei.* English translation from *Pontifical Commission for the Revision of the Code. Draft of the Canons of Book Two: The People of God,* trans. the Canon Law Society of America (Washington, DC: Canon Law Society of America, 1977) 62. All subsequent translations of this *schema* will be taken from this source unless otherwise stated.

14   Paul VI, motu proprio *Ministeria quaedam,* August 15, 1972: *AAS* 64 (1972) 529-534. Hereafter *MQ.* The pope had abolished the division of clergy into minor and major orders and replaced the four minor orders with two ministries, lector and acolyte. The rite of tonsure was suppressed, and the pope decreed that one now became a cleric with ordination to the diaconate.

15   Vatican II, decree *Presbyterorum Ordinis,* December 7, 1965: *AAS* 58 (1966) 1015, n. 16; decree *Perfectae caritatis,* October 28, 1965: *AAS* 58 (1966) 706-707, n. 12 and decree *Optatam totius,* October 28, 1965: *AAS* 58 (1966) 719-720, n. 10.

therefore celibacy common to all clergy. However, if the deacon's wife died he was bound by this obligation. Both unmarried and married permanent deacons were bound by the impediment of orders.

The Canon Law Society of America in its critique of canon 135 recommended that the prohibition of remarriage for permanent deacons be suppressed and questioned whether obligatory celibacy should continue in the Latin Church. The society stated:

> Paragraph 2 also explicitly precludes permanent deacons from remarrying after the loss of their spouse. While no official change in policy seems likely in the foreseeable future, it is questionable whether obligatory celibacy should continue in to be an integral part of the paradigm of priestly ministry throughout the Latin Church. This is true particularly but not exclusively in light of shifting ministerial imperatives and difficulties in adequately realizing the Church's mission in numerous parts of the world. Greater freedom should be accorded the Episcopal conferences in shaping ministerial forms with due regard for the delicacy of this issue and the significant change that would be involved in the ordination practice of the Latin Church. At least the prohibition of permanent deacons remarrying should be dropped if the *schema* is to deal more realistically with deacons' family obligations which involve remarriage. Dispensations for such marriages are normally granted in any event.[16]

The canon law societies of Australia and New Zealand,[17] Great Britain and

---

16   Canon Law Society of America, "Initial Report of the Task Force Committee on the Draft of the Canons of Book Two: People of God," in *Task Force Critiques of the Initial Schemata for the Revision of the Code of Canon Law* (Washington, DC: Canon Law Society of America, 1978) 17.

17   The Canon Law Society of Australia and New Zealand, *Report on the Schema de Populo Dei Libri II.* This report was not published and may be available by contacting the Society.

Ireland,[18] Canada[19] also studied the 1977 *Schema* and prepared critiques for their respective bishops' conferences.[20] In August and October, 1978, bishops and canonists representing ten episcopal conferences met in Ottawa, Canada to discuss the *Schema* and to share their critiques.[21] Many of the bodies that were consulted regarding the applicability of the impediment of orders for married deacons were in favor of its removal.[22]

In continuity with the 1917 code, canon 136 of the *schema* sought to protect the obligation of perfect and perpetual continence assumed by the cleric:

§1: Clerics must conduct themselves with prudence when they associate with persons whose company can endanger their observance of continence or cause scandal to the faithful.

§2: The decision to enact more specific rules in this matter belongs to the diocesan bishop, after hearing his presbyteral council, so that he may pass judgment in particular cases regarding the observance of this law. [23]

The canon obliged clerics to exercise due prudence in their relationships with others and to avoid any hint of scandal in this regard. The *schema* omitted all previous references to the cleric avoiding certain "women;" instead the term

---

18   The Canon Law Society of Great Britain and Ireland, *Report on the Schema de Populo Dei Libri II*. This report was not published and may be available by contacting the Society.

19   The Canon Law Society of Cananda, *Response of St. Paul Univeristy to the Pontifical Commisssion for the Revision of the Code of Canon Law on the Proposed "Schema Canonum Libri II de Populo Dei."* This report was not published and may be available by contacting the Society.

20   See Thomas J. Green, "Critical Reflections on the *Schema* of the People of God," *Studia canonica* 14 (1980) 236-238.

21   Ibid. 237-238. According to Green the following episcopal conferences were represented at Ottawa Symposium: Austalia, Canada, England and Wales, France, Germany, Ireland, Scotland, South Africa, the United States and Zaire. The Symposium produced an unpublished document *Schema Canon Libri II de Populo Dei. An Analysis Prepared by an Inter-Episcopal Conference Meeting in Ottawa, August, 1978.*

22   See *Communicationes* 9 (1977) 365.

23   *Schema de Populo Dei*, c. 136: "§1. Debita cum prudentia clerici se gerant cum personis quarum frequentatio suam obligationem ad continentiam servandam in discrimen vocare aut in fidelium scandalum cedere posit. §2. Competit Episcopo dioecesano ut hac de re, audito Consilio presbyterali, normas statuat magis determinatas utque de servata hac obligatione in casibus particularibus iudicium ferat."

"personis" is used which could mean male or female. Furthermore, unlike the former code, the canon did not attempt to regulate the living arrangements of clerics and any reference to concubinage is also omitted. The decision to enact further legislation on these matters and to pass judgment on particular cases was reserved to the diocesan bishop, previously local ordinary, with the added qualification that he had to hear the presbyteral council. The canon seemed to reflect a degree of confidence in the maturity of the cleric to exercise the necessary due prudence in his living of perfect continence.

3. 1980 *Schema Codicis Iuris Canonici:* Canons 250 and 251

In 1980, for the first time in the revision process, the *schemata* of each *coetus* were brought together into a single work. This allowed the work to be viewed in its entirety.[24] In preparation for this *schema* in January, 1980, the *coetus de sacra hierarchia* again discussed clerical celibacy. The *coetus* now considered the possibility of removing the prohibition against the remarriage of married deacons. One of the consultors proposed that rather than remove the prohibition they should keep the original wording and add: "unless the Apostolic See grants a dispensation in extraordinary cases and for very grave cause."[25] The consultor further suggested that perhaps such an extraordinary cause may well be a married deacon whose wife had died leaving him to care for minor children.[26] The secretary of the *coetus* reminded the group that the *coetus de matrimonio* had already removed the impediment of orders for married deacons. He argued that, therefore, there should be no reference to a prohibition of

---

24   *Incrementa,* XIII.
25   *Communicationes* 14 (1982) 77: "...nisi Apostolica Sedis in casibus extraordinariis atque ex gravissimus causis dispensationem concedat."
26   Ibid.: "Si deve infatti prevedere la possibilità di un novo matrimonio per cause gravissime come nel caso in cui si hanno figli minori e muore la madre."

Anthony McLaughlin

remarriage for married deacons.[27] The *coetus* agreed and approved canon 250 which stated:

§1. Clerics are bound by the obligation to observe perfect and perpetual continence for the sake of the kingdom of heaven and they are, therefore, held to celibacy.
§2. Men living a married life who have been promoted to the permanent diaconate are not held to the prescript of §1.[28]

All Latin clerics are bound to the obligation of perfect and perpetual continence and therefore celibacy. Married deacons, though clerics, are exempt from this obligation even if their wives die.

Cardinal Ermenegildo Florit, the retired archbishop of Florence, and Archbishop Luis Eduardo Henriquez, the bishop of Valencia, Venezuela, argued that the prohibition on remarriage after ordination for married deacons should be retained. They stated:

The norm given in canon 250, §2, which is connected with canon 1042, §2, is contrary to the motu proprio *Sacrum diaconatus ordinem,* n. 16, and the tradition of the entire Oriental Church (catholic and orthodox). Unless the norm of the preceding 1977 *schema* is restored ("which holds that one is to observe celibacy, even with the loss of a wife"), it

---

27   *Communicationes* 14 (1982) 77: "Mons. Segretario ricorda che già nel gruppo 'De Matrimonio,' a richiesta di molti Organi consultivi, si è soppresso l'impedimento per i diaconi vedovi; qui si deve quindi conformare il lesto a quanto già decisio, rimettendo la definitiva decisione all'autorità superiore. Il testo rimane: praescripto §1 non tenetur viri qui in matrimonio viventes ad diaconatum permanentem promoti sunt."
28   Pontificia Commissio Codici Iuris Canonici Recognoscendo, *Schema Codicis Iuris Canonici iuxta animadversions S. R. E. Cardinalium, Episcoporum Conferentiarum, Dicasteriorum Curiae Romanae, Universitatum Facultatumque ecclesiasticarum necnon Superiorum Institutorum vitae consecrata recognitum* (Vatican City: Typis Polyglottis Vaticanis, 1980) c. 250: "§1. Clerici obligatione tenentur servandi perfectam perpetuamque propter Regnum caelorum ideoque ad caelibatum adstringuntur. §2. Praescripto §1 non tenetur viri qui in matrimonio viventes ad diaconatum permanentem promoti sunt." Hereafter 1980 *Schema.* All translations of this *schema* are by this author unless otherwise indicated.

would be better to seek the will of the Fathers of the Pontifical Commission concerning this specific matter.[29]

These consultors urged that the exemptions for married deacons be removed and that the canon should be restored to its pre-1977 *Schema* state. If this did not happen, then the question should be turned over for the consideration of the *plenarium*.

In response the secretary agreed that the matter should be referred to the *plenarium*. He also pointed out that the *coetus de matrimonio* had voted unanimously not to bind married deacons to the impediment of orders and urged conformity with their decision:

> The question posed in the observations is deferred to the plenarium of the congregation. The consultors, however, consent to follow the consultors of the *coetus de matrimonio,* that the text of §2, can remain.[30]

Interestingly nothing was said about the possibility of a married deacon marrying more than once after ordination. Yet, if there is no prohibition on marriage after ordination then any argument to limit the number of marriages has less of a basis.

---

29   Pontificia Commissio Codici Iuris Canonici Recognoscendo, *Relatio Complectens Synthesim Animadversionum ab Em. Mis. atque Exc. mis. Patribus Commissionis ad Novissimum Schema Codicis Iuris Canonici Exhibitarum, cum Responsionibus a Secretaria et Consultoribus datis* (Vatican City: Typis Polyglottis Vaticanis, 1981) 64-65: "Norma quae datur in canon 250 §2, quae conectatur cum canon 1042 §2, est contraria sive motu proprio *Sacrum diaconatus ordinem,* n. 16, sive traditioni totius Ecclesiae Orientalis (catholicae et orthodoxae). Nisi restituatur norma praecedentis *schema*tis 1977 ('qui tamen et ipsa, amissa uxore, ad caelibatum servandum teneter'), optandum esset ut de re specifica votatio habeatur Patrem Pontificiae Commissionis." Hereafter 1981 *Relatio.*

30   1981 *Relatio,* 65: "Quaestio in animadversione posita defertur ad Congregationem Plenarium. Consultores autem consent, sicuti Consultores *Coetus De Matrimonio,* textus huius §2 manere posse."

4. *Coetus Studiorum de Matrimonio:* Canon 1040

The *coetus de matrimonio* was charged with revising the canons on marriage. In March 1975 the *coetus* published the *Schema de Sacramentis* that contained revisions to the canons governing matrimonial impediments including the impediment of orders. The *coetus* affirmed that a married deacon was incapable of contracting a new marriage. Canon 287 stated:

§1. Those who are in sacred orders invalidly attempt marriage.
§2. Even deacons who have been married, by reason of c. 211 §1, §2 are incapable of contracting a new marriage.[31]

Two years later in 1977 the *coetus* voted to exempt married deacons from the impediment of orders. They reasoned that it was unjust to expect a married man not to be able to marry again, particularly in view of the fact that he did not choose celibacy. Also the new marriage may be the best solution to the needs of his particular family. The *coetus* stated:

Regarding §2, very many organs of consultation complained that deacons who had been married are declared 'inhabiles' to contract a new marriage: which seems unjust to them both because such deacons did not choose celibacy, and because very often a new marriage provides a very good solution for the children that there might be. As the question is quite clear, a vote was taken whether it would be good to free

---

31   Pontificia Commissio Codici Iuris Canonici Recognoscendo, *Schema Documenti Pontifici Quo Disciplina Canonica de Sacramentis Recognoscitur* (Vatican City: Typis Polyglottis Vaticanis, 1975), c. 287: "§1. Invalide matrimonium attentat qui in sacris ordinibus sunt constituti. §2. Etiam diaconi qui coniugati fuerunt, de quibus in c. 211 §1, §2, ad novum matrimonium contrahendum inhabiles sunt. " All translations of this *schema* are by this author unless otherwise indicated.

In 1966 Paul VI had reserved the dispensation from the impediment of orders to the roman pontiff. See Paul VI, motu proprio *De Episcoporum muneribus* art. 9, June 15, 1966: *AAS* 58 (1966) 470: "Salvis facultatibus Legatis Romani Pontificis et Ordinariis specialiter tributis, nobis expresse reservamus dispensationes quae sequntur : 1. Ab obligatione caelibatus seu a prohibitione matrimonii contrahendi, qua diaconi et presbyteri astringuntur, etiam si ad statum laicalem legitime redacti aut regressi sint."

these deacons from the impediment: placet 6, non placet 2. Therefore two consultors proposed that §2 be modified in this way: *Diaconi qui coniugati ordinem sacrum receperunt impedimento de quo in §1 non tenetur.* The formula satisfied everyone.[32]

The *coetus* submitted that paragraph two of canon 287 of the *Schema de Sacramentis* should instead read: Deacons who are in marriage and receive sacred orders are not held to the precepts of §1.[33] Canon 287 developed into canon 1040 of the 1980 *Schema* which read:

§1. They who have been established in sacred orders attempt marriage invalidly.

§2. Married deacons who have received a sacred order are not held to the prescript of §1.[34]

Married deacons were not to be bound by the impediment of orders. However, their brother deacons who were unmarried were bound by the impediment.

Cardinal James Knox, Prefect of the Sacred Congregation for the Sacraments and Divine Worship, and Archbishop Henriquez argued that to permit clergy to marry after ordination was in contradiction to the constant canonical tradition observed equally in the East and the West. They argued that this would have a detrimental effect on the theology of orders. They stated:

---

32   *Communicationes* 9 (1977) 365: "Quoad §2 permulta organa consultationis conquest sunt eo quod diaconi, qui conjugati fuerint, inhabiles declarentur ad novum contrahendum matrimonium: quod iniustum ipsis videtur sive quia tales diaconi caelibatum non elegerunt, sive quia saepe saepius novum matrimonium optimam solutionem praebet proli quae forte habeatur. Cum quaestio sit omnio clara, habeatur suffragatio an placeat eximere illos diaconos ab impedimento: placet 6, non placet 2. Ideo duo Consultores preponunt ut §2 ita redigatur diaconi qui coniugati ordinem sacrum receperunt impedimento de quo in §1 non tenetur. Formula omnibus placet." English translation from Roman Cholji, The *Lex Continentiae* and the Impediment of Orders," *Studia canonica* 21 (1987) 414.

33   Ibid: "Diaconi qui coniugati ordinem sacrum receperunt impedimento de quo in §1 non tenetur."

34   1980 *Schema*, c. 1040: "§1. Invalide matrimonium attendant qui sacris ordinibus sunt constituti. §2. Diaconi qui coniugati ordinem sacrum receperunt impedimento de quo in §1 non tenetur."

The norm derogates from a canonical principle of more than a millennium, which has always been observed in both the Latin and Oriental Church, and which has an apostolic origin. This would cause grave consequences for the sacrament of orders because that 'total giving' which the sacrament of orders confers as a grace and demands as a response would be endangered.[35]

The *coetus* determined that it was not expedient to prohibit the second marriages of deacons. They stated that in fact many episcopal conferences had sought such an exemption for married deacons:

> The *coetus* unanimously determines that it is not expedient to prohibit the second marriages of deacons. For the norm from many Episcopal conferences and other consultative organs has been sought, ponderous and objective reasons are present (such as the care of education of children, because it is unjust to impose celibacy on one who did not choose it, etc.). The statements concerning the apostolic origin of this norm are without foundation, nor are the grave consequences to be feared for a celibate priesthood. If such are to be feared, they would be rather from the ordination of women deacons. Nor is there a rationale from the oriental discipline, nor the *Schema* of the Oriental code which assumes the same norm: c. 141.[36]

The *coetus* dismissed the arguments that the prohibition of marriage for

---

35   1981 *Relatio,* 253: "Norma derogate principium Canonicum plus quam millenarium, in Ecclesia sive Latina sive Orientali semper servatum et quod iuxta quosdam originem habet apostolicam. Gravia consectaria pro Sacramento Ordinis exinde prosui possunt, eo quod in discrimen ponatur illa 'donatio absoluta' quam Sacramentum Ordinis ut gratia confert et ut reponsum postulat."

36   Ibid.: "Unamiter censet *coetus* quod non expediat secundas nuptias diaconis uxoratis prohibere. Nam norma a pluribus Episcoporum Conferentiis aliisque organis consultationis petita est, adsunt ponderosae et obiectivae rationes convenientae (propter filios, alendos et educandos, quia iniustum est coelibatum imponere ei id non elegit, etc). Sine fundamento sermo fit de origine apostolica huius normae, neque gravia consectaria timenda sunt pro coelibatu sacerdotum. Si quae timenda essent, venirent potius ex ipsa ordinatione diaconorum uxoratorum. Neque valet ratio ex disciplina orientali, nam *Schema* Codicis Orientalis eandem normam assumit: c. 141.

those in sacred orders was of apostolic origin, and that permitting married deacons to remarry would have a detrimental effect on priestly celibacy. Throughout the remainder of the revision process, in canon 1040 of the 1980 *Schema* and in canon 1087 of the 1982 *Schema*, the consistent recommendation remained that married deacons not be bound by the impediment of orders.

Not much is discernible regarding the discussions within each *coetus*. Rarely does *Communicationes* relate in noteworthy detail the reasons why a particular *coetus* adopted a certain position.[37] Therefore, it is difficult to understand the reasons why the *coetus* recommended that married deacons should not be bound by the ancient prohibition on remarriage beyond the fact that such deacons did not choose celibacy and that in some cases the family would benefit from a new marriage. Any reference to the Church's long canonical tradition of perfect continence for married clergy was absent from the discussion.

5. The 1982 *Schema Codicis Iuris Canonici:* Canons 279 and 280

In 1981, Pope John Paul II convoked the final plenary session of the Pontifical Commission for the Revision of the Code to deliberate on the entire text of the new code and to cast a definitive vote. The plenary session took place in Rome from October 20-29.[38] A *relatio,* a report, was prepared containing the 1980 *Schema* along with the suggestions and recommendations of the commission members. The *relatio* was then submitted to all the members for further comment. Based on these comments the *plenaria* revised the 1980 *Schema* further and the 1982 *Schema* was born.

In the course of the *plenarium*, canons 250 §2 (exempted deacons from

---

37   See Thomas J. Green, "Revised *Schema De Matrimonio*," *The Jurist* 40 (1980) 61.
38   *Communicationes* 13 (1981) 255-270.

obligation of continence and celibacy) and 1040 §2 (permitted deacons to re-marry) of the 1980 *Schema* were reviewed. In support of its position the *relatio* cited canon 141 of the 1981 *Schema* for the Eastern code, *De Culto Divino et Praesertim De Sacramentis,* which also contained an exception for remarriage of deacons:

> Those who have been constituted in sacred orders attempt marriage invalidly, except married deacons who have received the sacred order.[39]

The matrimonial law that was the subject of revision was the motu proprio *Crebrae allatae sunt.*[40] Canon 62 of *Crebrae allatae sunt* stated:

> §1. Clerics promoted to a major order invalidly attempt marriage.
> §2. The power of invalidating marriage is attributed to the subdiaconate and also to the other major orders.[41]

The revision process for the Eastern code had from the beginning voted to exempt married deacons from the impediment of orders. In the second ses-sion of the commission to revise the canons on marriage, April 7-12, 1975, the commission voted to exempt married deacons from the impediment of orders.[42] Canon 26 of *De Impedimentis in Genere* stated:

> §1. Those who are constituted in sacred orders invalidly attempt marriage.
> §2. Deacons who are married and have assumed this sacred order are

---

39   Pontificia Commissio Codici Iuris Canonici Orientalis Recognoscendo, *Schema Cano-num De Normis Generalibus et de Bonis Ecclesiae Temporalibus* (Vatican City: Typis Polyglottis Vaticanis, 1981), c. 141: "Invalide matrimonium attentant qui in sacris ordinibus sunt constituti, exceptis diaconis qui coniugati ordinem sacrum receperunt."

40   Pius XII, motu proprio *Crebrae allatae sunt,* February 22, 1949: *AAS* 41 (1949) 89-117. This motu proprio established the marriage law to be followed by the Eastern Catholic Churches. Hereafter *CA.*

41   *CA,* c. 62: "§1. Invalide matrimonium attentant clerici maiore ordine aucti. §2. Subdia-conatui, aeque ac maioribus ordinibus, vis dirimendi matrimonium tribuitur." All translations of this text are by this author unless otherwise indicated.

42   Pontificia Commissio Codici Iuris Canonici Orientalis Recognoscendo, *Nuntia* 8 (1979) 13. Hereafter *Nuntia.*

not held to the impediment in §1.[43]

This text conformed to the text of the *coetus de matrimonio* which had voted to exempt married deacons from this impediment as early as March 1975. However, in the 1986 *Schema Codicis Iuris Canonici Orientalis* the exemption for married deacons had been removed.[44] When the Eastern code came into effect on October 1, 1991, it contained no exemption from the impediment of orders for married deacons. Canon 804 decreed: "Persons who are in sacred orders invalidly attempt marriage."[45] It is interesting that eight years after the promulgation of the 1983 code, the supreme legislator was still determined that married deacons were not to be exempted from the impediment of orders.

The *plenarium* subsequently voted, 38 to 13 that widowed deacons should be permitted to remarry and remain in ministry without any need of a dispensation.[46] With the further revision, canons 250 and 251 of the 1980 *Schema* were now numbered 279 and 280 respectively in the 1982 *Schema*. Canon 279 §1 had another qualifying clause added. It now read:

§1. Clerics are obliged to observe perfect and perpetual continence for the sake of the kingdom of heaven and therefore are bound to celibacy which is a special gift of God by which sacred ministers can adhere more easily to Christ with an undivided heart and are able to dedicate themselves more freely to the service of God and humanity.

---

43   *Nuntia* 8 (1979) 13: c. 62: "§1. Matrimonium invalide attentant qui in sacris ordinibus sunt constituti. §2. Diaconi qui coniugati ordinem sacrum assumpserunt, impedimento de quo in §1 non tenetur." All translations of this text are by this author unless otherwise indicated.

44   *Nuntia* 24-25 (1987) 146: c. 799: "Invalide matrimonium attentat, qui in ordine sacro constitutus. "

45   *Codex Canonum Ecclesiarum Orientalium auctoritate Ioannis Pauli PP. II promulgatus* (Vatican City: Libreria Editrice Vaticana, 1990), c. 804: "Invalide matrimonium attentat, qui in ordine sacro est constitutus." Hereafter *CCEO*. English translation from *Code of Canon Law, Latin-English Edition: New English Translation* (Washington, DC: CLSA, 1995). All subsequent English translations of canons from this code will be taken from this source unless otherwise indicated.

46   *Communicationes* 14 (1982) 170.

§2. Men who are living in marriage and have been promoted to the permanent diaconate are not bound to the prescript of §1.[47]

All Latin clerics are obliged to observe perfect an perpetual and are therefore bound to celibacy. Married deacons are exempt from this obligation.

Canon 280 urged clerics to protect their continence by behaving prudently in the relations with other persons and empowered the bishop to enact legislation to protect the continence of clerics. The canon stated:

§1: Clerics must conduct themselves with prudence when they associate with persons whose company can endanger their observance of continence or cause scandal to the faithful.

§2: The decision to enact more specific rules in this matter belongs to the diocesan bishop, after hearing his presbyteral council, so that he may pass judgment in particular cases regarding the observance of this law. [48]

In summary we can state the following concerning the revision of canon 132 of the 1917 code concerning the obligation of clerical celibacy:

- *Schema De Populi Dei*: Canon 135 § 1 obliged Latin clerics to observe perfect and perpetual continence and therefore celibacy. Paragraph § 2 exempted married deacons from the obligation of continence and

47   Pontifica Commissio Codici Iuris Canonici Recognoscendo, *Codex Iuris Canonici: Schema Novissimum Iuxta Placita Patrum Commissionis Emendatum atque Summo Pontifici Praesentatum* (Vatican City: Typis Polyglottis Vaticanis, 1982), c. 279: "§1. Clerici obligatione tenentur servandi perfectam perpetuamque propter Regnum coelorum continentiam, ideoque ad coelibatum adstringuntur, quod est peculiare Dei donum, quo quidem sacri ministri indiviso corde Christo facilius adhaerere possunt
   atque Dei hominumque servitio liberius sese dedicare valent. §2. Praescripto §1 non tenetur viri qui in matrimonio viventes ad diaconatum permanentem promoti sunt." Hereafter 1982 *Schema*. All translations of this *schema* are by this author unless otherwise indicated.
48   1982 *Schema*, c. 280: "§1. Debita cum prudentia clerici se gerant cum personis quarum frequentatio ipsorum obligationem ad continentiam servandam in discrimen vocare aut in fidelium scandalum vertere posit. §2. Competit Episcopo dioecesano ut hac de re, audito Consilio presbyterali, normas statuat magis determinatas utque de servata hac obligatione in casibus particularibus iudicium ferat."

celibacy; however, upon the death of their wives deacons were bound to observe celibacy.

- The 1980 *Schema Codicis*: Canon 250 § 1 obliged Latin clerics to observe perfect and perpetual continence and therefore celibacy. Paragraph § 2 exempted married deacons from the obligations continence and celibacy even if their wives die.

- The 1982 *Schema Codicis*: Canon 279 § 1 obliged Latin clerics to perfect and perpetual continence and therefore celibacy, but added a qualifying clause that celibacy is also a gift in its own right. Paragraph § 2 exempted married deacons from the obligations of continence and therefore celibacy even if their wives die.

Based on the above *schema,* two principles are clear. First the code commission affirmed absolute continence and therefore celibacy for Latin clergy, and second the commission believed that permanent married deacons should be exempt from this obligation.

We can also state the following concerning the revision of canon 1072 of the 1917 code concerning the impediment of orders:

- *Schema De Sacramentis*: Canon 287 § 1 declared that those in sacred orders invalidly attempt marriage. Paragraph § 2 expressly stated that married deacons were also incapable of contracting a new marriage.

- The 1980 *Schema Codicis*: Canon 1040 declared that those on sacred orders invalidly attempt marriage. Paragraph § 2 exempted married deacons from the impediment of orders.

- The 1982 *Schema Codicis*: Canon 1087 declared that those in sacred orders invalidly attempt marriage. Paragraph § 2 exempted married deacons from the impediment of orders.

Based on the above *schema,* two principles are clear. First the code commission affirmed the impediment of orders for those in sacred orders. Second the commission believed that married deacons should be exempt from this impediment.

B. 1983 Code of Canon Law

The 1982 *Schema Codicis Iuris Canonici* was submitted to Pope John Paul II for personal examination and approval on April 22, 1982.[49] The pope studied the text with the help of a small number of canonists including Archbishop Rosalio Castillo Lara, pro-president of the commission.[50] Eight months later in December 1982 the pontiff declared that he would promulgate the code on January 25, 1983 to take effect on the first Sunday of Advent, November 27, 1983.

A comparison of the 1982 *Schema* with the 1983 code indicates that there was "considerable legislative activity during the eight months of papal review."[51] Some new canons were added, others were modified, some others were removed and still others had certain texts removed. The *schema's* proposed canon 279 on clerical celibacy and 1087 on the impediment of orders were among the canons that were significantly revised.[52] The pope removed canon 279 §2 that exempted married deacons from perfect and perpetual continence. He also removed canon 1087 §2 that exempted married deacons from the impediment of orders. Further when the *schema* for the Eastern code was presented to him for approval he also removed an exemption for married deacons from the impediment of orders from canon 141 of that *schema.*

Canons 132 and 133 of the 1917 code became canons 135 and 136 of the

---

49   *Communicationes* 15 (1983) 27-35.
50   See Umberto Betti, "In margine al nuovo codice di diritto canonico," *Antonianum* 58 (1983) 628-647.
51   *Incrementa,* XII.
52   Alesandro, "The Revision of the Code of Canon Law," 128.

1977 *Schema de Populo Dei,* which became canons 250 and 251 of the 1981 *Schema,* which became canons 279 and 280 of the 1982 *Schema.*

1. Canon 277: The Obligation of Continence and Celibacy

With the revision process complete, canons 132 and 133 of the 1917 code had now become canon 277 of the 1983 code. Canon 277 is found in Book Two: People of God, chapter three, "The Rights and Obligations of Clerics." Canon 277 §1 states:

> Clerics are obliged to observe perfect and perpetual continence for the sake of the kingdom of heaven and therefore are bound to celibacy which is a special gift of God by which sacred ministers can adhere more easily to Christ with an undivided heart and are able to dedicate themselves more freely to the service of God and humanity.[53]

A man becomes a cleric upon ordination to the diaconate.[54] Clerics-deacons, presbyters and bishops-are obliged to observe perfect and perpetual continence for the sake of the kingdom of heaven and therefore celibacy. By using the phrase "perfect and perpetual continence" the canon not only borrows from *Presbyterorum ordinis* 16, but also recovers a long standing canonical expression.[55] For most of the Church's legislative history the terms continence, perfect

---

[53]   *Codex Iuris Canonici auctoritate Ioannis Pauli PP. II promulgatus* (Vatican City: Libreria Editrice Vaticana, 1983), c. 277: "§1. Clerici obligatione tenentur servandi perfectam perpetuamque propter Regnum caelorum continentiam, ideoque ad caelibatum adstringuntur, quod est peculiare Dei donum, quo quidem sacri ministri indiviso corde Christo facilius adhaerere possunt atque Dei hominumque servito liberius sese dedicare valent." Hereafter 83 *CIC.* English translation from *Code of Canon Law, Latin-English Edition: New English Translation* (Washington, DC: CLSA, 1998). All subsequent English translations of canons from this code will be taken from this source unless otherwise indicated.

[54]   83 *CIC,* c. 266 §1: "Per receptum diaconatum aliquis fit clericus et incardinatur ecclesiae particulari vel praelaturae personali pro cuius servitio promotes est."

[55]   See Jorge de Otaduy, "Obligaciones y derechos de los clérigos," in *Comentario Exegético al Código de Derecho Canónico,* ed. Angel Marzoa et al. (Pamplona: Ediciones Universidad De Navarra, 1997) 1: 337.

continence, chastity and perfect chastity were commonly used.[56] According to the canon clerics have two distinct obligations, the observance of perfect and perpetual continence, minimally no sexual relations, and the commitment to celibacy, minimally no contracting of marriage. Continence is presented as the fundamental norm. Celibacy is presented as a secondary good, which, among other things, offers the best protection for the obligation of perfect and perpetual continence.[57] One must be careful to recognize when the law refers to the obligation of continence and when it refers to the obligation of celibacy.[58]

Unlike the former canon 132, celibacy is not described negatively as a prohibition on marriage but positively as a "special gift of God" that disposes the cleric to more worthy service of God and neighbor. There is also no reference to the cleric's violation of chastity constituting a sacrilege. The following exchange concerning this issue is recorded in *Communicationes:*

Let it be stated that the violation of the perfect continence entails the sin of sacrilege (some Father).

Response. This is true, but it is a matter for moral theology.[59]

The secretariat relegated this issue to the area of moral theology not canon law. The removal of canon 119 of the 1917 cod e that declared the physical violation of a cleric to be a sacrilege[60] assured that any reference to sacrilege

---

56   See Council of Carthage (390), in *Sacrorum Conciliorum: Nova et Amplissma Collectio,* ed. Ioannes Dominicus Mansi (Paris: Herbert Welter, 1902) 3: 692-693. Hereafter Mansi.
57   See Edward Peters, "Canonical Considerations on Diaconal Continence," *Studia Canonica* 39 (2005) 150-151.
58   Ibid.
59   *Communicationes* 14 (1982) 170: "Dicatur quod violatio perfectae continentiae de qua in §1 secumfert peccatum sacrilegii (aliquis Pater). R. Hoc verum est, sed pertinet ad theologiam moralem." English translation is my own.
60   17 *CIC*, c. 118: "Omnes fideles debent clericis, pro diversis eorum gradibus et muneribus, reverentiam seque sacrilegii delicto commaculant, si quando clericis realem iniuriam intulerint."

would be omitted.[61]

Canon 277 §1 as it is written contains no exemption for married deacons. In fact as previously stated Pope John Paul II removed the paragraph that exempted married deacons just before the promulgation of the code. A plain reading of the canon would bind married permanent deacons to perfect and perpetual continence from the moment of ordination. In examining this canon the author is mindful of the methods of interpretation contained in canon 17 of book one of the code, "General Norms," which states:

> Ecclesiastical laws must be understood in accord with the proper meaning of the words considered in their text and context. If the meaning remains doubtful and obscure, recourse must be made to parallel places, if there are such, to the purpose and circumstances of the law, and to the mind of the legislator.[62]

Laws are to be understood according to the proper meaning of words, both their text and context. Only if meaning remains doubtful or obscure may one have recourse to other interpretative aids.[63] Javier Otaduy in his commentary on this canon observes:

> One must not suppose that the intention of the legislator is other than the one manifested in his words otherwise "frustra ferrentur leges." The words, then, are "quasi legis substantia," and one must not look for artificial reasons to discredit their proper sense.[64]

---

61   John E. Lynch, "The Obligations and Rights of Clerics," in *The Code of Canon Law: A Text and Commentary*, ed. James A. Coriden et al. (New York/Mahwah, NJ: Paulist Press, 1985) 210.
62   83 *CIC*, c. 17: "Leges ecclesiasticae intellegendae sunt secundum propriam verborum significationem in textu et contextu consideratam; quae si dubia et obscura manserit, ad locos parallelos, si qui sint, ad legis finem ac circumstantias et ad mentem legislatoris est recurrendum."
63   See Javier Otaduy, "Ecclesiastical Laws," in *Exegetical Commentary on the Code of Canon Law,* ed. Angel Marzoa et al. (Chicago, IL: Midwest Theological Forum, 2004) 1:325.
64   Ibid., 362.

As we will see some canonists contend that the text and context of canon 277 §1 are indeed doubtful. James Provost argues that canon 277 as it is written is problematic. He states:

> There remains the problem of canon 277. This is the canon which imposes perfect and perpetual continence on all clerics. No exception is made for permanent deacons, although one had been included in the earlier drafts of the canon. Does this mean that married permanent deacons as of November 27, 1983 had to cease having marital relations with their wives? The text of the law would seem to impose this 'for the sake of the kingdom of heaven.' However, through matrimony each of the spouses acquires 'equal obligations and rights to those things which pertain to the partnership of conjugal life' (c.1135) and sexual cooperation is part of that permanent consortium (c. 1096 §1). *Since the new code does not take away acquired rights unless they were expressly revoked by the code (c. 4), and since even canon 277 does not explicitly state it is revoking the acquired marital rights of married deacons, continence is not being imposed on them even though the law reads that way.*[65]

Joseph W. Pokusa argues similarly to Provost:

> Married couples enjoy a mutual and 'acquired right' to marital relations. Such an acquired right' is without doubt protected from any change which may have been introduced by the 1983 Code of Canon Law.....Nowhere does the 1983 code expressly revoke a married deacon's right to proper marital intimacy. Canon 1031 §2, moreover, continues to require the consent of the wife prior to ordination. Only if the Church explicitly advised the wife (and the deacon candidate) that they would be expected to renounce sex and live continently could there be

65   James H. Provost, "Permanent Deacons in the 1983 Code," *CLSA Proceedings* 46 (1985) 186.

any juridic basis for supporting she has given up her right to a proper married life in virtue of her husband's ordination. Certainly, the argument against canon 277 being literally applied to married permanent deacons ordained before the 1983 code could be justified on the basis of canon 4's exception for acquired rights. Just how facilely such an argument could be directed in the case of deacons who were ordained after November 23, 1983 may be questioned.[66]

Robert M. Garrity agrees with Provost and Pokusa. He asserts:

Despite the letter of the law, married deacons clearly are not bound to continence. They have an acquired right to marital relations with their wives.[67]

Peters responds to Provost arguments:

There are some key acknowledgements of major points in this passage, including: first, that c. 277 clearly imposes continence on all clerics, including permanent deacons; and second, that an exception to the law of continence for permanent deacons was proposed but was dropped from the 1983 code before promulgation. Yet there is no suggestion in Provost's remarks that permanent deacons ordained under the 1983 code are not included in the scope of c. 277. The most Provost argues, and I think correctly, is that one cannot lose a fundamental or acquired right without consent, and that consent cannot have been obtained from men (and their wives) who were unaware that a fundamental right (conjugal relations) would be lost upon ordination. Provost's argument, however, that permanent deacons are immune by law from the obligation of continence because no express mention of them is made in c. 277 fails for

66   Joseph H. Pokusa, "The Diaconate: A History of Law Following Practice," *The Jurist* 45 (1985) 125-126. See also *A Canonical-Historical Study of the Diaconate in the Western Church,* Canon Law Studies 495 (Washington, DC: Catholic University of America, 1979).
67   Robert M. Garrity, "Spiritual and Canonical Values in Mandatory Priestly Celibacy," *Studia canonica* 27 (1993) 241.

the simple reason that law, having imposed (or better here, reiterated) a given obligation on a class of persons, does not need to engage in the redundant exercise of expressly saying, in effect, that "no exception for a subset of those persons is granted" in order for that obligation to be binding on the subset of persons in the class.[68]

While canon 277 *§1 states an obligation for clerics, c*anon 288 expressly exempts permanent deacons, married or unmarried, from various clerical obligations, but the obligations prescribed in canon 277 are not among them.[69] In his commentary on canon 288, William Woestmann contends that married deacons are not bound by the obligations of canon 277 when he states:

> Although this canon (288) makes no reference to canon 277, *§1 and the obligation of clerics to observe celibacy and perpetual continence, legitimately married permanent deacons are not bound by celibacy and perpetual continence. However they are bound to conjugal chastity.*[70]

Woestmann does not cite any source to justify this mitigation. Edward Peters disagrees with Woestmann's contention:

> First, one should observe that all married Christians, not just permanent deacons, are bound to observe "conjugal chastity," but since neither c. 277 nor c. 288 even mentions "chastity," clerical or otherwise, reading an explicit canonical obligation of "chastity" into the terms of these canons is unsupportable. More importantly, though, it seems a conclusion exactly the opposite of Woestmann's should be drawn regarding the failure of c. 288 to include an exemption from the obligation of continence imposed on all clerics in c. 277, i.e., not that such an exemption

---

68   Peters, "Canonical Considerations on Diaconal Continence," 176-177.

69   83 *CIC*, c. 288: "Diaconi permanentes praescriptis canonum 284, 285 §§3 et 4, 286, 287 §2 non tenentur, nisi ius particulare aliud statuat."

70   William H. Woestmann, *The Sacrament of Orders and the Clerical State: A Commentary on the Code of Canon Law* (Ottawa, St. Paul University, 1999) 202.

should be recognized, but that an exemption on this precise point was clearly withheld.[71]

Provost, Pokusa and Garrity argue that married clerics, whether deacons or priests, are exempt from the obligations of canon 277, because in accord with canon 4[72] they cannot be deprived of their acquired right to conjugal relations within marriage.[73] Peters points out that canon 4 refers to rights granted to physical persons by the Apostolic See. Can one argue that conjugal rights are granted to the couple by the Apostolic See? Rather are not conjugal rights given by natural law or even divine law?[74] Yet we also know from the code that certain fundamental rights including conjugal ones can be freely surrendered. An unmarried man freely surrenders his natural and fundamental right to marry in order to receive holy orders. Could a married couple surrender their conjugal rights in order for the husband to be admitted to holy orders? While one can argue that married persons do have a right[75] to conjugal relations, can one also argue that this conjugal right can be surrendered by mutual consent for the sake of ordination? After all that was the practice of the Church for much of her canonical history. Conversely, can one not argue that there is no right for a cleric and his wife to have sexual relations after ordination?

Peters does admit that, while canon 4 may not be applicable to the issue

---

71   Edward Peters, "Canonical Considerations on Diaconal Continence," *Studia canonica* 39 (2005) 176.

72   83 *CIC*, c. 4: "Iura quaesita, itemque privilegia quae, ab Apostolica Sede ad haec usque tempora personis sive physicis sive iuridicis concessa, in usu sunt nec revocata, integra manent, nisi huius Codicis canonibus expresse revocentur."

73   83 *CIC*, c. 1135: "Utrique coniugi aequum officium et ius est ad ea quae pertinent ad consortium vitae coniugalis."

74   See Peters, "Canonical Considerations on Diaconal Continence," 174-175.

75   See Francisco Javier Urrutia, *De Normis Generalibus, Adnotationes in Codicem: Liber 1* (Rome: Tipographia Pontifical Gregorian University, 1983) 12, explains that acquired rights are assured in an act already posited and recognized by law. Acquired rights are considered established in the highest degree: "sed iura acquisita posito iam facto a lege agnito....Iura quaesita maxime stabilia habebtur."

of continence for married deacons, there is the deeper question that one cannot surrender fundamental rights without being expressly aware of it. Just as the unmarried candidate for orders is expressly aware that he is surrendering his natural and fundamental right to marry, so to if married clergy are bound to surrender their conjugal relations, should they not be made aware of this obligation?[76]

Furthermore canon 1135 which speaks of each spouse having an equal duty and right to those things which belong to the partnership of conjugal life, obviously including sexual relations, is speaking of married persons in general and not of 'married clergy' in particular.[77]

Canon 277 §2 seeks to protect the continence of clergy. In doing so the primary good of continence is affirmed. It states:

Clerics are to behave with due prudence towards persons whose company can endanger their obligation to observe continence or give rise to scandal among the faithful.[78]

This seems a natural and practical consequence of the preceding paragraph. Peters observes that there is a noticeable shift in language from canon 133 of the 1917 code.[79] The former canon exhorted clerics to avoid certain "mulieres" (women) and clerics who were contumacious in this regard were presumed to be living in concubinage. The 1983 code warns clerics to avoid certain "perso-

---

76   See Peters, "Canonical Considerations on Diaconal Continence," 177.
77   Ibid., 175.
78   83 *CIC*, c. 277 §2: "Debita cum prudentia clerici se gerant cum personis, quarum frequentatio ipsorum obligationem ad continentiam servandam in discrimen vocare aut in fidelium scandalum vertere possit."
79   17 *CIC*, c. 133: "§1. Caveant clerici ne mulieres, de quibus suspicio esse possit, apud se retineant aut quoquo modo frequentent. §2. Eisdem licet cum illis tantum mulieribus cohabitare in quibus naturale foedus nihil mali permittit suspicari, quales sunt mater, soror, amita et huiusmodi, aut a quibus spectata morum honestas, cum provectiore aetate coniuncta, omnem suspicionem amoveat. §3. Iudicium an retinere vel frequentare mulieres, etiam illas in quas communiter suspicio non cadit, in peculiari aliquo casu scandalo esse possit aut incontinentiae aferre periculum, ad Ordinarium loci pertinet, cuius est clericos ab hac retentione vel frequentatione prohibere. §4. Contumaces praesumuntur concubinarii."

nis" (persons). 'Women' could threaten the cleric's obligation of celibacy, i.e., attempted marriage, while the use of the word "person" (male/female) seems to aimed more at the protection of continence rather than the obligation of celibacy. "This shift in language towards 'persons' and 'continence' is consistent with the argument that continence and not celibacy is the primary canonical obligation for clerics."[80] Also, not all clerics are bound to celibacy, i.e., married deacons, hence the canon's emphasis on continence.[81]

Canon 277 §3 deals with the authority of the bishop to safeguard the observance of continence. It states:

> The diocesan bishop is competent to establish more specific norms concerning this matter and to pass judgment in particular cases concerning the observance of this obligation.[82]

This canon goes further than the 1917 code and gives the diocesan bishop authority to issue specific norms on this matter. Earlier drafts had included a reference to the bishop consulting the presbyteral council before establishing or issuing such norms.[83] However, this requirement was removed because of the delicate and confidential nature of such matters.[84] The canon is silent on what shape these norms might take.

2. Canon 1042: The Impediment of Marriage

Under the 1917 code, a married man was simply impeded from the recep-

---

80   Peters, "Canonical Considerations on Diaconal Ministry," 150.
81   Ibid.
82   83 *CIC*, c, 277 §3: "Competit Episcopo dioecesano ut hac de re normas statuat magis determinatas utque de huius obligationis observantia in casibus particularibus iudicium ferat."
83   1977 *Schema De Populo Dei*, c. 136; 1989 *Schema De Codicis Iuris Canonici*, c. 251 §1.
84   See Aiden McGrath, "The Obligations and Rights of Clerics," in *The Canon Law: Letter & Spirit*, ed. Gerard Sheehy et al. (Collegeville, MN: Liturgical Press, 1995) 158.

tion of orders.[85] The impediment could be dispensed from by the Holy See but only if perpetual continence could be guaranteed.[86] With the restoration of the permanent diaconate and the admission of married men to this order canon 987 would need to be revised. As prescribed in canon 277 clerics in the Latin Church are ordinarily obliged to celibacy. Therefore being married is an impediment to the reception of orders. Though canon 1042 affirms this norm it also establishes an exception for married men who are legitimately destined for the permanent diaconate. These men are not impeded from the reception of orders. Yet married men who are destined for the presbyterate must petition the Holy See for a dispensation from this impediment.[87]

The impediment of marriage arises from a valid bond which distinguishes this canon from canon 1041, 3°.[88] The impediment ceases with a declaration of nullity, a dissolution of marriage, or the death of a spouse. In the 1917 code all married men had to have a dispensation from the impediment of marriage in order to receive orders. Now only those married men not legitimately destined for the permanent diaconate must do so. A married man who receives holy orders without a dispensation does so validly but illicitly. Such a man becomes irregular for the exercise of orders already received.[89] Interestingly, Coriden and Provost do not see an exception in this canon to the canonical obligation of continence for married clergy. They argue:

---

85   17 *CIC*, c. 987, 2°: "Sunt simpliciter impediti: Viri uxorem habentes." See also Roman Cholji, "The *Lex Continentiae* and Orders," *Studia canonica* 21 (1987) 413.

86   See Udalricus Beste, *Introductio in Codicem: quam in usum et utilitatem scholae et cleri ad promptam expeditamque canonum interpretationem,* 3rd ed. (Collegeville: St. John's Abbey Press, 1946) 580; Mattheaus Conte A Coronata, *Institutiones Iuris Canonici* (Turin: Marietti, 1947) 2:191; Eduardus Regatillo, *Institutiones iuris canonici* (Santander: Sal Terrae, 1946) n. 968, 539.

87   Donal Kelly, "Holy Orders," in *The Canon Law: Letter & Spirit*, ed. Gerard Sheehy et al. (Collegeville, MN: Liturgical Press, 1995) 565. See also 83 *CIC*, c. 1047 *§2, 3°*.

88   83 *CIC*, c. 1041, 3°. This canon speaks of an attempted or invalid marriage.

89   83 *CIC*, c. 1044 §2, 1°: "Ab ordinibus exercendis impediuntur: qui impedimento ad ordines recipiendos detentus, illegitime ordines recepit."

The dispensation from the impediment of canon 1042, 1° which permits a married man to be ordained to the priesthood does not explicitly include with it a dispensation from the obligations of canon 277 §1. Neither is there an explicit exception in the law for married men ordained to the diaconate.[90]

Coriden and Provost do believe that, while an exception is not found in canon 1042, it is found elsewhere in the code. We will examine their claim later in this chapter.

3. Canon 1031 §2: Married Men Seeking Orders

As outlined above, ordinarily a validly married man is impeded from the reception of orders. Yet a married man who is legitimately destined for the permanent diaconate is not so impeded. Canon 1031 §2 states:

A candidate for the permanent diaconate who is not married is not to be admitted to the diaconate until after completing at least the twenty-fifth year of age; one who is married, not until after completing at least the thirty-fifth year of age and with the consent of his wife.[91]

The canon distinguishes between married and unmarried candidates for the permanent diaconate. In the case of unmarried candidates the age for ordina-

---

90   See James A. Coriden and James H. Provost, "Canonical Implications Related to the Ordination of Married Men to the Priesthood in the United States of America," *CLSA Proceedings* 58 (1996) 448.

91   83 *CIC*, c. 1031 §2: "Candidatus ad diaconatum permanentem qui non sit uxoratus ad eundem diaconatum ne admittatur, nisi post expletum vigesimum quintum saltem aetatis annum; qui matrimonio coniunctus est, nonnisi post expletum trigesimum quintum saltem aetatis annum, atque de uxoris consensu."

tion is established at twenty-five, the same as for the presbyterate.[92] A married candidate must have completed his thirty-fifth year,[93] and the law additionally requires that his wife consent to his ordination.[94] The requirement of the consent of the wife is stated in two different canons.[95] This consent is to be given in writing and included in the documents required for the husband's ordination.[96]

4. Spousal Consent[97]

The only time the code requires the consent of another, who is neither the authorized sacred minister nor the recipient, for an adult to licitly receive a sacrament, is in the case of a married man's ordination to the diaconate.[98] The wife of a man legitimately destined for the permanent diaconate must consent to his ordination. As noted earlier two canons specifically mention the necessity of this spousal consent. Furthermore, the code does not admit of the possibility that the ordination of a permanent deacon is licit without the consent of his wife. This is truly an extraordinary circumstance. What if the wife does not consent? Should the ordination of her husband not proceed? According to the

---

92   See Paul VI, motu proprio *Sacrum diaconatus ordinem,* June 18, 1967, n. 5: *AAS* 59 (1967) 699. Hereafter *SDO.* In the United states the particular law establishes the minimum age for the reception of diaconate at thirty-five for married and unmarried candidates. See United States Conference of Catholic Bishops, *National Directory for the Formation, Ministry, and Life of Permanent Deacons in the United States* (Washington, DC.: United States Conference of Catholic Bishops, 2005) n. 87. Hereafter *NDFD.*

93   See *SDO* 12.

94   See *SDO* 11.

95   83 *CIC,* cc. 1031§2, 1050, 3°.

96   83 *CIC,* c. 1050, 3°: "Ut quis ad sacros ordines promoveri possit, sequentia requiruntur documenta: 3° si agatur de promovendis ad diaconatum, testimonium recepti baptismi et confirmationis, atque receptorum ministeriorum de quibus in can. 1035; item testimonium factae declarationis de qua in can. 1036, necnon, si ordinandus qui promovendus est ad diaconatum permanentem sit uxoratus, testimonia celebrati matrimonii et consensus uxoris."

97   See Peters, "Canonical Considerations on Diaconal Continence," 153-156. Peters raises this question in great detail. The author of this book bases much of section B.4. of this chapter entitled "Spousal Consent" on Peters observations.

98   See Peters, "Canonical Considerations on Diaconal Continence,"154.

national directory for the formation of permanent deacons in the United States, it would seem that consent is also required of a woman who marries a widowed permanent deacon.[99]

The requirement of the wife's consent raises a fundamental question. To what is the wife being asked to consent? "Few commentators have asked this question, and those that have either passed over it in silence or simply mentioned it without further analysis."[100] Daniel Cenalor states that the wife's consent is required, because "any opposition by the candidate's wife would make, to a greater or lesser degree, the ministry difficult to exercise."[101] Robert J. Geisinger suggests:

> A wife's agreement to her husband's diaconal ordination does not imply that she intends to participate actively in his ministry, although she may wish to do so; the consent rather suggests simply that she will support him in his exercise of sacred ministry. Most fundamentally, the wife's consent assures the parties that she foresees no threat to her marriage.[102]

McGrath contends that the consent of the wife is to ensure that she knows the "nature and the extent of the obligations to be undertaken by her husband."[103] Some commentators, for example, Woestmann and Althaus, simply state the

---

99   United States Conference of Catholic Bishops, *National Directory for the Formation, Ministry and Life of Permanent Deacons in the United States* (Washington, DC: United States Conference of Catholic Bishops, 2005) n. 75, 36.

100   See Peters, "Canonical Considerations on Diaconal Continence," 153-156.

101   See Daniel Cenalmor, "The Requirements for Ordination," in *Exegetical Commentary on the Code of Canon Law,* ed. Angel Marzoa et al. (Chicago, IL: Midwest Theological Forum, 2004) 3/1: 960.

102   See Robert J. Geisinger, "Article 4: The Required Documents and Investigation," in the *New Commentary on the Code of Canon Law,* ed. John P. Beal et al. (New York/Mahwah, NJ: Paulist Press, 2000) 1229.

103   See Aiden Mc Grath, "The Obligations and Rights of Clerics," in *The Canon Law: Letter and Spirit,* ed. Gerard Sheehy et al. (Collegeville, MN: Liturgical Press, 1995) 558.

requirement of uxorial consent without further analysis.[104] Others such as Manzanares and Chiapetta make no mention of it at all.[105]

Most commentators believe that the requirement of uxorial consent is simply a matter of domestic practicality. This author wonders how the ministry of a permanent deacon would in the majority of cases impact a marriage and family more than his secular job already does. While his diaconal ministry makes additional demands of him, it is interesting to note that only thirty percent of permanent deacons are involved in full-time ministry.[106] Full-time ministry in most of these cases means no more than twenty-one hours a week.[107] Moreover sixty-two percent of married permanent deacons were not employed in secular work.[108]

Peters suggests that perhaps the requirement of uxorial consent has a more fundamental basis:

> But the extraordinary and twice mentioned requirement of uxorial consent to the husband's ordination would be understandable, indeed, wholly justified, if as a result of the husband's ordination, the wife were to suffer the loss of one of her own fundamental marital rights as would be the case if all clerics, including married permanent deacons, were bound under c. 277 §1, to the obligation of "perfect and perpetual continence for the sake of the kingdom of heaven." In that case, obviously,

---

104   Woestmann, *The Sacrament of Orders and the Clerical State,* 50-51; Rüdiger Althaus, "Begrenztes Recht auf Priesterweihe," in *Münsterischer Kommentar zum Codex Iuris Canonici* (Essen, 1985) Band 4, 1031/2.

105   Julio Manzanares, "De la función de santificar de la Iglesia," in *Codigo De Derecho Canonico,* ed. Juan Luis Acebal et al. (Madrid: Biblioteca De Autores Cristianos, 2004) 532; Luigi Chiappetta, *Il Codice di diritto canonico: commento giuridico-pastorale* (Naples: Edizioni Dehoniane, 1996) 2: 229.

106   Center for Applied Research in the Apostolate Georgetown University, *Profile of the Diaconate in the United States: A Report of Findings from CARA's Deacon Poll* (Washington, DC: CARA, 2004) 20.

107   Ibid., 21.

108   Ibid., 14.

the husband's choice to accept ordination and to assume its burdens, including continence (albeit without celibacy) would leave the wife without the opportunity to exercise her legitimately acquired conjugal rights. It is in the face of her own loss of conjugal rights, I suggest, and not because of some vague notions of marital harmony, and even less to canon law having granted one person a power of personal preference over another's ability to receive a sacrament, that the 1983 code recognizes a wife's extraordinary power of veto over her husband's desire to seek the sacrament of orders.[109]

For much of the Church's canonical history uxorial consent was directly related to the surrendering of conjugal rights and the embracing of absolute continence.

5. Canon 1037: Public Acceptance of Celibacy

The obligation of celibacy is to be assumed in a public rite before the reception of diaconate. This requirement was first introduced in 1972 by Paul VI in the motu proprio *Ad pascendum*.[110] Prior to this time, the acceptance of celibacy was implicit in the ordination to the subdiaconate. In *Ad pascendum* article 6 the pope stated:

> The special consecration of celibacy for the sake of the kingdom of heaven, and its obligation for candidates to the priesthood and for unmarried candidates to the diaconate, are in fact linked with the diaconate. The public commitment to holy celibacy before God and the Church is to be celebrated in a particular rite, even by religious, and is to precede ordination to the diaconate. Celibacy accepted in this way

---

109   Peters, "Canonical Considerations on Diaconal Continence, 155.
110   Paul VI, motu proprio *Ad pascendum,* August 15, 1972: *AAS* 64 (1972) 534-540. Hereafter *AP.*

is a diriment impediment to marriage. In accordance with traditional church discipline, a married deacon who has lost his wife cannot enter a new marriage.[111]

Accordingly a public rite of the acceptance of celibacy was inserted into the ordination rite. This requirement found juridic expression in canon 1037 which states:

> An unmarried candidate for the permanent diaconate and a candidate for the presbyterate are not to be admitted to the order of diaconate unless they have assumed the obligation of celibacy in the prescribed rite publicly before God and the Church or have made perpetual vows in a religious institute.[112]

An unmarried candidate for sacred orders is bound to make an explicit acceptance of the obligation to celibacy. The canon does not require these men to make an explicit promise of continence. Unmarried men are already bound to continence by the moral law, but they are not bound to celibacy. In order to protect the fundamental obligation to observe perfect and perpetual continence, an explicit acceptance of celibacy is necessary.

Married candidates for the permanent diaconate or the presbyterate are not obliged to promise celibacy. This would make no sense because they are already married. Yet could it be argued that married men implicitly make a conditional

---

111   *AP* art. 6, *AAS* 64 (1972) 539: "Consecratio proprio caelibatus, propter regnum caelorum servati, huiusque obligatio pro candidatis ad sacerdotium et pro candidatis non uxoratis ad diaconatum reapse conectuntur cum diaconatu. Publica ipsius sacri caelibatus assumptio coram Deo et Ecclesia etiam a religiosis celebranda est speciali ritu, qui ordinationem diaconalem praecedat. Caelibatus hoc modo assumptus impedimentum dirimens est adnuptias ineundas. Diaconi quoque uxorati, amissa uxore, ex tradita Ecclesiae disciplina ad novum matrimonium ineundum inhabiles sunt."

112   83 *CIC*, c. 1037: "Promovendus ad diaconatum permanentem qui non sit uxoratus, itemque promovendus ad presbyteratum, ad ordinem diaconatus ne admittantur, nisi ritu praescripto publice coram Deo et Ecclesia obligationem caelibatus assumpserint, aut vota perpetua in instituto religioso emiserint."

acceptance of celibacy with the reception of ordination, because upon the death of their wives each is bound to celibacy? Gianfranco Ghirlanda argues that permanent deacons upon the death of their wives are bound to observe the perfect and perpetual continence prescribed in canon 277 §1.[113]

In 1989 John Paul II revised the rite of ordination of deacons. In the revised rites even religious who had taken perpetual vows are now bound to make a public acceptance of celibacy before ordination.[114] Thus the pope derogated from the prescripts of canon 1037.

The juridic effects of the obligation of continence-celibacy prescribed in canon 277 and supported by canon 1037 are basically threefold: (1) The obligation lays the foundation for the impediment of orders, canon 1087; (2) Violation of the obligation is subject to penalties, canons 1394-1395; (3) The obligation may be the object of dispensation, canon 291.

6. Canon 1087: The Impediment of Sacred Orders

Those who are in sacred orders invalidly attempt marriage. In the revision process canon 1072 of the 1917 code became canon 1087. In fact the wording of the canon 1087 is virtually verbatim that of the former canon 1072.[115] The impediment of sacred orders arises from the valid reception of the orders of bishop, presbyter and deacon and is related to the obligation of clerical celibacy.[116] Yet this invalidating law is not rooted in the law of celibacy *per se* but in the valid reception of orders. The law of celibacy provides a basis and a justification for

---

113   Gianfranco Ghirlanda, *De Ecclesiae Munere Sanctificandi: De Ordine* (Rome: Pontifical Gregorian University, 1983) 31: "Se diaconus coniugatus permanes qui uxorem amittit, obligatione servandi perfectam et perpetuam continentiam tenetur.... "

114   Congregation for Divine Worship and the Discipline of the Sacraments, decree *Ritus ordinationem* n. 5, June 29, 1989: *AAS* 82 (1990) 827.

115   17 *CIC*, c. 1072: "Invalide matrimonium attentant clerici in sacris ordinibus constituti."

116   83 *CIC*, c. 277 §1.

this canon, but it does not imply or constitute it.[117] The impediment of sacred orders applies to all clerics whether they were married or unmarried when they received them. An exemption from this impediment for married deacons was removed by the legislator before the promulgation of the code.

As Richard Lyons observes:

> The question now arises whether or not married permanent deacons who became widowers, might be allowed to remarry. In the present law, the answer appears to be negative, barring the possibility of a dispensation. Another interesting problem with this canon is in its relation to canon 288 of the 1983 code, which lists those canons which do not bind permanent deacons. Canon 277 is not among those listed. Therefore, unless this was an oversight which might be corrected in the future, canon 277 obliges permanent deacons who become widowers to remain unmarried.[118]

A dispensation from the impediment of sacred orders is reserved to the Apostolic See.[119] According to the *praxis curiae* bishops are not dispensed from this impediment. Presbyters are only dispensed as part of the laicization process,[120] and until recently deacons were also only dispensed as part of the laicization process.[121] In danger of death situations those mentioned in canon 1079 §2 can

---

117   See Cantón, "Impedimento de Orden Sagrado," 85.

118   Richard Lyons, "The Permanent Diaconate: A Commentary on its Development from the End of the Second Vatican Council to the 1983 Code of Canon Law," *CLSA Proceedings* 49 (1988) 94.

119   83 *CIC*, c. 1078 §2: "Impedimenta quorum dispensatio Sedi Apostolicae reservatur sunt: 1° impedimentum ortum ex sacris ordinibus aut ex voto publico perpetuo castitatis in instituto religioso iuris pontificii."

120   The author acknowledges that the term 'laicization,' though not used explicitly in the code, is used in common parlance to denote the process, voluntary or imposed, by which a cleric loses the clerical state. This term will be used for the sake of convenience to denote loss of the clerical state.

121   John P. Beal, "Diriment Impediments Specifically," in *New Commentary on the Code of Canon Law*, ed. John P. Beal et al. (New York/Mahwah, NJ: Paulist Press, 2000) 1289.

dispense a deacon from this impediment but not a priest or bishop.[122] This dispensation can be granted even if the danger is applicable to the perspective wife.[123]

In the years between the restoration of the permanent diaconate and the 1983 code, the Holy See rarely granted a dispensation for deacons from the impediment of orders. Such a dispensation would permit a permanent deacon to marry again validly and remain in ministry. Ordinarily, deacons who wished to remarry were encouraged to petition for laicization and a dispensation from the impediment of orders. Between the restoration of the permanent diaconate and the 1983 code, only eighteen laicizations were granted for permanent deacons.[124]

In 1984 *Roman Replies* recorded the first case of a permanent deacon receiving a dispensation from the impediment of orders to remarry.[125] The dispensation was granted eight days after the promulgation of the code. The case involved a widowed African-American deacon in a diocese in the southern United States. He was the only African-American deacon in a diocese where one-fifth of the faithful were African-American. The dispensation was granted on the basis of the ministerial need and the needs of his children. The deacon was permitted to marry validly and to remain in ministry. However, the congregation cautioned the bishop that this dispensation should not become an example to others.[126]

---

122   83 *CIC*, c. 1079 §1: "Urgente mortis periculo, loci Ordinarius potest tum super forma in matrimonii celebratione servanda, tum super omnibus et singulis impedimentis iuris ecclesiastici sive publicis sive occultis, dispensare proprios subditos ubique commorantes et omnes in proprio territorio actu degentes, excepto impedimento orto ex sacro ordine presbyteratus."

123   Thomas P. Doyle, "Diriment Impediments in General," in *The Code of Canon Law: A Text and Commentary*, ed. James A. Coriden et al. (NewYork/Mahwah, NJ: Paulist Press, 1985) 761-762.

124   *Diaconal Quarterly* 9 (1983) 22.

125   "Celebration of Marriage: 1. Dispensation from canon 1087 for a permanent deacon," in *Roman Replies and CLSA Advisory Opinions 1984*, eds. William A. Schumacher and Richard A. Hill (Washington, DC: CLSA, 1984) 3. Hereafter *RRAO.*

126   Ibid.

Anthony McLaughlin

In the subsequent years most requests for a dispensation from the impediment of orders were met with the suggestion from the Holy See that the deacon
should request laicization and a dispensation from the impediment of orders. It
was very rare that a deacon would be dispensed from the impediment of orders
and remain in ministry. In some cases where a deacon petitioned solely for a dispensation from the impediment of orders the reply was usually that the situation
did not meet the standard of grave ministerial and familial need.[127] Requests for
readmission to the clerical state by deacons who had been laicized and dispensed
from the impediment of orders and had remarried were generally denied.[128]

The situation underwent a significant development in 1997. The Congregation for Divine Worship and the Discipline of the Sacraments issued a circular
letter on June 6 which was sent to diocesan ordinaries and to Superiors General
of Institutes of Consecrated Life and of Societies of Apostolic Life.[129] The letter
announced that up to that point widowed deacons who sought a dispensation
from the impediment of orders had had to meet three cumulative and simulta-
neous conditions, a requirement that led to grave difficulties for widowed deacons who wanted to continue their ministry. The congregation decreed that such
deacons would only have to satisfy any one of the three conditions. (1) There
is a great and proven usefulness for the ministry of the deacon to the diocese to
which he belongs. (2) He has children of such a tender age as to be in need of

<hr/>

127 "Canons 1037, 1041, 1042: The Permanent Diaconate and the Sacrament of Marriage."
RRAO 1991, eds. Kevin Vann and Lynn Jarrell, 16-25.
128 Ibid.
129 Congregation for Divine Worship and the Discipline of the Sacraments, circular letter to
Diocesan Ordinaries and to Superiors General of Instituties of Consecrated Life and of Societies
of Apostolic Life *Concerning dispensation from the obligations of ordination and from vows with
dismissal from the clerical state for priests under the age of 40 and, concerning this dispensation
for priests who are in danger of death and, concerning dispensation from the diriment impediment
of entering into a second marriage and remaining in the ministry on the part of permanent deacons
who are widowed,* June 6, 1997. Prot. No. 263/97. In *Origins* 27, no. 11 (August 28, 1997) 169-
171. The English text is that published by the congregation.

motherly care. (3) He has parents or parents-in-law who are elderly and in need of care.[130] Any one of these conditions taken singly is sufficient for granting a dispensation from the diriment impediment of entering into a second marriage and still remaining in the ministry. With these new regulations it was now more likely that widowed deacons would receive a dispensation to marry and remain in ministry. Consequently, requests from deacons for laicization declined drastically, since most of these requests were based on a desire for remarriage. Petitions to be readmitted to the clerical state from deacons who had been laicized in order to remarry were denied. Requests made by unmarried deacons for a dispensation from the impediment of orders have been denied. Such deacons can only receive a dispensation as part of the process of laicization. It is apparent that these norms apply only to widowed deacons.

On July 13, 2005 the congregation issued another circular letter outlining the conditions necessary for the granting of a dispensation from the impediment of orders for a widowed deacon.[131] This time the conditions were much more restrictive. Unlike the 1997 circular which established that the fulfillment of any of the three given conditions was enough to warrant a favorable response, now petitions from widowed deacons would be considered only when three conditions were fulfilled concurrently. The conditions were: (1) great pastoral usefulness of the deacon's ministry; (2) attestation by the bishop; (3) the care of minor children.

The previous conditions of pastoral usefulness and the care of minor children remain in place. The specific requirement of the *votum* of the diocesan

---

130   Ibid., 170.
131   Congregation for Divine Worship and the Discipline of the Sacraments, circular letter *Competency for Priestly and Diaconal Dispensation,* July 13, 2005. Prot. N. 1080/05. See also Woestmann, *The Sacrament of Orders and the Clerical State,* 456.

bishop is made explicit, and the former condition of the care of elderly parents or parents-in-law has been dropped. This document marks another shift.

From 1967 and the restoration of the permanent diaconate up until 1997, a dispensation from the impediment of orders was generally only granted to widowed deacons as part of a laicization process. In other words it was exceptional for a widowed deacon to remarry and remain in ministry. In the rare case where a dispensation was granted, it was generally granted only when grave circumstances such as ministerial need or care of minor children were present.

With the congregation's circular letter of 1997 the possibility of a widowed deacon receiving a dispensation to remarry and remain in ministry was broadened. The petitioner had to meet only one of three conditions. As a consequence petitions for laicizations decreased rapidly with many widowed candidates now qualifying for the dispensation. However, in the congregation's 2005 circular letter the conditions for granting a dispensation were more restrictive. All three conditions outlined in the letter would need to be fulfilled concurrently. Consequently it became more difficult for a widowed deacon to receive a favorable response from the congregation and an increasing number simply sought laicization.

The United States Bishops' Committee on the Diaconate and the Center for Applied Research in the Apostolate published a research report in 2000. They concluded that since 1968, one hundred and fifty-seven deacons have left the clerical state, thirty-seven deacons have been granted dispensations to remarry, one hundred and ten deacons have remarried without a dispensation and two hundred and twenty-four deacons have divorced or separated since ordination.[132] This amounts to less than one percent of all permanent deacons in the United States. More than nine in ten deacons are married. Only three percent have never been married. This differs from the figures for Catholic men as a whole, because deacons tend to be older and more likely to be married. The marital status of deacons remains unchanged over the past three years. Most candidates, ninety-five percent, are married. About three percent are single and have never been married. About one percent have been divorced and are not remarried, and less than one percent are widowed.[133]

The fact that the congregation is willing at all to grant a dispensation for a widowed deacon to remarry and remain in ministry raises fundamental questions concerning any contention that married deacons are bound to observe the perfect and perpetual continence prescribed in canon 277. This either demonstrates that the Church does not believe that married deacons are bound to absolute continence or that there still remains some doubt concerning the matter.

7. Canon 1394 §1: Penalties for Violation of Celibacy

A cleric's violation of the obligation to observe celibacy is subject to various penalties not excluding dismissal from the clerical state. Canon 1394 §1 states:

> Without prejudice to the prescript of can. 194, §1, n. 3, a cleric who attempts marriage, even if only civilly, incurs a *latae sententiae* suspension. If he does not repent after being warned and continues to give scandal, he can be punished gradually by privations or even by dismissal from the clerical state.[134]

---

132 *A Research Report by the Bishops' Committee on the Diaconate and the Center for Applied Research in the Apostolate,* May 2000 (Washington, DC: USCCB & CARA, 2000).

133 Ibid.

134 83 *CIC,* c. 1394 §1: "Firmo praescripto can. 194, §1, n. 3, clericus matrimonium, etiam civiliter tantum, attentans, in suspensionem latae sententiae incurrit; quod si monitus non resipuerit et scandalum dare perrexerit, gradatim privationibus ac vel etiam dimissione e statu clericali puniri potest."

Canon 2388 §1 of the 1917 code established the penalties of excommunication and possible degradation for a cleric who violated celibacy by attempting marriage either civilly or canonically.[135] The female accomplice also incurred the same penalty of excommunication as the cleric.

According to canon 1394 §1 of the new code a cleric violates his obligation to observe celibacy by "attempting marriage" either civilly or canonically, "*etiam civiliter tantum.*" The law speaks of "attempted marriage," because it considers the act as a conscious and voluntary attempt. Yet, the act itself lacks all juridical value. A civil "marriage" though civilly valid, would be canonically non-existent,[136] because of the impediment of orders and lack of canonical form.[137]

The cleric who attempts marriage incurs a *latae sententiae* penalty of suspension. He is prohibited from all acts of the power of orders and all acts of governance.[138] Furthermore, the cleric loses any ecclesiastical office he may hold, and he is irregular for the exercise and reception of orders.[139] If the cleric does not repent after being warned he can be punished gradually by successive *ferendae sententiae* penalties[140] including dismissal from the clerical state. Dismissal from the clerical state can only be imposed by a collegiate tribunal or

---

135   17 *CIC*, c. 2388 §1: "Clerici in sacris constituti vel regulares aut moniales post votum sollemne castitatis, itemque omnes cum aliqua ex praedictis personis matrimonium etiam civiliter tantum contrahere praesumentes, incurrunt in excommunicationem latae sententiae Sedi Apostolicae simpliciter reservatam; clerici praeterea, si moniti, tempore ab Ordinario pro adiunctorum diversitate praefinito, non resipuerint, degradentur, firmo praescripto can.188, n. 5."

136   83 *CIC*, c. 1108 §1: "Ea tantum matrimonia valida sunt, quae contrahuntur coram loci Ordinario aut parocho aut sacerdote vel diacono ab alterutro delegato qui assistant, necnon coram duobus testibus, secundum tamen regulas expressas in canonibus qui sequuntur, et salvis exceptionibus de quibus in cann. 144, 1112 §1, 1116 et 1127 §§1-2." See also John Martin, "Offenses Against Special Obligations," in *The Canon Law: Letter & Spirit*, ed. Gerard Sheehy et al. (Collegeville, MN: Liturgical Press, 1995) 803-804.

137   83 *CIC*, c. 1087.

138   83 *CIC*, cc. 1333 §1; 1334 §1.

139   83 *CIC*, cc. 194 §1, 3°; 1041, 3° ; 1044, 3°.

140   83 *CIC*, c. 1336 §1, 2°.

administratively by the Holy See.[141] Unlike the former law the canon does not determine a penalty for the female accomplice.[142] She can however be punished by a *ferendae sententia* penalty for her role in the commission of a delict.[143]

8. Canon 1395: Penalties for Violation of Chastity

A cleric's violation of the obligation to observe perfect and perpetual continence may be subject to various penalties not excluding dismissal from the clerical state. Canon 1395 states:

§1. A cleric who lives in concubinage, other than the case mentioned in can. 1394, and a cleric who persists with scandal in another external sin against the sixth commandment of the Decalogue is to be punished by a suspension. If he persists in the delict after a warning, other penalties can gradually be added, including dismissal from the clerical state.

§2. A cleric who in another way has committed an offense against the sixth commandment of the Decalogue, if the delict was committed by force or threats or publicly or with a minor below the age of sixteen years, is to be punished with just penalties, not excluding dismissal from the clerical state if the case so warrants.[144]

---

141   83 *CIC*, c. 1425 §1, 2°.

142   Giuseppe Di Mattia, "De los delitos contra obligaciones especiales," in *Comentario Ex-egético al Código de Derecho Canónico*, ed. Angel Marzoa et al. (Pamplona: EUNSA, 1996) 4/1: 578-579. Always excepting, of course, the general norm on accomplices in offenses under canon 1329. This is especially so when the partner has consented *ex dolo* to celebrating the attempted marriage.

143   William H. Woestman, *Ecclesiastical Sanctions and the Penal Process,* 2nd ed. (Ottawa: St. Paul University, 2003) 146.

144   83 *CIC*, c. 1395: "§1. Clericus concubinarius, praeter casum de quo in can. 1394, et clericus in alio peccato externo contra sextum Decalogi praeceptum cum scandalo permanens, suspensione puniantur, cui, persistente post monitionem delicto, aliae poenae gradatim addi possunt usque ad dimissionem e statu clericali. §2. Clericus qui aliter contra sextum Decalogi praeceptum deliquerit, si quidem delictum vi vel minis vel publice vel cum minore infra aetatem sedecim annorum patratum sit, iustis poenis puniatur, non exclusa, si casus ferat, dimissione e statu clericali."

Canon 2359[145] of the 1917 code prescribed penalties not excluding deposition for a cleric's violation of chastity. Canon 1395 §1 considers external offenses other than attempted marriage committed by a cleric against the sixth commandment. In the first paragraph two separate offenses are mentioned. The first is a cleric living in concubinage. The second is a cleric who continues in a sin against the sixth commandment which causes scandal. Concubinage can be defined as:

> A permanent or quasi permanent and continuing relationship between
> a cleric and a woman, whether married or single, which involves the
> component of their having sexual intercourse together.[146]

While a cleric may not be living in concubinage, he may well be sinning against the sixth commandment in other ways. These acts are not isolated or occasional sins.[147] The canon, unlike its 1917 counterpart, does not list possible sins but speaks in more general terms.

The punishment for certain separate violations of clerical chastity is the same, mandatory *ferendae sententiae* suspension. If the cleric does not repent after being warned, he can be punished gradually by successive *ferendae sententiae* penalties[148] including dismissal from the clerical state. Again dismissal

---

145   17 *CIC*, c. 2359: "§1. Clerici in sacris sive saeculares sive religiosi concubinarii, monitione inutiliter praemissa, cogantur ab illicito contubernio recedere et scandalum reparare suspensione a divinis, privatione fructuum officii, beneficii, dignitatis, servato praescripto can. 2176-2181. §2. Si delictum admiserint contra sextum decalogi praeceptum cum minoribus infra aetatem sexdecim annorum, vel adulterium, stuprum, bestialitatem, sodomiam, lenocinium, incestum cum consanguineis aut affinibus in primo gradu exercuerint, suspendantur, infames declarentur, quolibet officio, beneficio, dignitate, munere, si quod habeant, priventur, et in casibus gravioribus deponantur. §3. Si aliter contra sextum decalogi praeceptum deliquerint, congruis poenis secundum casus gravitatem coerceantur, non excepta officii vel beneficii privatione, maxime si curam animarum gerant."

146   John Martin, "Offenses Against Special Obligations," in *The Canon Law: Letter & Spirit*, ed. Gerard Sheehy et al. (Collegeville, MN: Liturgical Press, 1995) 803, par. 2809.

147   Di Mattia, "De los delitos contra obligaciones especiales," 4/1: 581.

148   83 *CIC*, c. 1336 §1, 2°.

from the clerical state can only be imposed by a collegiate tribunal or administratively by the Apostolic See.[149]

Paragraph two of the canon addresses other sins against the sixth commandment committed by a cleric with aggravating circumstances. These circumstances include sexual offenses committed with the use of force, threats, in public or with minors.[150] The legislator does not establish a determinate penalty due to the range of aggravating circumstances. He merely establishes that a just penalty should be imposed not excluding in the most serious cases dismissal from the clerical state.[151]

9. Canon 291: Dispensation from Celibacy

The clerical obligations of perfect and perpetual continence and therefore celibacy prescribed in canon 277 may be subject to dispensation. Canon 291 states:

Apart from the case mentioned in can. 290, n. 1, loss of the clerical state does not entail a dispensation from the obligation of celibacy, which only the roman pontiff grants.[152]

Theologically one cannot cease being an ordained deacon, presbyter or bishop, but one may lose the legal state of being a cleric.[153] The 1917 code spoke

---

149   83 *CIC,* c. 290.

150   In 1994, particular law for the United States established that a minor was one who had not completed his eighteenth year. This was established as universal law in 2001; see the Congregation for the Doctrine of the Faith, *Ad exsequendam ecclesiasticam,* May 18, 2002: *AAS* 93 (2001) 785-788.

151   De Mattia, 582. See also William H. Woestmann, *The Sacrament of Orders and the Clerical State: A Commentary on the Code of Canon Law* (Ottawa: St. Paul University, 1999) 149.

152   83 *CIC,* c. 291: "Praeter casus de quibus in can. 290, n. 1, amissio status clericalis non secumfert dispensationem ab obligatione caelibatus, quae ab uno tantum Romano Pontifice conceditur."

153   83 *CIC,* c. 1008: "Sacramento ordinis ex divina institutione inter christifideles quidam, charactere indelebili quo signantur, constituuntur sacri ministri, qui nempe consecrantur et deputantur ut, pro suo quisque gradu, in persona Christi Capitis munera docendi, sanctificandi et regendi adimplentes, Dei populum pascant."

of the loss of the clerical state as "a reduction to the lay state."[154] With the teaching of *Lumen gentium* on the radical equality of all the faithful,[155] the 1983 code avoids this phrase choosing instead to say "loss of the clerical state." For these same reasons the former canonical penalty of degradation[156] is now known as dismissal. Under the 1917 code a cleric who had lost the clerical state no longer had the rights and privileges of being a cleric. However, he was still bound by the obligations of celibacy and recitation of the divine office.[157]

In the 1983 code, as in the 1917 code, a cleric can lose the clerical state in one of three ways: (1) by judicial sentence or administrative decree declaring the invalidity of sacred ordination, (2) by the penalty of dismissal legitimately imposed, or (3) by rescript from the Holy See. Rescript is granted to deacons for grave causes and to presbyters for most grave causes.[158] Loss of the clerical state does not ordinarily include a dispensation from celibacy. The cleric must petition the roman pontiff for this favor. In cases of a declaration of the invalidity of ordination no dispensation is needed inasmuch as the person was never ordained and therefore never was a cleric. As we noted in chapter two, prior to the Second Vatican Council though some clerics were "reduced to the lay state," dispensations from celibacy were rarely granted. During the pontificate of Paul VI well-prepared petitions with strong arguments were normally granted even for younger priests who had only been ordained a short while.[159]

154   17 *CIC*, cc. 211-214.
155   Second Vatican Council, dogmatic constitution *Lumen gentium*, November 21, 1964: *AAS* 57 (1965) 5-67. Hereafter *LG*.
156   17 *CIC*, c. 2298, 12°.
157   17 *CIC*, cc. 211-214.
158   83 *CIC*, c. 290: "Sacra ordinatio, semel valide recepta, numquam irrita fit. Clericus tamen statum clericalem amittit: 1° sententia iudicali aut decreto administrativo, quo invaliditas sacrae ordinationis declaratur; 2° poena dimissionis legitime irrogata; 3° rescripto Apostolicae Sedis; quod vero rescriptum diaconis ob graves tantum causas, presbyteris ob gravissimas causas ac Apostolica Sede conceditur."
159   Woestmann, *The Sacrament of Orders and the Clerical State,* 208-209.

However, under John Paul I and John Paul II such dispensations were granted with less frequency.

On October 14, 1980 the Congregation for the Doctrine of the Faith issued new norms regarding the processing of dispensations from the obligations of priestly ordination including celibacy.[160] These are the norms currently in force. The current norms restored the separate processing of petitions for dispensation from celibacy and loss of the clerical state. This change was given juridic expression in canon 291 of the 1983 code. The norms are more restrictive than the previous norms. In general two types of cases will be given consideration: (1) cases involving elderly priests who have long since left the ministry and in many cases have "married" and have children, and (2) cases involving causes that existed before ordination that demonstrate that ordination should never have been received. The congregation affirmed in the letter introducing this legislation that a dispensation from celibacy was not to be seen as a right. The expectation was that priests were to be faithful to their commitment even in the midst of difficulties.[161]

In 1989 competence for the handling of all cases of dispensation from clerical celibacy was transferred to the Congregation for Divine Worship and the Discipline of the Sacraments.[162] The processing of dispensations from celibacy for deacons is distinct from that for priests. The process generally follows a short informative process with the Cardinal Prefect having been granted the habitual faculty to laicize deacons.[163] A dispensation is never granted to a laicized

---

160   The Sacred Congregation for the Doctrine of the Faith, letter *Per Litteras ad universos,* October 14, 1980: *AAS* 72 (1980) 1132-1137. Hereafter *PLa.* See also previous norms issued by this same congregation, *Normae ad apparandas in Curiis dioecesanis et religiosis causas reductionis ad statum laicalem cum dispensatione ab obligationibus cum sacra Ordinatione conexis,* January 13, 1971: *AAS* 63 (1971) 303-308.

161   *PLa* 1133.

162   John Paul II, apostolic constitution *Pastor bonus* 62, June 28, 1988: *AAS* 80 (1988) 876.

163   *Notitiae* 25 (1989) 486.

transitional deacon who after entering a canonical marriage wishes to exercise his diaconal ministry.[164] As of August 1, 2005 this competence was transferred to the Congregation for the Clergy.[165] On January 30, 2009 Pope Benedict granted the Congregation for the Clergy faculties to resolve grave violations of clerical celibacy or situations where clerics have freely and illicitly abandoned the ministry for an extended period.[166]

A dispensation from the obligation of celibacy is granted not as a reward for bad behavior but is granted for several reasons: for the sake of the salvation of the individual; to safeguard the commitment of celibacy; to protect the faithful from further scandal; to demonstrate mercy and only as a last measure when the person's priesthood cannot be saved.[167] The practice continues of speedily processing a dispensation from priestly celibacy in situations where there is imminent danger of death.[168] The local ordinary and in his absence those mentioned in canon 1078 can dispense from celibacy for a deacon in danger of death.[169]

10. Readmission to the Clerical State

A person who has lost the clerical state can be readmitted to that state only

---

164 See *RRAO* 1986, 20-22.

165 Congregation for Divine Worship and the Discipline of the Sacraments, circular letter *Competency for Priestly and Diaconal Dispensation,* July 13, 2005. Prot. No. 1080/05.

166 Congregation for the Clergy, letter to Ordinaries, April 18, 2009. Prot. No. 2009/0556.

167 Paul VI, encyclical *Sacerdotalis caelibatus,* June 24, 1967: *AAS* 59 (1967) Art. 84-90, 690-692.

168 Francis J. Schneider, "Chapter VI: Loss of the Clerical State," in *New Commentary on the Code of Canon Law,* ed. John P. Beal et al. (New York/Mahwah, NJ: Paulist Press, 2000) 387.

169 83 *CIC,* c. 1078: "§1. Ordinarius loci proprios subditos ubique commorantes et omnes in proprio territorio actu degentes ab omnibus impedimentis iuris ecclesiastici dispensare potest, exceptis iis, quorum dispensatio Sedi Apostolicae reservatur. §2. Impedimenta quorum dispensatio Sedi Apostolicae reservatur sunt: 1° impedimentum ortum ex sacris ordinibus aut ex voto publico perpetuo castitatis in instituto religioso iuris pontificii; 2° impedimentum criminis de quo in can. 1090. §3. Numquam datur dispensatio ab impedimento consanguinitatis in linea recta aut in secundo gradu lineae collateralis."

with a rescript from the Holy See.[170] In theory this applies not only to those who voluntarily sought removal from the clerical state, but also to any whose ordination was declared invalid, and to those who were dismissed. The person would first have to find a bishop or religious superior who was willing to accept him into his diocese or institute. He would then petition the pope for readmission to the clerical state. If the person never married, a favorable decision is more likely. If he married, the question of natural obligations to his former wife and children would arise.[171] It does not seem to be the practice of the Holy See to readmit a deacon who has lost the clerical state.[172] Upon readmission to the clerical state the cleric would again be bound to observe perfect and perpetual continence and therefore celibacy.[173]

11. The Pastoral Provision

In recent decades the Holy See has more frequently granted dispensations from celibacy for former non-Catholic ministers who are married and wish to be ordained Catholic priests. Two conditions have to be present. The person had to have already served as a minister in another church or ecclesial community before being received into full communion with the Catholic Church, and there needed to be sufficient pastoral cause for a dispensation to be granted.[174] Initially this phenomenon, with few exceptions, concerned Episcopalian ministers.[175]

---

170   83 *CIC*, c. 292: "Praeter casus de quibus in can. 290, n. 1, amissio status clericalis non secumfert dispensationem ab obligatione caelibatus, quae ab uno tantum Romano Pontifice conceditur."

171   Woestmann, *The Sacrament of Orders and the Clerical State,* 216.

172   Ibid.

173   83 *CIC*, c. 277 §1.

174   See James A. Coriden and James H. Provost, "Canonical Implications Related to the Ordination of Married Men to the Priesthood in the United States of America," *CLSA Proceedings* 58 (1996) 451.

175   For a fuller treatment of the pastoral provisions see Richard A. Hill, "The Pastoral Provision: Ordination of Married, Protestant Ministers," *CLSA Proceedings* 51 (1989) 95-96.

On June 20, 1980 the Congregation for the Doctrine of the Faith established "pastoral provisions"[176] to provide pastoral care to ministers and laity of the Episcopal Church who were seeking full communion with the Catholic Church. On March 31, 1981 the contents of the June 1980 document were summarized in a statement from the congregation.[177] The provisions provided for the possibility of ordaining to the presbyterate former Episcopal ministers, most of whom were married. The Holy See was at pains to point out that though an exception to celibacy would be made for such ministers this was an exception and would never be the norm. The congregation stated:

> In accepting former Episcopal clergy who are married into the Catholic priesthood, the Holy See has specified that this exception to the rule of celibacy is granted in favor of these individual persons and should not be understood as implying any change in the Church's conviction of the value of priestly celibacy, which will remain the rule for future candidates for the priesthood from this group.[178]

This exception led Frank Bonnike, leader of Corps of Reserve Priests United for Service (CORPUS), to ask whether "a Roman Catholic priest who left the Catholic priesthood to marry and become an Episcopalian priest now can be accepted back into the Church."[179] According to Joseph H. Fichter the explanation why the Episcopal minister may bring his wife with him and why the resigned Catholic priest may not has been put in the bluntest moral terms. He states:

---

176   See *Enchiridion* 7 (1980-1981) par. 1213. Also, letter to the President of National Conference of Catholic Bishops, Archbishop John R. Quinn, from the Sacred Congregation for the Doctrine of the Faith outlining the Pastoral Provision, July 22, 1980. Prot. No. 66/77. For a detailed treatment of the Pastoral Provisions see Joseph H. Fichter, *The Pastoral Provisions: Married Catholic Priests* (Kansas City, MO: Sheed & Ward, 1989).

177   See Sacred Congregation for the Doctrine of the Faith, private statement, March 31, 1981. Published in *L'Osservatore Romano*, English edition, April 1, 1981.

178   Ibid. See also Woestman, *The Sacrament of Orders and the Clerical State*, 395.

179   Fichter, *Pastoral Provisions*, 57.

The man who abandons the Episcopal Church to join the true Church of Rome is to be praised for good moral behavior. He deserves commendation and rewards. The man who abandons the Catholic priesthood to take a wife is to be blamed for reprehensible moral behavior. He is to be scolded and penalized. In the former case, it does not matter that the priest is married; in the latter case, it is the only thing that matters. In the first case, he has to leave his Church but retains his wife; in the second, he has to leave his wife to retain his Church.[180]

Fichter's observations are simplistic. It must be pointed out that a Catholic priest who attempts marriage does not remove himself from the Church. He is still a member of the Church though his living arrangements are irregular.

In the pastoral provision and in the various rescripts granted by the Holy See there is no reference to how a married priest and his wife are to exercise sexual relations in their marriage.[181] There is no reference to the ancient discipline of continence for married clergy in major orders, either the absolute continence required in the West or the temporary continence as is the practice in the East. Unlike widowed deacons who may receive a dispensation from the impediment of orders to remarry, it is not the practice to grant such dispensations to married priests.

Along with attaining the necessary *debita scientia* (knowledge) the former Episcopalian minister is not to be assigned to the ordinary care of souls and is not permitted to transfer to another country to take up priestly duties without the approval of the Holy See.[182]

The pastoral provision had originally not been extended to members of other Christian denominations. In 2005, it was extended to include ministers

---

180   Ibid.
181   For examples of such rescripts, see *RRAO* 1989, 7-10.
182   Ibid.

from so-called "continuing Anglican churches." This specifically included ministers from the Reformed Episcopal Church that split from the Episcopal Church in the 19th century. Protestant ministers from other ecclesial communities (Lutheran, Methodist, etc) who have been received into full communion with the Catholic Church may be ordained, but they are not included under the pastoral provision process. In their case the necessary dispensation from the impediment of marriage must be sought from the Holy See.[183] Since the establishment of the pastoral provision, over eighty former Episcopalian ministers, most of who are married, have been ordained Catholic priests in the United States.[184]

12. Vatican Statement on the Ordination of Married Men

During the 1990 Synod of Bishop on the Priesthood, Cardinal Aloisio Lorscheider of Brazil, in an interview with the Italian Catholic magazine, *Famiglia Cristiana*, stated that Pope John Paul II had approved the ordination of two married Brazilian men on condition that they severed the conjugal life.[185]

---

183   83 *CIC*, c. 1042, 1°; 1047 § 2, 3°.

184   On November 4, 2009, after the research for this book was complete, Pope Benedict XVI promulgated the apostolic constitution *Anglicanorum coetibus*. The constitution was published November 9, along with specific norms governing the establishment and governance of personal ordinariates, structures similar to dioceses, for former Anglicans who become Catholic.

Concerning the possibility of ordaining married former Anglican clergy to the presbyterate, the prescripts of the 1980 Pastoral Provision remain unchanged. As a rule, only celibate men will admitted to the presbyterate. Yet an ordinary may petition the roman pontiff for a dispensation to ordain a married man to the presbyterate, on a case by case basis. Once ordained the cleric would be bound by the impediment of orders and therefore unable to enter marriage *post ordinationem*. See section 6, articles 1 & 2. *Origins* 39, no. 25 (November 19, 2009) 389. As with the pastoral provision there is no reference to the ancient discipline of continence for married clergy in major orders, either the absolute continence required in the West or the temporary continence as is the practice in the East.

185   See *Famiglia Cristina*, October 14, 1990.

The Obligation of Perfect and Perpetual Continence

Shortly afterwards, on October 18, 1990,[186] the Vatican issued a statement acknowledging that the pontiff had permitted married men to become priests in an "extremely limited number of cases" on three conditions: (1) total separation from the wives in the matter of cohabitation; (2) a free and conscientious acceptance by the candidate for ordination of the celibate way of life and (3) the explicit and written consent of the wife and children, if any, to the ordination. Their marriages were not dissolved or annulled. The pontiff obliged them to suspend the exercise of their marital rights.

Furthermore, the statement said exceptions had also been made in the case of married clergy of other ecclesial communities who joined the Catholic Church. These exceptions allowed these men to be ordained and continue having sexual relations with their wives. But even in these cases, "the law of celibacy has been reaffirmed" as the standard for the Latin Church.

This Vatican statement is extremely significant. It states that married clergy of other ecclesial communities who joined the Catholic Church and were ordained Catholic priests were permitted to continue their conjugal life. While lifelong Catholic men who were ordained priests were obliged to separate from their wives and observe perfect and perpetual continence. This raises the question as to whether Catholic men legitimately destined for the diaconate are also bound to observe perfect and perpetual continence. Though, admittedly, this has not been explicitly stated as a condition for ordination as in the aforementioned cases of married men being ordained priests.

---

186   See Vatican statement of October 18, 1990 in *Origins* 20, no. 21 (November 1, 1990) 334. An article in the Oct. 18 edition of the Italian newspaper, *Corriere delta Sera*, said one of the priests, Father Ivo Schmidt, 69, was ordained in 1987. It quoted Schmidt and his wife, 67-year-old Adulina, as saying they had not had sex together in 20 years, after she lost a baby in childbirth and, after multiple operations, was no longer able to have sexual relations. "We wanted to have a child. Now we have an enormous flock," his wife said.

C. Conclusion

The code commission affirmed the obligation of perfect and perpetual continence and therefore celibacy for Latin clergy, but believed that permanent deacons should be exempt from this obligation. Further, the commission also affirmed the impediment of orders for Latin clergy, but believed that permanent deacons should be exempt from this impediment. Shortly before the promulgation of the code, Pope John Paul II removed both of these exemptions for permanent deacons.

Canon 277 §1 of the 1983 code states: "Clerics are obliged to observe perfect and perpetual continence for the sake of the kingdom of heaven and therefore are bound to celibacy...."[187] Accordingly, clerics have two distinct obligations, the observance of perfect and perpetual continence, minimally no sexual relations, and the commitment to celibacy, minimally no contracting of marriage. Continence is presented as the fundamental norm. Celibacy is presented as a secondary good, which is ordered to the protection of the primary good of perfect and perpetual continence.

While the law is clear that married deacons are not bound by the secondary obligation of celibacy (c. 1037), unless their wife dies, some argue that it seems less clear whether they are bound by the primary obligation of perfect and perpetual continence. The code does exempt permanent deacons from some of the obligations common to all clerics (canon 288) yet it does not list canon 277 §1 among them.

Others argue that married deacons are not bound to observe perfect and perpetual continence because as married persons they have an acquired right

---

[187]   83 *CIC*, 277 §1: "Clerici obligatione tenentur servandi perfectam perpetuamque propter Regnum coelorum continentiam, ideoque ad coelibatum adstringuntur...."

to conjugal relations (cc. 4, 1135, 1055 §1). Yet is there an acquired right to conjugal relations for married deacons and their wives when there is such a long canonical history to the contrary?

Another category of married clergy became a reality in the Church in the early 1980's. The pastoral provision permitted former Protestant ministers, most of whom were married, to be ordained to the presbyterate. Here too it is clear they are not bound to celibacy unless their wives die. Some argue that again it seems less clear whether they are bound to observe perfect and perpetual continence within their marriages. Though such a position is now untenable following the Vatican statement of October 18, 1990.[188]

So while married clergy are not bound to celibacy unless their wives die, it is less clear whether they are bound to observe perfect and perpetual continence. Yet, it must be stated that married candidates for the diaconate or the presbyterate and their wives are not obliged to observe absolute continence within their marriages. Surely such a surrender of a fundamental right cannot be simply implicitly assumed.

Furthermore, all those in sacred orders- married or unmarried- are bound by the impediment of orders. For much of the Church's canonical history the impediment of orders, some argue, presupposed the existence of the law of continence. So if on the one hand the impediment presupposes continence, yet the fact that a dispensation from this impediment is possible seems to mitigate against the existence of the law of continence. Additionally, if the legislator does not intend to bind married clergy to observe perfect and perpetual continence, then the applicability of the impediment of orders for married clergy may need to be reevaluated.

---

188   See footnote 183.

While one may argue for or against the prescriptions of canon 277 §1 obliging married clergy, the fact remains that the current praxis does not bind married deacons to observe continence. If a change in discipline was intended, then this needs to be more clearly enunciated. If, however, a change was not intended then the current situation needs to be addressed.

CHAPTER FIVE

THE OBLIGATION OF PERFECT AND PERPETUAL CONTINENCE AND MARRIED DEACONS IN THE LATIN CHURCH: CANONICAL CONCLUSIONS

It is nonetheless important to situate this chapter by restating the more significant elements of our research. This is essential in order to anchor our analysis of the implicit suppositions of particular authors.

For at least the first millennium married men were admitted to every degree of the hierarchy in the Latin Church, both to minor and major orders. Beginning not later than the Council of Elvira, 305 it was increasingly the norm in the Latin Church that married major clerics, with the consent of their wives, were obliged to observe the *lex continentiae*. They were prohibited from having sexual relations and from entering a new marriage *post ordinationem*.[1] The *lex continentiae* was the fundamental obligation that bound all major clerics married and unmarried.

The obligation to observe the *lex continentiae* was enforced by penalties for all violations of the law. The gravity of the penalties varied over the centuries

---

1   Council of Elvira, c. 33. In *Sacrorum Conciliorum: Nova et Amplissma Collectio,* ed. Ioannes Dominicus Mansi (Paris: Herbert Welter, 1902) 2:11. Hereafter Mansi.

from excommunication to loss of the clerical state. Major clerics who attempted marriage *post ordinationem* incurred grave penalties. In 1139, the Second Lateran Council declared such marriages to be not only illicit but invalid.[2] With the institution of seminaries by the Council of Trent the Church now had a wealth of young unmarried candidates for orders.[3]

In 1610, the Sacred Congregation for the Council declared that a married man could no longer be admitted to tonsure.[4] The diocesan bishop could tonsure a married man and admit him to all orders only if he and his wife promised to refrain from sexual relations and have no more children. In the eighteenth century, Pope Benedict XIV (1740-1758) reserved to himself the cases of young married men petitioning for tonsure.[5] With the promulgation of the 1917 code, marriage *per se* was established as an impediment to the reception of orders.[6] Though it was still possible for a married man to receive major orders, a dispensation from the impediment was granted only on condition that he, with the consent of his wife, observed the law of continence.

Through the centuries the ordination of married men gradually decreased and after Trent candidates for orders were almost exclusively unmarried. In the 1950's there was a movement in Germany to restore the permanent diaconate

---

2   Second Lateran Council, c. 7. See Norman T. Tanner, ed., *Decrees of the Ecumenical Councils* (London and Washington: Sheed & Ward and Georgetown University Press, 1990) 2:198. Hereafter Tanner.

3   Council of Trent, session 23, July 15, 1563, *de sacramento ordinis,* c. 18. Tanner, 2:750.

4   Sacred Congregation for the Council, *Tricaricen* 23, January 1610, n. 2385: "Coniugatos, durante coniugio non posse ad primam tonsuram promoveri." In *Codicis Iuris Canonici Fontes,* Pietro Gasparri (Rome: Typis Polylottis Vaticanis, 1923-1939) 5:211. Hereafter *Fontes.*

5   Benedict XIV, *Libri Octo de Synodo Diocesana* (Rome: Excudebant Nicolaus et Marcus Palearini, 1748) 13: 12, nn. 14-15.

6   *Codex Iuris Canonici Pii X Pontificis Maximi iussu digestus Benedicti Papae XV auctoritate promulgatus* (Rome: Typis Polyglottis Vaticanis, 1917), c. 132 §3: "Coniugatus qui sine dispensatione apostolica ordines maiores, licet bona fide, suscepit, ab eorundem ordinum exercitio prohibetur." Hereafter 17 *CIC.*

and admit married men to the order.[7] Prior to this time the diaconate as a perma-

nent order in the Church had not existed for nearly twelve hundred years.[8] For

much of that time the diaconate was ceremonial, transitory, and subordinate to

the presbyterate.[9] In 1964, against a backdrop of much debate regarding the ob-

ligation of celibacy and married deacons, Alfons Cardinal Stickler published an

article on the continence of deacons in the first millennium. In it he discussed the

importance of understanding celibacy not only in the sense of prohibiting clerics

from marrying but also in the sense of absolute continence for those already

married.[10] He examined ecclesiastical legislation and magisterial teaching from

the fourth century to the close of the first millennium and concluded that it was

the uninterrupted tradition of the Church that all clergy in major orders, married

or unmarried were obliged to absolute continence.[11] Stickler further asserted that

to permit married deacons the use of their marriages would rupture the unity of

the celibacy-continence obligation that had bound all grades of major clerics

equally.[12] In the dogmatic constitution on the Church, *Lumen gentium,* the Sec-

ond Vatican Council (1962-1965) approved the restoration of the permanent di-

---

7   For an excellent treatment of this movement to restore the permanent diaconate see José L. Casañas Medina, *The Law for the Restoration of the Permanent Diaconate: A Canonical Commentary,* Canon Law Studies 460 (Washington, DC: Catholic University of America, 1968) 35-63; William T. Ditewig, *The Emerging Diaconate: Servant Leaders in a Servant Church* (New York: Paulist Press, 2007) 94-122 and Edward P. Echlin, *The Deacon in the Church: Past and Future* (New York, NY: Alba House, 1971) 95-124.

8   See Kenan B. Osborne, *The Permanent Diaconate: Its History and Place in the Sacrament of Orders* (New York: Paulist Press, 2006) 93. A transitional diaconate had continued to exist during this period of time.

9   See Echlin, *The Deacon in the Church,* 93.

10   Alfons Maria Stickler, "La continenza dei diaconi specialmente nel primo millennio della chiesa," *Salesianum* 26 (1964) 301: "Attualita della questione non solo del celibate nel senso di divieto di sposarsi ma anche nel senso della Continenza perfetta per gli sposati precedentemente."

11   Ibid.

12   Ibid., 298: "Il trinomio costante che sin dall'inizio associa sempre vescovi, sacerdoti e diaconi quando si parla dell'obbligo della Continenza, è inoltre una delle prove più chiare, ma nella letteratura contemporanea meno avvertita, della motivazione spirituale di questo obbligo come inerente alla natura intrinseca di ogni ministero sacro."

aconate and established that married men could be admitted to the order.[13] With the motu proprio *Sacrum diaconatus ordinem*[14] of June 18, 1967, Paul VI issued "certain and definite norms"[15] for the restoration of the permanent diaconate. Among them were two requirements significant to the history of married deacons and continence, the consent of the candidate's wife and her possession of certain moral qualifications.[16] Additional legislation was promulgated in the motu proprios *Ad pascendum*[17] and *Ministeria quaedam,*[18] August 15, 1972.

There was no reference in conciliar or post conciliar documents to the discipline of continence for married clergy in major orders, either the absolute continence required in the West or the temporary continence as it is practiced in the East. Nor was there any comment on whether the discipline that had bound all major clerics equally was now changed, if indeed a change was intended or needed. The issue was posed in exclusive terms, as celibacy versus married clergy, and as a consequence any discussion of continence was absent. The non applicability of the obligation of celibacy to married deacons was understood, therefore, to legitimize conjugal relations.

The code commission affirmed the obligation of perfect and perpetual continence for Latin clergy but recommended that married deacons should be exempt from this obligation. The commission also affirmed the impediment of or-

---

13   Vatican II, dogmatic constitution *Lumen gentium*, November 21, 1964: *AAS* 57 (1965) 36. Hereafter *LG*.

14   Paul VI, motu proprio *Sacrum diaconatus ordinem,* June 18, 1967: *AAS* 59 (1967) 697-704. Hereafter *SDO*.

15   *SDO* Introduction, *AAS* 59 (1967) 698: "…ut certae ac definitae hac de re normae edantur ad eam…." English translation from *TPS* 12 (1967) 238.

16   The research presented in chapter one demonstrated that the consent of the wife and her moral qualities were directly related to the promise of absolute continence expected of both spouses after the husband's ordination.

17   Paul VI, motu proprio *Ad pascendum,* August 15, 1972: *AAS* 64 (1972) 534-540. Hereafter *AP*.

18   Paul VI, motu proprio *Ministeria quaedam,* August 15, 1972: *AAS* 64 (1972) 529-534. Hereafter *MQ*.

ders for Latin clergy but recommended that married deacons should be exempt from the impediment. Both of these exemptions were removed by John Paul II shortly before the promulgation of the 1983 code.

Concerning clerics and the obligation of continence canon 277 §1 states: "Clerics are obliged to observe perfect and perpetual continence for the sake of the kingdom of Heaven and therefore are bound to celibacy...."[19] While canon 288[20] of the 1983 code exempts permanent deacons from some obligations common to all clerics canon 277 §1 is not one of these. A fundamental question thus arises: "Are married deacons obliged to observe perfect and perpetual continence?"

A. The Two "Schools"

The research in the previous four chapters indicates that how one approaches the question of married deacons and continence depends on two principle factors: (1) whether one believes that celibacy is of apostolic or ecclesiastical origin and (2) whether one accepts celibacy understood narrowly as a prohibition on marriage or broadly as the *lex continentiae,* no sexual relations *post ordinationem.*

If celibacy is of apostolic origin then the teaching cannot be changed. If it is of ecclesiastical origin then change is possible. If celibacy is understood narrowly, as a prohibition on marriage, then it is a tautology to bind a married man, unless his wife dies. In this narrow view a married man cannot be bound to

---

19   *Codex Iuris Canonici auctoritate Ioannis Pauli PP. II promulgatus* (Vatican City: Libreria Editrice Vaticana, 1983), c. 277 §1: "Clerici obligatione tenentur servandi perfectam perpetuamque propter Regnum caelorum continentiam, ideoque ad caelibatum adstringuntur...." Hereafter 83 *CIC.* English translation from *Code of Canon Law, Latin-English Edition: New English Translation* (Washington, DC: CLSA, 1998). All subsequent English translations of canons from this code will be taken from this source unless otherwise indicated.

20   83 *CIC,* c. 288: "Diaconi permanentes praescriptis canonum 284, 285 §§3 et 4, 286, 287 §2 non tenentur, nisi ius particulare aliud statuat."

celibacy and can continue conjugal relations. If celibacy is understood broadly, as a prohibition on sexual relations *post ordinationem,* then a married man can be ordained but only on condition that he observe the *lex continentiae* common to all clerics.

One can therefore discern two "schools" of thought, or two approaches in regard to continence and married deacons. One "school" that holds that married deacons are obliged to the continence prescribed in canon 277 §1, which we will call the "Continence School"[21] and the other which holds that they are not so bound, which we will call the "Celibacy School." [22]

In the proceeding chapters we outlined the arguments of each "school" so there will be no need to repeat them here. For the purposes of this section we will examine the practical implications of the theses adopted by both "schools" for the interpretation and implementation of the prescripts of canon 277 §1.

B. The "Continence School"

The early Church had an entire network of interconnected laws that sought to guarantee and safeguard the continence of major clerics. It should follow that if married deacons are bound to observe continence that many of these laws would need to be restored.

1. Married Deacons and the Obligation of Perfect and Perpetual Continence

The obligation of married deacons to observe perfect and perpetual conti-

---

21   Many of those who ascribe to this "school" also hold that celibacy is of apostolic origin. See chapter one, 21-23; 29-33.

22   The proponents of this "school" believe that celibacy is of ecclesiastical origin. See chapter one, 21-23; 29-31.

nence has a long canonical history.[23] The teachings of the Second Vatican Council do not mitigate this obligation. No exemption from continence is granted in the language of *in matrimonio viventibus* (living in marriage); the phrase used in *Lumen gentium* 29[24] and *Sacrum diaconatus ordinem* 26[25] to describe both married candidates to the diaconate and married deacons. This terminology may be read either as descriptive of the candidate simply or of the married state of life in which he is expected to continue. The obligation to observe continence would also not be contrary to the teaching of *Gaudium et spes,*[26] despite its emphasis on the personalist dimension of marriage.[27] Married persons each have equal obligations and rights to those things which pertain to the partnership of conjugal life, and sexual cooperation is part of the permanent consortium.[28] The obligation of continence always requires the mutual consent of the spouses, thus respecting the rights and obligations of each spouse. Without mutual consent the candidate cannot proceed to ordination as a deacon. Canon 277 §1 reads as if the obligation of perfect and perpetual continence is applicable to married deacons, because it is. This obligation has canonical precedent and is not mitigated anywhere else in the code.[29]

---

23   From the fourth century the Church admitted married men to major orders on condition that they, with the consent of their wives, observe the *lex continentiae,* i.e., that they refrain from sexual relations and have no more children. See chapter one for ample documentation in this regard.

24   *LG* 36.

25   Paul VI, motu proprio *Sacram diaconatus ordinem* 26, June 18, 1967: *AAS* 59 (1967) 697-704. Hereafter *SDO.*

26   Vatican II, pastoral constitution *Gaudium et spes*, December 7, 1965: *AAS* 58 (1966) 1025-1115. Hereafter *GS.* See also chapter three, 37-45.

27   See commentary on personalist approach chapter three, 183-187.

28   See 83 *CIC*, cc. 4, 1055, 1056, 1096 §1 and 1135.

29   See chapter four, 235-240. The various arguments for and against married deacons being bound to continence are discussed in more detail.

2. The Impediment of Digamy to Orders[30]

From the time of the pastoral letters the Pauline injunction for ministers, "husband of one wife," provides us with the fundamental and perennial reference point for the discussion of clerical celibacy:

A bishop must be irreproachable, the husband of one wife.[31]
A presbyter must be irreproachable, the husband of one wife.[32]
A deacon must be irreproachable, the husband of one wife.[33]

The pastoral letters to Timothy and Titus catalogue those factors that would make a candidate unsuitable for ministry. At first sight these scripture passages appear to have nothing whatsoever to do with celibacy and continence and instead everything to do with marriage and family. One could even argue that they speak against celibacy-continence. Some, as was the case with the Protestant reformers, saw these passages as even requiring clergy to be married, others, that it was an injunction against polygamy.

However, since the earliest times, the predominant interpretation of these passages by the Church was that the injunction excluded from major orders any man who had taken a second wife. Candidates for orders were not required to be married. In fact the injunction against a second marriage was considered by the Church to be "for the sake of future continence." Christians were not forbidden to enter a second marriage, yet one's entry into a second marriage was generally considered to be a demonstration of one's inability to live continently.[34]

---

30   The impediment of digamy has been treated in chapter one, 55-60; and chapter two, 126-128. What will follow is a summary of this treatment. Any new source will be cited in the footnotes. Otherwise please refer back to the relevant pages in chapters one and two.
31   *NAB*, 1 Tim 3:2 ('mias gynaikos andra').
32   *NAB*, Tit 1:6 ('mias gynaikos aner').
33   *NAB*, 1 Tim 3:12 ('mias gynaikos andres').
34   *NAB*, 1 Tim 5:14; 1 Cor 7:1-40.

Monogamy was considered a strong indication that the candidate had the ability to practice the absolute continence that would be required of him at ordination. The digamy prohibition was necessary because of the obligation of continence after ordination. Accordingly, a candidate for major orders who had been married more than once was prohibited from the reception of orders. The impediment of digamy, "twice married," appeared in church legislation as early as the middle of the third century.

If married deacons are bound to observe perfect and perpetual continence it would follow that the impediment of digamy for the reception of orders should be restored. This would be necessary to ensure the suitability of candidates for the obligation of absolute continence.

3. Moral Qualities

The Council of Elvira prohibited a candidate who had been guilty of adultery or fornication after baptism from the reception of subdiaconate.[35] A short time later the Council of Neocaesarea prohibited the husband of an adulterous wife from the reception of orders. The council declared that if the wife committed adultery *post ordinationem,* then the cleric was obliged to separate from her. If he failed to do so he would be excluded from the ministry.[36] Later councils legislated in like manner to establish the suitability of the candidates for major orders and their wives to live the continence that would be required of them.[37]

As part of the formation process it would be necessary to determine the suitability of the candidate and his wife for the obligation of absolute continence.

---

35   See Council of Elvira, c. 30. Mansi, 2: 10.
36   See Council of Neocaesarea, c. 8. Mansi, 2:541; Council of Arles, c. 25. Mansi, 2:474 and Council of Elvira, c. 65. Mansi, 2:16. Arles and Elvira obliged the cleric to separate from his adulterous wife.
37   See chapter one.

It would seem necessary to inquire about the sexual history of each before and during their marriage. A history of incontinence on the part of either would be a strong indication of either party's probable inability to practice the perfect and perpetual continence required by canon 277 §1.

If a candidate and/or his wife have committed adultery or fornication after baptism this could also prohibit the candidate's ordination. The law would need to prohibit a candidate who had committed adultery or fornication from receiving orders. He would also be prohibited if his wife committed either of these offenses. A major cleric whose wife committed adultery *post ordinationem* would be required to separate from her or else cease from ministry. Such legislation would be necessary to protect and foster the obligation of perfect and perpetual continence.

4. Age of Ordination

It has been argued that the pastoral letters presuppose a certain maturity in married candidates.[38] They were expected to be *viri probati*. For the first several centuries the minimum age for ordination to the diaconate was thirty years old.[39] Though the minimum age requirement bound both married and unmarried candidates, it was not unusual for an unmarried candidate to be ordained at a younger age.[40]

---

38   See Henri Kruse, "Eheverzucht im Neuen Testament und in der Frühkirche," *Forum für Katholische Theologie* 1 (1985) 113, n. 63. Kruse sets the age for priestly ordination at sixty years old. It was precisely the usual higher age of clerics that made it necessary for the Church Fathers to explain why Timothy, who was unmarried, was a bishop at such a young age. (1 Tim 4:12; 2 Tim 2:22).

39   Council of Neocaesarea 314-325, c. 11 required that no one be ordained a priest before his thirtieth year. Mansi 2, 547-548. See also Pope Siricius, *Decreta*, February 10, 385, *Patrologia Cursus Completus: Series Latina*, ed. Jacques-Paul Migne. 13: 1143a. Hereafter *PL*. The pope wanted the age for deacons to be thirty, for presbyters to be thirty-five and for bishops to be forty-five.

40   See Stefan Heid, *Celibacy in the Early Church* (San Francisco, CA: Ignatius Press, 2000) 323-326. See Council of Carthage, 397, c. 18. Mansi 3: 693.

The Obligation of Perfect and Perpetual Continence

When one considers that it was common, at this time, for people to marry in their lower to mid-teens,[41] the minimum age for diaconal ordination made it likely that the cleric had consummated his marriage, lived a number of years as a married man and had reared his family.[42] Such men with a completed family were then ordained.[43] The minimum age for ordination came after the phase of raising a family and presupposes an obligation of perpetual continence.[44] Such a candidate could now devote himself entirely to ecclesiastical and liturgical concerns. He could also embrace this new way of living his marriage with greater hope of perseverance.

The 1983 Code of Canon Law establishes the minimum age for ordination to the permanent diaconate at thirty-five years for married candidates and twenty-five for unmarried ones.[45] Particular law for the United States has established the minimum age for both married and unmarried candidates at thirty-five years.[46] The Unit-

---

41   "The Church adopted Roman Law's identification of the age for marriage with the age of puberty. The presumption of law was that a boy had attained puberty when he had completed his fourteenth year, and a girl upon the completion of her twelfth year." John C. O'Dea, *The Matrimonial Impediment of Nonage: An Historical Synopsis and Commentary*, Canon Law Studies 205 (Washington, DC: Catholic University of America, 1944) 1. See also See Keith Hopkins, "The Age of Roman Girls at Marriage," in *Population Studies* 18 (1965) 309-327.

It is worth noting that the lower age for marriage is related to a high mortality rate. According to Peter Brown, the age expectancy of an individual at the height of the Roman Empire was less than twenty-five years, in Peter Brown, *The Body and Society: Men, Sex and the Body: Men, Women and Sexual Renunciation in Early Christianity* (New York, NY: Columbia University Press, 2008) 6. Furthermore, only four out of every hundred men, and fewer women, lived beyond the age of fifty. See Keith Hopkins, "On the Probable Age Structure of the Roman Population," in *Population Studies* 20 (1966) 245-264.

42   Heid, *Celibacy in the Early Church,* 323.

43   Ibid.

44   Ibid.

45   83 *CIC*, c. 1031: "§2. Candidatus ad diaconatum permanentem qui non sit uxoratus ad eundem diaconatum ne admittatur, nisi post expletum vigesimum quintum saltem aetatis annum; qui matrimonio coniunctus est, nonnisi post expletum trigesimum quintum saltem aetatis annum, atque de uxoris consensu. §3. Integrum est Episcoporum conferentiis normam statuere, qua provectior ad presbyteratum et ad diaconatum permanentem requiratur aetas. §4. Dispensatio ultra annum super aetate requisita ad normam §§1 et 2, Apostolicae Sedi reservatur."

46   United States Conference of Catholic Bishops, *National Directory for the Formation, Ministry, and Life of Permanent Deacons in the United States* (Washington, DC.: United States Conference of Catholic Bishops, 2005) n. 87. Hereafter *NDFD.*

ed States Conference of Catholic Bishops further decreed that the establishment of a maximum age for ordination to the permanent diaconate is at the discretion of the diocesan bishop.[47] The rationale for the minimum age for married candidates is to allow sufficient time for the candidate to have lived in the married state.[48]

So if married deacons are bound to observe perfect and perpetual continence then it would seem reasonable that the minimum age be set higher than thirty-five. This would of course depend on the local custom. A higher age would allow the candidate to rear his family, and perhaps he and his wife could assume the obligations of continence with greater likelihood of persevering. In this regard it may be necessary to establish the minimum amount of years a candidate should have lived in the married state. A married candidate for the diaconate should be one who has lived as a married man for a number of years.[49] It would be appropriate to determine further what constitutes a suitable "number of years." With the deacon and his wife being obligated to observe absolute continence it would seem prudent that a candidate have lived as a married man until at least he no longer has care of minor children.

Regarding unmarried candidates the age could be lowered to conform to the minimum age limit established by universal law of twenty-five years. It may even be reasonable to lower the minimum age limit to twenty-three years in conformity with that for transitional deacons.[50]

---

47   Ibid.
48   See *SDO* 13 and *NDFD* 37.
49   *NFPD* n. 37.
50   83 *CIC*, c. 1031 §1: "Presbyteratus ne conferatur nisi iis qui aetatis annum vigesimum quintum expleverint et sufficienti gaudeant maturitate, servato insuper intervallo sex saltem mensium inter diaconatum et presbyteratum; qui ad presbyteratum destinantur, ad diaconatus ordinem tantummodo post expletum aetatis annum vigesimum tertium admittantur."

5. Spousal Consent[51]

Only with the Council of Orange (441) was a candidate for major orders obliged to make an explicit promise of continence.[52] The husband's obligation of absolute continence obviously affected his wife and their marriage. A fundamental right was being surrendered, the right to conjugal relations. It was a matter of justice that the wife be informed of her husband's obligation and consent to it. Obviously, the ability of the cleric husband to live his commitment of absolute continence depended in no small measure on the cooperation of his wife. The Council of Agde, 506 required not only the profession of perfect continence of the ordinand but the explicit consent of the spouse given through her promise of continence.[53]

Deacon candidates and their wives must be made aware that from the day of ordination the deacon is obliged to observe perfect and perpetual continence. This involves the surrendering of the fundamental right, shared by each spouse, to conjugal relations. The wife is primarily consenting to her husband's obligation which will obviously affect her and in which she must necessarily acquiesce. The promise of perfect and perpetual continence should be made explicitly by both parties before the ordination. Appropriate formation before and after ordination should be given to assist the couple in living this commitment.

6. The Impediment of Orders

As mentioned earlier in this chapter, the "husband of one wife" passages in Paul's letters to Timothy and Titus were understood as legislating for the mo-

---

51 See also chapter one, 62-64; and chapter four, 245-248.
52 The Council of Orange, c. 21. In *Corpus Christianorum, Series Latina* (Turnhout: Brepols Press, 1954-) 148:84. Hereafter *CCL*.
53 The Council of Agde, c. 16. *CCL* 148:201.

nogamy of clergy. This emphasis on the monogamy of clergy was interpreted as a safeguard for absolute continence and a prohibition on further marriage.

The prohibition of marriage for major clergy *post ordinationem,* when all other Christians could lawfully marry again, has its roots in the clerical obligation to observe continence. The obligation of absolute continence would prohibit major clergy from marrying after ordination as they could not in theory consummate such a bond. The very raison d'être for the impediment of orders is found in the obligation of absolute continence. It would therefore offend against the nature of the continence obligation to dispense married deacons from the impediment of orders. The prohibition on a new marriage would have to be absolute. The only way a married deacon could be dispensed from the impediment of orders would be as part of the laicization process.

7. Penalties for Violation of Continence

The Council of Elvira and subsequent councils imposed severe penalties for a cleric's violation of continence, including, deprivation of office, deposition and degradation.[54] An incontinent cleric was not permitted to exercise his ministry and was ordinarily removed from the ranks of the clergy. Yet a violation of continence was not so easily established and could never be based on mere rumor or hearsay. There were only several ways of proving such a violation (1) the cleric's wife became pregnant; (2) the cleric admitted his incontinence; (3) the cleric's incontinence became public knowledge.

In order to protect and foster the obligation of perfect and perpetual continence non-observance would necessarily be subject to penalty. Following the

---

54   See Council of Elvira, c. 33. Mansi, 2:11; Council of Arles, c. 29. Mansi, 2:474; Council of Ancyra, c. 10. Mansi, 2:518; Council of Nicea, c. 1. Mansi 2:546 and Third Council of Carthage, c. 3. Mansi, 3:969.

former legislation a deacon proven to be incontinent would be suspended, and if he persisted in the delict after a warning, other penalties could gradually be added, including dismissal from the clerical state. Other violations against continence would depend on whether one interpreted continence narrowly as "no sexual relations" and "having no more children" or broadly as any interaction, including passionate kissing and touching that might place the cleric in the occasion of incontinence.

8. Legitimacy of Children

Previous legislation considered children born of clerical marriages to be illegitimate because they were fathered by one who had an obligation of continence. A married man who had received major orders was obliged to observe absolute continence. Therefore he was forbidden the use of his marriage. If he had any more children they were illegitimate on account of this obligation. The 1917 code declared that children born after the taking up of sacred orders were illegitimate.[55] This was removed in the revision process.[56] But with married deacons being bound to observe continence should this declaration of illegitimacy be restored?

9. The Obligation of Those Already Ordained Permanent Deacons

Since the restoration of the permanent diaconate, married deacons have not been obliged to observe perfect and perpetual continence and have even been

---

55   *Codex Iuris Canonici Pii X Pontificis Maximi iussu digestus Benedicti Papae XV auctoritate promulgatus* (Rome: Typis Polyglottis Vaticanis, 1917), c. 1114: "Legitimi sunt filii concepti aut nati ex matrimonio valido vel putativo, nisi parentibus ob sollemnem professionem religiosam vel susceptum ordinem sacrum prohibitus tempore conceptionis fuerit usus matrimonii antea contracti." Hereafter 17 *CIC.*

56   This may indicate that children born to licitly ordained married men are in fact legitimate, seeming to suggest that they are therefore not prohibited from conjugal relations.

dispensed from the impediment of orders to marry again and remain in ministry. To my knowledge and based on the research of available sources, no bishop, no superior, no formator, no ecclesiastical authority has urged married deacons to observe any form of continence. So what is the responsibility to observe the law of continence for those many married deacons who have already been ordained without any knowledge of this obligation?

As Edward Peters rightly observes: "one cannot be held to have surrendered fundamental rights without an express awareness that it is being done."[57] Those who were never informed that the obligation of perfect and perpetual continence was binding upon them, cannot be considered bound by the obligation. The surrendering of a fundamental right without one's knowledge would not be just and could not possibly be imposed retroactively. To impose this obligation would offend against the marital rights and obligations of each of the spouses. Those who have already been ordained deacons could be encouraged to embrace the obligation though they could not be obliged.

Candidates who are presently in formation would need to be made expressly aware that they would be obliged to observe the prescripts of canon 277 §1 upon ordination to the diaconate. Both spouses would be asked explicitly to consent to these obligations prior to ordination. Candidates and their wives would need to receive the necessary formation and to live assistance this commitment. It would be essential to determine each spouse's suitability for the continence obligation which would necessarily include an inquiry into their sexual history. A candidate would be prohibited from orders for the following reasons: twice married, fornication or adultery after baptism, if his wife was

---

57   Edward Peters, "Canonical Considerations on Diaconal Continence," *Studia canonica* 39 (2005) 177.

guilty of adultery or fornication, or was twice married. Such candidates would have to withdraw or risk being dismissed from the program. Others may be unwilling to accept the obligation of continence, and they could withdraw from the program voluntarily.

Ninety-two percent of active deacons are currently married. Four percent are widowers, and one percent have never been married.[58] The overwhelming majority of men who petition for ordination to the diaconate are married men.[59] It seems probable that enrollment for the permanent diaconate would decrease dramatically if married deacons were bound to refrain from sexual relations.

10. The Unity of the Obligation

Pope Leo (440-461) expressly stated: "The law of continence is the same for the ministers of the altar (the deacons) as for the bishops and for the presbyters."[60] It is this unity of discipline of the major clergy that tests the unity of the sacramental ministry of the Church, both of the *sacerdotium* (episcopate and presbyterate) and of the *ministerium* (diaconate). The Church consistently bound all those in major orders to observe the same discipline of continence. Otherwise, why should unmarried deacons not marry if there are married deacons that do not respect clerical continence and can, in exceptional cases, even marry a second time? Why are presbyters and bishops continent if there are married permanent deacons who do not respect clerical continence? Why is an exception being made for married deacons and not for the other grades? With

---

58   Center for Applied Research in the Apostolate Georgetown University, *Diaconate Post Ordination Survey, 2008-2009* (Washington, DC: CARA, 2009) 16.

59   Ibid.

60   Pope Leo the Great, letter to Bishop Rusticus: "Lex continentiae eadem est ministris altaris quae episcopis atque presbyteris, qui cum essent laici sive lectores, licito et uxoris ducere et filios procreare potuerunt. Sed cum ad praedictos pervenerunt gradus, coepit eis non licere quod licuit." *PL* 54:1204a.

married deacons being bound to the prescripts of canon 277 §1 the unity of this obligation would be preserved, thus reflecting the oldest canonical tradition.

C. The "Celibacy School"

While previous legislation obliged married deacons to observe perfect and perpetual continence, such an obligation could not be imposed on them today and therefore the prescripts of canon 277 §1 could not possibly oblige married deacons. Only unmarried candidates for holy orders can be obliged to celibacy. Married candidates cannot and therefore continue to enjoy their marriage after ordination. The current praxis seems to accept the thesis of this "school."[61] Yet there are some additional implications that are worthy of note.

1. Married Deacons and the Obligation of Perfect and Perpetual Continence

From the fourth century the Latin Church increasingly ordained married men to major orders on condition that they observe the *lex continentia*. With the Second Vatican Council and *Gaudium et spes* a more personalist understanding of marriage emerged. Married persons each have equal obligations and rights to those things which pertain to the partnership of conjugal life, and sexual coop-eration is part of the permanent consortium.[62] Each spouse has an acquired right to the conjugal life. This right has not been expressly revoked by the code. As

---

61   Practically no canonists have written in defense of a married deacon's right to have conjugal relations perhaps because so few seem to be aware of the arguments that can be adduced against the practice. Any arguments in support of a married deacons right to conjugal relations have been generally raised in the context of the applicability of canon 277 § 1. See Edward Peters, "Ca-nonical Considerations on Diaconal Continence," *Studia canonica* 39 (2005) 174-177; James H. Provost, "Permanent Deacons in the 1983 Code," *CLSA Proceedings* 46 (1985) 175-191 and James A. Coriden and James H. Provost, "Canonical Implications Related to the Ordination of Married Men to the Priesthood in the United States of America," *CLSA Proceedings* 58 (1996) 438-451.

62   83 *CIC*, c. 4.

a consequence the obligation of continence cannot and should not be obliged as a condition for a married man to be ordained. To oblige married persons to observe perfect and perpetual continence would be a tautology. It would offend against these rights and obligations and do grave harm to the nature of marriage itself. Therefore, even though canon 277 §1 reads as if the obligation is applicable to married deacons, the obligation for them has been mitigated elsewhere in the code.[63]

2. Age of Ordination

As already stated the universal law establishes the minimum age of the reception of diaconate at thirty-five years for married candidates and twenty-five for unmarried ones.[64] Particular law for the United States has established the minimum age for both married and unmarried candidates at thirty-five years. The rationale for this minimum age for married candidates is to allow sufficient time for the candidate to have lived in the married state.[65] While the "Continence School" could argue that a higher minimum age is more suited to the obligation of perfect and perpetual continence, it would follow that if there is no such obligation, as the "Celibacy School" would hold then the minimum age could be lowered.

The Eastern code establishes that the minimum age for the diaconate is the completion of twenty-three years.[66] The same code makes no special pro-

---

63   See 83 *CIC*, cc. 4, 1055, 1056, 1096 §1 and 1135.
64   83 *CIC*, c. 1031 § 2.
65   See *SDO* 13 and *NDFD* 37.
66   *Codex Canonum Ecclesiarum Orientalium auctoritate Ioannis Pauli PP. II promulgatus* (Vatican City: Libreria Editrice Vaticana, 1990), c. 759: "Aetas praescripto ad diaconatum est vicesimus tertius annus expletus,…."

vision for so-called married deacons.[67] In principle the Eastern Churches have always admitted married men to the diaconate, be it transitional or permanent. The canon makes no distinction between married and unmarried candidates. All candidates to the diaconate have to be at least twenty-three years old at the time of ordination. From the Council of Trullo, 692, the Eastern Churches have had the tradition of married deacons who were not obliged to absolute continence.[68] The minimum age for ordination to the permanent diaconate in the Latin Church could be lowered to reflect the Eastern practice.

Or, conversely, perhaps the minimum age could be raised. The demands of diaconal ministry could place an additional strain on a marriage. Hence the consent of the wife is required. An increase in the minimum age would permit a married candidate to live a number of years in his marriage and no longer have minor children or at least no longer have the care of very young children. That way the stability of his marriage would be more firm, and his availability for diaconal ministry would be more assured. The minimum age could be raised not because there is an implied obligation of continence, but simply because it is immanently practical.

3. The Impediment of Orders

During the revision process the various *coetus* recommended that married deacons not be bound by the impediment of orders.[69] Shortly before the prom-

---

67   See Victor J. Pospishil, "Requirements of Ordination, cc. 743-775," *Eastern Catholic Church Law* (New York, Saint Maron Publication, 1996) 429.

68   Council of Trullo, c. 13. Mansi, 11: 947. Canon 13 remains the continence discipline of the Eastern Churches. Presently, nineteen of the twenty-one Eastern Catholic Churches permit all clergy below the rank of bishop to be married and to have conjugal relations, though these clergy are obliged to observe periodic continence. The Syro-Malabar Church and the Syro-Malankara Church do not have married clergy.

69   See discussion of the revision process concerning the applicability of the impediment of orders for married deacons. Chapter four, 250-256.

ulgation of the 1983 code, John Paul II removed this exception. It would seem that if married deacons have no obligation of continence then the impediment of orders should not bind them. This appeared to be the connection made by the various *coetus* when they treated the exemption from celibacy alongside the exemption from the impediment of orders. If a married cleric was not bound to celibacy, he should not be bound to the impediment of orders.

Married deacons should enjoy the rights of all other married members of the Christian faithful to enter another marriage upon the death of their spouse. The impediment of orders has its raison d'être in the obligation of clerical celibacy. A married man is not obliged to celibacy, so he should not be bound by the impediment of orders.[70] Therefore a married deacon could marry again with a declaration of nullity or upon the death of his spouse without the need for a dispensation and without incurring any penalties. If the impediment of orders has its raison d'être in orders *per se* and not continence then this needs to be enunciated more clearly.

A decision to permit married deacons who were not obliged to continence to exercise their ministry and to exempt them from the impediment of orders may not be without consequences for the Latin Church's relationship with the Eastern Catholic and Orthodox Churches. These Churches accept the legislation of the Council of Trullo in regard to married clergy being bound to periodic

---

70   See Juan Ignacio Bañares, "Chapter III: Individual Diriment Impediments, c. 1087," in *Exegetical Commentary on the Code of Canon Law,* ed. Angel Marzoa et al. (Chicago, IL: Midwest Theological Forum, 2004) 3/2: 1187.

continence.[71] They also do not ordinarily permit a deacon to marry after the reception of orders.

4. The Unity of the Obligation

According to previous legislation, bishops, presbyters and deacons were equally bound to observe the discipline of absolute continence.[72] But now that an exception has been made for married deacons this raises further questions. What about unmarried deacons? If their married brothers are not bound to observe perfect and perpetual continence, why are unmarried deacons so obliged? We know that they are obliged to continence because they are not married, but could they, like their married brothers, enter marriage after ordination? Could they make their desire to marry known before ordination as was understood by some to be the legislation of the Council of Ancrya, 314-325?[73] Furthermore what might be the implications for presbyters and bishops?

C. Conclusion

The answer to the question of whether married deacons are obliged to ob-

---

71   Council of Trullo 692, c. 13: "Quoniam in Romanum ecclesia pro canonis ordine traditum esse cognovimus, ut diaconi vel presbyteri, qui ut ordinentur digni existimati sunt, profiteantur se non amplius suis uxoribus coniungendos, nos antiquum canonum apostolicae perfectionis ordinisque servantes, hominum qui sunt in sacris coniuga etiam ex hoc temporis momento firma et stabilia esse volumus, nequaquam eorum cum uxoribus coniunctionem dissolventes vel eos mutual tempore convenienti consuetudine privates....Scimus autem, quod et qui Carthagine convenerunt, ministrorum gravitatis in vita curam gerentes dixerunt: 'Ut subdiaconi, qui sacra mysteria contrectant, et diaconi et presbyteri secundum easdem rationes a consortibus abstineant'...." Mansi, 11:947. See also D. Cummings, *The Rudder (Pedalion) of the Metaphorical Ship of the One Holy Catholic and Apostolic Church of Orthodox Christians* (Chicago: The Orthodox Christian Educational Society, 1957) 305-307. *The Rudder* (Greek: Πηδάλιον) is a codification of Orthodox canon law by St. Nicodemus of the Holy Mountain. It was first translated into English by D. Cummings, and published by the Orthodox Christian Educational Society in 1957 under the title of *The Rudder*.

72   See chapter one. The common obligation for deacons, presbyters and bishops is examined from Council of Elvira 305 until the Council of Trent.

73   See discussion of Council of Ancyra, chapter one, 35-38.

serve the perfect and perpetual continence prescribed in canon 277 §1 will ultimately depend on how one understands celibacy. If celibacy is understood narrowly as the legal condition of being unmarried then only celibate clerics are bound to observe the law of continence. Married clerics, who are obviously not celibate, are not bound to observe the law of continence. This in turn implies the legitimization of conjugal relations for married clerics (the "Celibacy School"). However, if celibacy is understood broadly in terms of the *lex continentiae,* no sexual relations *post ordinationem,* then there is the canonical precedent of at least a millennium that married deacons are bound to observe the law of continence ("the Continence School"). The law of continence, not celibacy, is the fundamental norm that binds all clerics, married or celibate. As we have demonstrated, when the thesis of each "school" is taken to its logical conclusions there are significant implications for the current interpretation and implementation of the prescripts of canon 277 §1.

The purpose of the book is twofold: 1) to offer a broad overview of the development of the law of chastity, continence and celibacy and its applicability to married deacons in the Latin Church; 2) to provide an interpretation of the law concerning the obligation of continence for married deacons and, consequent to such an interpretation, the practical implications of that law.

This book will contribute to canonical studies by offering a deeper understanding of the relationship between continence, chastity and celibacy. In clarifying the fundamental issues and analyzing the implicit suppositions of the two "schools" this book will help to illustrate why the obligation of continence and married deacons is even a question. Furthermore, if a change in discipline was intended, then this needs to be more clearly enunciated. If, however, a change was not intended then the current situation needs to be addressed.

BIBLIOGRAPHY

A. PRIMARY SOURCES

Abbott, Walter M, ed. *The Documents of Vatican II: In a New and Definitive Translation.* New York: Herder and Herder, 1966.

Acta Apostolicae Sedis: Commentarium Officiale. Rome: Typis Polyglottis Vaticanis, 1908-1928. Vatican City: Typis Polyglottis Vaticanis, 1929-.

Acta Sanctae Sedis. 41 vols. Rome: Ex Typographia Polyglotta S. C. de Propaganda Fide, 1865-1908.

Alberigo, Joseph, et al., eds. *Conciliorum Oecumenicorum Decreta.* Third edition. Bologna: Institutio per le Scienze Religiose, 1973.

Baronius, Caesar. *Annales Ecclesiastici.* 12 vols. Paris: Barri-Ducis, 1864.

Benedict XIV. Apostolic constitution *Eo quamvis tempore,* May 4, 1745. *Iuris Pontificii De Propaganda Fide.* Rome: Ex Typographia Polyglotta S. C. de Propaganda Fide, 1888-1909. 3: 221-232.

_____. Apostolic constitution *Allatae sunt,* June 26, 1755. *Iuris Pontificii De Propaganda Fide.* 3:598-621.

_____. Apostolic constitution *Etsi pastoralis,* May 26, 1742. *Magnum Bullarium Romanum.* Luxemburg: Sumptibus Andreae Chevalier, 1752. 15:94-104.

_____. *Libri Octo de Synodo Diocesana.* Rome: Excudebant Nicolaus et Marcus Palearini, 1748.

Benedict XV. Allocution *Cum multa hoc*, December 16, 1920. *AAS* 12 (1920) 585-588.

_____. Apostolic constitution *Providentissima Mater Ecclesia,* May 27, 1917. *AAS* 9 (1917) 2:5-7.

_____. Motu proprio *Cum iuris canonici,* September 15, 1917. *AAS* 9 (1917) 483-484.

Bruns, Herman. T. *Canones Apostolorum et Conciliorum: Saeculorum IV-VII.* Berlin: G. Reimeri, 1839.

Canon Law Digest. 13 vols. Vols. 1-3 edited by T. Lincoln Bouscaren, vols. 4-6 edited by T. Lincoln Bouscaren and James O'Conner. Milwaukee: The Bruce Publishing Co., 1934-1967. Vols. 7-10 edited by James O'Connor. Mundelein: Chicago Province of the Society of Jesus, 1967-1983. Vol. 11 edited by Edward G. Pfnausch, Washington: Canon Law Society of America, 1983-1985. Vol. 12 edited by Arthur Espelage, Washington: Canon Law Society of America, 1986-1990. Vol. 13 edited by Patrick Cogan, Washington: Canon Law Society of America, 1991-1995.

Carlen, Claudia., et al., eds. *Papal Pronouncements: A Guide, 1740-1978.* Ann Arbor: MI: The Pieran Press, 1990.

_____. *The Papal Encyclicals.* Raleigh, NC: The Perian Press, 1981.

Code of Canon Law: Latin-English Edition: New English Translation. Washington, DC: Canon Law Society of America, 1998.

Code of Canons of the Eastern Churches: Latin-English Translation: New English Translation. Washington, DC: Canon Law Society of America, 2001.

Codex Canonum Ecclesiarum Orientalium auctoritate Ioannis Pauli PP. II promulgatus. Vatican City: Libreria Editrice Vaticana, 1990.

Codex Iuris Canonici auctoritate Ioannis Pauli PP. II promulgatus. Vatican City: Libreria Editrice Vaticana, 1983.

Codex Iuris Canonici Pii X Pontificis Maximi iussu digestus Benedicti Papae XV auctoritate promulgatus. Vatican City: Typis Polyglottis Vaticanis, 1917.

Codicis Iuris Canonici Fontes. Ed. Pietro Card. Gasparri. 9 vols. Rome: Typis Polylottis Vaticanis, 1923-1939.

Concilium Tridentinum Diariorum, Actorum, Epistularum, Tractum Nova Collectio. The Commission of Theologians of the Council of Trent. Ed. Societas Goerresiana. Freiburg: Herder Press, 1901-.

Congregation for Catholic Education, *Basic Norms for the Formation of Permanent Deacons.* Washington, DC: United States Catholic Conference, 1998.

Congregation for Clergy. *Directory on the Life and Ministry of Priests*, March 31, 1994. Vatican City: Libreria Editrice Vaticana, 1994.

_____. *Directory for the Ministry and Life of Permanent Deacons.* Washington, DC: United States Catholic Conference, 1998.

Congregation for the Doctrine of the Faith. Declaration *Persona humana,* December 29, 1975. *AAS* 68 (1976) 77-96.

_____. Instruction *Ad exsequendam ecclesiasticam,* May 18, 2002. *AAS* 93 (2001) 785-788.

_____. Circular letter *Substantial and Procedural Norms,* October 14, 1980. *AAS* 72 (1980) 1132-1137.

Congregation for Divine Worship and the Discipline. Decree *De Regulis Servandis Ad Nullitatem Ordinationis Declarandum,* October 26, 2001. *AAS* 94 (2002) 292-300.

_____. Decree *Ritus ordinationem*, June 29, 1989. *AAS* 82 (1990) 826-827.

Coram Jullien, January 13, 1928. *Sacra Romanae Rotae Decisiones Seu Sententiae.* 20 (1928) 1-13.

Corpus Iuris Canonici. Ed. Emil Friedberg. 2 vols. Graz: Akademische Druck-u. Verlagsanstalt, 1959.

Coustant, Pierre, ed. *Epistolae Romanum Pontificum.* Farnborough: Gregg Press, 1967.

Decisiones seu sententiae. Vatican City: Libreria Editrice Vaticana, 1909-.

Decretum Gratiani emendatum et notantibus illustratum una cum glossis, Gregorii XIII. Pont. Max issu editum. Rome, 1582.

Denzinger, Heinrich. *Enchiridion Symbolorum: Definitionum et Declarationum de Rebus Fidei et Morum.* Fortieth edition. Paris: Éditions du Cerf, 2005.

Enchiridion Vaticanum: Documenti ufficiali della Santa Sede, testo ufficiale e versione Italiana. 23 vols, 3 Supplements. Bologna: Edizioni Dehoniane, 1962-2006.

Flannery, Austin, ed. *Vatican Council II: The Conciliar and Post Conciliar Documents.* 2 vols. Northport, NY: Costello Publishing, 1996.

_____. *Vatican Council II: More Postconciliar Documents.* 2 vols. Collegeville: The Liturgical Press, 1982.

Funk, Francis X., ed. *Didascalia et Constitutiones Apostolorum.* Paderborn: Libraria Ferdinand Schöningh, 1905.

Gratian. *Concordia Discordantium Canonum.* In *Corpus Iuris Canonici.* Ed. Emil Friedberg. Vol 1. Graz: Akademische Druck- u. Verlagsanstalt, 1959.

Iuris Pontificii De Propaganda Fide. Rome: Ex Typographia Polyglotta S. C. de Propaganda Fide, 1888-1909.

Jaffé, Philippus, ed. *Regesta Pontificum Romanorum.* 2 vols. Graz: Akademische Druck-U. Verlagsanstalt, 1956.

Joannou, Périclès-Pierre, P., ed. *Les canons des synodes particuliers.* 2 vols. Pontificia Commissione per la Redazione del Codice di Diritto Canonico Orientale. Grottaferrata, 1962.

John XXIII. Allocution *Questa festiva,* January 25, 1959. *AAS* 51 (1959) 65-69.

_____. Encyclical *Sacredotii Nostri primordia,* August 1, 1959. *AAS* 51 (1959) 545-579.

John Paul II. Apostolic constitution *Pastor bonus,* June 28, 1988. *AAS* 80 (1988) 841-912.

_____. Apostolic constitution *Sacrae disciplinae leges*, January 25, 1983. *AAS* 75/2 (1983) ix-xiv.

_____. Apostolic exhortation *Familiaris consortio,* November 22, 1981. *AAS* 74 (1982) 81-191.

_____. Encyclical *Redemptor hominis,* March 4, 1979. *AAS* 71 (1979) 257-324.

_____. Letter *Novo incipiente,* April 8, 1979. *AAS* 71 (1979) 393-417.

_____. *Original Unity of Man and Woman: Catechesis on the Book of Genesis.* Boston, MA: St. Paul Editions, 1981.

Julius III. Papal bull to Cardinal Reginald Pole. *Caelibatus et Breviarum: Duo*

The Obligation of Perfect and Perpetual Continence

Gravissima Clericorum Officina, e Monumentis Omnium Seculorum Demon-strata. Ed. Augustino De Roskovány. 11 vols. Pestini: Typis Beimel et Basilii Kozma, 1861. 2: n. 1333.

Leo XIII. Encyclical *Satis cognitum,* June 29, 1896. *AAS* 28 (1895-96) 708-739.

Mansi, Ioannes Dominicus. *Sacrorum Conciliorum: Nova et Amplissma Collectio.* 53 vols. Florence and Venice, 1757-1798; Paris: Herbert Welter, 1899-1927.

Migne, Jacques-Paul, ed. *Patrologia Cursus Completus.* Series Graeca. 162 vols. Turnhout, Belgium: Brepols Press, 1857-1887.

_____. *Patrologia Cursus Completus.* Series Latina. 221 vols. Paris 1844-1865.

Munier, Charles, ed. *Corpus Christianorum Series Latina.* 176 vols. Tornhout, Belgium: Brepols Publishers, 1953- 1975.

National Conference of Catholic Bishops. *Foundations for the Renewal of the Diaconate.* Washington, DC: United States Catholic Conference, 1986.

_____. *Permanent Deacons in the United States: Guidelines on their Formation and Ministry.* Washington, DC: United States Catholic Conference, 1971.

_____. *Permanent Deacons in the United States: Guidelines on their Formation and Ministry.* Washington, DC: United States Catholic Conference, 1984.

New American Bible. Nashville: Catholic Bible Press, 1987.

Paul VI. Allocution *Singulari cum,* November 20, 1965. *AAS* 57 (1965) 985-989.

_____. Apostolic constitution *Pontificalis Romani Recognitio,* June 17, 1968. *AAS* 60 (1968) 369-373.

_____. Encyclical *Sacerdotalis caelibatus,* June 24, 1967. *AAS* 59 (1967) 657-697.

_____. Motu proprio *Ad pascendum,* August 15, 1972. *AAS* 64 (1972) 534-540.

_____. Motu proprio *De Episcoporum muneribus*, June 15, 1966. *AAS* 58 (1966) 467-472.

_____. Motu proprio *Ministeria quaedam,* August 15, 1972. *AAS* 64 (1972) 529-534.

_____. Motu proprio *Sacrum diaconatus ordinem,* June 18, 1967. *AAS* 59 (1967) 697-704.

PCLT 12959/2011. Roman Replies and CLSA Advisory Opinions 2011. Canon Law Society of America, 2011.

PCLT 13095/2011. Roman Replies and CLSA Advisory Opinions 2012. Canon Law Society of America, 2012.

Percival, Henry R., ed. *The Seven Ecumenical Councils of the Undivided Church: Their Canons and Dogmatic Decrees.* New York, NY: Charles Scribner's Sons, 1901.

Peters, Edward N., ed. *The 1917 Pio-Benedictine Code of Canon Law: In English Translation with Extensive Scholarly Apparatus.* San Francisco, CA: Ignatius Press, 2001.

_____, ed. *Incrementa in Progressu 1983 Codicis Iuris Canonici.* Montréal: Wilson & Lafleur, 2005.

Pius VII. Papal bull to the papal legate to France, Cardinal Caprara. Roskovány, 3: n. 1969.

Pius X. Apostolic exhortation *Haerent animo,* August 4, 1908. St. Pii X Acta 4: 242-244.

_____. Motu proprio *Arduum sane munus,* March 19, 1904. *AAS* 36 (1904) 193-198.

Pius XI. Encyclical *Ad Catholici Sacerdotii,* December 20, 1935. *AAS* 28 (1936) 390-395.

_____. Encyclical *Cast connubii,* December 31, 1930. *AAS* 22 (1930) 539-592.

Pius XII. Address to newlyweds *Un giogo,* March 18, 1942. In *Discorsi e Radiomessagi de Sua Santità Pio XII.* Vatican City: Tipografia Poliglotta Vaticana, 1955-1959. 4 (1942-1943) 3-8.

_____. Address to newlyweds *A un alto concetti,* April 22, 1942. In *Discorsi* 4 (1942-1943) 45-49.

_____. Allocution to Roman Rota *Gia per la terza volta,* October 31, 1941. *AAS* 33 (1941) 421-426.

_____. Allocution to World Congress of the Lay Apostolate in Rome *Six ans se sont,* October 5, 1957. *AAS* 49 (1957) 922-939.

_____. Apostolic exhortation *Menti Nostrae,* September 23, 1950. *AAS* 42 (1950) 657-702.

_____. Encyclical *Mystici Corporis,* June 29, 1943. *AAS* 35 (1943) 193-248.

_____. Encyclical *Sacra virginitas,* March 25, 1954. *AAS* 46 (1954) 161-191.

_____. Motu proprio *Cleri sanctitati,* June 2, 1957. *AAS* 49 (1957) 433-603.

_____. Motu proprio *Crebrae allatae,* February 22, 1949. *AAS* 41 (1949) 89-117.

Pontificia Commissio Codici Authentice Interpretando. *Codex Iuris Canonici: auctoritate Ioannis Pauli PP. II Promulgatus.* Vatican City: Liberia Editrice Vaticana, 1989.

Pontificia Commissio Codici Iuris Canonici Recognoscendo. *Schema Documenti Pontifici Quo Disciplina Canonica de Sacramentis Recognoscitur.* Vatican City: Typis Polyglottis Vaticanis, 1975.

_____. Pontificia Commissio Codici Iuris Canonici Recognoscendo. *Codex Iuris Canonici: Schema Novissimum iuxta placita Patrum Commissionis Emendatum atque Summo Pontifici Praesentatum.* Vatican City: Typis Polyglottis Vaticanis, 1982.

Pontificia Commissio Codici Iuris Canonici Orientalis Recognoscendo, *Nuntia.* 35 vols. Vatican City: Typis Polyglottis Vaticanis, 1975-1990.

_____. *Communicationes.* Rome, 1969-.

_____. *Schema Canonum Libri II De Populo Dei.* Vatican City: Typis Polyglottis Vaticanis, 1977.

_____. *Schema Codicis Iuris Canonici iuxta animadversions S. R. E. Cardinalium, Episcoporum Conferentiarum, Dicasteriorum Curiae Romanae, Universitatum Facultatumque ecclesiasticarum necnon Superiorum Institutorum vitae consecrata recognitum.* Vatican City: Typis Polyglottis Vaticanis, 1980.

_____. *Schema Documenti Pontificii quo Disciplina Canonica de Sacramentis Recognoscitur.* Vatican City: Typis Polyglottis Vaticani, 1975.

_____. *Relatio complectens synthesim animadversionum ab Em. mis. atque Exc. mis. Patribus Commissionis ad Novissimum Schema Codicis Iuris Canonici Exhibitarum, cum Responsionibus a Secretaria et Consultoribus datis.* Vatican City: Typis Polyglottis Vaticanis, 1981.

_____. *Codex Iuris Canonici: Schema novissimum post consultationem S. R. E. Cardinalium, Episcoporum Conferentiarum, Dicasteriorum Curiae Romanae, Universitatum Facultatumque ecclesiasticarum necnon Superiorum Institutorum vitae consecrata recognitum, iuxa placita Patrum Commissionis deinde emendatum atque Summo Pontifici praesentatum.* Vatican City: Typis Polyglottis Vaticanis, 1981.

Pontificale Romanum. Ex decreto sacrosancti Oecumenici concilii Vaticani II instauratum, auctoritate Pauli PP. VI promulgatum. De institutione lectorum et acolythorum; De admissione inter candidatos ad diaconatum et presbyteratum; De sacro caelibatu amplectendo. Editio typica altera. Vatican City: Typis Polyglottis Vaticanis, 1990.

Romita, Florence, ed. *Concilii Oecumenici Vaticani II: Constitutiones, Decreta, Declarationes.* Rome: Desclée et Socii, 1966.

Sacred Apostolic Penitentiary. Decree *Lex Sacri Caelibatus,* April 18, 1936. *AAS* 28 (1936) 242-243.

Sacred Congregation for the Doctrine of the Faith. Public statement on *Pastoral Provision.* March 31, 1981. Published in *L'Osservatore Romano*, English edition, April 6, 1981, 2.

Sacred Congregation for the Oriental Church. Decree *Cum data fuerit,* March 1, 1929. *AAS* 21 (1929) 152-159.

_____. Decree *Graeci-Rutheni Ritus,* December 23, 1929. *AAS* 22 (1930) 346-354.

_____. Decree *Quo faciliter,* September 26, 1932. *AAS* 24 (1932) 344-346.

_____. Decree *Qua sollerti,* May 24, 1930. *AAS* 22 (1930) 102-103.

Sacred Congregation for the Propagation of the Faith. Decree *Romanae Ecclesiae*, May 1, 1897: *ASS* 30 (1897-1898) 635-636.

Sacred Congregation for Religious. Instruction *Quantum Religiones,* December 1, 1931. *AAS* 24 (1932) 74-81.

Sacred Congregation of the Roman and Universal Inquisition. Letter to Ordinaries Concerning Matrimonial Dispensations, February 20, 1888. *AAS* 20 (1888) 543-544.

Sacred Congregation of the Sacraments. Decree *Regulae servandae in processibus super nullitate sacrae ordinationis,* June 9, 1931. *AAS* 23 (1931) 457-492

_____. Decree *Venetiarum* August 16, 1909. *AAS* 1 (1909) 656.

_____. Instruction *Quam ingens,* December 27, 1930. *AAS* 23 (1930) 120-129.

_____. Instruction *De Ordinariorum munere sedulo scrutandi mores candidatorum ante Ordinationem,* December 27, 1930. *AAS* 23 (1930) 120-127.

Schroeder, H. J. *Disciplinary Decrees of the General Councils.* St. Louis: B. Herder Book Co., 1937.

Synod of Bishops, Second General Assembly. *Ultimus temporibus,* November 30, 1971. *AAS* 63 (1971) 898-1024.

Tanner, Norman T. ed. *Decrees of the Ecumenical Councils.* 2 vols. London and Washington: Sheed & Ward and Georgetown University Press, 1990.

United States Conference of Catholic Bishops, *National Directory for the Formation, Ministry and Life of Permanent Deacons in the United States.* Washington, DC: United States Conference of Catholic Bishops, 2005.

Vatican Council I. *Prima Schema Constitutionis Dogmaticae de Ecclesia Christi Patrum Examini Propositum.* In *Sacrorum Conciliorum: Nova et Amplissma Collectio.* Ed. Ioannes Dominicus Mansi (Paris: Herbert Welter, 1901-1927) 51:539-553.

_____. *Schema Constitutionis Dogmaticae Secundae de Ecclesia Christi Secundum Reverendissimorum Patrum Animadversiones Reformatum.* In *Sacrorum Conciliorum: Nova et Amplissma Collectio.* Ed. Ioannes Dominicus Mansi (Paris: Herbert Welter, 1901-1927) 53: 308-317.

Vatican Council II. *Acta et Documenta Concilio Oecumenico Vaticano II Apparando.* Series 1 Antepraeparatoria. 4 vols. Vatican City: Typis Polyglottis Vaticanis, 1960-61.

_____. *Acta et Documenta Concilio Oecumenico Vaticano II Apparando.* Series 2 Praeparatoria. 7 vols. Vatican City: Typis Polyglottis Vaticanis, 1964-1969.

_____. *Acta Synodalia Sacrosancti Concilii Oecumenici Vaticani II.* 6 vols. Vatican City: Typis Polyglottis Vaticanis, 1970-1996.

_____. Decree *Ad gentes,* December 7, 1965. *AAS* 58 (1966) 947-990.

_____. Decree *Optatam totius,* October 28, 1965. *AAS* 58 (1966) 713-727.

_____. Decree *Orientalium Ecclesiarum,* November 21, 1964. *AAS* 57 (1965)

_____. Decree *Perfectae caritatis,* October 28, 1965. *AAS* 58 (1966) 702-712.

_____. Decree *Presbyterorum Ordinis,* December 7, 1965. *AAS* 58 (1966) 991-1024.

_____. Dogmatic Constitution *Dei verbum,* November 18, 1965. *AAS* 58 (1966) 817-830.

_____. Dogmatic constitution *Lumen gentium,* November 21, 1964. *AAS* 57 (1965) 5-67.

_____. Pastoral constitution *Gaudium et spes,* December 7, 1965. *AAS* 58 (1966) 1025-1115.

B. Secondary Sources

1. Commentaries

Abbass, Jobe. *Two Codes in Comparison.* Kanonika 7. Rome: Pontifical Oriental Institute, 1997.

Abbo, John A. and Jerome D. Hannan. *The Sacred Canons: A Concise Presentation of the Current Disciplinary Norms of the Church.* Second edition revised. 2 vols. St. Louis: B. Herder Book Co., 1952.

Alesandro, John A. "General Introduction." In *The Code of Canon Law: A Text and Commentary,* eds. James A. Coriden et al., 1-22.

Althaus, Rüdiger. "Begrenztes Recht auf Priesterweihe." In *Münsterischer Kommentar zum Codex Iuris Canonici,* ed. Klaus Lüdicke et al., Band 4: 1030/1-1054/2.

Bachofen, Charles Augustine, *A Commentary on the New Code of Canon Law.* Second edition. 8 vols. London: B. Herder Book Co., 1919.

Bañares, Juan Ignacio. "Chapter III: Individual Diriment Impediments, c. 1087." In *Exegetical Commentary on the Code of Canon Law,* eds. Angel Marzoa et al., 3/2: 1187-1190.

Beal, John P. "Diriment Impediments Specifically." In *New Commentary on the Code of Canon Law,* ed. John P. Beal et al., 1282-1296.

Beal, John P., et al., eds. *New Commentary on the Code of Canon Law.* New York/Mahwah, NJ: Paulist Press, 2000.

Beste, Udalricus. *Introductio in Codicem.* Fourth edition. Naples: M. D'Auria Pontificius Editor, 1956.

Blat, Alberto. *Commentarium Textus Codicis Iuris Canonici.* Second edition. 5 vols. Rome: Ex Typographia Pontificia in Instituto Pii IX, 1921-24.

Bouscaren, T. Lincoln and Adam C. Ellis. *Canon Law: A Text and Commentary.* Milwaukee: The Bruce Publishing Company, 1946.

Canon Law Society of America. "Initial Report of Task Force Committee on the Draft of the Canons of Book Two: The People of God." In *Task Force Critiques of the Initial Schemata for the Revision of the Code of Canon Law.* Mimeographed: Canon Law Society of America, 1978.

_____. "Second Report of Canon Law Society of America Task Force Committee on the *Schema Canonum Libri II De Populi Dei.*" In *Task Force Critiques of the Initial Schemata for the Revision of the Code of Canon Law.* Mimeographed: Canon Law Society of America, 1978.

_____. "Report of the Task Force Committee on the *Schema Canonum Libri II De Populo Dei.*" In *Task Force Critiques of the Initial Schemata for the Revision of the Code of Canon Law.* Mimeographed: Canon Law Society of America, 1978.

Cantón, Alberto Bernárdez. "Impedimento de orden sagrado." In *Compendio de Derecho Matrimonial Canónico,* 84-87. Madrid: Tecnos, 1989.

Cappello, Felix M. *Summa Iuris Canonici.* Fourth edition. 3 vols. Rome: Universitas Gregorianae, 1945.

_____. *Tractatus Canonico-Moralis de Sacramentis.* 5 vols. Turin: Marietti, 1943-50.

_____. *Tractatus Canonico-Moralis de Censuris iuxta Codicem Iuris Canonici.* Fourth edition. Rome: Marietti, 1950.

Caparros, Ernest, et al. eds. *Code of Canon Law Annotated.* Second edition. Montreal: Wilson and LaFleur Limitée, 2004.

Cenalmor, Daniel. "The Requirements for Ordination," in *Exegetical Commentary on the Code of Canon Law,* ed. Angel Marzoa et al. Chicago, IL: Midwest Theological Forum, 2004. 3/1: 960.

Chelodi, Ioannes. *Ius Canonicum de Matrimonio et de Iudiciis Matrimonialibus.* Ed. Pio Ciprotti. Fifth edition. Vicenza: Società Anonima Tipografica Editrice, 1947.

_____. *Ius de Personis Iuxta Codicem Iuris Canonici.* Second Edition. Trent: Libreria Edit. Tridentum, 1927.

Chiappetta, Luigi. *Dizionario del nuovo codici di diritto canonico.* Second edition. Naples: Edizione Dehoniane, 1986.

_____. *Il Codice di diritto canonico: commento giuridico-pastorale.* Second Edition. 3 vols. Rome: Edizioni Dehoniane, 1996.

Coriden, James A., et al., eds. *The Code of Canon Law: A Text and Commentary.* New York/Mahwah, NJ: Paulist Press, 1985.

Coronata, Matthaeus Conte, A. *Institutiones Iuris Canonici.* Fourth edition. 5 vols. Turin: Marietti, 1939-47.

_____. *Compendium Iuris Canonici.* Fifth edition. 3 vols. Rome: Marietta, 1950.

Di Mattia, Giuseppe. "De Los delitos contra obligaciones especiales." In *Comentario Exegético al Código de Derecho Canónico*, ed. Angel Marzoa et al., 4/1: 573-584.

Del Valle, José María González. "Irregularidades y otros impedimentos." In *Comentario Exegético al Código de Derecho Canónico*, ed. Angel Marzoa et al., 3/1: 973-1006.

De Otaduy, Jorge. "Obligaciones y derechos de los clérigos." In *Comentario Exegético al Código de Derecho Canónico,* ed. Angel Marzoa et al., 2/1: 336-339.

Doyle, Thomas P. "Title III: Marriage (cc. 1055-1165)." In *The Code of Canon Law: A Text and Commentary,* ed. James A. Coriden et al., 737-833.

Eichmann, Eduard and Klaus Mörsdorf, eds. *Lehrbuch des Kirchenrechts auf Grund des Codex Iuris Canonici.* 3 vols. Munich: Verlag Ferninand Schöningh, 1964-1979.

Gasparri, Pietro. *Tractatus de Sacra Ordinatione.* 2 vols. Paris: Delhomme et Briquet, 1893.

_____. *Tractatus Canonicus de Matrimonio.* 2 vols. Vatican City: Typis Polyglottis Vaticanis, 1932.

Gasparri, Pietro and Jusztinian Györg eds. *Codicis Iuris Canonici Fontes.* 9 vols. Rome: Typis Polyglottis Vaticanis, 1923-.

Geisinger, Robert J. "Article 4: The Required Documents and Investigation." In *The New Commentary on the Code of Canon Law,* ed. John P. Beal et al. 1229.

Jombart, Émile. *Manuel de droit canon: conforme au Code de 1917 et aux plus récentes décisions du Saint-Siège.* Paris: Beauchesne et Ses Fils, 1949.

Jone, Heriberto. *Commentarium in Codicem Iuris Canonici.* 3 vols. Paderborn: Officina Libraria Ferdinand Schöningh, 1950-55.

Lombardía, Pedro, et al., eds. *Código de Derecho Canónico, Edición Anotada.* Pamplona: EUNSA, 1983.

Lüdicke, Klaus, et al., eds. *Münsterischer Kommentar zum Codex Iuris Canonici.* 6 vols. Essen: Ludgerus, 1985-.

Lynch, John. "Chapter III: The Obligations and Rights of Clerics." In *The Code of Canon Law: A Text and Commentary,* eds. James A. Coriden et al., 198-229.

McGrath, Aiden. "The Obligation and Rights of Clerics." In *The Canon Law: Letter & Spirit*, ed. Gerard Sheehy et al., 115-209.

Manzanares, Julio. "De Los requisitos previos para la ordenación." In *Codigo De Derecho Canonico,* ed. Juan Luis Acebal et al., 533-535.

Martin, Andrés, ed. *Comentarios al Decreto Optatam Totius Sobre la Formación Sacerdotal.* Madrid: Editorial Católica, 1970.

Martin, John. "Offenses Against Special Obligations." In *The Canon Law: Letter & Spirit,* ed. Gerard Sheehy et al., 802-807.

Marzoa, Angel, et al., eds. *Comentario Exegético al Código de Derecho Canónico.* Pamplona: EUNSA, 1996.

Michiels, Gommarus. *De Delictis et Poenis Commentarius Libri V Codicis Iuris Canonici.* 3 vols. Paris: Typis Societatis St. Joannis Evangelistae, Desclée et Socii, 1961.

_____. *Normae Generales Iuris: Commentarius Libri I Codicis Iuris Canonici.* 2 vols. Rome: Desclée et Socii, 1949.

Naz, Raoul, ed. *Traité de droit canonique.* 4 vols. Paris: Librairie Letouzey et Ané, 1948.

Ojetti, Benedetto. *Commentarium in Codicem Iuris Canonici.* 2 vols. Rome: Pontificia Universitas Gregoriana, 1927.

Pospishil, Victor J. *Eastern Catholic Church Law According to the Code of Canons of the Eastern Churches.* Second edition. Brooklyn: St. Maron Publications, 1996.

Regatillo, Eduardus F. *Institutiones Iuris Canonici.* 2 vols. Santander: Sal Terrae, 1946.

Reiffenstuel, Anacletus. *Ius Canonicum Universum: Complectens Tractatum de Regulis Iuris.* 7 vols. Paris: Ludovicum Vivès, 1864-1870.

Schneider, Francis J. "Chapter VI: Loss of the Clerical State." In *New Commentary on the Code of Canon Law,* ed. John P. Beal et al., 382-393.

Sheehy, Gerard, et al., eds. *The Canon Law: Letter and Spirit.* Collegeville: Liturgical Press, 1995

Urrutia, Francisco Javier. *De Normis Generalibus, Adnotationes in Codicem: Liber 1.* Rome: Tipographia Pontifical Gregorian University, 1983.

Van Hove, Alphonse. *De Legibus Ecclesiasticis.* 2 vols. Mechlin/Rome: H. Dessain, 1930.

Vermeersch, Arthur. *Theologiae Moralis Principia: De Personis, De Sacramentis, De Legibus Ecclesiae et Censuris.* Rome: Universitatas Gregoriana, 1923.

Vermeersch, Arthur and Joseph Creusen, eds. *Epitome Iuris Canonici.* Fourth edition. Rome: H. Dessain, 1930.

Wernz, Franz X. *Ius Decretalium.* 6 vols. Rome: Ex Typographia Polyglotta S. C. de Propaganda Fide, 1898-1904.

Wernz, Franz X. and Petrus Vidal, *Ius Canonicum.* 7 vols. Rome: Apud Aedes Universitas Gregoriana, 1944.

Woestmann, William H. *The Sacrament of Orders and the Clerical State: A Commentary on the Code of Canon Law.* Third edition. Ottawa: St. Paul University, 2006.

_____. *Ecclesiastical Sanctions and the Penal Process.* Second edition. Ottawa: St. Paul University, 2003.

Woywod, Stanislaus. *A Practical Commentary on the Code of Canon Law.* Revised by Callistus Smith. New York: Joseph F. Wagner, Inc., 1957.

2. BOOKS

Alberigo, Joseph, and Joseph Komonchak, eds. *History of Vatican II.* 5 vols. Leuven: Belgium; Maryknoll, NY: Orbis, 1995-2006.

Aubert, Roger. *Vatican I.* Paris: Éditions de l'Orante, 1964.

Audet, Jean Paul. *Mariage et c*élibat dans le *service pastorale de L'Église: histoire et orientations.* Paris: Éditions de L'Orante, 1967.

_____. *Structures of Christian Priesthood: A Study of Home, Marriage and Celibacy in the Pastoral Service of the Church.* Trans. by Rosemary Sheed. New York: The Macmillan Company, 1968.

Ayer, Joseph C. *A Source Book for Ancient Church History.* NewYork: Charles Scribner's Sons, 1913.

Barnett, James Monroe. *The Diaconate: A Full and Equal Order.* Revision of 1981 edition. Pennsylvania: Trinity Press International, 1995.

Bassett, William and Peter Huizing eds. *Celibacy in the Church.* New York, NY: Herder and Herder, 1972.

Baum, Gregory. *The Teachings of the Second Vatican Council.* Westminster, MD: The Newman Press, 1966.

Beltrando, Piercarlo. *Diaconi per la: itinerario ecclesiologico del ripristino del ministero diaconale.* Milano: Istituto Propaganda Libraria, 1977.

Bohr, David. *Catholic Moral Tradition.* Eugene, OR: Wipf & Stock, 2006.

Boni, Andrea. *Sacralità del celibato sacerdotale.* Genova, 1979.

Bonivento, Cesare. *Priestly Celibacy: Ecclesiastical Institution or Apostolic Tradition.* Papua New Guinea: Vanimo, 2006.

Brockman, Norbert. *Ordained to Service: A Theology of the Permanent Diaconate.* Hickville, NY: Exposition Press, 1976.

Brown, Peter. *The Body and Society: Men, Sex and the Body: Men, Women and Sexual Renunciation in Early Christianity.* New York, NY: Columbia University Press, 2008.

Brundage, James A. *Medieval Canon Law.* London and New York: Longman Group, 1995.

Brunini, Joseph B. *The Clerical Obligations of Canons 139 and 142: An Historical Synopsis and Commentary.* Canon Law Studies 103. Washington, DC: Catholic University of America, 1937.

Chizzoniti, Erminia. *Il diaconato permanente.* J.C.D. dissertation. Rome: Pontifical University of the Lateran, 2006.

Cholij, Roman. *Clerical Celibacy in the East and West.* Second edition. Hereford, England: Fowler Wright Books, 1989.

Cochini, Christian. *Origines apostoliques du célibat sacerdotal.* Paris: Dessain et Tolra, 1981.

Cochini, Christian. *The Apostolic Origins of Priestly Celibacy.* Trans. by Nelly Marans. San Francisco, CA: Ignatius Press, 1990.

Collins, John N. *Diakonia: Re-Interpreting the Ancient Sources.* New York: Oxford University Press, 1990.

Colson, Jean. *La fonction diaconale, aux origines de L'Église.* Paris: Desclée de Brouwer, 1962.

Confoy, Mary. *Religious Life and Priesthood: Perfectae Caritatis, Optatam Totius, Presbyterorum Ordinis.* New York: Paulist Press, 2008.

Congar, Yves. *Jalons pour une théologie du laïcat.* Paris: Éditions du Cerf, 1954.

_____. *Vatican II: Le concile au jour.* Paris: Éditions du Cerf, 1963.

Connolly, R. Hugh, ed. *Didascalia Apostolorum.* Oxford: Clarendon Press, 1929.

Costello, Con. *In Quest of an Heir: The Life and Times of John Butler Catholic Bishop of Cork Protestant Baron of Dunboyne.* Cork: Ireland: Tower Books of Cork, 1978.

Cowdrey, Herbert Edward John. *Pope Gregory VII.* Oxford: Clarendon Press, 1998.

Cummings, Owen F. *Deacons and the Church.* Mahwah, NJ: Paulist Press, 2004.

Dale, Alfred William Winterslow. *The Synod of Elvira and Christian Life in the Fourth Century.* London: Macmillan, 1882.

Davis, Leo Donald. *The First Seven Ecumenical Councils 325-787: Their History and Theology.* Collegeville: The Liturgical Press, 1990.

Deen, Henri. *Le célibat des prêtres dans les premiers siècles de L'Église.* Paris: Éditions du Cèdre, 1969.

Delacroix, Simon. *La réorganisation de L'Église de France après la révolution 1801-1809.* Paris: Éditions du Vitrail, 1962.

Denzler, Georg. *Das Papsttum und der Amtszölibat.* 2 vols. Stuttgart: Hiersemann, 1973-1976.

_____. *Die Geschichte des Zölibats.* Freiburg: Herder, 1993.

De Roskovány, Augustino. *Caelibatus et Breviarum: Duo Gravissima Clericorum Officina, e Monumentis Omnium Seculorum Demonstrata.* 11 vols. Pestini: Typis Beimel et Basilii Kozma, 1861-1881.

Ditewig, William T. *The Emerging Diaconate: Servant Leaders in a Servant Church.* New York, NY: Paulist Press, 2007.

Ditewig, William T. and Richard Gaillardetz, eds. *Theology of the Diaconate: The State of the Question.* Mahwah, NJ: Paulist Press, 2005.

Donovan, John Thomas. *The Clerical Obligations of Canons 138 and 140.* Canon Law Studies 272. Washington, DC: Catholic University of America, 1948.

Doms, Herbert. *Vom Sinn und der Ehe.* Breslau: Ostdeutsche Verlagsanstalt, 1935.

Echlin, Edward, P. *The Deacon in the Church, Past and Future.* New York, NY: Alba House, 1971.

Faivre, Alexander. *Emergence of the Laity in the Early Church.* New York, NY: Paulist Press, 1990.

Favale, Agostino, ed. *Magisterio Conciliare.* 14 vols. Turin: Società Editrice International, 1966-1970.

Fernandez, Aurelio and James Socias. *Our Moral Life in Christ: A Basic Course on Moral Theology.* Princeton, NJ: Scepter Press, 1997.

Fichter, Joseph H. *The Pastoral Provisions: Married Catholic Priests.* Kansas City, MO: Sheed & Ward, 1989.

Findlay, Stephen Findlay. *Canonical Norms Governing the Deposition and Degradation of Clerics: An Historical Synopsis and Commentary.* Canon Law Studies 130. Washington, DC: Catholic University of America, 1941.

Gaillardetz, Richard. *The Church in the Making.* New York/Mahwah, NJ Paulist Press, 2006.

Galot, Jean. *Theology of the Priesthood.* San Francisco: Ignatius Press, 1985.

Ghirlanda, Gianfranco. *De Ecclesiae Munere Sanctificandi: De Ordine.* Rome: Pontifical Gregorian University, 1983.

Gibaut, John St. H. *The Cursus Honorum: A Study of the Origins and the Evolution of Sequential Ordination.* New York, NY: Peter Lang Publishing, 2000.

Goracy, Joseph. *The Diriment Matrimonial Impediment of Major Orders.* Canon Law Studies 233. Washington, DC: Catholic University of America, 1920.

Gryson, Roger. *Les origines du c*élibat *ecclésiastique du premier au septième siècle.* Gembloux: J. Duculot, 1970.

Guevin, Benedict M. *Christian Anthropology and Sexual Ethics.* Lanham, MD: University Press of America, 2002.

Healy, Edwin. *Moral Guidance.* Chicago, IL: Loyola University Press, 1943.

Hefele, Charles J. *Histoire des conciles d'après les documents originaux.* 11 vols. Paris: Letouzey et Ané, 1907-1952.

_____. *A History of the Councils of the Church from the Original Documents.* 5 vols. New York: AMS Press, 1972.

Heid, Stefan. *Zölibat in der frühen Kirche: Die Anfänge einer Enthaltsamkeitspflicht für Kleriker in Ost und West.* Paderborn: Ferdinand Schöningh GmbH, 1997.

_____. *Celibacy in the Early Church: The Beginnings of a Discipline of Obligatory Continence for Clerics in East and West.* Trans. by Michael J. Miller. San Francisco, CA: Ignatius Press, 2000.

Hickey, John J. *Irregularities and Simple Impediments in the New Code of Canon Law.* Canon Law Studies 7. Washington, DC: Catholic University of America, 1920.

Hildebrand, Dietrich Von. *Celibacy and the Crisis of Faith.* Washington, DC: Franciscan Herald Press, 1971.

Hornef, Joseph. *The New Vocation.* Techny, IL: Divine Word Publications, 1963.

Jedin, Hubert. *Ecumenical Councils of the Catholic Church: An Historical Outline.* New York: Herder and Herder, 1960.

Jörgensen, Johannes. *St. Francis of Assisi: A Biography.* New York, NY: Longmans Press, 1913.

Anthony McLaughlin

Journet, Charles. *The Church of the Word Incarnate*. Trans. by A. H. C. Downes London and New York: Sheed and Ward, 1955.

Kempf, Friedrich et al. eds. *The Church in the Age of Feudalism: History of the Church*. 3 vols. New York: Seabury Press, 1980.

Kleist, James. *The Epistles of St. Clement of Rome and St. Ignatius of Antioch*. Westminster, MD: The Newman Bookshop, 1949.

Knapp, James. *Celibate Chastity in the Life of the Priest in the Light of the Teaching of Karol Wojtyla/John Paul II*. The Pontifical John Paul II Institute for Studies on Marriage and Family. S.T.D. dissertation. Washington, DC: Catholic University of America, 1998.

Kung, Hans. *The Council, Reform and Reunion*. Trans. by Cecily Hastings. New York, NY: Sheed and Ward, 1961

Laeuchli, Samuel. *Power and Sexuality: The Emergence of Canon Law at the Synod of Elvira*. Philadelphia: Temple University Press, 1972.

Laplante, André. *La formation des prêtres: genèse et commentaire du décret conciliaire Optatam totius*. Paris: P. Lethielleux, 1969.

Lehmkuhl, Augustino. *Theologiae Moralis*. Seventh edition. Freiburg: Herder, 1893.

Lercaro, Giacomo. *Lettere dal concilio*. Ed. Giuseppe Battelli. Bologna: Edizione Dehoniane Bologna, 1980.

Lewis, Charlton T. and Charles Short, eds. *A Latin Dictionary*. Oxford, England: Clarendon Press, 1962.

Lexikon für Theologie und Kirche. 9 vols. Freiburg: Herder, 1998.

Loitta, Filippo. *La continenza dei chierici nel pensiero canonistico classico da Graziano a Gregorio IX*. Milan: Giuffre, 1971.

Maassen, Friedrich. *Geschichte der quellen und der literatur des canonischen rechts im Abendlande bis zum ausgange des mittelalters*. Graz: Leuschner & Lubensky, 1870.

Mackin, Theodore. *What is Marriage?* New York: Paulist Press, 1982.

_____. *The Marital Sacrament.* New York: Paulist Press, 1989.

Mathieu, Françoise-Désiré. *Le concordat de 1801: ses origines son histoire d'après des documents inédits.* Paris: Perrin et Cie, 1903.

McBride, James. *Incardination and Excardination of Seculars: An Historical Synopsis and Commentary.* Canon Law Studies 145. Washington, DC: Catholic University of America, 1941.

McDevitt, Gilbert Joseph. *Legitimacy and Legitimation: An Historical Synopsis and Commentary.* Canon Law Studies 138. Washington, DC: Catholic University of America, 1941.

McGovern, Thomas. *Priestly Celibacy Today.* Princeton, NJ: Scepter Publishers, 1998.

Medina, José L. Casañas. *The Law for the Restoration of the Permanent Diaconate: A Canonical Commentary.* Canon Law Studies 460. Washington, DC: Catholic University of America, 1968.

Moriarty, Francis. *The Extraordinary Absolution from Censures.* Canon Law Studies 113. Washington, DC: Catholic University of America, 1945.

Naz, Raoul, ed. *Dictionnaire de droit canonique.* 7 vols. Paris: Librairie Letouzey et Ané, 1935-1965.

Nedungatt, George. *A Guide to the Eastern Code: A Commentary on the Code of Canons of The Eastern Churches*, Kanonika 10. Rome: Pontificio Istituto Orientale, 2002.

Nedungatt, George and Michael Featherstone eds. *The Council in Trullo Revisited,* Kanonika 6. Rome: Pontificio Istituto Orientale, 1995.

Nichols, Aidan. *Holy Order: The Apostolic Ministry from the New Testament to the Second Vatican Council.* Dublin: Veritas Publications, 1990.

Nowell, Robert. *The Ministry of Service: Deacons in the Contemporary Church.* New York, NY: Herder and Herder, 1968.

Odahl, Charles Matson. *Constantine and the Christian Empire.* New York: Routledge, 2004.

O'Dea, John, C. *The Matrimonial Impediment of Nonage: An Historical Synopsis and Commentary.* Canon Law Studies 205. Washington, DC: Catholic University of America, 1944.

Osborne, Kenan B. *The Permanent Diaconate: Its History and Place in the Sacrament of Orders.* New York, NY: Paulist Press, 2006.

_____. *Priesthood: A History of Ordained Ministry in the Roman Catholic Church.* New York/Mahwah: Paulist Press, 1988.

Pagé, Roch. *Diaconat permanent et diversité des ministères: perspective du droit canonique.* Montréal, Québec: Éditions Paulines, 1988.

Palazzini, Pietro, ed. *Dictionarium Morale et Canonicum.* Rome: Officium Libri Catholici, 1962-1968.

Paska, Walter. *Sources of Particular Law for the Ukrainian Church in the United States,* Canon Law Studies 485. Washington, DC: The Catholic University of America, 1975.

Patterson, Charles. *The Obligation of Spiritual Retreats for Secular Clergy According to Canon 126.* J.C.D. Dissertation. Rome: Pontifical University of St. Thomas, 1956-1957.

Pelikan, Jaroslav and Helmut T . Lehmann, eds. *Luther's Works American Edition.* 55 vols. Augsburg: Augsburg Fortress, 1967.

_____. *The Spirit of Eastern Christendom: The Christian Tradition.* Chicago: University of Chicago Press, 1974.

Plöger, Josef G. and Hermann Joh. Weber. *Der Diakon: Wiederentdeckung und Erneuerung seines Dienstes.* Freiburg: Herder Press, 1980.

Pokusa, Joseph H. *A Canonical-Historical Study of the Diaconate in the Western Church.* Canon Law Studies 495. Washington, DC: Catholic University of America, 1979.

Probst, Ferdinand. *Kirchliche Disciplin in den drei ersten Christlichen Jahrhunderten.* Tübingen: H. Laupp, 1873.

Prümmer, Dominic M. *Handbook of Moral Theology.* Trans. by Gerald W. Shelton. Cork, Ireland: Mercier Press Ltd., 1956.

Quasten, Johannes. *Patrology.* 2 vols. Westminster, MD: The Newman Press, 1951.

Quasten, Johannes and Joseph Plumpe. *Ancient Christian Writers.* Westminster, MD: The Newman Press, 1946-.

Rahner, Karl and Herbert Vorgrimler, eds. *Diaconi in Christo.* Freiberg: Herder Verlag, 1962.

Richardson, Cyril C. ed. *Early Christian Fathers.* New York, NY: Collier Books, 1970.

Reichert, Eckhard. *Die Canones der Synode von Elvira: Einleitung und Kommentar.* Dissertation. University of Hamburg: 1990.

Renken, John A. *The Contemporary Understanding of Marriage: A Historico-Critical Study of Gaudium et spes, 47-52, and It's Influence Upon the Revision of the Codex Iuris Canonici.* JCD Dissertation. Rome: Pontifical University of St. Thomas, 1981.

Roberts, Alexander and James Donaldson, eds. *Ante-Nicene Fathers: The Writings of the Fathers Down to A.D. 325.* 10 vols. Peabody, MA: Hendrickson, 1994.

Schamoni, Wilhelm. *Married Men as Ordained Deacons.* London: Burns & Oates, 1955.

Schillebeeckx, Edward. *Der Amtszölibat: Eine Kritische Besinnung.* Dusseldorf: Patmos Verlag, 1967.

_____. *Celibacy.* New York, NY: Sheed & Ward, 1968.

_____. *Christliche Identität und kirchliches Amt.* Düsseldorf: Patmos Verlag, 1985.

Shotwell, James T. and Louise Ropes Loomis, eds. *The See of Peter.* New York: Columbia University Press, 1991.

Singles, Donna. *Des diacres parlent: originalités et enjeux du diaconat aujourd'hui.* Paris: Éditions du Cerf, 1985.

Stickler, Alfons Maria. *The Case for Clerical Celibacy.* Trans. by Brian Ferme. San Francisco: Ignatius Press, 1995.

_____. *Il celibato ecclesiastico: la sua storia e i suoi fondamenti teologici.* Vatican City: Libreria Editrice Vaticana, 1994.

_____. *Historica Iuris Canonici Latini: Historia Fontium.* Turin: Augustae Taurinorum,1950.

Sweeney, Francis. *The Reduction of Clerics to the Lay State: An Historical Synopsis and Commentary.* Canon Law Studies 223. Washington, DC: Catholic University of America, 1945.

Vacant, Alfred et al., eds. *Dictionnaire de théologie catholique.* 15 vols. Paris: Letouzey et Ané, 1903-51.

Vermeersch, Arthur. *Theologiae Moralis Principia: De Personis, De Sacramentis, De Legibus Ecclesiae et Censure.* Rome: Universitas Gregoriana, 1923.

Vogels, Heinz-Jürgen. Priester dürfen heiraten: Biblische, geschichtliche und rechtliche Gründe gegen den Pflichtzölibat. Bonn: Köllen, 1992.

Vogelpohl, Henry. *The Simple Impediments to Holy Orders: An Historical Synopsis and Commentary.* Canon Law Studies 224. Washington, DC: Catholic University of America, 1945.

Von Hillebrand, Dietrich. *Die Ehe.* München: Ars Sacra, 1929.

Vorgrimler, Herbert ed. *Commentary on the Documents of Vatican II.* 5 vols. New York: Herder and Herder, 1967-69.

Waldstein, Michael. *Theology of the Body.* Boston, MA: Pauline Books & Media, 2006.

Watkins, Edward, I. *The Church in Council.* New York : Sheed and Ward, 1960.

Wiltgen, Ralph. *The Rhine Flows into the Tiber: The Unknown Council.* New York, NY: Hawthorn Books Inc., 1967.

Winninger, Paul. *Vers un renouveau du diaconat.* Paris: Desclée de Brouwer, 1958.

_____. et al. eds. *Le diacre dans l'Eglise et le monde d'aujourd'hui.* Paris: Éditions du Cerf, 1966.

Wojtyla, Karol. *Love and Responsibility.* Trans. by H. T. Willetts. San Francisco, CA: Ignatius Press, 1993.

Wrenn, Lawrence G., *Authentic Interpretations on the 1983 Code*. Washington, DC: CLSA, 1993.

Wuerl, Donald. *The Priesthood: The Doctrine of the Third Synod of Bishops and Recent Theological Conclusions*. S.T.D. dissertation. Rome: Pontificia University of St. Thomas Aquinas, 1974.

3. ARTICLES

Abbo, John A. "The Problem of Lapsed Priests." *The Jurist* 23 (1963) 153-179.

Alesandro, John A. "The Revision of the Code of Canon Law: A Background Study." *Studia canonica* 24 (1990) 91-146.

Bauer, Francis C. "The Admission of Previously Married and Annulled to Sacred Orders, Diaconate and Religious Life." in *Canon Law Society of America: Proceedings* 47 (1985) 126-129.

Betti, Umberto. "In margine al nuovo codice di diritto canonico," *Antonianum* 58 (1983) 628-647.

Bickell, Gustav. "Der Cölibat eine apostolische Anordnung." *Zeitschrift für Katholische Theologie.* 2 (1878) 26-64.

_____. "Der Cölibat dennoch eine apostolische Anordnung." *Zeitschrift für Katholische Theologie.* 3 (1879) 792-799.

Bilaniuk, Petro B. T. "Celibacy and Eastern Tradition." In *Celibacy: The Necessary Option*. Edited by George H. Fein, 32-72. New York: Herder and Herder, 1968.

Chadwick, Henry. "Enkrateia." In *Reallexikon für Antike und Christentum Sachwörterbuch zur Auseinandersetzung des Christentums mit der antiken Welt.* Stuttgart: Hiersemann, 1950-. 5 (1962) 343-365.

Cholij, Roman. "Priestly Celibacy in Patristics and in the History of the Church." In *For Love Alone: Reflections on Priestly Celibacy*. Maynooth, Ireland: St. Paul's Publications, 1993.

_____. "Clerical Celibacy in the Western Church: Some Clarifications," *Priests and People* 3 (1989) 301-313.

_____. "The *Lex Continentiae* and Orders." *Studia canonica* 21 (1987) 391-418.

Anthony McLaughlin

_____. "Married Clergy and Ecclesiastical Continence in Light of the Council of Trullo." *Annuarium Historiae Conciliorum* 19 (1987) 71-230, 241-299.

_____. "Observaciones críticas acerca de los cánones que tratan sobre el celibato en el Código de Derecho Canónico de 1983." *Ius Canonicum* 31(1991) 291-305.

_____. "An Eastern Catholic Married Clergy in North America." *Studia canonica* 31 (1997) 311-339.

Chiappetta, Luigi. "L'Ordine Sacro." In *Il matrimonio: nella nuova legislazione canonica e concordataria.* Rome: Edizione Dehoniane, 1990. 151-158.

Claeys-Bouuaert, F. "Clercs." In *Dictionnaire de droit canonique,* ed. Raoul Naz. Paris: Librairie Letouzey et Ané, 1935-1965. 3:828.

Cnudde, Matthieu. "L'ordination des diacres." *La Maison Dieu: revue de pastorale liturgique.* 98 (1969) 73-94.

_____. "Laïc et laïcat." In *Dictionnaire de spiritualité ascétique et mystique: doctrine et histoire.* Ed. Marcel Viller et al. Paris : G. Beauchesne et fils, 1976.

Connell, Francis J. "The Catholic Doctrine of the Ends of Marriage." *The Catholic Theological Society of America: Proceedings of the Foundation Meeting.* New York, NY: The Catholic Theological Society of America, 1946. 34-35.

Constantelos, Demetrios. "Marriage and Celibacy of the Clergy in the Orthodox Church." *Concilium* 78 (1972) 30-38.

Coriden, James A. and James H. Provost, "Canonical Implications Related to the Ordination of Married Men to the Priesthood in the United States of America." *CLSA Proceedings* 58 (1996) 438-451.

Coyle, John Kevin. "Recent Views on the Origin of Clerical Celibacy: A Review of the Literature from 1980-1991." *Logos* 34 (1993) 480-531.

Crouzel, Henri. "Celibacy in the Early Church." In *Priesthood and Celibacy.* Ed. Joseph Coppens et al, 451-502. Milan: Editrice Anora Milano, 1972.

De la Potterie, Ignace. "L'origine et le sense primitive du mot 'laïc.'" *Nouvelle revue théologique* 80 (1958) 840-853.

Doskey, Clinton J. "Annulments and Entrance into Religious Life, Priesthood and Diaconate." *CLSA Proceedings* 47 (1985) 115-125.

Dulles, Avery. "The Church." In *The Documents of Vatican II.* Ed. Walter M. Abbott. New York: Herder and Herder, 1966.

Dura, Nicolae. "The Ecumenicity of the Council in Trullo: Witnesses of the Canonical Tradition in the East and the West." *The Council in Trullo Revisited,* Kanonika 6. Eds. George Nedungatt & Michael Featherstone, 229-262. Rome: Pontificio Istituto Orientale, 1995.

Eber, Jochen. "Zölibat," *Evangelisches Lexikon für Theologie und Gemeind* 3 (1994) 2217.

Epagneul, Michel Dominique. "Du role des diacres dans L'Église d'aujourd'hui." *Nouvelle revue theologique* 79 (1957) 153-168.

Erikson, John H. "The Council of Trullo: Issues Relating to the Marriage of Clergy." *The Greek Orthodox Theological Review* 40 (1995) 183-199.

Fedele, Pio. "Ancora sulla definizione del matrimonio in diritto canonico." *Ephemerides Iuris Canonici.* 33 (1977) 54.

Fellhauer, David E. "The *Consortium Omnis Vitae* as a Juridical Element in Marriage." *Studia canonica* 13 (1979) 3-171.

Ford, John C. "Marriage: Its Meaning and Purposes." *Theological Studies* 3 (1942) 372.

Fox, Joseph. "A General Synthesis of the Work of the Pontifical Commission for the Revision of the Code of Canon Law." *The Jurist* 48 (1988) 800-840.

Funk, Franz X. "Der Cölibat keine apostolische Anordnung." *Theologische Quartalschrift* 61 (1879) 208-247.

_____. "Der Cölibat noch lange keine apostolische Anordnung." *Theologische Quartalschrift* 62 (1880) 202-221.

_____. "Cölibat und Priesterehe im christlichen Altertum." *Kirchengeschichtliche Abhandlungen und Untersuchungen.* 1: 121-155. Paderborn: Ferdinand Schöningh, 1897.

Gangi, Bonaventure. "Coelibatus." In *Dictionarium Morale et Canonicum*. Ed. Pietro Palazzini. Rome: Officium Libri Catholici, 1962-1968. 1: 722-725.

Garrity, Robert M. "Spiritual and Canonical Values in Mandatory Priestly Celibacy." *Studia canonica* 27 (1993) 217-260.

Gaudemet, Jean. "Gratien et le **célibat** ecclésiastique." *Studia Gratiana* 13 (1967) 341-369.

Gessel, Wilhelm. "Besprechungen." *Annuarium Historiae Conciliorum* 2 (1970) 422-423.

Goethe, Rudolf. "Die offene Tur," in *Bekenntnis zur Katholische Kirche*. Würzburg : Echter-Verl, 1956. 117-165.

Green, Thomas, J. "The Revision of Marriage Law: An Exposition and Critique." *Studia canonica* 10 (1976) 363-411.

_____. "Critical Reflections on the *Schema* on the People of God."*Studia canonica* 14 (1980) 235-314.

_____. "Revised *Schema De Matrimonio:* Texts and Reflections." *The Jurist* 40 (1980) 57-127.

Griffe, Elie. "À propos du canon 33 du Concile d'Elvire." *Bulletin de littérature ecclésiastique* 74 (1973) 142-145.

_____. "Le Concile d'Elvira et les origines du célibat ecclésiastique." *Bulletin de littérature ecclésiastique* 77 (1976) 123-127.

Gryson, Roger. "Dix ans de recherches sur les origines de célibat ecclésiastique. Réflexion sur les publications des années 1970-1979." *Revue théologique de Louvain* 11 (1980) 160-164.

Hill, Richard A. "The Pastoral Provision: Ordination of Married, Protestant Ministers." *CLSA Proceedings* 51 (1989) 95-100.

Hödl, Ludwig. "Lex Continentiae: A Study on the Problem of Celibacy." In *Priesthood and Celibacy*, ed. Joseph Coppens et al., 693-727. Milan: Editrice Anora Milano, 1972.

Hofinger, John. "The Case for Permanent Deacons." *Catholic Mind* 57 (1959) 114-125.

_____. "The Deacon in the Parish." *Life of the Spirit* 14 (1959) 161-167.

_____. "Rebirth of the Diaconate in the Roman Catholic Church." *Dominicana* 47 (1962) 20-31.

Hofinger, John and Paul Winninger, "Le renouveau du diaconat: situation présent de la controverse." *Nouvelle revue theologique* 83 (1961) 337-366.

Hopkins, Keith. "On the Probable Age Structure of the Roman Population." *Population Studies* 20 (1966) 245-264.

_____. "The Age of Roman Girls at Marriage." *Population Studies* 18 (1965) 309-327.

Huels, John M. "Classifying Authentic Interpretations of Canon Law," *The Jurist* 72 (2012): 605-640.

Jombart, Émile. "Celibat des clercs." In *Dictionnaire de droit canonique.* Ed. Raoul Naz. Paris: Librairie Letouzey et Ané, 1935-1965. 3: 132-145.

_____. "Excommunication." In *Dictionnaire de droit canonique.* Ed. Raoul Naz. Paris: Librairie Letouzey et Ané, 1935-1965. 5: 615-628.

Jounel, Pierre. "Ordinations." *The Church at Prayer: An Introduction to the Liturgy.* Ed. Aimé George Martimort. Collegeville, Minnesota: The Liturgical Press, 1987. 3: 178.

Knetes, Christophores. "Ordination and Matrimony in the Eastern Orthodox Church." *Journal of Theological Studies* 11 (1910) 348-400 and 481-509.

Kottje, Raymond. "Das Aufkommen der täglichen Eucharistiefeier in der Westkirche und die Zölibatsforderung." *Zeitschrift für Kirchengeschichte* 82 (1971) 218-228.

Kruse, Henri. "Eheverzucht im Neuen Testament und in der Frühkirche." *Forum für Katholische Theologie* 1 (1985) 94-116.

Leclerq, Henri. "La législation conciliaire relative au célibat ecclésiastique." In *Dictionnaire d'archéologie Chrétienne et de liturgie* 2: 2068-2088.

Lécuyer, Joseph. "Decree on the Ministry and Life of Priests: History of the Decree." In *Commentary on the Documents of Vatican II.* Ed. Herbert Vorgrimler. New York: Herder and Herder, 1967. 3: 183-205.

L' Huillier, Peter. "Episcopal Celibacy in the Orthodox Tradition." *St. Vladimir's Theological Quarterly* 35 (1991) 271-300.

_____. "Critique of the Law of Celibacy in the Catholic Church from the Period of the Reform Councils." In *Celibacy in the Church*. Eds. William Bassett and Peter Huizing. New York: Herder and Herder, 1972.

_____. "Marriage and Celibacy of the Clergy, The Discipline of the Western Church: An Historical-Canonical Synopsis." *The Jurist* 32 (1972) 210.

Luther, Martin. "An Appeal to the Ruling Class of German Nationality as to the Amelioration of the State of Christendom." Trans. in *Martin Luther: Selections from His Writings*. Ed. John Dillenberger. New York: Doubleday, 1961. 448-449.

Lyons, Richard. "The Permanent Diaconate: A Commentary on its Development from the End of the Second Vatican Council to the 1983 Code of Canon Law." *CLSA Proceedings* 49 (1988) 77-100.

Mackin, Theodore. "Conjugal Love in the Magisterium." *The Jurist* 36 (1976) 263-301.

McGarrity, Robert M. "Spiritual and Canonical Values in Mandatory Priestly Celibacy." *Studia canonica* 27 (1993) 217-260.

McIntyre, John P. "Optional Priestly Celibacy." *Studia canonica* 29 (1995) 103-153.

Martin, Francis. "Marriage in the New Testament Period." *Christian Marriage: A Historical Study*. Ed. Glenn W. Olsen, 80-82. New York: The Crossroad Publishing Company, 2001.

Meigne, Maurice. "Le concile d'Elvire et les origines du célibat ecclésiastique." *Revue d'histoire ecclésiastique* 70 (1975) 361-387.

Möhler, John, A. "Beleuchtung der Denkschrift für die Aufhebung des den Katholischen Geistlichen Vorgeschriebenen Cölibates. Mit drei Actenstucken." *Gesammelte Schriften und Aufsatze*. Regensburg: Dollinger, 1839. 1:177-267.

Nedungatt, George. "The Temporal Goods of the Church in the Legislation of the Ecumenical Councils." *Folia Canonica* 4 (2000) 117-133.

Neuner, Josef. "Decree of Priestly Formation." In *Commentary on the Documents of Vatican II.* Ed. Herbert Vorgrimler. New York: Herder and Herder, 1967. 2: 371-404.

_____. "Priestly Formation." In *From Trent to Vatican II: Historical and Theological Investigations.* Ed. Raymond F. Bulman et al. Oxford, NY: Oxford University Press, 2006. 117-136.

Palazzini, Pietro. "Castitas." In *Dictionarium Morale et Canonicum.* Rome: Officium Libri Catholici, 1962-1968.

Peri, Vittorio. "Introduction." *The Council in Trullo Revisited.* Kanonika 6. Eds. George Nedungatt & Michael Featherstone. Rome: Pontificio Istituto Orientale, 1995. 15-41.

Peters, Edward. "Canonical Considerations on Diaconal Continence," *Studia canonica* 39 (2005) 147-180.

Philips, Gerard Philips. "Dogmatic Constitution on the Church." In *Commentary on the Documents of Vatican II.* Ed. Herbert Vorgrimler. New York: Herder and Herder, 1967. 1:

Pitsakis, Constantin. "Clergé marié et célibat dans la législation du Concile in Trullo: le point de vue Oriental." *The Council in Trullo Revisited.* Ed. George Nedungatt and Michael Featherstone. Kanonika 6: 263-306. Rome: Pontificio Istituto Orientale, 1995.

_____. "Le droit matrimonial dans les canons du concile in Trullo." *Annuarium Historiae Conciliorum* 24 (1992) 158-185.

Pokusa, Joseph H. "The Diaconate: A History of Law Following Practice." *The Jurist* 45 (1985) 95-135.

Provost, John H. "Offenses against the Sixth Commandment: Toward a Canonical Analysis of Canon 1395." *The Jurist* 55 (1995) 632-663.

_____. "Some Canonical Considerations Relative to Clerical Sexual Misconduct." *The Jurist* 52 (1992) 615-641.

_____. "Permanent Deacons in the 1983 Code." *CLSA Proceedings* 46 (1985) 175-191.

Ratzinger, Joseph. "Priestly Ministry: A Search for its Meaning." *Emmanuel* 76 (1970) 490.

Roberts, William. "Christian Marriage." In *From Trent to Vatican II: Historical and Theological Investigations.* Ed. Raymond F. Bulman et al. Oxford, NY: Oxford University Press, 2006. 209-226.

Schmaus, Michael. "Commentary of Decree *Presbyterorum ordinis.*" In *Commentary on the Documents of Vatican II.* Ed. Herbert Vorgrimler. New York: Herder and Herder, 1967. 4: 210-298.

Schumacher, William A. and Richard A. Hill. "Celebration of Marriage: Dispensation from Canon 1087 for a Permanent Deacon." *Roman Replies and CLSA Advisory Opinions 1984.* Washington, DC: CLSA, 1984. 3.

Simon, Constantin. "The First Years of Ruthenian Church Life in America." *Orientalia Christiana Periodica.* Rome: Pontifical Institute for Oriental Studies, 1935-.

Sloyan, Gerard. "Biblical and Patristic Motives for Celibacy of Church Ministers." *Concilium* 78 (1972) 13-29.

Stickler, Aflons Maria. "The Evolution of the Discipline of Celibacy in the Western Church from the End of the Patristic Era to the Council of Trent." In *Priesthood and Celibacy.* Ed . Joseph Coppens et al. Milan: Editrice Ancora Milano, 1972. 503-597.

_____. "La continenza dei diaconi specialmente nel primo millennio della chiesa." *Salesianum* 26 (1964) 275-302.

_____. "Tratti salenti nella storia del celibate." *Sacra Doctrina* 15 (1970) 585-620

_____. "Historical Note on the Celibacy of Clerics in Major Orders." *Osservatore Romano,* March 19, 1970.

Tocanel, Petrus. "Clerci." In *Dictionarium Morale et Canonicum.* Ed. Pietro Palazzini. Rome: Officium Libri Catholici, 1962-1968. 1: 705-706.

Troianos, Spyros N. "The Canons of the Trullan Council in the Novels of Leo VI." *The Council of Trullo Revisited.* Ed. George Nedungatt and Michael Featherstone. Konanika 6: 189-198. Rome: Pontificio Istituto Orientale, 1995.

Urrutia, Francisco Javier. "De Pontificio Consilio de legume textibus interpretandis," *Periodica* 78 (1989): 503-521

Vacanard, Elphège-Florent. "Les origines du célibat ecclésiastique." Études de *critique et d'histoire religieuse* 1 (1905) 71-120.

Van Bekkum, Wilhelm. "Le renouveau liturgie au service des missions." *La Maison Dieu: revue de pastorale liturgique* 45 (1956) 174-175.

Vann, Kevin W. and Lynn Jarrell. "Canons 1037, 1041, 1042: The Permanent Diaconate and the Sacrament of Marriage." *Roman Replies and CLSA Advisory Opinions 1984*. Washington: Canon Law Society of America, 1984. 16-25.

Varvaro, William A. "Legislation for Permanent Deacons: Developments and Difficulties." *Diaconal Quarterly* 10 (1984) 4-21.

Velari, Mauro. "Completing the Conciliar Agenda." *History of Vatican II*. Eds. Giuseppe Alberigo and Joseph Komonchak. Maryknoll, NY: Orbis, 1995. 4: 231-237.

Verkamp, Bernard. "Cultic Purity and the Law of Celibacy. " *Review for Religious* 30 (1971) 199–217

Winklemann, Friedhelm. "Paphnutios, der Bekenner und Bishof." In *Probleme der Koptischen Literatur.* Wittenburg, Germany: Institut für Byzantinsk der Martin Luther Universitat Halle-Wittenberg, 1968. 1: 145-153.

Wulf, Friedrich. "Commentary on the Decree Presbyterorum Ordinis." In *Commentary on the Documents of Vatican II.* Ed. Herbert Vorgrimler ed. New York: Herder and Herder, 1969. 4: 183-297.

www.ingramcontent.com/pod-product-compliance
Lightning Source LLC
Chambersburg PA
CBHW031423270326
41930CB00007B/558